Essays on
THE TEACHING OF ENGLISH

Essays on
THE TEACHING OF ENGLISH

Reports of the Yale Conferences
on the Teaching of English

Edited by

Edward J. Gordon

Edward S. Noyes

A Publication of the National
Council of Teachers of English

 APPLETON-CENTURY-CROFTS, INC.

New York

808
G65e
Oct. 1966
55682

Preface

This is a book for the high school teacher of English. In it, good teachers try to say in concrete language how they have handled problems relevant to any English classroom: in the teaching of language, writing, and literature. As they do, the central motif of the book emerges: the problem of thinking; from this all else grows.

The essays offered here are drawn from Reports of four of the annual Yale Conferences on the Teaching of English, financed by the Yale Master of Arts in Teaching Program as a part of its in-service training. These meetings began in 1955 to bring together teachers of English—mainly from secondary schools, but always with higher education represented—to consider topics of special importance in the classroom.

For each Conference, working committees of outstanding teachers were assembled, meeting at intervals during the year. Their discussion of a particular topic culminated in a report to which all had contributed from their experiences and which was then disseminated at the Conference, first by being read by the Committee Chairman and discussed from the floor, and second by being included in a Conference Report distributed to all in attendance. Included also were talks by distinguished university teachers on topics central to a given Conference. The Reports have usually been taken home by those in attendance to be shared with other members of the Department of English. From them the present selection has been made in the hope, shared by the National Council of Teachers of English, that it will prove useful to an even wider audience.

Questions with which the committees were asked to grapple were such as these: What kind of language teaching should be going on in the secondary school? What is grammar? How should it be taught? How should new ideas on linguistics influence the traditional teaching of grammar?

Again: How can writing be taught? What writing skills are most needed? What acts of thought must a student perform in order to

v

write well? What makes a piece of writing interesting? How should a piece of expository prose be evaluated? What should be done about creative writing?

As for literature: How can poetry be taught? What approaches can we make to the long narrative poem? What can be done with the novel, and what techniques does the novelist use? How can we rise above the level of teaching only what happens? As examples, our speakers and committees used works often taught in secondary schools.

To these questions our committees and speakers put their minds. No teacher need agree with their answers as given here, any more than the individual authors agree with one another. We are merely presenting ways found useful by teachers in solving their own dilemmas. On certain basic principles, however, the reports do agree, and these principles the editors have tried to express in their introductions to the essays.

To make their reports more useful, each committee offered in an appendix to its report bibliographies, classroom exercises, and, sometimes, accounts of the ways in which students had reacted to the exercises. These documents, slightly modified, are included in the present volume.

Most remarkable is the fact that many teachers gave up many week ends to come to New Haven from all corners of New England to work on this material. Their only motive was to improve their own teaching and that of others who may read their efforts. To them the editors are most grateful: those teachers are the producers of this book. To see the time and care that went into their work is to make one proud to be a teacher.

The editors also extend their thanks to the Committee on Publications of the National Council of Teachers of English: Professor George Arms, University of New Mexico; Richard Corbin, Peekskill High School, Peekskill, New York; Elizabeth Guilfoile, Cincinnati Public Schools; and Professor J. N. Hook, University of Illinois, Chairman. Professors George Henry of the University of Delaware and Silvy Kraus of the University of Oregon also gave a critical reading to the manuscript.

E. J. G.
E. S. N.

Yale University

Table of Contents

III. THE TEACHING OF LITERATURE

I

THE TEACHING
OF LANGUAGE

We turn first to language, the genesis of all our other work, and we try to show how thinking in semantics, grammar, and descriptive linguistics should change the concepts that determine our teaching.

Our main concern is that the words which we and our classes use should have roots in reality, that words should have a connection with the operations they are describing. If words are used to convey ideas, then ideas must underlie the words. If words are a way of communicating, what do we communicate when we use them?

The study of grammar (and not many people agree on what grammar is) will not solve these problems; it tells us rather how words go together. The good teacher will always relate the grammar to the situation being described. He will not say that this sentence is right or wrong, but will ask, "What are you trying to say, and have you said it?" Our students should be forced in all their speaking and writing to define key words, to expand abstractions, to minimize jargon; in short, to make clear what they are trying to say. It is then that we are teaching thinking.

1

What Kinds of Language Teaching?

Louis Zahner, *Groton School, Massachusetts*

Was ever such a coy mistress as English! Well may we English teachers, along with Andrew Marvell, complain of the whimsies of this unpredictable creature we try to woo, and with him exclaim, "At my back I always hear Time's winged chariot." Where do we get time—time even to think about the principles, the theories, the philosophy from which all our work must grow if it is to be any good?

We don't.

The theoretical aspect of language and its teaching is limitless in itself, and reaches out in all directions into subjects and fields that we do not generally think of as having anything to do with language. I shall touch this vast subject only here and there. I can give no answers. I shall try only to raise and suggest questions. If, under pressure of time I seem to be making categorical assertions, I ask you to take them as tentative, as suggestive, not conclusive.

First off, let's get theory into its place. What do theories and principles have to do with us hard-headed, practicing, down-to-earth teachers? There are at least two compelling reasons for our considering theory.

First, no classroom practice is sound unless it stems from sound theory and can be traced back to it.

Second, although we may stoutly deny being theorists, we are, nevertheless, willy-nilly, theorists. We cannot avoid it. We are theorists at every moment that we are in school—in class and out; good theorists, middling theorists, or bad theorists—but certainly theorists.

For at every moment in the school day we are dealing with our students *as if* certain principles and theories were true. We are always teaching *as if*. If I am teaching a grammar lesson, for example, I am teaching it *as if* certain things were true about language and its operation in general, about the English language and a native language in particular, about a pupil, about society. Implicit in all our teaching there are theoretical assumptions of all sorts, probably hidden, unrecognized. Sound teaching demands of us that we know not only what we are teaching, but why; that every moment of our work be based consciously on a theory we believe to be valid. The theory may be—should be, perhaps—tentative, constantly under revision as we learn more. But it must be explicit.

I grant that theory isn't worth much unless it can be applied in practice. But this does not mean that theory has to be directly translated into classroom devices and exercises if it is to justify itself. Much of it does not come directly into the classroom. We don't have to teach theory. But a teacher should have theoretical reserves upon which to call, and to call quickly and confidently, when those unexpected questions and opportunities flash out in the classroom, and when he is planning a day's unit or a four-year curriculum.

These *as if's*, these assumptions, lie in many different but interrelated fields. For us English teachers there are perhaps four main ones: *The Individual; Society; Language; Literature*. Whenever we teach "English," we teach as if certain things were true about the individual pupil and his development. I do not suggest that in our precipitate descent from the ivory tower we plumb the depths of the Freudian pit; but I do hold that it is our job to know how a normal adolescent develops; in particular, how he naturally learns his native language, and how his language operates in his development. We teach as if certain things were true about his society—the groups in which he lives, from gang, family, and school up through the whole human race; and about language, what it is, and what it isn't, what it does and how it does it; and of course about literature, but that isn't our subject here.

This looks like a tall order; but this isn't all. For all these fields have their interrelationships, and these too have their theories that are part of our *as if's*. We are always teaching English as if, for example, certain relationships exist between a pupil and his society, or between language and society—what language is doing to our culture, and our culture to language. But the end is not yet. This whole business, our four bases and their interrelationships, are coming at us through time. *Time,* that we can neither define nor escape, is an inexorable ingredient in our witches' brew of *as if's*. Nothing but toil and trouble for us English teachers! We are always teaching, for example, as if certain things were true about the influences of the past upon the present, and the present upon the future, of the individual, society, language, and literature; about the change of an individual through time (a split second, a class hour, a year, a lifetime) and about the effect of his learning of language upon this change. We say, perhaps, that we are teaching language at it is now to this pupil as he is now, that he can live in the world as it is now. But we don't; we can't. For before our sentence is finished this "now" is in the past. Do we sometimes teach, I wonder, as if our pupil, our language, our society, were all static?

We cannot even begin to spell out here these intricate relationships, all conditioned by time, and the principles on which they seem to be operating. I have simply tried to suggest that we cannot consider language and its teaching as if it were something apart from everything else, however we may seem to do so when we talk about it at conferences, or set it up in a curriculum.

But it is time to dive in. What *is* this English language that I've been talking about; and, perhaps more important, what *isn't* it?

It is not grammar alone; though one of our most questionable *as if's* is that it *is* grammar alone; for most of the time that we put in consciously teaching "language" is spent on whatever it is we call "grammar."

It *is* the native language of our pupils. Do we stop to examine the way a native learns his own language, without benefit of schoolteachers, and do we build our methods consistently upon these natural ways of learning, the ways through which even our youngest pupils, before any study of grammar at all, have acquired an amazing ability to make language work for them with entire adequacy? Or do we go at it as if it were something new to them, making a complicated mystery of it? Do we proceed as if it were a foreign language, to be taught to beginners by rules, paradigms, definitions, and word lists?

English is a living language. It lives and grows within the native son, bone of his bone. It is a part of him, an indispensable means of his understanding himself and his world. It is through words that an individual first is able to make order of a sort out of a chaotic world, to organize it into manageable classifications and abstractions. This power of ordering a complex and seemingly chaotic world by imposing words upon it begins at birth and never stops. It is a part, a very large part, of growth and personal development. Our words and word patterns condition our world, set the limits of our thinking, and determine our modes of thought.

A living language also, like all other living things, grows and changes through the process of death and birth, decay and rejuvenation. Old words go, or change their meanings; new words arise to meet new needs. It lives also in its literature, in its masses of men and women, in living voices. Do we ever teach it as if it were a dead language, to be imposed upon a pupil by fiat from without? As if its "rules" were sanctions that should and can confine it, not merely descriptions of social practice, full of exceptions, constantly changing? Do we teach it as if there were a universal grammar, best exemplified by Latin, and try to cram its living structure into dead Latin grammatical categories, terminology, and definitions?

English is an analytic language. In an inflected language, like Latin, the word carries the idea; in English, it is the word group. In Latin, we get first the grammar and from that, the meaning. In English, it is the other way around. We get grammar from meaning. For example, if I say, "I saw an antique Persian strip in a mosque," you can't tell the part of speech or construction of "Persian," "strip," or "in a mosque" until you know whether I am talking about a carpet or an old man. Or if somebody says, "Uncle Sam has made me a soldier," you can't get his grammar until you know whether a small boy is talking about his toy-making uncle, or whether the speaker is his older brother home on furlough. Even structure and "signal words" do not always help us out. A recent number of an alumni magazine had this caption under a picture: "Mr. X watches a baseball arch through the air." Take the same structure and signals: "Mr. X watches a Roman arch through an airplane window." We can't differentiate between the grammar and structure of these two sentences until we see what they mean. We can tell what they mean only by relating them to our experience in the world we know. Examples could be multiplied: "He looked up the word in a dictionary." "He looked up the shaft in a hurry." In an inflected language the word form would give the whole meaning away at once, no questions asked. But word form accounts for only about five per cent of the pattern of English; and we give it about ninety-five per cent of our teaching time.

We are perhaps too likely, then, to teach language as if there were nothing but grammar that really matters; to teach a grammar that is not an English grammar; and to teach it as if it were completely independent of meaning, as if language were form without substance. We may throw in a little drill on vocabulary and usage. What else is there?

"Well," you will say, "there are the language arts."

I agree. But I do not accept the current definition of this shibboleth, "the language arts." It has come to mean little more than "language activities," activities in which language is used—telephoning, running a meeting, listening to the radio, writing a business letter, carrying on a conversation. Now these, some of them, are useful activities. If they have to be taught, and can't be taught in the home, I suppose we must teach them in the school. But they are no more language arts than painting a magazine cover, or painting a fish, painting a portrait, painting a landscape, are the arts of painting. These are activities employing the arts of painting to produce artifacts. The arts of painting are such arts as the use of color, design, perspective, composition, drawing. Once these arts are mastered, the artist is ready for whatever comes along—still life, portrait, all the rest. He can meet new problems of painting as they arise; he doesn't have to go running back to art school and wail to his teacher, "I have a commission to paint a picture of a fully dressed man ascending a staircase. We never did this one. Teach me quick."

Are there not, similarly, language arts that can be understood and taught, and that, once mastered, will put a pupil on his own in his use of language, while he is in school and afterwards, in any situation? We can, of course, practice such arts in any classroom activity we wish, but never with the assumption that the activity is the art, or the illusion that we can introduce into the classroom more than a pitiful fraction of the vast number of the demands that life makes upon language.

But what are these language arts? Can we list them? No, probably not. But we are all teachers of English, and we have a right, a responsibility, even, to try. I am inclined to start out something like this:

The art of making sense.
The art of getting the effects we are after.
The art of making discriminations.

There are more than these, of course, but these will keep us busy for a while, and will serve as examples. Of course, too, these overlap: one of the effects we are after, for example, is to make sense, and one of the discriminations we want to make is sense from nonsense. Then, too, they all have subdivisions—just as the art of color in painting has its subdivisions: hue, intensity, and value. Logical patterns, inductive and deductive, for example, might be included under the art of making sense. But these will serve well enough for now. Let's take a look at them.

How about making sense?

It doesn't make sense to say, "I am coming to New Haven if I had time," but change the verb form *had* to *have*, and we are all right. This is a matter of formal grammar—the grammar of form. In some sentences making sense demands "right," or consistent, forms.

Now take this one: "Order and pattern some have must they sense make to are words if." Here, if you will take my word for it, our forms are all right. But all we have is a random list of words. They do not have a recognizable pattern or order. Read them the other way around, and all is well: "If words are to make sense, they must have some pattern and order." So to our grammar of form we must add the grammar of pattern, of word groups, of order—order within the word group and between the word groups.

Now let's try another: "The firmly imbedded stone gathered speed as it rolled up the steep cliff until it came to a slow stop at the foot of the mountain." Form, perfect. Order and pattern, impeccable—quite a lovely sentence, in fact. But it doesn't make sense to me. I might build around it a nightmare or fairy-tale context creating an unreal world in which it would make sense; but just as it is it is senseless. The trouble is that it has no correspondence at all with the real world as we know it. We have nothing within our experience to which to connect it.

(It may be worth noting here parenthetically that words don't make sense or fail to make sense just in themselves, absolutely. They make sense, or not, *to* somebody. This bit about the stone makes no sense to anybody here, because not one of us has any experience to tie it to. But some other sentence might make sense to some of us and not to others, because experience differs. This is an important point in communication and human relations. This is a point worth making to our pupils.)

This, then, seems to be our trinity for making sense: word form, word order and pattern, reference to human experience in the world as we know it. In discourse, they operate inseparably together. Any teaching of one of the three that does not take into full account the other two is not a teaching of language. Any grammatical analysis or manipulation of a sentence that is not at pains to examine just what the sentence is saying in terms of realities of our experience stultifies the pupil and falsifies the language. Just as far as the art of making sense goes, I have put them in an ascending order. Of least importance is the grammar of form. Who could possibly misunderstand the sense of "Him and me done it"?

Word order is of more importance, for changing it can cause nonsense, ambiguity, a change in sense, or a rhetorical change. We don't give enough teaching time to word order; there is much to be learned from experimenting with different word orders. Our pupils come to us, to be sure, with an almost miraculous sense of word order. And for this we can be thankful. What we can teach them about language is really an infinitesimal part of what they know already or will learn without us. We can add only a few of the refinements, a few working principles. Take that sentence that I read backwards a while ago. It was a thirteen-worder—not very long. A seventh-grader could easily get through one of equal length with no trouble at all, without stopping to think: "When I left for camp last summer, my mother kissed me good-bye." Suppose now that we were to take that sentence and try it out with every possible different order of its thirteen words, as we might, for example, with the three-worder "I am here." *I am here. I here am. Here I am. Here am I. Am here I. Am I here.* And let's keep at this thirteen-worder until it is done, twenty-four hours a day, if the job runs over a day. Let's allow ourselves five seconds to think up each new order and to write it down. No time out for meals. You might like to try this out when you get home. On second thought, perhaps you had better not—not unless you have some spare time. It would take you—how long do you think? Almost exactly one thousand years. Yet, out of the billions of possible word orders that could be made from those thirteen words, our seventh-grader—for all I know, our first-grader—picks one of the half-dozen or so sensible ones, without hesitation. How a child learns, without formal schooling, to handle the intricacies of form and meaning is an important thing for us language teachers to know and to build upon—an essential part of our theoretical reserves.

Now for our third, most important, requisite for making sense: reference to human experience in the world as we know it.

This is the hardest of the arts to teach; in fact, much of our teaching weakens or even destroys it. It is hard, even, to diagnose the lack of it, to see the need of teaching it at all. A mistaken form or order is obvious; we can see it, isolate it, prescribe directly for it. It is not so when words lose touch with reality. To be sure, when a pupil is talking about the sensory, physical world, there is no trouble, or if there is, we can spot it. He will not seriously write about a stone rolling up a cliff. He may, in writing a story, forget his point of view, and tell about the look of fear he sees on the face of a mountain climber whom he is watching from half a mile below; but this again is obvious, and easily set straight. It is when he gets into abstractions, into generalizations, into the whole world of ideas, that the rub comes; and this is the world that his school and his maturing life lead him into. And it is hard to spot this trouble, and to help him see it and prevent it. In fact, we ourselves are the worst sinners. The disease is epidemic in books on education, even in official reports written by English teachers. And, in our emphasis on form and elegance, we accept with joy from a pupil something like this:

The cynical attitude of the common adolescent borders closely on the fatalism of Henchard. A connection may be seen if one notices that the cynic ascribes the lowest motives to an act. The fatalist says, "These things will invariably be so." In saying this, he assumes the lowest motives for man's actions, because higher motives would inevitably tend to change the evil that the fatalist says is irrevocably so. Thus I should call Hardy even more a cynic than a fatalist, because he takes cynicism for granted, but writes about fatalism.

Excellent. Just what we are after. Mature vocabulary, accurately used. Sentence-sense of a high order—variety, balance—the works. A compelling logical pattern. Spelling and punctuation perfect. But it is nonsense—a stone rolling up a cliff. All the skills of writing that this twelfth-grader has been so carefully taught were brought to bear in making nonsense sound convincing to himself and to his reader. I am not objecting to his criticism of a novel or novelist as such; he is entitled to his own critical views. But he ignored his own experience by making statements about the relationships in this world between motives and outcomes that just are not so, and that, a conference revealed, he did not believe.

These word-world relationships are hard to teach. But one thing is in our favor. Just as a twelve-year-old (or a three-year-old, for that matter) comes to us with uncanny control over the forms, structures, and meanings of words, so he comes to us with his language surely rooted in his firsthand experience. He has learned language simply by using it to exist effectively in this workaday world. What use is it to him—or to anybody—if it won't do that? As the ideas he wants to talk about move further and further from sensory experience, it is our job as English teachers to multiply and strengthen the connections he has already made between words and reality. But most of our teaching of language works in exactly the opposite direction.

We ask him to define "school spirit." "School spirit," he replies, "is when somebody gives up something he wants to do to cheer at an unimportant football game." There we have at hand the first natural beginnings of operational definition of an abstraction, certainly one of the most important elements of mature use of language in clear statement and clear thinking. We could jump at the chance: "Good. Let's have some more things you have seen people do that show that they have school spirit." But we don't. We jump on him. "You mustn't say 'something is when . . .' Turn to page 96. 'Something is' must be followed by a predicate adjective or substantive in the nominative case, never by an adverb. Try again." And at last we get:

"School spirit is loyalty to the highest ideals of the institution." "Good. 'A' plus." Form and no content. A mist was about to be lifted, but we have saved it and got it wrapped up safely in a fog. Salvage form, of course; but do not jettison content. The content is the priceless cargo; start with it, find and teach its appropriate form. Let's try it again. "When I see somebody do thus and so, and not do this and that, I say he has school spirit." Even the fog lifts. Our job is to wed form and content.

Or we give him sentences to piece together by using participles, gerunds, subordinating conjunctions—almost anything for sentence variety, regardless of what he himself thinks about relationships he sees in the situation he is writing about. Combine, combine. Avoid "and's." This is the way to write it: "Since the house was founded upon a rock, it did not fall, even though floods caused by descending rains, as well as winds, beat upon it." How much better this is than the barbarous original: "And the rains descended, and the floods came, and the winds blew and beat upon that house and it fell not, for it was founded upon a rock." Well, thank you very much; I'll string along with the King James version if you don't mind.

Getting a pupil to do any such work on writing different versions of sentences without at the same time asking him (not telling him) which version would be better, when, and why, is assault and battery upon his intelligence and libel against the language.

And so it goes. Our grammatical categories, "rules," and definitions are based on arbitrarily assumed norms, which are for the most part derived from simple, physical and sensory situations, at a level at which grammatical form reflects reality well enough. "My dog bit my cat." *Dog* is the subject; we are talking about it. It acted. *Cat* is the object—it received the action, was the object of the action. That tells what really happened. That is all right. But then we go on to extend our grammatical descriptions to situations and sentences that they no longer describe. "You should have seen the trout I saw yesterday." I am talking not about you or myself, but the trout. The grammatical subject is no longer the logical subject. The word *trout* is the grammatical object, but the trout itself received no action at all; I didn't catch it.

We could spell out this misrepresentation of reality by our usual grammatical categories, definition by definition, rule by rule, through almost every item of grammar that we teach. But this is to our advantage; for it is just here, in laying bare to our students and with them the nature of grammatical "rules" and definitions, and in finding and discussing the countless cases to which they do not apply, that we can find some of our best materials and methods for our teaching of language—and of life.

Our absorption with grammatical terminology and analysis blocks us, and our pupils, from much of what matters most about language. We give them the idea that if they can diagram a sentence, or tell the part of speech and construction of every word in it, they have mastered it.

Let me take one example—one that came up in my seventh grade a while ago: the sentence (one of theirs) "Long books are dull." That's an easy one. Structurally, it is a simple sentence, so its meaning must be simple. (Superstition.) A seventh grader can give it the complete grammatical treatment, so of course he knows all about what it says, and how what it says corresponds with reality. (Superstition number two.) But before moving on to a harder, complex sentence, like, "My father got mad at me when I broke a window," let's take a closer look. There are several most important things to notice about this "Long books are dull." They are not easy, but a seventh-grader can get them.

It is a generalization. On what specific firsthand particulars is it based? Are there enough? How many might be enough?

It is in form a "declarative statement," like "this book is rectangular in shape." How does it differ? It is, of course, a value judgment, not, like the other, a statement of fact, "dull" being the key word.

It is a relative statement. Here the clue is "long." "Long" makes sense only in relation to something else. How long, exactly, is "long?"

"Long" may be subjective, not objective. It may refer to the way books seem, not to the number of pages.

And before we go on to the next one, let them take a try at this one again. We may get something like this: "The longest story I ever tried to read was X, and it didn't interest me. I didn't finish it." All sorts of useful and vital language work can lead naturally out of a lesson in formal and structural grammar—even out of the forms of pronouns. "Who, in this or that sentence, is *we?*" That is always a crucial question. Don't settle for the answer that it is the nominative case first person plural of the pronoun.

The compelling job in all teaching of language (or for that matter of everything we teach through language—history, science, business practice, or anything else, including literature and composition) is to get at truth, reality, the world as we know it and believe it to be, through words. It is the specific and special job of language teaching to establish the methods by which this can be done, and the conviction that it is worth doing. It is our job to strengthen, refine, and multiply the links between what we consider to be reality, the total world outside ourselves, and the words by which we think about it and communicate our expanding ideas about it; by which we manipulate it in our thinking and discourse. Acquisition of one's native language is at once the means and measure of one's development as a person. Good language teaching is the forward cutting edge of the pupil's growth toward maturity. Poor language teaching can stunt his growth, and perhaps fix him permanently in adolescence. Good language teaching creates two-way highways between words and experience, and keeps the traffic going.

But we must get on to another language art: the art of getting the effects we are after. Language is intended to have certain effects on certain people. It if it successful, it has these effects without at the same time having undesirable, unintended effects. In this view, good English is effective English. English is most likely to be effective if it is appropriate in at least five directions: to the purpose; to the subject; to the occasion; to the receiver; and to the speaker or writer. What are these possible effects, which, for convenience, we can call "meanings"? One we have discussed: making plain sense. This is sometimes called a "referential" or "intellectual" effect.

Language can also have nonintellectual effects. My words can let you know, directly or by suggestion, what my feelings or attitudes are toward anyone or anything. Or they can, with or without my conscious intent, stir your feelings, implant in your mind attitudes toward anyone, including myself, or anything. A while ago I defended the sentence "Him and me done it" as making clear sense. It is "substandard" English, but I do not call it bad English until it gets into a situation in which it is ineffective. Sooner or later it will; for, although it makes plain sense, it is likely to give some listener feelings and opinions about the speaker that are unintended, and damaging; damaging, perhaps, even to his career. Substandard English is not *per se* bad English; it is simply impoverished English, limiting the situations in which the speaker can take part with confidence and effectiveness. English that is confined to superstandard, prissy idiom and usage has the same sort of impoverishment and limitation.

We need not pause for long on the only other effect of language that I shall mention: the effect of influencing action. Let me say only that it operates, like all uses of language, through suggestion as well as statement. In fact, language generally operates more effectively by suggestion than by statement in this particular use of influencing action. The imperative mood is often its least effective instrument. Often, too, it is inextricably fused with giving factual information, with stirring emotions, and with influencing attitudes.

Very rarely, in fact, does language operate with only a single effect.

The other language art that I mentioned was the art of discrimination—pertinent and useful discrimination. I am not happy about the name I have given it, but it will do as a caption for a few illustrations of the sort of thing I have in mind. I have said "pertinent discrimination," because sometimes we do not have to stop to make discriminations at all. We don't want to make linguistic analysis a matter of captious hairsplitting, and knowing when to make discriminations is in itself an art. Discriminations should also be usable since making them at all implies that we know what to do about them once we have made them. There is no point in learning the difference between a domestic cat and a skunk unless I can use what I have learned in appropriate action.

Here, then, are some of the distinctions that call for this art of discrimination:

Between literal and metaphorical language. This implies the ability to interpret metaphor, once it is recognized. Within metaphor, a further distinction may be useful: that between metaphor used to expand and clarify meaning and for rhetorical effects, and that used in an attempt to prove. Metaphor cannot prove; but when it is used in the attempt, it requires a special sort of interpretation.

Between kinds of statements and kinds of questions. The rote classification of sentences by form only, as "declarative," "interrogative," or "imperative," obscures vital logical and rhetorical distinctions, particularly those between statements of fact, statements of opinion or value judgments, and normative statements.

Between kinds of questions: scientific questions (those with verifiable answers), exploratory questions (those capable of leading to useful discussion or research, but not to immediate scientific answers), and bootless or meaningless questions that pose as scientific or exploratory.

Between degrees of generalization. This involves the knowledge that a statement is not general or specific in an absolute sense, but only relative to another statement. It requires a decision as to what degree of generalization is appropriate to the subject and purpose, and what specific cases, and how many, are necessary for support or illustration. (An ancillary art here is that of discrimination between an "all" and a "some" generalization.)

Between abstractions and words that refer to picturable objects; that is, between abstract language and language that refers more directly to the physical world. Once the distinction is made, and the abstraction recognized, the art of defining it is put to use. I have already touched lightly on the art of operational definition; you may remember my illustration of defining "school spirit." These abstractions come from the realities of our experience as surely as do words like *chair* and *cow*. They stand just as surely for realities. And they can be defined, understood, and made clear in the same way—by tracing them back to their source in our world. The way back is more devious and intricate, but it can be followed—that is, if the word has any meaning for its user or receiver.

Between tones of voice, and their analogous tones in written discourse. The tone can determine the sense, even to the point of completely changing it. It is a decisive factor also in the use of the other effects of language.

I spoke earlier of the importance of a teacher's having theoretical reserves. I have made no attempt to go into any theories with any depth, nor even to mention all those that I believe are important. You surely have noticed great gaps in my fabric. Nowhere have I mentioned the theories of fact or the theories of proof; nowhere discussed the formal or inductive logical patterns; nor the theory as to how words get meaning only from experience; nor the principles of definition, nor definition by context (with its important bearing on shifts of meaning); nor the theory of language as symbol; nor the principles of classification, which underlie much of what I have been discussing here. Nor have I touched on the principle that we have words only for what we need to talk and think about—*we* as individuals, *we* as a society; that there is more in the world for which we have no words than we have classified to our satisfaction and imposed words upon, and more escapes us than we capture.

So in closing, let me say that I have tried only to mention a few of the elements of language that I believe we can introduce with profit into our classrooms, to suggest only a few principles and theories against which we may test our current practices, and to indicate promising subjects for further thought and for the experiment and research that every one of us can carry on in the laboratory of his own classroom.

Finally, this seems to me to be the conclusion of the whole matter: try to teach them so to control language that experience, reality as it is given us to know it, is not mutilated in its precarious passage through words.

And so I come at last to the queen of the language arts, the hardest of all to win: the art of stopping, the art of silence.

2

Some Definitions of Terms:
Report of the Language
Committee

PHILIP BURNHAM, *St. Paul's School, Concord, New Hampshire, Chairman*

ROBERT BOYNTON, *Germantown Friends School, Pennsylvania*

FREDERICK PETERSON, *Phillips Academy, Andover, Massachusetts*

DOROTHY SHAPLEIGH, *New Britain High School, Connecticut*

ALMA WATERHOUSE, *Hall High School, West Hartford, Connecticut*

This committee has been asked to report to you on language, to say something meaningful about language study in secondary schools—an assignment for which we quickly recognize our limitations both of time and of authority. Yet because of our variety of background and training and experience, and because we are motivated by the same hopes and aspirations that bring teachers from all over New England to this conference, we think we present some considerations of great importance to us all.

For our purposes, language study needs definition and illustration.

The committee considers language study to include at least eight subdivisions, not of equal weight or value (nor can we devote an appropriate share to each in this report). Six are to be considered and briefly discussed before we move into fuller consideration of the two which need most concern.

We consider language study to be the description and discussion of why we talk and write the way we do. The eight subdivisions of language study are:

1. Grammar
2. Usage
3. Rhetoric
4. Vocabulary
5. Spelling
6. Punctuation and capitalization
7. History of the English language and of other languages
8. Semantics

Our reasons for the teaching of language are familiar ones:

1. To help students to use language effectively in speaking, writing, listening, and reading.
2. To help students to use language effectively in thinking.
3. To give students a terminology.
4. To enrich for students their whole cultural point of view, to help them better to understand who they are and what they are.

Now the arbitrary division into eight parts is not entirely satisfactory, neither to the committee nor, perhaps, to you. For some will be of the opinion that these eight are, after all, what we really mean when we name the first listed—"grammar"; and when we call semantics "the study of words and meanings," you will be confirmed in your opinion, or you will say, "Well, that's just the problem of usage." We hope we have here immediately illustrated the importance of semantics, of the concern over words and their meanings, for we do think that the *grammar* of these last few sentences is at least reasonable, and the *usage* tolerable.

Since almost everything has to be learned through words, it has often been said that every teacher is a teacher of English—a statement to which this report will return. The converse we need to consider: "The teacher of semantics," remarked F. A. Philbrick in his *Understanding English: An Introduction to Semantics*, "may find that he has become a teacher of everything." Provided he touches on topics which are "part of a general explanation of meaning, this seems to be not a drawback but an advantage. Generations of teachers have deplored the isolation of studies from each other—'in watertight compartments' as the common but inappropriate, metaphor has it—and the power of semantics to spill over dikes and dams is one of the best reasons for teaching it." S. I. Hayakawa's *Language in Thought and Action*, one of the books in the list of suggested readings for the conference, thoroughly explores "the role of verbal communication in human affairs."

On spelling or on punctuation and capitalization this committee now has little to say. We urge, however, that they get no more attention than they deserve. They are, to be sure, two parts of the eight we have chosen, but the mathematics of English teaching does not make them one fourth of the total importance of language study. What we will have to say in detail about grammar may appropriately be applied to spelling and to punctuation and capitalization.

This committee does consider highly important some knowledge— on the part of the teacher as indeed of the student—of the history of the English language and of other languages, not for its own sake, but as illumination, often by contrast, of present practices, and as another of the many means to help us all better to understand who and what we are.

Students are interested in knowing where language comes from, with the inevitable human curiosity that asks where anything and everything "comes from." Human beings, like animals, used sounds before they developed a language, sounds that were a sort of humming or singing, and that were uttered in a spirit of play or an overflow of emotion. The nearest thing to them which we know is probably the cooing or gurgling of a baby before it learns its parents' language. Leonard Bloomfield's *Language* makes some very illuminating remarks about the earliest languages.

And more important for the study of language is language's analytical development. Except in a few "reply" words such as *yes* and *no*, we no longer have anything even resembling sentence-words. We analyze the same sentence idea into parts, and have several words make up a sentence, which the hearer has to put together in the right way in order to create in his own mind the idea of the speaker. No one knows what analytical division occurred first, but the result has been surprisingly uniform throughout all the languages which we now know. But being a folk creation, language is not a completely logical analysis, and we need to make students aware of its probable origins and its history—especially its constant and continuing change, its perverseness (or, lest we mistake the word for the thing, the perverseness of its users).

On vocabulary, as one of the eight parts of language study, this committee has two comments to make. We are uneasy about the "learning-one-word-a-day-and-using-it-in-your-composition" practice. If we are to teach semantics, we cannot overlook the contexts of words. Important as the enlargement of useful and potential vocabulary is, this committee is convinced that interest in language—especially in semantics and language history—and attention to words in context are the means by which vocabularies are enlarged. The virtue of words is in appropriateness and meaning rather than in number. The second comment on vocabulary has to do with dictionaries. We are disturbed that the high competition among makers of desk dictionaries has led to an apparent concern on the part of editors and publishers not with "What's the latest word?" but with "Who has the latest word?" The representative of the dictionary publisher says, "Look! We have the most recently revised dictionary. We now include the word *tizzle*, first used just yesterday by the American ambassador. Of course it may have been a misprint, but we have it, anyhow! What other dictionary has *tizzle*?" If this is to continue, we may soon find *The New York Times* keeping us up to date. This might be a good thing, ironically enough, for it would at least emphasize the constant change in language; but it is surely not such a frantic concern of the dictionary maker.

In the teaching of usage this committee is anxious to report its dissatisfaction with the doctrine of *rightness* and *wrongness*, of the *correct* and the *incorrect*. That usage differs with individuals—even the individual—is readily observable, sometimes too readily. Language scholars discuss these differences in terms of the occasion where language is used and the purpose for which it is intended.

Following their practice, but altering the terms of classification, Robert C. Pooley, in another of the books on the list of suggested readings for this conference, *Teaching English Usage*, enumerates five levels of usage: (1) illiterate—outside the pale of cultured society; not for the classroom; (2) homely—not illiterate and not acceptable; to be modified for the classroom; (3) standard English on the informal level —the usage of cultured, educated people; for the classroom and all ordinary occasions; (4) standard English on the formal level—the goal of expression showing care and restraint; also for the classroom and more formal occasions; (5) literary—usage revealing beauty and grace.

The National Council of Teachers of English has accepted as the definition of good English "that form of speech which is appropriate to the purposes of the speaker and listener." This particular definition admits a very considerable leeway; pushed to extremes, it permits forceful, if inelegant, telling of where to head in. The definition of bad English makes the criteria sense and meaning and stresses the occasion rather than the individual: "Bad English is that use of language which is unclear, ineffective, and inappropriate to the language occasion." These definitions bring to mind analogies frequently employed: language is the garment or vehicle for thought. Like clothes or vehicles, which differ according to the demands of the occasion, language styles differ according to the needs of the occasion. The judgment of usage must be in terms of meaning for the situation rather than in any other terms.

Of the eight items in this committee's discussion of language, we are left with but two—grammar and rhetoric. With these two the committee would like to complete its report in some detail.

Knowing full well that the discussion of grammar is that place where angels fear to tread, this committee rolled up its collective sleeves and—perhaps to carry out the full phrasing of the proverbial wisdom—gladly rushed in. Grammar, we came to feel, was something like Robert Frost's "The Secret Sits":

> We dance around in a ring and suppose,
> But the Secret sits in the middle and knows.

We were plagued by reports that grammar, like Conrad's "Mr. Kurtz—he dead," was no longer among the living, and we were plagued by inquiries as to who or what had "this ill deed done." We recollected Chaucer's "I lerne song, but I kan but smal grammeere," as well as Artemus Ward's "Why care for grammar as long as we are good?"

We came out of the semantic difficulties mentioned earlier in this report through this definition: grammar, as a part of language study, is a description of how we talk and write. We considered the National Council of Teachers of English definition of grammar as the description of the formation of English sentences and the explanation of choice in inflectional words. We talked of the grammar of language as the devices that signal structural meaning. And we said that grammar had to do with word forms and the organization of those words in sentences, that grammar describes how words are used together to convey meaning. We threw out the consideration of grammar as correctness opposed to incorrectness. Always we came back to *description* as our key word, and through that word to the definition of grammar as the description of how we talk and write.

And as a committee we agreed that grammar is but one part of the study of language—one eighth in our strict mathematics. And though we do not ask you to apply here a mathematics that we asked you to reject earlier, we do ask that grammar be put into its appropriate perspective in language: neither to be ignored, nor to be allowed to grow to such leviathan-like proportions that it absorbs more Jonahs than the Biblical whale probably ever dreamed of.

Now in the barrage of attacks upon grammar, the emphasis seems to have been upon what is wrong with grammar itself; as if somehow this innocent description of how we talk and write had an evil mist more deadly than atomic dust surrounding it, and even to mention its name was to re-enact the opening of Pandora's box, letting out "Hope" in the bargain. Better yet, to double the curse one simply put "formal" in front of it; "formal grammar" can make one see "more devils than vast hell can hold." And so we see those who have attempted to exorcise it, sometimes by putting "functional" in place of "formal," sometimes by calling the rose by any other name.

This committee wishes to report its view that modern linguistic study does not pose a question regarding the teaching of traditional grammar but a question regarding the traditional teaching of grammar.

By traditional teaching of grammar we refer to the secure, safe, but invalid assumption that grammar has to do with absolutes of right and wrong, with a monotonous chanting of identifications of parts of speech wholly unrelated to the real problems of oral or written expression; that grammar can be of use to students through dogmatic pronouncements of "correct" and "incorrect" in regard to the use or identification of sentence elements. Instead, if we concentrate on the operations of our language (as our definition suggests), we shall encourage the realization that language is not a static form controlled by exercises, but a flexible arrangement of words and structures, usually in constant flow and fluctuation in the utterances of a single person as well as in utterances throughout the history of the language. Language, as an art form, is a mobile.

In our description (or grammatical interpretation) of language we may continue to use the traditional grammar but with reservations concerning the validity of many of our long-accepted practices. Such reservations should serve to guide the teacher in determining the approach, portion of time, and extent of the possibilities for the teaching of grammar.

One misconception should be noted, since the misconception directly affects the practice in many schools. Too often teachers have felt that they have solved the problem and "kept abreast of modern trends" if they either disregard traditional grammar or hoodwink themselves by using a term such as "functional grammar," a term which has come to mean simply "less grammar." Of the two misconceptions, the latter is probably the more misleading. Those who disregard traditional grammar eventually find themselves handicapped in their description of language skills (unless they have been more successful than modern linguists in their attempts to find substitutes for the commonly accepted classifications and structures). Those who have convinced themselves that they have achieved a modern approach by the magic of *functional* grammar, however, are likely to continue complacently with an ample set of drill exercises and testing devices which, even when carefully avoiding the terms of traditional grammar, are no more functional than any drill materials which might include the terms of traditional grammar.

The magic cannot be accomplished merely by a variation of the type of drill nomenclature nor by the use of a term such as *functional*. In short, there is no magic other than a fully informed and re-sourceful teacher who can present traditional grammar in a flexible, significant, and purposeful manner.

Such a view suggests that as teachers we have failed to supply imagination and thought to our teaching of language, particularly to our teaching of grammar. We readily agree that there is no virtue in grammar for its own sake, and yet because it is said to have rela-tionship to effective speaking and writing, we drum through the drill books, and the work books, and the interminable lists, and we fill-in-the blanks for pages innumerable, and we stop there.

But the grammar that can profitably be taught is that which has direct use in speaking and writing. To list the adjectives or to pick out the appositives or identify the participles and stop there is to get out the cake pan and the flour and other ingredients and then walk out of the kitchen, expecting the cake to be baked when the company suddenly appears and the need is upon us.

The purpose of the activity in the kitchen is to get the cake; just as surely the purpose of the activity in grammar is to get clear-cut, effective communication. We want to show that knowing something about adjectives makes better sentences, that appositives and par-ticiples are some of the devices that sometimes signal meaning more exactly than, say, two sentences. But we don't want students to take this on faith, expecting them somehow to perform the miracle with grammar that we did not expect of the cake pan and flour. Grammar is for sentence improvement, and only when it is directed toward improving sentences—particularly the students' own sentences—does it have a validity as one part, surely not the whole, of language study.

We think students should understand grammatical relationships for insight into the ways in which words are put together to make effective sentences. We think they should be concerned with indi-vidual words—parts of speech and function words, with word order, inflection, and, in speaking, intonation and stress. And, above all this, of course, they must be concerned with meaning. Better perhaps it is to say that all these considerations for grammar and for all language study move constantly toward meaning. The purposes for the study of grammar are those for language study; terminology is only the means we use to teach students to use language effectively, to sharpen thinking and in turn make speaking and writing come as close to intention as possible, and to help students better to understand what and who they are.

This means, too, that as teachers we must be aware of the significant studies of language, for example, of the work of Charles Fries, whose *Structure of English* is on the list of suggested readings for this conference, as well as of the thorough book-length study by a committee for the Progressive Education Association, *Language in General Education*, published in 1940. And those more general but significant studies, such as *General Education in a Free Society* (1945), and *General Education in School and College* (1952).

Teachers of English must, like all teachers and members of all professions, keep up with the times. When we talk of "standards" we must not mean the arbitrary rules of correctness that never were on sea or land, but we must mean the practices that the real world recognizes and accepts. We must get out of the unreal classroom world of an inflexible "It is I" or "shall-and-will" dogma or an angry clucking at the current use of "like" as a subordinating conjunction, into the real world. Let us replace our ivory towers with steel towers when we are dealing with the world most of us and most of our students know. We need not demolish every ivory tower, but we need not build one or maintain one where ivory is too precious for, and too far removed in usefulness from, the practical everyday affairs of heart and mind and hand.

To move from discussion of grammar to discussion of rhetoric is to move only a short space, for the very close relationship of grammar and rhetoric—indeed of all eight of the subdivisions in language that we have made—is quite apparent. Rhetoric is simply the art of using words effectively in speech or in writing, and frequently the problems of rhetoric become problems in usage or semantics or grammar, or even in the history of the language.

The seven deadly sins of rhetoric—or perhaps seventy-times-seven—are indicated by the need for rooting out jargon and cliché, for recognizing the importance of connotation and the confusion of ambiguity. To name the devices or the problems is to show the scope of learning which rhetoric involves. In addition to those mentioned, we can name at least these: transition, parallelism, logical comparison, point of view, subordination, diction, wordiness and repetition, monotonous structure, excessive or inappropriate use of the passive voice, the use of figurative language, and fine writing. Such a listing can be no more than a reminder of the variety of considerations in the study of rhetoric, yet it can serve as evidence to support the practical suggestions which now follow.

In a relatively short space, this committee has tried to make three statements, perhaps even conclusions:

1. That grammar is important, but that grammar is only one part of language study and needs to be taught as such, particularly with thought and imagination constantly moving the study of grammar toward effective speaking and writing.
2. That language study comes out of students' own speaking and writing.
3. That language power grows from students' own critical thinking.

Very well, you may say, and yet how is all this to be done? And what of composition, of intensive reading, of extensive reading? And the home rooms, the study halls, and the lunchrooms to supervise, the department meetings, the committee meetings, the school plays and newspapers and magazines? Not to mention the dozen and one other things that teachers as responsible members of the school group and of their whole communities are expected and want to do?

We move toward a solution by showing that as a profession we are informed and competent, that we are alert to the real needs of our students (a need not generally met by the substitution of dreary "activities" for direct and imaginative concern with the real problems in language which students face), and that we know what is important and alive rather than dogmatic and parroted.

We move toward a solution by showing that we need writing and more writing from our students. Harold Martin, Director of the required English course at Harvard, "General Education A," and a teacher of wide experience in public secondary schools in New York, has described "How the American Boy Learns to Write." Mr. Martin concludes:

Today, by and large, the American boy does not learn to write. If he becomes able to, it is because he has stumbled upon it. We can change that. We can change it by requiring him to write and write and write; by becoming writers ourselves, even to that unlistening audience whom one addresses as 'Dear Reader'; by putting precision and handsomeness and honesty of expression at the center of our teaching; by sacrificing the immediate popularity of the teacher-buddy to the satisfaction of knowing that the student who leaves our charge is better equipped to live because he has become habituated to inquiry and has gained some skill in the use of the only instrument that makes inquiry possible—the grubby pen that is clenched between ink-soiled fingers on a weary arm attached to aching shoulders topped by a head swimming with the combinations and permutations of an idea that will have its way, an idea that will out.[1]

And we move toward a solution by showing that present teacher loads—120 to 150 students in four or five classes—won't allow adequate attention to all of the writing we ought to have. We need to show that more than two different classes per day—that is, more than two preparations—is an absurdity, especially when added to the problem of class size. The mathematics of correction is effective: even one 150-word paper per week (which in itself is not enough writing) from 120 to 150 students would take six to eight hours of correction time and this is to assume that teachers, unlike members of other professions, do not have their working hours in any way interrupted, even by the need to stretch or to eat.

We move toward a solution by constantly reminding teachers of other subjects that even as we, especially in discussing semantics, become teachers of other subjects, so they, whenever they ask a student to speak or to write, are teachers of English; and if they need the language they ought to know and do something about it.

Even within present conditions we can show our awareness and concern: there is no reason why a class cannot be reading in class

[1] Harold Martin, "How The American Boy Learns to Write," *The English Leaflet*, The New England Association of Teachers of English (March, 1955).

time while the teacher talks to individual students about their own writing. But this is only a finger in the dike. Chairmen of departments, superintendents, school boards, and parents must be shown, practically, that our problems can be solved not by a glorious reception room or a new gym or another activities unit on how to set the table for a party of six, but by adequately paid teachers dealing creatively with a reasonable number of students in a reasonable daily program that leaves time and energy for professional stimulation and growth through discussion and reading and thought.

The demands and responsibilities others ask us to assume when we teach English, and indeed the demands and responsibilities we put upon ourselves, have an interesting and close parallel in the remarks made at the end of James Gould Cozzens' fine novel *The Just and The Unjust*. A young lawyer says to his father, a judge, that things just won't work out. If a war breaks out, he says in 1939, "all bets are off." It is the father's reply that says as much to us as English teachers as it says to the young man, Abner Coates, or, for that matter, to every one of our students today and tomorrow:

"Don't be cynical," Judge Coates said. "A cynic is just a man who found out when he was about ten that there wasn't any Santa Claus, and he's still upset. Yes, there'll be more war; and soon, I don't doubt. There always has been. There'll be deaths and disappointments and failures. When they come, you meet them. Nobody promises you a good time or an easy time. I don't know who it was who said when we think of the past we regret and when we think of the future we fear. And with reason. But no bets are off. There is the present to think of, and as long as you live there always will be. In the present, every day is a miracle. The world gets up in the morning and is fed and goes to work, and in the evening it comes home and is fed again and perhaps has a little amusement and goes to sleep. To make that possible, so much has to be done by so many people that, on the face of it, it is impossible. Well, every day we do it; and every day, come hell, come high water, we're going to have to go on doing it as well as we can."

"So it seems," said Abner.

"Yes, so it seems," said Judge Coates, "and so it is, and so it will be! And that's where you come in. That's all we want of you."

Abner said, "What do you want of me?"

"We just want you to do the impossible," Judge Coates said.[2]

[2] (New York, Harcourt, Brace & Co., 1950).

Appendix

Excerpts from the Secondary Education Board's
DEFINITION OF THE REQUIREMENTS
in English [2]

English is a language. For the pupils in our schools it is the native language—the language on which they rely, in school and out, both in their own thinking and in their dealings with others. The part played by language in general, and by the native language in particular, in the development of the young is the common concern of all teachers. The operation of language in communication is the special concern of the teacher of English.

This operation of language is the common root of the teaching and learning of all the branches of English, the classroom subject. Written and oral expression, general reading, the interpretation of literature, listening with understanding—these are not isolated, discrete subjects or parts of an English course, however necessary it may be to treat them as such in the construction of teaching units or in setting standards and requirements. They are indivisibly unified into a whole by virtue of the fact that they are alike processes and outcomes of language in operation, stemming from common principles of language. Each of these branches, to be sure, requires its own techniques of teaching, learning, and practicing; but these are simply the specialized techniques of applying language principles common to all uses of language.

As a teacher of the native language the teacher of English has also another special responsibility. The native language is not merely a means of communication. It is an integral part of the entire development of the pupil and of his growing ability to organize and understand his world, and to cope with it. It is perhaps the central part, at once the means and index, of this growth. It is, furthermore, both the material and process of his thinking. A working knowledge of the

2 Copies of the *Definition of the Requirements for 1955, with the Examinations of March and May, 1954,* may be obtained at a small charge from The Secondary Education Board, Milton 86, Massachusetts, by whose permission these excerpts have been used.

operations of language is therefore essential to education. It is the first concern of the English class.

To what extent theoretical knowledge of the operations of language is essential or useful to the acquisition of this working knowledge is a moot question; but it is a question that concerns teaching methods rather than end results.

It has been the intent of the Committee to incorporate this concept of English and its teaching in the statement of requirements. In specifying the different parts of the requirement, the Committee has kept in mind the common root of language operation, and the interrelationship of the parts, each to the others. The parts of the requirement, furthermore, have been graded, as far as possible, to the stages of the all-round development of the pupil.

In this concept, English grammar becomes one part of language operation—but only one. Grammatically considered, English is primarily a language of word-order which nevertheless makes full use of its few surviving inflected forms. It is an analytic rather than a synthetic language. It is also a living language, hence a language inevitably undergoing change in structure, form, vocabulary, and idiom —that is, in usage. A teaching of grammar that is not consistent with these qualities of English is not a teaching of English grammar. But an understanding of grammar and usage alone is only a partial understanding of the operation of language. In fact, grammar itself cannot be fully understood apart from the full operations of language. Grammar functions as only one of the essential components of language operating to achieve its effects; and like all of these components, in any context it is what it is because each of the others is what it is.

Similarly, in this view vocabulary should keep pace with a pupil's experience and development, his ability to understand concepts, and his natural opportunity and need to use these in communication. This implies the teaching and learning of new words, and new meanings and applications of familiar words, in situations, or "settings," and in full verbal contexts, rather than in lists dissociated alike from the pupil's experience and his desire or need to understand others or to express himself. The pupil, furthermore, should have, and be able to use, a vocabulary, as well as a knowledge of idiom and usage, appropriate to any situation, formal or informal, in which he may naturally find himself.

Bibliography

FRIES, Charles C., *American-English Grammar* (National Council of Teachers of English Publication; New York, Appleton-Century-Crofts, Inc., 1940).

An authoritative study of the language habits of the American public, demonstrating failure of rules to explain common usage; advocates speech as criterion for standard English.

————, *The Structure of English* (New York, Harcourt, Brace & Co., 1952).

One of the newest and most controversial works on "the grammar of structure"; proposes a new approach to "sentence analysis" and a new terminology for grammar.

HAYAKAWA, S. I., *Language In Thought and Action* (New York, Harcourt, Brace & Co., 1939).

Concerned with language as a symbolic system, stressing affective language as an instrument for understanding; replete with illustration of misconception in meaning.

HOOK, J. N., and MATHEWS, E. G., *Modern American Grammar and Usage* (New York, The Ronald Press Company, 1956).

An analysis, largely in traditional terms, of modern American grammar and usage in writing rather than in speaking.

JESPERSEN, Otto, *Language: Its Nature, Development, and Origin* (New York, Henry Holt & Co., 1933).

Supporting the idea of language as human behavior; amply provided with concrete example and historic anecdote regarding changing conditions and interpretations of language.

LaBRANT, Lou, *We Teach English* (New York, Harcourt, Brace & Co., 1951).

An explanation of the composite language program, including all phases of the study within its framework; theory and illustration from actual classroom practice.

MARCKWARDT, Albert, *Introduction to the English Language* (New York, Oxford University Press, Inc., 1942).

A recapitulation of the history of the English language, the occasion of its changes, and an exposition of reasons for its current pattern.

OGDEN, C. K., and RICHARDS, I. A., *Meaning of Meaning* (London, Kegan Paul, Trench, Trubner and Co., Ltd., 1936).

Accepts semantics as key to intelligent usage; queries possibility of finding "respectable nomenclature" for grammar; stresses need of analyzing structure for sense.

POOLEY, Robert C., *Teaching English Usage* (National Council of Teachers of English Publication; New York, Appleton-Century-Crofts, Inc., 1946).

Concerned with language as behavior; classifies usage on five levels; in accepting a "standard English," accepts considerable content, but advocates teaching in relation to need.

ROBERTS, Paul, *Understanding Grammar* (New York, Harper & Brothers, 1954).

A comprehensive discussion of both traditional grammar and the new linguistics.

ZAHNER, Louis, and others, *Language in General Education* (Progressive Education Association Publication; New York, D. Appleton-Century Company, Inc., 1939).

Emphasizes social nature of language as expression and means of interpretation; differentiates between formal grammar and grammar of meaning, but accepts some traditional content and practice.

3

What About Grammar?
Report of the Grammar
Committee

THOMAS RAGLE, *Phillips Exeter Academy, New Hampshire, Chairman*
ROBERT BOYNTON, *Germantown Friends School, Pennsylvania*
HAZEL GUYOL, *Concord High School, New Hampshire*
DALTON McBEE, *Phillips Academy, Andover, Massachusetts*
OLIVE MacPHERSON, *Somerville High School, Massachusetts*

Let us begin by stating unequivocally that this Committee believes grammar should be taught in the secondary schools. This statement is not so unnecessary as it might first appear: there are teachers today who seem to deny that grammar should be taught. Some profess not to teach grammar because they believe it is not necessary. Upon examination, we discover that they do teach grammar, but under a different name: "sentence structure" they call it, or "mechanics." They mean only that they do not teach grammar as they were taught it. Nevertheless their statement, "grammar is unnecessary," is quoted in the press and has a pernicious effect: it misleads inexperienced teachers, and misrepresents our position before the public.

Others profess to teach no grammar in school because they believe the ability to comprehend and to articulate can be, should be, picked up by osmosis, a sort of absorption by imitation. Read enough, imitate enough, they argue, and you will absorb all the tools you need to write well. They point to Greek literature, which flourished before grammar had been analyzed and dignified as a subject for formal study, or to some British public schools, where the study of English does not mean what we should call composition and grammar, but what we should call literature—the study of English authors from Chaucer through the nineteenth century. In such schools the art of composition is learned largely in the process of writing critical or historical essays which are corrected more for content than form. Yet these British students learn to write well.

The answer to these critics is that there are two kinds of grammar, and we as teachers frequently confuse them. What these last critics mean is that the teaching of what used to be called "Formal Grammar," and what we now might call "Theoretical Grammar," is unnecessary. They do not deny usage, only principles. We may draw an analogy here with the machine gun. One member of our Committee remembers trying desperately a few years ago to explain to a recruit how to adjust the barrel of his machine gun. He was making no progress whatsoever; the recruit stared in uncomprehending amazement. At this point a combat veteran, using unprintable words perfected in a long army career, blew the oververbal teacher aside and said, "Look, Mac, this way." Thereupon, using no more than the monosyllabic "see," he taught the recruit what to do. Then, turning a withering gaze upon the former instructor, he spat, "If we tried to explain *how* everything works, we'd never win a war. Show 'em and let 'em copy."

A good point: show 'em and let 'em copy. Isn't that what happens much of the time anyway? Homer, we may presume, spoke excellent Greek before the science of grammar had been invented. Children speak English before they come to school; indeed, they often handle sentence structure remarkably well, particularly if they come from a literate family. We ourselves use the complicated English tense systems without conscious effort, yet it is doubtful that we could explain the complicated theory behind them—so complicated that Jesperson spends sixty-five pages or so classifying them. How did Homer learn? How do the children learn? How did we learn? By imitation. Thus in the sense we have been using the term *grammar* up to this point, Homer, the children, and we did not learn theoretical grammar, but usage—not principles, but practice.

Now we all believe that correct usage should be taught—because it is useful, directly useful to the student. Similarly all our grammar teaching in school, of whatever sort, should be directed toward eventual use, toward application—toward improved comprehension and improved articulation: listening, reading, speaking, writing. We are not teaching students how to cut out paper dolls to represent parts of speech. We are not primarily teaching morals, however admirable these morals may be. We are not even teaching grammar for its own sake, or for fun, as some learned and dedicated grammarians would have us believe. It might be laudable for Americans to know how their language operates, but if the knowledge has no eventual application, however laudable the knowledge may be, we do not have room for it in the school curriculum. There just is not room. Therefore, if we believe that theoretical grammar should be taught in school, we must so believe because a knowledge of theoretical grammar is useful, because it helps comprehension and articulation.

It does. At least some of it does. When this Committee said that we believe grammar should be taught in school, we were not thinking of usage—though what we have already said should indicate that we believe usage also should be taught—we were thinking of principles. But let's be clear about one thing here: there are two points at question—whether a knowledge of principles is necessary, and whether teaching of principles is necessary. Critics of the kind we have been discussing are guilty of confusing the two, but the problems are quite separate. If we pause to consider, however, the first should cause us little trouble. Beyond a very narrow range, knowledge of principles is necessary if the student is to have any mobility in the language at all. Return for a moment to our analogy of the machine gunner: either he must fire all types of machine gun, a tedious if not impossible task, or he will be able to adjust the barrel only of the type he has been taught. If his unit captures a foreign machine gun, he cannot use it, and his usefulness to his company is greatly reduced. If he learns the theory of his adjustments, however, he can figure out any machine gun. Knowledge of grammatical theory, or principles, as we have been calling them, serves the same purpose. Faced with the involved sentences and nonsentences of Dickens, after having read little more than the daily paper, the student can still figure out what Dickens is saying because the grammatical principles are sufficiently the same. In the same way, when he is faced with the elaborate periodic sentences of Milton and has read only the loose sentences of Hemingway, he can still puzzle out what Milton is saying. The prose of Joyce, on the other hand, presents difficulties because a sufficient number of principles are not the same.

Knowledge of the principles, therefore, is necessary if the student is to have any mobility in the language at all. Upon reflection, most of us would not quarrel with that. The real problem comes when we try to decide how the student is to learn them. But again, let's be clear about what actually happens: if our good students gain mobility through imitation, they have done more than just copy: they have induced the principles from their own experience. Homer, the children, and we learned to copy usage, but we also induced some principles at the same time. All but the slowest child learns ultimately that the subject normally precedes the verb in English; he learns this much even if he cannot learn to identify in class a subject and a verb. Therefore some critics ask, "If he can induce principles, why should he be taught them at all? Why not spend time on other things which must be taught?"

This Committee believes that principles should be taught for at least two reasons. First, convenience. Even if we can learn to write good English by induction, we can more quickly and more easily learn to write good English by being taught. To learn, we must be critical of our work, and to be critical, we must understand principles as well as usage. The sooner the student understands the principles of grammar, the sooner he can correct, and thus improve his own work. Consider a simple error, so obvious you may think unnecessary any attempt to understand the principle behind it: "This morning I found a fountain pen coming up the stairs to class." You smile. Obvious. Of course the error's obvious; if you repeat the sentence before the students, they all immediately know what's wrong. Yet we take time out to explain the principle of the dangling modifier because the next example may not be so obvious. "This morning I met John coming up the stairs to class." Who is coming up the stairs? John should be, but you know and we know from experience that students are capable of writing that sentence and meaning, "When I was coming up the stairs to class this morning, I met John, who was going down the stairs." How much more easily we can correct this error after we have discussed the principle; how much more easily can the student, through self-criticism, correct it for himself, or avoid it altogether. In this connection we might do well to quote a comment by The Commission on the English Curriculum of the National Council of Teachers of English. In the chapter on grammar in their book, *The English Language Arts in the Secondary School*, they write, "The teaching of grammar (i.e., theoretical grammar) cannot be ignored, for through a functional knowledge of the basic structure of the English sentence and the terms used in identifying language forms, an intelligent student can be assisted in the revision of his writing and the self-analysis of recordings of his speech." [1]

First, convenience. Second, accuracy. As we have implied, students are able to correct the error we have just been considering through induction—they are able, that is, if they make the error often enough and are misunderstood often enough. And there is value in such induction, since a principle learned for oneself is not so easily forgot; but there is danger, also. The principle may be imperfectly learned, thus imperfectly applied. Therefore, at the very least an explicit statement of the principle is eventually helpful, even necessary. It is this explicit statement that we teach. Haven't you ever had the experience of putting an incorrect sentence on the board, of asking the students to state what is wrong with it, of having them identify it but remain unable to correct it? For example, "Watching the side of the road, his car went out of control."

"There's something wrong with the participial phrase," says a student.
"What?" we reply.
"It doesn't sound right."
"In what way? Why?"
"I don't know, but I know it's wrong."

1 Angela Broening, ed., *The English Language Arts in the Secondary School* (National Council of Teachers of English Curriculum Series; New York, Appleton-Century-Crofts, Inc., 1956), p. 357.

"Correct it, then."

"Due to watching the side of the road, his car went out of control."

And on and on. The student correctly located the error, but since he incorrectly diagnosed its nature, he substituted a construction equally bad.

Learning entirely by imitation, then, implies either that we use only those constructions we have heard several times, or that we eventually induce the principle for ourselves. The first is undesirable because it strictly limits us—witness the limitations of those who cannot grasp the principles of grammar even when taught; the second is undesirable, unless supported by teaching, because it is inconvenient, and because it leads to imperfect understanding of the principles. May we add one caution here, however. We are not suggesting that students be discouraged from inducing their own principles (it might be good for them, if the principles are then checked for accuracy), nor are we stating that all principles should be taught. Some elements of grammar are best learned by simple imitation, because, paradoxically enough, such imitation is more convenient. Thus, although there are complicated principles governing the vowel changes in Anglo-Saxon strong verbs, and therefore governing the principal parts of some modern English verbs, it is much easier for us to learn these principal parts by heart. On the other hand, it is easier, more convenient, to learn the principles of subordination than to copy only those sentences we have heard and can imitate.

Already some of the veteran teachers among you may feel uneasy. "Is that Committee going to say," they are thinking, "that we can teach theoretical grammar to everyone? It can't be done." These teachers are correct: It can't be done. Scientific evidence on this point is not yet conclusive, but experience strongly supports the belief that the ability to profit by a knowledge of theoretical grammar improves as the I.Q. rises. Why shouldn't it? The I.Q. is basically a measure of the mind's ability to handle abstractions, to see pattern behind apparently disparate things, and theoretical grammar is nothing but pattern underlying usage. It is logical to assume, therefore, that those students with little ability to reason will profit little from instruction in theoretical grammar. The difficulty with our machine gunner, to return to our analogy, was that he could not theorize; he could not relate abstract ideas, expressed by words alone, to the physical object before him. He could learn only by imitation. Now, do you see where our thinking is leading us? If all that we have said is true, those who are least able to profit by an intensive course in grammar—theoretical grammar, that is —are those who often are given the most instruction in it; on the other hand, those who stand to profit most from such instruction are those who receive the least of it.

Ironic, bitterly ironic—a situation we are in a position to do something about right now. We can, for instance, gear our teaching of grammar to the student. For the slow student, our approach should be less abstract. That same Commission of the English Curriculum expresses our point very clearly:

> The slower the student is . . . the less reliance should be put on grammatical generalizations and classifications as a means of improving his understanding or use of English. He is likely to profit more from direct teaching and habit formation of a particular detail of good usage. It does little good to remind John of a rule concerning agreement of subject and predicate if he is still unable to identify predicates and has no concept of agreement. Much teaching done by gifted verbalists is completely lost on students of limited verbal ability who have little appreciation of the meaning of grammatical rules or who do not recognize an example or a violation of a grammatical rule which has been formally stated by the teacher or the textbook.[2]

By the same token, the amount of grammar we give students should vary as their ability to absorb it varies. A few, in other words, will be capable of learning no theoretical grammar, some only a little, the majority a moderate amount, and a few gifted linguists perhaps even more than we, as teachers, are competent to teach. Until we have more scientific evidence of how much grammar a certain intelligence can grasp, the answers to two simple questions might guide our judgment of how much to teach: first, what principles would immediately help the student better to express what he is trying to express; second, can he apply the principles we have already given him. Obviously it is foolish to teach the intricacies of a periodic sentence to a boy who has trouble writing a simple sentence. Equally, if we have spent considerable time discussing parallel construction, and one student continually fails to handle it correctly on his themes, it might be time to slow down, to substitute imitation and practice, lots of practice. Show 'em and let 'em

[2] *Ibid.*, p. 368.

copy. It also follows that we give even the more able students only so much theoretical grammar as they can profitably use. Knowledge of the principles behind the vowel changes in strong verbs, for instance, cannot be profitably used by high school students. Therefore we should not—and do not—teach these principles, even to those students able to understand them.

What, then, have we established so far? That we should teach grammar in the secondary schools. That we should teach both usage and theory. That all students do not profit from theory, and therefore all students should not be taught theory—only those who can understand it sufficiently to apply it. Now we turn to another question: what theoretical grammar should we teach? Here, before we get too involved, let us narrow the field within recognizable and practicable bounds. After all, since the word *grammar* first came into technical use in the fourth century B.C., it has included such varied studies as orthography, etymology, prosody, phonology, morphology, syntax, and even literary criticism and literary history. We shall restrict—somewhat arbitrarily—our discussion of grammar to the theory of word form (or "morphology") and the theory of word groups (or "syntax"). Morphology and syntax. We shall not include—at the peril of our lives— the theory of word sounds (or *phonology*), even though morphology and syntax may ultimately rest on a basis of phonology.

Well then, what morphology and what syntax should we teach? In order to answer this question, we must turn to the only primary source we have: the language itself. And here we come to the problem that has vexed teachers for many years now. Who sets the standards of English? The answer is not, as many of us have always assumed, the grammarians—at least in their role of grammarian. Rather they act as reporters, investigators, research men. As the physicist in the laboratory studies the laws of mechanics, the grammarian studies the laws of language. He does not make these laws; he defines them. He does not even judge them. The teacher, on the other hand, must every day exercise judgment in the use of language. It follows that if he is to judge wisely, he must know the laws the grammarian discovers; therefore he should understand how the grammarian operates, and just how far his "law" or principles are valid. Let's pause for a moment to see.

One of the first facts which a grammarian must face is that language changes. Since Dr. Johnson stated this fact clearly in the eighteenth century, even the public has recognized that word meanings change. The etymologies in the dictionaries demonstrate the change: the word *nice* now commonly means 'well-mannered,' 'pleasant,' 'agreeable.' In the eighteenth century it commonly meant 'fine,' 'demanding close discrimination,' as in the phrase, "a nice point." In Shakespeare's time it commonly meant 'overrefined,' 'shy,' and, surprisingly, 'lascivious.' When it entered the language in Middle English it meant 'foolish,' 'stupid,' since it comes from the Latin *nescius*, 'ignorant.' We all recognize such semantic changes. We also recognize spelling changes, although they are often disguised for us by modern editors: a random page of Elizabethan prose reveals these spellings in one sentence: *againe* for 'again,' *findeinge* for 'finding,' *wee* for 'we,' *pittie* for 'pity,' and these are not all the curious spellings in this one sentence. We even recognize some changes in form: *climb* was originally a strong verb, like *drink*, and had simple past forms *clumb* and *clambon;* now it is a weak verb with the simple past *climbed*. But do we recognize how far these changes have gone? In some twentieth century grammars you can still find the statement that there are three cases in the English noun: subjective, possessive, and objective. This is not true. Our first or third person pronoun still has three forms (I, my, me; he, his, him), but not the noun. And modern adjectives no longer decline at all although in Anglo-Saxon they had more endings than the nouns. How significant these form changes are we shall see later.

Incomplete as our knowledge may be, however, we have all come to recognize that changes have occurred in meaning, spellings, and forms. But have we recognized how great a change has come about in syntax? The use of the participle is a good example. According to Mr. G. H. Vallins, a prominent British grammarian, the participle was used in Anglo-Saxon as an adjectival complement of the verb.[3] At first this participle was inflected to agree with the object. Thus, translated into modern English, we find the sentence "they have slain him," in which the past participle actually is an adjective modifying "him," with which it agrees, as though the sentence were "They have him slain" or "They have him in the condition of having been slain." He quotes as analogous our sentence, "I have the books properly arranged for you," which is not quite the same construction as "I have properly

[3] G. H. Vallins, *The Pattern of English* (London, Andre Deutsch Ltd., 1956), pp. 66–71.

arranged the books for you." Slowly, however, this "adjective," or participle, began to lose its strictly adjectival force and gained more verbal force, so that the participle was not always inflected to agree with the object of the sentence. The loss of inflections further obscured the agreement, until the participle broke free and our present compound tenses were born. Had syntax been fixed, the compound tenses never would have been born.

In one construction, then, the participle lost its adjectival inflections and became attached to the verb. In another, it kept its adjectival force and gradually broke completely away from the verb—mostly under the influence of Latin, which had highly developed participial phrases. When Anglo-Saxon monks translated Latin texts, they recognized the value of these phrases, and began to use the English participle in a similar manner. What must have seemed a barbarism at the time caught on. By the time of the King James Bible in 1611, the participial phrase was in general use ("and he rebuking them suffered them not to speak" —Luke 4:41), but rarely at the beginning of the sentence. A century and a half later, the participial phrase had moved to the beginning of the sentence, where it often, without rebuke, dangled. Vallins quotes the eighteenth century grammarian Cobbett, who did not hesitate to employ a dangling participle in his own grammar, published in 1817: "Having been taught by the rules of *Etymology*, what are the relationships of words, Syntax will teach you how to give all your words their proper situations."

Changes have occurred, then, in forms and sentence structure, in morphology and syntax. It is the role of the grammarian to record these changes, the duty of the teacher to recognize them. And this duty brings us to an important point: usage precedes grammatical principles; language precedes any description of language. Grammatical principles are formed after the fact. Grammar in this sense does not control language; language controls grammar. Difficulty arises, and has arisen for us, when a principle is hardened into a rule and hangs on after the principle no longer accurately describes the language. Consider for a moment our description of the participle above: to the purist in the court of King Alfred, the use of the participle as a complement of the verb, without agreement with the object, must have been a shocking violation of a rule. Even worse must have sounded the independent use of a participle as an adjective, after the Latin. To an Elizabethan, beginning a sentence with a participle must have seemed odd. Yet each time, grammarians finally caught up with usage, and the revolutionary constructions were found acceptable, even formulated into new rules. We now teach our students to use the participial phrase as a weapon, to move it about for emphasis and rhythm. On the other hand, the double negative and the second person singular, *thou*, with its forms *thine* and *thee*, which were once acceptable, have fallen out of good usage; their lapse has been noted by the grammarians, and we no longer teach them.

To some, the notion that grammar does not legislate, but merely describes, means the end of all teaching, as the notion of government without a king meant to some colonists in the eighteenth century the end of all government. But just as we learned to govern without a king, we must learn to teach without an arbitrary grammar. We must recognize that the grammarian—as grammarian—does not legislate that a certain construction must be used. He merely describes which constructions are found in the language; he describes which constructions follow certain principles and which do not. He explains that one construction is clearer than another, or is more common in one community than another. He even describes which construction is preferred by the best speakers. On this latter description we found our teaching, for in effect the forms and constructions of the best users of our language set our standards. If grammatical principles do not legislate, good usage —with emphasis on *good*—does. It sets the standards in the sense that we as teachers select those constructions which appear in good usage and legislate that they should be used by our students. The basis on which we judge good usage lies largely outside the spectrum of grammar. We legislate usually on the basis of semantic meaning and propriety—does the construction make sense, and is it acceptable usage in its context. These are not, we repeat, essentially grammatical concerns, yet they are based on grammar. They are the same concerns which guide the best writers. In other words, the grammarians tell us what ways of saying something are at our disposal; we as teachers or as good writers decide which ways to use, normally for reasons outside the strict confines of grammar. The professional grammarian is the mapmaker who charts all the known roads of the English language; grammar is the map; the teacher is the driving instructor who chooses the most useful roads recorded on the map and teaches them to his students. Ultimately the students develop their own judgment and read the map for themselves. The mapmaker does not say to the driving instructor, "You must use this road and no other." He says, "Here is the map of the roads," and he may, by the red and black lines on his map, indicate which are most used and which are in good condition. The instructor looks and sees that one is better for his purpose than another. The teacher says to his student, "Use this one." Eventually the student says to himself, without the help of the instructor, "This is the best road for my purpose. Because it is the best—not because anyone told me to, but because it is the best—I shall use it." At this point the student has become a good writer, and helps create good usage himself. The grammarian describes *his* language, and the circle begins again.

We have labored over this relationship between grammarian and teacher and writer because it has been so widely misunderstood. It is important, very important, that we recognize the descriptive nature of grammar as grammar, and reject what might be called its prescriptive nature—it does not command. At the same time we must recognize that grammar does show us the way. Although it does not say, "Take this road," it does indicate where roads exist, and if we do not follow the map, we may get into a deal of trouble. A simple example comes immediately to mind. Much ink has been spilt over the split infinitive. May we use it or not? According to the process outlined above, we first look to the grammarian. He will give the facts; on his facts we shall make our decision. Here is what Mr. Vallins has to say about it: "This construction . . . had existed, though it was not common, in English from late mediaeval times. . . . But it was not until the middle of the nineteenth century that it was called in question." [4]

Mr. Vallins goes on to point out that even then it was not condemned outright. Finally in 1905 the grammarian Nesfield had what Vallins called "a dogmatic, but historically unsound," note on it: "An adverb should not be placed between the *to* and the infinitive. The usage is springing up, but it is not sanctioned by the usage of any good writers." Mr. Vallins continues:

To the generation who were educated in the early years of this century the split infinitive is still suspect; and indeed it still arouses the displeasure of the schoolmaster and the examiner. . . . The fact is that the position of the adverb in relation to the *to* and the verb is only one aspect of, and follows the principle governing, the position of the adverb generally. It

[4] *Ibid.*, pp. 131–133.

is to be noted that the splitting of the infinitive by anything more than a single adverb ("To at all times and in all circumstances be ready") is regarded as a solecism.

One member of this Committee knows precisely what Mr. Vallins means here by "the displeasure of the schoolmaster." He remembers not long ago reading his weekly essay to an instructor at college. At one point during the reading the instructor leaned over to pick up a pencil; just as he reached out to grasp it, he emitted an agonizing groan. The student stopped, somewhat alarmed, and asked, "Are you all right, sir? Did you wrench your back or something?"

"No," came the voice from the depths, as the instructor slowly straightened up, "You split an infinitive."

Once taught like this, we feel it hard not to perpetuate the displeasure. But if we are to be good teachers, we should not. We should teach what grammar actually tells us. Here, grammar tells us that a split infinitive was sometimes good usage until late in the nineteenth century, that the law against it is modern and largely the result of imperfect knowledge, that the objection to it now is not based on sense, but on propriety. We should recognize it as such. We should recognize that it is often better English to split an infinitive than to use an awkward expression that does not split an infinitive. Furthermore, we should remember what we have learned from experience. When we apply for some jobs, for instance, we are judged by our language. The split infinitive is considered wrong, however incorrectly, by some businessmen; therefore, if we are prudent, we do not split an infinitive in the presence of such men. Or consider an example closer to home. You are English teachers. As English teachers, some of you may have your ears tuned to pick up split infinitives—sort of a reflex action. We have compiled a report which we hope you will take seriously; but if we used a split infinitive, you might be so upset you might not listen attentively, or might dismiss us as ignorant and callow. So we don't split infinitives. Absurd?

Recently one member of our Committee lent a new grammar book to a colleague—a colleague, be it noted, who was ill disposed to consider any changes in his present teaching methods. He opened the book, read the first sentence, and shut the book. "The author of this book," he said, "cannot write good English; he split an infinitive in the first sentence. Therefore his book is no good." Before we condemn, before we recommend, therefore, it is important that we as teachers know the facts about our language. Then, when we teach, we can teach with confidence and not feel the loss of prescriptive grammar.

Shall we pause for another breath? We set out a few minutes ago to decide what morphology and what syntax we should teach. Before we could decide, however, we had to discover who sets the standards of English. We discovered that those who use the language most effectively set the standards; this effectiveness is determined largely on considerations outside the spectrum of grammar—on semantic meaning and propriety. The grammarian reports all usage, indicates its conditions, and describes its principles. As grammarian he does not prefer, he does not prescribe; he does establish the grounds on which preference and prescription may be made. The teacher, on the other hand, selects good usage, provides its conditions, and teaches its principles. Absolutely necessary for this process is accurate knowledge by the teacher, and ultimately by the student, of how the English language is used by the most effective speakers and writers; we cannot teach sound principles unless we know the facts of usage.

Now we are ready to answer our question: what morphology and what syntax do we teach? We teach the morphology and syntax which the grammarian tells us best describes good usage in the language. In this connection some years ago grammarians and teachers became uneasy with traditional grammar. It was certainly not all wrong, but it did not adequately describe constructions which were perfectly acceptable usage, and it continued to describe some which no longer were. On the one hand, it did not adequately explain the function of words like *looks* or *feels* in the sentences "He looks good," or "He feels good." On the other, it talked of an objective case in the noun and a second person pronoun *thou*. The reasons for the discrepancy were not far to seek. Traditional English grammar descended from Latin and Greek; it never did *completely* describe the English language, even when it was first introduced. And, as we have seen, the language has been slowly but continuously changing; grammar has been slower to change than the language, until finally the discrepancy has become very noticeable. Scholars like Jespersen, Sapir, Bloomfield, and Fries began to study the language more carefully. They did not study it in isolation, however, but in relation to other fields of knowledge, such as cultural anthropology. In addition, they were aided by scientific methods. For this reason they and their associates are known as linguistic scientists, or linguists, rather than grammarians. It is to them, as the mapmakers, to whom we are now asked to turn. Perhaps, as we turn, it would be well to remind ourselves that these men are not inventing the language. They are merely offering what they believe to be, after serious and prolonged study, a better description of it. Like all revisions of something with which we have long been familiar, some parts seem strange, but much is familiar, even if occasionally it looks different under new terminology. Let's consider, very briefly, what sort of map these men offer.

They point out that there is a trend behind the morphological changes in English, a trend intimately connected with the concurrent changes in syntax. Anglo-Saxon was a highly inflected language, like Latin. Nouns and adjectives declined. For this reason, word order, though it usually followed established patterns, could vary widely without destroying the meaning of the sentence. At the least, many more patterns were possible than are now possible in modern English. But even in the Anglo-Saxon period, the inflections were becoming less important; some disappeared or coalesced with others. Then, aided by the confusion of vocabulary and forms which followed the Norman invasion of 1066, the loss of inflections was accelerated until today word order is more important to convey semantic meaning than are forms. That is, the meaning of "Him and me ain't going" is clearer than the meaning of "Going I aren't and he." We are not saying that inflections now have *no* significance—merely that they are now not so significant (and do not present so many problems) as they once were. To help make up for their loss, word order and auxiliary words have become more important. At one time, for instance, forms were decisive in this sentence, "Whom seest thou?" This was clearly distinct from "Who sees thee?" because the forms *whom* and *who*, *thou* and *thee* were distinctive. But consider what has happened. We have lost the second person singular in ordinary speech. What shall we say, then? "Whom see you?" and "Who sees you?" We might, still distinguishing the meaning through the forms of the interrogative pronoun. But we don't. The first noun or pronoun in a sentence is so regularly the subject that we need more than the inflection of a pronoun to distinguish subject from object. The forms are no longer sufficiently distinctive. We can say, "Whom sees you?"; we do say "Whom do you see?", adding the auxiliary word *do*. Indeed, the objective form *whom* is so little stressed here that we often, if not usually, say, "Who do you see?" This last version is creeping into good usage even now. Sapir goes so far as to predict that *whom* will ultimately disappear from English speech.[5]

The changes can be explained by the increased importance of word order and other syntactical matters, as opposed to forms. Position has become so important that in some cases it may even be said to control form—position instead of function. Thus we find "Whoever I saw isn't here," but "He gave the books to whomever was there," "Who do you refer to," but "To whom do you refer." In other words, *who* is becoming the accepted form whenever it heads its clause, except when it immediately follows a preposition.

Actually most of what we have been saying is already familiar to us; most of us in our teaching have recognized implicitly, if not explicitly, the need for emphasis on sentence structure or syntax in secondary school English courses. We spend most of our time, not giving the principal parts of verbs—though some verb forms still cause trouble— but teaching the proper use of subordination and parallel constructions, the clear reference of pronouns and the clear dependence of modifying elements. Certainly at the level in which we are particularly interested today—that is, theoretical grammar or grammatical principles—most of our teaching is syntactical rather than morphological. Except for number and agreement, morphological principles—such as the theory behind vowel changes in strong verbs—are too complex for students in secondary school.

The grammarians have done more than throw weight on the teaching of syntax. They have redefined the elements out of which a sentence is composed. We are all familiar with the parts of speech. As an example of what is happening to them, consider the old description of a noun: "The English noun is the name of a person, place or thing. It may be divided into two classes, proper and common. It has three genders—masculine, feminine, and neuter. It has three cases—subjective, possessive, objective—according as it is employed. It has two numbers—singular and plural." But this description is inaccurate. Grammatical gender does not exist in English; we have only natural

[5] Edward Sapir, *Language* (Harvest Books #7; New York, Harcourt, Brace & Co., 1949), p. 162.

gender, which is a matter of semantics. And the English noun has only two cases—common and possessive. Finally, the very definition of a noun as the name of a person, place, or thing leads to semantic difficulties. Because of these difficulties, linguists approach the definition from an entirely different direction.[6] They define it morphologically and syntactically—in terms of its possible changes in form and its possible position in the sentence. A noun, Professor Roberts says, is a word that "behaves" like the words *apple, beauty*, and *desk*. Linguists usually say "patterns" like these words; indeed, *pattern* is a key word for them, since their whole concept of grammar is based on the "pattern" of English speech, of English sentences. All right, then, a noun is a word which patterns like *apple, beauty, desk*. Thus we find it in patterns like this:

I saw the *apple*.
I was disappointed in the *desk*.
Her *beauty* is gone.
Desks, apples, and *beauties* are plentiful in Washington.

Any word which can behave like this belongs to the noun class. Thus *dog* is a noun, but *go* isn't. We can say, "I saw the dog," but we can't say, "I saw the *go*." The major morphological features of this class of words (i.e., *noun*) are the plural ending, and the possessive ending; that is, we are helped in recognizing them if we see that they can take either of these endings.

If this approach to a noun seems strange to us, we might consider the possibility that we actually learned how to use nouns this way, rather than through a semantic definition. A child learning to talk does not learn first that a noun is a person, place, or thing; that would involve a philosophical distinction. The child learns that the word *doll* can occur in certain constructions, not in others. "I see the *doll*," but not "I *doll* the see."

This approach to parts of speech has led to a revision of word classification in general. Although this revision is not yet complete, although the names of the classifications have not yet been agreed upon, the general outline of the revision is clear, is not likely to change greatly. Professor Paul Roberts, as an example, speaks of *form classes* and *structure groups*. *Form classes* include all those words which inflect. *Structure*

[6] This discussion is taken largely from Paul Roberts, *Patterns of English* (New York, Harcourt, Brace & Co., 1956), pp. 1–16, 288–289.

groups include all those words which do not inflect, but act as signals to indicate sentence structure or pattern. Examination shows us that nouns, verbs, adjectives, and adverbs inflect; articles, conjunctions, and prepositions do not. Thus we have four form classes—nouns, verbs, adjectives, and adverbs—which contain most of the words in the language. Many of these words can be members of more than one form class. Some two hundred important words however, such as *the*, *but*, and *with*, do not inflect. These fall into several different structure groups. They indicate the relationship between words in the sentence.

Now the relevance of such classifications is apparent as soon as we turn to something like Lewis Carroll's *Jabberwocky*. This odd poem tantalizes us because it seems to make sense, yet it doesn't. But it does, say the linguists; it makes syntactical or grammatical sense. By examining endings, by attending to word order and structural words, we can parse every stanza. Witness:

> 'Twas brillig, and the slithy toves
> Did gyre and gimble in the wabe:
> All mimsy were the borogoves,
> And the mome raths outgrabe.

"Brillig" is an adjective. "Toves" is a noun. "Gyre" and "gimble" are verbs. What word order, inflections, and structure words have done here is reveal the pattern of the language, reveal it quite apart from semantic meaning. In general, understanding of the pattern helps us puzzle out the meaning of sentences obscure because some of the words are obscure, and helps us vary pattern in order to attain clarity and emphasis on our writing.

This is what the linguists tell us. This is our map. Now we as teachers have a considerable responsibility at this point. Most of us are not qualified to judge the accuracy of the map, at least until we have tried it, but we are qualified—even obligated—to decide what parts of it are relevant to our teaching, what parts of it can make us better teachers. And it is just this problem of relevancy which we cannot at this time answer. Few school teachers—and they are to be commended—have done more than play with linguistics. The rest of us have proceeded slowly, and rightly so. We are the guardians of a tradition, and we do not wish to lose what is good in the old. At the same time most of us have at one time or another become dissatisfied with parts of the tradition, and the discoveries of the linguists seem to help. Therefore, in the light of what has been said here this afternoon, we have a twofold obligation: first, to recognize that since language changes, and since modern scientific methods permit more accurate descriptions of even those elements which do not change, we must not be satisfied with a static approach to grammar; second, to recognize that we should examine the material offered us by the linguists. They are the experts, experts in a sense we can never be. At the very least we have the obligation of listening to them so that we may decide, on rational grounds, if and how their discoveries may be applied to teaching English in schools. This Committee believes that we shall find linguistic science useful.

And so our structure at last falls into place. What have we said? First, that knowledge of theoretical grammar makes comprehension and articulation easier, and beyond a very elementary level makes it possible at all; therefore, we should teach as much theoretical grammar as our students can profitably learn. Second, that language changes, and grammarians report this change; therefore it is our duty as teachers to examine what changes the grammarians record so that we can teach an accurate, useful grammar. Third, that the linguists are now urging more emphasis on syntax, and a redefinition of parts of speech in terms of their form and position in a sentence; therefore we should study what the linguists have to say to see how what they say might help us become better teachers.

Our last point leads this Committee to make specific recommendations which we hope will be taken seriously by you and other teachers of English. First, that each of us increase his efforts to learn what these new theories are all about—we might, for instance, read the books recommended in the highly select and critically annotated bibliography of this report. Second, that the universities be encouraged to give courses, particularly summer courses, in linguistics, courses specifically designed for teachers. Third, that some group like the National Council of Teachers of English or a university school of education sponsor a group of experienced school teachers to go to the source of these linguistic studies, learn what the new theories are, return to the classroom, experiment with them, reassemble with the results of the experiment, and write textbooks which embody the new theories and are pedagogically sound. This last recommendation is analogous to what is already happening in high school physics, particularly nuclear physics, where new theories have been slow to filter down to the classroom. In this way we shall be assured that the new theories get a proper hearing, and that when they finally reach the average classroom, they will be useful for our purposes. In this way, we shall be prepared, shall not waste time on duplicating experiments. Educate ourselves first; then educate our pupils.

Appendix

The Committee discussed at some length the problem of *how* grammar should be taught. On occasion, too much emphasis has been placed on grammar for the simple reason that it can be taught, or perhaps we should say, can be tested. As we stated in the main body of the report, however, we teach English in secondary school so that the students may better understand and better articulate; therefore we should teach grammar with a view to application. This does not mean that separate units in grammar are not useful; it does mean that these units should be carefully integrated in the end with the student's reading and writing.

Several approaches were suggested. Some of the more useful follow:

1. Each year following that in which the basic principles of grammar are introduced, the teacher may begin by reviewing what the class is already supposed to know. This review should not take long, and has the advantage later of making comprehensible the teacher's corrections on themes. It also helps the transfer students adjust to the requirements of a new school. There is danger, however, that this approach may isolate grammar from its application.

2. The teacher may note the most frequent errors on written work, then pause at a convenient time and direct his teaching for a few days, even a week, to the elimination of these particular errors. This method insures that the principles taught are those which the

is cut off from fact and is plunged into a philosophical definition of terms that has no resting place." [1]

Granted words may be more accurately classified apart from meaning, does it follow that we should teach them apart? At least one teacher on this Committee, otherwise enthusiastic about linguistics, is hesitant here, because his teaching is based on the technique of getting a student to say something, and then working on it until it is said as well as possible. Grammar thus becomes a tool to convey meaning. What happens if you "put meaning aside"? Surely there are good answers to this and similar problems, but we should know what they are before committing ourselves. For this reason we suggested that the group of experienced teachers study linguistics for the express purpose of discovering how it can be put to good use in secondary schools.

Bibliography

FRIES, Charles C., *The Structure of English* (New York, Harcourt, Brace & Co., 1952).

Unlike his earlier (1940) *American English Grammar* which centered upon the " 'grammar of usage'—the problems of social class difference," this book deals primarily with the " 'grammar of structure'—the construction of our utterances"—and offers an approach to the problems of " 'sentence analysis' that differs in point of view and in emphasis from the usual treatment of syntax."

———, *Teaching of English* (Ann Arbor, Mich., George Wahr, 1949).

Excellent advice on the teaching of language and literature; particularly good is the first section, "What Is Good English?"; a book every English teacher should reread yearly.

HALL, Robert A., *Leave Your Language Alone!* (Ithaca, N.Y., Linguistica, 1950).

The title indicates the bias; in the Preface, Hall says that the book is "addressed to the general public, in favor of a scientific attitude toward

[1] *op. cit.*, p. 17.

language and of linguistic relativism and tolerance, but including only as much detailed scientific analysis as is necessary to justify or exemplify its statements and conclusions"; the technique is the frontal assault, good for those who like to argue with authors.

*JESPERSEN, Otto, *Growth and Structure of the English Language* (Oxford, Basil Blackwell & Nott, Ltd., 1952).

Any book by Jespersen on English is invaluable to the teacher of English; this one-volume study attempts "to characterize the chief peculiarities of the English language, and to explain the growth and significance of those features in its structure which have been of permanent importance"; full of examples.

*NIDA, Eugene A., *Linguistic Interludes* (Glendale, Calif., Summer Institute of Linguistics).

Among other things these "Interludes" are intended "to introduce the beginning student or layman to (1) the conflicting attitudes toward linguistics, and (2) the fundamental principle of the descriptive linguistic approach."

*POTTER, Simeon, *Our Language* (Baltimore, Md., Penguin Books, Inc.).

Another inexpensive book on language by a leading British linguist; "a popular study of our language—its sources, its history, its peculiar genius, and how it is and should be used in speech and writing."

ROBERTS, Paul, *Patterns of English* (New York, Harcourt, Brace & Co., 1956).

A textbook for high school students built according to "the principles of linguistic science"; a valuable first that should get the respectful attention of all high school English teachers; based largely on the Fries and Whitehall books mentioned; the teacher's edition has a 39-page Teacher's Guide that is clear and convincing. An earlier book by Roberts, *Understanding Grammar* (New York, Harper & Brothers, 1954), gives a very complete and edifying discussion of the problems of traditional grammar.

*SAPIR, Edward, *Language* (New York, Harcourt, Brace & Co., 1921).

Perhaps the most revealing and most readable of the general treatments of linguistics; relates linguistics to other fields of knowledge and stimulates thinking about language as a worldwide human phenomenon; worth reading particularly if you have doubts about the motives of linguistics.

*SCHLAUCH, Margaret, *The Gift of Language* (New York, Dover Publications Inc.)

Not very strong on descriptive linguistics but excellent on "the relation of language to society and to literature."

SMITH, Henry Lee, Jr., *Linguistic Science and the Teaching of English* (Cambridge, Mass., Harvard University Press, 1956).

A short (61 pages) introduction to the linguist as cultural anthropologist; a clear, readable insight into the structure of English with implications for teaching; a good book to read carefully three or four times.

*VALLINS, G. H., *The Pattern of English* (London, Andre Deutsch, Ltd., 1956).

A historical study of the English language, directed toward showing, "by illustration and example, the changing pattern of English from the time of King Alfred to the present day." Short (188 pages), readable, and easily understood without knowledge of linguistic theories; uses old terminology.

WHITEHALL, Harold, *Structural Essentials of English* (New York, Harcourt, Brace & Co., 1956).

Probably the most useful book for the teacher wanting a compressed but thorough analysis of the linguistic's approach to English structure; the book is short (154 pages) and can therefore be read several times (which is necessary); Whitehall makes good sense and points the way to productive self-study by the teacher.

* The starred books are inexpensive paperback editions; for a little over $5.00 anyone can buy five excellent books covering a wide range of modern linguistic thinking.

II

THE TEACHING
OF WRITING

*Any teacher knows that teaching writing is his most diffi-
cult job. Too many and too large classes aggravate the problem, but
often the chief trouble is failure to adopt the right method for a given
class. To the question "What is the right method?" our authors offer
various answers, each of which seems to work well for its proponent;
each essay proposes a somewhat different method. It is clear that the
paths to teaching writing effectively are numerous, but they must be
paths, not random bushwhacking.*

*Professor Richard B. Sewall is a teacher in one of the country's most
famous courses in writing, Yale's "Daily Themes," in which each student writes a three-hundred-word paper every day for a whole term.
We do not suggest that you do precisely the same unless, like Mr. Sewall, you are one of a staff teaching the course. What is important for
our purposes is the method. The material for the course is "the blank
page which the student must face every evening." Interesting and valuable to any teacher are the critical principles of the course, which Mr.
Sewall expounds with examples: personal experience, specific and significant detail, sensory appeal, consistency of point of view, characterization by the indirect method, and appropriate connotation of words.
A teacher who leads his class to an understanding of these principles is
teaching writing, not merely having pupils write. For, in the best creative writing a student uses, not only his emotions, but also his head.*

4

The Content of Student Writing

RICHARD B. SEWALL, *Yale University*

We all agree heartily that one of the first purposes of
education is to lead our students to a decent competency in written
expression; but we differ—and there are signs that we are beginning
to differ sharply—as to methods. Let me state the opposition bluntly.
On the one hand are those who believe that a student must know how
to say something before he is in a position to say it. These are the
formalists. They stress the necessity for a solid grounding in grammar, the mechanics of the sentence, and (as the student advances)
the laws of logic and the principles of rhetoric. Their tools are the
grammar book, the drill book, exercises in the diagraming and parsing
of sentences, and (later on) the assigned theme in "description," "exposition," "narration," and "argumentation"; worthy disciplines all,
and no pedagogical system ought to be entirely without them. The
weight of tradition is on this side, and it can be said to dominate the
field at present.

On the other hand are those who, discouraged with the results of
the old disciplines, see the problem as more of a psychological than a
disciplinary one and are reaching out for techniques that would release inhibitions, provide the student with inner compulsions that
would in the end (but not entirely of themselves, of course) conquer
technical obstacles. The belief is that if the student has something to

say and wants to say it, he will learn with a minimum of technical guidance *how* to say it: the *what* will find a *how*. The task of the teacher, then, is to kindle laggard imaginations, open up possibilities, provide a congenial milieu, and, as the pressure and command of content grow in the individual student, point out ways and means by which he can say more clearly and more cogently what he wants to say. But always the *what* precedes the *how*. These people would concentrate, first of all and at all costs, on getting the student to write, and keep on writing, and write more. They would rely more heavily than the traditionalists on the student's native sense of the mother tongue, his ability to talk in grammatical sentences, even at an early age, with surprising accuracy, if in limited range. They would bend their efforts on breaking down that mysterious barrier between oral and written competency. They would make the formal study of grammar less abstract, less *a priori*, and more practical, allowing the student to grow into an understanding of the structure and possibilities of the sentence and paragraph as the expressive needs develop.

Theoretically, I am solidly on the side of this latter group; and, although I see many practical hazards, I am convinced that progress lies in this direction, not to the exclusion of the traditional disciplines but to their considerable mitigation. I base my conviction on what I see of the work being done in the schools and on the product that comes to me every year in the freshman class in college. Quite frankly, the student writing that I see, except for the products of a few noble but isolated experimental programs, strikes me as little short of appalling. It is dull and lifeless, stultifying to the imagination, and blighting to the spirit. The old disciplines, I should say, are perilously near bankruptcy. They come nowhere near, by themselves, developing the available human resources.

For the boys and girls I see are anything but dull and lifeless; they are far from dispirited (except on the subject of "English Comp"); and they are by no means deficient in imagination. Aldous Huxley once said that every child under ten is a genius. I would give him a couple of more years, and I would add that our schooling in America (public and private) has been singularly successful in killing off, as far as written expression is concerned, this tremendous potential. Why does the marvelous imaginative life of most children under ten —the hour-long monologues they hold with themselves when left

alone, the imaginary playmates (sometimes whole families) they conjure up and converse with—come to such a dead end in the early
teens? The imagination is still there; but the outlets get clogged and
jammed.

I saw this cycle work out dramatically a few years ago in our
neighborhood. Telling about it may suggest both an object-lesson
and a cure. The nine- and ten-year-olds round-about suddenly decided to start what they were pleased to call a newspaper. The press
was to be a postcard mimeographing machine, and the newsprint
came from ten-cent, 4″ x 6″ pads of varying colors. The neighborhood was electrified. Contributions poured in; nobody wanted to be
left out. The prose was startling and fascinating; the spelling bold
and imaginative. The subjects ranged from how to grow feathers on
a bald-headed canary to "How it Feels to have Your TONSELES Out."
There was freshness of vision and direct, uncluttered phrasing. For
instance, the piece on the TONSELES:

You go to the hospitle in the morning and get put in bed for about five
hours and then they opporate on you. The ether smells pretty good to me
but not to you maybe. You feel very bad when you wake up. Its all red
when you throw up. Your mother comes and gets you about nine oclock
next morning. It's awful having your tonceles out. The elevator is the
only fun.

Or another, under the heading "Rare Tooth Pulled":

Billy Lucianni has had a rare tooth pulled. When the dentist pulled it out
the baby tooth and the real tooth came out stuck together. It was so rare
the dentist is going to take it to a meeting. The worst part was that Billy
got an infacshen and had to miss a scout trip.

Each issue had an original design on the cover. Adults kept strictly
out, except for an occasional helping hand with the machine. The
little paper sold like hotcakes and is now a collector's item.

Many people have had similar experiences in their neighborhoods,
but I venture to say that most of them came like this one to an early
end as "the world became more and more." There was no carry-over
in school, where the good woman who taught most of this brood
made only one comment, "But you can spell better than *that*." And
so spelling, grammar, punctuation, the parsing of sentences—one line

under the subject, two under the predicate, three under the predicate modifier—took over, creative impulses withered in source themes on such subjects as "The Story of Chewing Gum"; in pompous little book reports, covering "plot," "setting," and "character"; and in juvenile moralizing on prefabricated topic sentences like "Shallow men believe in Luck."

What can we do about it? How make the carry-over? How keep the spring bubbling sweet and clear? Of course, we can't—with complete success, anyway. The water is bound to get muddied. But my conviction is that we can do better than we've done. Exhibit *A* in my talk tonight is simply another method, on a much more mature level and in a more organized way, of harnessing, directing, and making something of the same creative energies and impulses that made our little neighborhood newspaper such a roaring success. I know that every school situation presents unique and often insurmountable problems; the vision of forty squirming, itching, restless kids in a single classroom haunts me. My Exhibit *A* may strike many of you as wildly impractical. But the principle is the thing, and I am convinced that it can be applied, in part if not in whole, with vital results to almost any level of education.

My story is of Yale's only mass-production creative writing course —that is, the only nonseminar course in this kind of writing, the only one open to all comers. It was founded about 1912, by Professor John Berdan, and was called, and still is, Daily Themes. It is one of the few courses whose title means precisely what it says. It means a theme a day, Monday through Friday, to be deposited by nine o'clock each morning in a receptacle established for the purpose. At 9:15 every morning the box is opened and every theme is stamped with the date for that day. The emphasis in the title is on the word *daily:* not two themes every other day, or five themes every Friday morning. The belief is that no one has more than one theme in him per day. Two would mean a serious dilution of effort and concentration; five on Friday means nonsense. There are weekly five-minute conferences in which every theme of each student for the past week is discussed with him in quick review. Often the comments in so brief a time can be little more than "This is good," "This is bad," "Do this," "Don't do that,"—short, swift, even a little brutal; but perhaps more effective, through their shock-effect, than the long, often sentimental heart-to-heart conferences of many creative writing courses I know of.

The course uses no books, no syllabi, no examinations. The heart of the matter is the blank page which the student must face every evening, Sunday through Thursday. There are two lectures a week. There are prohibitions and principles, but they provide the most flexible, least arbitrary guidance imaginable and leave ample room for the individual. Pedagogical changes have been rung on them for forty years by various instructors of widely differing tastes. It is significant that they have outlived the several major shifts of literary fashion that have taken place in America since the course was founded. These principles, which I shall presently describe, are somewhat loosely strung together by a series of slogans which, as the course progresses, are advanced *seriatim* at about two week intervals in the lectures. From the very beginning no subjects are ever assigned. We simply make clear that we do not want expository writing. We want "creative" writing, the kind you get in stories and novels. We do not want to hear how to lay a railroad track, or paint a house, or build a smudge. We advise something close to home, and we place an arbitrary limit of three to four hundred words—a physical necessity in view of the immense task of correcting the papers, but also a good discipline in economy and emphasis. The opening lecture in the course usually concludes with some such sentiments as these: "Above all, *interest* us. Remember that we bore easily. We are not interested in grade *B* movies or in your brand of science fiction. But the chances are that we will be interested in *you*, not your whole life-story, because you can't make it interesting in three hundred words, but in something that you personally have observed, or thought about, or lived through—an hour, a moment, a single impression."

The inevitable result of this, the second day out, is a rash of grade *B* movie scenarios, science fiction, and horror stories. For instance:

The quiet of the night was torn asunder by the shrill of sirens, and the darkness in the alley was shattered by spotlights and torches. A group of uniformed men stood over Stan's body. The blood from his body still fed a river of red which ran among the cobblestones. A shower of splintered glass made a pillow for his head.

"You damn punk!" Stan had spotted Jerry sitting on a box in the dead-end alley. "If you ever mess around with my girl again I'll kill you."

By this time he was standing over Jerry. He grabbed him by the collar and jerked him to his feet. Jerry jerked away, falling to his knees, and it was then that he saw the others.

"You ain't gonna get the chance. I'm going to finish you right now."

"You guys can't get away with this. Do you want to spend the rest of your lives in jail?"

"No stupid copper can catch me, I'll spit in their faces."

A bottle crashed against the back of Stan's head, and he fell forward onto the tarnished blade of Jerry's knife.

"Hey, Lieutenant, we found this guy hiding in a doorway at the end of the alley. Do you want him?"

"What's your name, son?"

"Jerry—sir. I don't know anything. I just heard a fight and came to see what was going on."

"Why were you hiding?"

"I heard the sirens and got scared—but I didn't do nothing."

"Just the same, you'd better come down to the station with us."

The last grain of Jerry's composure disappeared.

"I didn't mean to do it," he shrieked. "He was hitting me. I didn't mean to do it."

"Sure, Kid."

It started to rain and they put a canvas over Stan's body.

As well as such harrowing tales as this, there usually is an elaborate account of how to lay a railroad track, or paint a house, or build a smudge. (Don't think for a minute that college seniors, any more than school boys, listen to directions.) On these papers goes a large red *W*, orginally standing for *Worthless* but in recent years commonly designating *W awful;* and the next lecturer reaffirms (with controlled emotion) that "What is likely to interest us is *you.*"

He then may break into the second leading principle of the course, the first on the Grand List of slogans: INDIVIDUALIZE BY SPECIFIC DETAIL. This is the "eye-opener" of the course. It is the major weapon against the stereotype, the stock description, the imitated grade *B* movie, the third-hand horror story of the sort I've just read. The details, to be individualized, must have been seen; they must have been experienced in all their living reality. It must not be *any* foot-ball game that you describe, it must be *a particular* football game;

not *any* pretty girl whom you are sitting next to, but a *particular* girl, wearing not just any fur coat, but an aging mink and a hat which you saw on her roommate at the Cornell game last weekend.

As the eyes get wider open, and the vision becomes sharper, the writing becomes more interesting. The twenty-odd papers which the instructor reads every night begin to throb with a new life. The students begin to see that they do not have to smash their father's Cadillac, or murder their grandmother, or take a rocketship to the moon to get materials for daily themes. They can get one from as unlikely to a source as a slide rule and a book of logarithms:

"Look, with tables, a slide rule, and good solid numbers, you've damn well got to be right." He took the slide rule from its case and waved it before us. "See, just slide the thing, and there's your answer—when you read a poem, how do you know what the prof thinks the thing's about. And then you spend all that time writing a theme—what the hell, *you* think it's good, but he can flunk you if he doesn't like it." He took a book filled with nothing but columns of numbers. "Look, here they are, take these and maybe a graph or two—both the prof and I know they're right, no opinion to it—if I use 'em right, he's got to give me a hundred. Ever get a hundred in an English course?" I admitted that I hadn't. "Ever expect to, or know anybody who did?" Again I admitted that he was right. "My God, what a waste of time—how do you expect to make a living?" I pointed out to him that any number of men who majored in English are still living quite comfortably. "Nuts, you can't really learn anything solid." Again the slide rule waved before us. "Don't even see how you pass every term—can't see how you and the prof always agree on that hazy stuff—too much opinion in there." He riffled through the book of tables again. "With these tables, a slide rule, and good solid numbers, you've damn well got to be right."

Again, here's one on nothing more exotic than a visit to one's mother at the hospital. It's haunted my slumber ever since I read it two years ago.

"There she is," said Dad pointing through the windshield to a tall bunch of buildings huddled together above Riverside Drive. I lost sight of the hospital buildings for a minute as we pulled up in front of them. Getting out, we walked into the efficient lobby and followed the sign marked "Elevators."

She was lying on the bed with a black bandage-like cup over both of her eyes, the operated one marked with a little white X in the middle. I sat down in the straight-backed chair and asked her how she was doing. "No, no pain," she replied, "it's just this horrible itching under the bandage."

I felt relieved that this was all and looked at the figure on the bed again. Her hands were wringing each other in an effort to control the desire to scratch. I tried to take my conversation far afield of this hospital, but it always wound back to the expressionless figure on the bed who wrung her hands and seemed to be counting the endless seconds. "If only they could do something about this itching," she said and Dad replied that the doctor would be here soon. The minutes wormed forward, my own life having shrunk into a childish test-tube existence next to this.

The doctor finally came and we left the room while he changed her dressings. He left and offered us the usual noncommital phrases outside the door.

We re-entered and Mother was lying there, her face still drawn. "Well, does that feel better?" we asked.

"That itching, that damn itching," she said and I left, thinking dully of the long hours of the coming night, and the itching . . .

As someone put it, the British explorer, Sir Hubert Wilkerson, could find more interesting things in his own backyard than most other explorers could find in the whole Antarctic. The first weeks go largely to opening up the possibilities of your own backyard—the sharpening of the visual sense to everyday reality and, second, to the search for the *significant* detail which will best reveal that reality, like the book of tables and the slide rule in the theme just read. Mere cataloguings of detail won't do, mere lists of what you see from your back window. They must be selected for meaning: The little humanizing touch (to get back to the Yale Bowl) of the beautifully turned-out girl, "the tailored woman" down for the week end from Smith, who had forgotten to clean her fingernails. The thrill of wonder when the impossible blind date, the roommate's sister, reveals astonishing powers in her technical grasp of the science of football, even unto wing-backs and T-formations. But above all, the details must make the picture sharp and clear—the episode recreated in its own unmistakable individuality and uniqueness. Here's one that I submit as only mildly successful, but a great advance over the shilling shocker I read first:

I felt the stone-boat lurch and drag heavily in the freshly plowed earth. I hated the thought of rolling on that heavy stone again. But when I turned around in my seat, I saw that it had rolled over the small boy who had been tagging along with me that day. I pulled the tractor out of gear and raced back to the spot. The weight had passed over his legs, and a corner of the stone pinned him to the ground. I had no doubt but that it weighed a half-ton and thought surely that the boy's legs had been crushed. On freeing him I saw an ugly gash on his shin. There was little blood, and I suddenly noticed that the boy had made no sound above a soft, moaning, whimper. I gently lifted his leg to find any possible fracture. Miraculously there was none.

His dirty, brown cheeks were streaked with tears and his lips quivered as he asked me if he would be all right. I told him that I was certain he would be but that I must pick him up and take him to the house and put a bandage on. This was a bit of a lie, but I knew he was afraid of doctors. Thinking that *I* would take care of him cleared all worry from his face. He reached up and put his arms around my neck as I carried him back to the farm. The shock had made him drowsy, and he fought to keep his eyes open. I knew he was on the verge of unconsciousness but he was still making plans for his own safety. I had to promise that if he did go to the hospital where there were doctors, I would go with him.

I would call attention to several specific and telling details which give the theme a fair degree of individuality and make us sense its reality: the "lurch" of the stone-boat; the nicely moderated handling of the wound; the excellent description of the little boy's state of shock—no screams, only a "soft, moaning, whimper"—the drowsiness that made him "fight to keep his eyes open," and his childish fear of doctors. This has the breath of life.

To get the general run of themes even approximating this one involves at least a dozen false starts for most students. The grip of the grade *B* movie and fourth-rate journalistic culture is hard to loosen. It is hard to learn all over again to see things with your *own* eyes. Even after a month, the clichés will creep in; but by the end of three weeks we find it possible to turn to the second of our major slogans: VIVIFY BY RANGE OF APPEAL. Under this slogan we show that the sense of sight is not enough. The other senses—smell, hearing, touch, taste— are important means which the writer has at his disposal. We often introduce this slogan in an unannounced class exercise, putting on the blackboard a single word, such as *Skunk*, or *Garbage*, or *Chanel No. 5*. The results of a half hour's go at such a project are, as you may imagine, catastrophic. The students, as Professor Berdan used to say, turn into elephants, all noses. The themes reek; the stench is intolerable. The text of the next lecture is *moderation in all things*. But the principle is never forgotten: that any description of the Maine coast neglects at its peril a whiff of the clam flats at low tide; that, if you're describing a boyhood adventure in your grandmother's attic, you'd better say what it smelled like.

So far, as you can see, the course is simply an invitation toward a little more perceptive and sensitive living—or, rather, a return to the vivid, honest, and direct observation of children: "It's all red when you throw up." Most of us go through life half blind, half deaf, insensitive to taste and color and smell—to the feel of the texture of everyday life, to much of what makes life—and writing—interesting.

But there is more to it than mere sense impressions, of course, although it is surprising how insensitive or inhibited even the early adulthood of college students can be. After the scene has been chosen and the details visualized, there comes the problem of organization and arrangement. This is the problem of the craftsman. It involves strategy, a sense of field-generalship. How to deploy your details to the best possible advantage? This involves the principles inherent in the third slogan: CLARIFY BY POINT OF VIEW. A scene at the Yale Bowl, or an after-game cocktail party, or a remembered moment at a high school prom must be described from a well-established point of view. The reader must, in his mind's eye, know where he is and visualize his position. Is he on the fifty-yard line or behind the goal posts? Is he seeing the cocktail party from a position in a corner, a bit aloof, or are we in the midst of a chattering group sitting on the floor in front of the fire? Are we swirling in the center of the gymnasium or viewing the scene from behind the punch bowl? The point of view, then, must be clear; and in a three-hundred-word theme *it had better not shift*. Nothing is more irritating to the reader, comfortably oriented on the fifty-yard line, than to find himself suddenly behind the goal posts. We emphasize here, also, another aspect of *point of view:* psychological point of view. This too, in a three-hundred-word theme, had better be both clear and single, since here, in the attitude of the writer toward his subject, the main meaning of the theme may lie. In fact, a theme with no clearly implied attitude is subject to the most withering comment in our arsenal of critical terms: "So what?" The reader wants not only to see and hear and smell the immediate reality of the scene; he wants to be guided into a hint of its meaning—or what it meant to the author. The shilling shocker I read earlier is, among other things, a "So what?" theme, a mere spate of pseudo sensationalisms. If the reader has nothing but a hodge-podge of details, or a dead-pan description with no more life than an architect's drawing, he may well turn aside with the muttered curse, "So what?"

Such is the nature of artistic communication that this meaning is usually most effectively conveyed, not by direct *ex cathedra* statement by the author, but indirectly, by suggestion. Hence the fourth of our slogans: USE THE INDIRECT METHOD. The reader will share more immediately and deeply in the mood or emotion or experience of the writer if he is led into the heart of the matter almost without his knowing it—by indirection and suggestion. Here we put the student writer through a stern artistic discipline: he must do it all without *telling* us what he is doing. Thus the unforgivable sin is such a passage as this: "His eyes bulged. His face grew livid. His fists clenched. *He was angry*." During the few weeks when we emphasize this discipline, the key critical term after such a passage is "Telling." We are met with the inevitable complaints: "But doesn't Hardy *tell*, and Dickens?" And the answer is "Of course they do": in the freer context and loose structure of the novel, the author can do as he pleases in the large imaginative world he has created. Provided his larger reality is secure, he can analyze, and explain, and make pronouncements at will. In a three-hundred-word theme the little illusory world may be shattered by even one unnecessary intrusion by the author, one moralistic tag, one bit of *obiter dicta*.

This principle is perhaps most clearly illustrated in the presentation of character. Hence the next slogan: CHARACTERIZE BY SPEECH AND GESTURE. In other words, let the character speak for himself. Describe just that significant gesture which reveals the inner reality: the nervous clasping and unclasping of the hands; the slight twitch in the corner of the mouth; the quick, averted glance, and let the detail tell its own story. No field is richer for purposes of creative writing than this of character. Students now realize (for one thing) how futile was their initial worry about finding subjects to write on. They need no longer smash their father's Cadillac or murder their grandmother. There are as many theme subjects as there are people they know—or even people they don't know, like the nervous little old lady who sat opposite them in the bus that morning. Here, of course, the danger is that the clichés take over, that the little old lady becomes any little old lady, a stock character constructed from one or two poorly observed details. The first themes on roommates (an annual project) usually trot out a small regiment of campus types: the loafer, the dead-beat, the Don Juan, the party boy—generally in contrast to the author, who invariably emerges as studious, conscientious, never in debt, neat in his ways, and misunderstood. But a little dynamite in the form of a few *W*'s usually cures this tendency, and we send the authors back to write about a *man,* not a comic-strip caricature. Here's a theme that came through the mill a little while ago that hits off a character nicely, I think, without "telling" and by the skillful use of speech and gesture. Let's call it "The Good-Natured Roommate":

Art was sick of studying for a minute, so he came to the door that separated our studies and stood there looking at me. I, too, wanted a break, but pretended to ignore him. He cleared his throat; ignored. He walked over to the mirror, patted his tie; and, running his hand through the heavy stubble of his crew cut, said to the mirror, "Now there's a fine-looking lad."

"Art," I said, closing my book, "you're Irish and you're ugly."

He turned back to the mirror and scratched his beard with a square fingertip. "I think he's wrong," he said to the mirror.

"How about a beer or two, Art?"

"Now there's a man who talks sense," and he spun around with a broad smile on his pleasant, policeman's face.

Even if our students never develop into professional story-writers and novelists—although not a few of them have—they at least know the difference between a living fictional creation and a cliché, or a monster. Here is another, an admitted *tour de force,* but as sophisticated a bit of characterization as I've had in some time. The author, then a senior, went on to journalism and was at last account writing a novel:

"*Not* Lois Jamison's brother! Why isn't this a wonderful coincidence. Do sit down and talk to me." She patted the cushion beside her. "Goodness, we were at Miss Porter's for three years, and I never even realized Lois had a brother. A sweet, sweet girl. And now I find her long-lost brother at a cocktail party at Yale."

"Cigarette?" I asked. As she bent forward, I caught the scent of jasmine. She gripped my hand to steady the lighter and thanked me with an intimate blink of her blue eyes. She settled back in the couch, luxuriously stretching out her arms and exhaling a cone of smoke. "Just what I needed," she murmured. "You must be a mind reader." She twisted toward me, her long chestnut hair brushing against my shoulder. "Can you blow smoke rings? I'm just dying for someone to teach me how to blow smoke rings."

I shook my head. "Sorry, I always choke when I try it."

A blonde fellow stopped before the couch, silently profferring a tray of martinis. The girl turned to him, blinking her eyes. "Grand," she exclaimed. "A traveling oasis. You *are* a life saver."

She flicked the stem of the glass with a maroon-tipped finger and chuckled at the tinkling sound. "Music with our drink. How wonderful can wonderful get?" She rubbed the frosted glass against her smooth brown forehead. "Mmmn . . This is delightful." She closed her eyes and settled her head against my shoulder. "Tell me, Henry . . . It is Henry, isn't it? Do you like to go iceskating when the air is cold and crisp in the woods and the snow is piled on the branches like lazy white cats?"

The latter weeks of the course are devoted to stylistic matters. From vividly imagined detail and the manipulation of detail in an ordered whole, we go to matters of diction, the choice of words. Under the slogan USE WORDS FOR CONNOTATION, we call attention to the rich dynamics of the individual word, how a single word misused may ruin an entire theme, or how a single word—apt, vivid, suggestive—may make a theme, like the image of the young mathematician "waving" his slide rule to emphasize his point, or the snow "like lazy white cats" of the theme I just read. Matters of the sound of words and the possible variations of their rhythm in prose sequence are stressed, and here we make ample use of the resources of the best in English poetry and prose for illustration—or an occasional student example like the last sentence of the "Lois Jamison" theme. But it is one thing to see how Keats did it, or Ernest Hemingway; it is another to do it yourself. And for students this may be one of the most educational aspects of the entire course. They see the things they read from an entirely new perspective. They even achieve a rule-of-thumb standard of criticism and a new appreciation for a job superbly done. As an antidote to the prevailingly bookish and absorptive aspect of our formal education, such an experience is invaluable.

Now the question is, how much of all this is applicable to the years of formal education prior to college? My claim at the outset was that the principles and some of the techniques of daily themes are relevant to even the early years of grade school—as soon, I should say, as the child can put words together to form even the simplest sentence. There is the whole world of nature for him to observe and record, the world of his own childish experience, from how it felt to have his tonsils out to the time he threw up all over the kitchen floor. There are friends to write about and to write to. There are grandmothers, uncles, aunts, cousins, (not to mention mothers and fathers) who love getting letters; there are diaries to keep and little newspapers to write. A few years beyond this early stage, when the range of commitments is larger and daily stints of writing reach such proportions that teachers no longer have time to correct them, I am aware that a new problem enters. How to correct the daily themes of eighty to one hundred students? The answer usually is that it's impossible and the result is total abandonment. But I think we have given up too quickly. We haven't begun to use all our resources, from parental (or grandmotherly) co-operation, on down.

In some way or other we must get our young people to write and keep them writing. No one knows who he is until he has tried to put himself on paper. And no one knows what his world is until he has tried to describe it. I would have the study of formal grammar come along in due course, but *as auxiliary to the creative process, rather than vice-versa.* The dominance by the study of formal grammar over the English work of the middle and late grades is, to my way of thinking, a shocking reversal of values. The endless workbooks and filling-in of blanks are a blight on those magic creative years of childhood and adolescence. They often are excuses for teachers who don't know what else to do. Let me say that I am not a "self-expressionist." I would have our students know the mechanics of the sentence. I do not look upon creative writing as a cure-all. But I am interested in rearing generations of young Americans who will be able to face a job of writing with readiness and some delight, who will be more keenly alive to the world in which they live—see it more clearly, sense its passing and permanent values more deeply, and be able to record it with some precision. I cannot resist some final examples illustrating the kind of values that can accrue, under ideal conditions, from this discipline of creative writing. Here's a well-realized moment, I think, snatched from just before lunch on a football week end:

"I suppose you get lots of letters from young girls?" she asked, tapping a fresh cigarette on her red thumbnail.

The boy and girl were sitting on a dark leather couch in the common room. The autumn sun streamed through the windows behind them.

"I'm sorry," he said. "I guess I'm not being very polite. You don't mind if I read this, do you?" He looked up from the envelope and over to the girl beside him.

"Nonsense. Go ahead."

"Your dress shines in the sunlight," he said.

"Yes, I know," she smiled.

"Don't worry about the time. It's only 12:15. The game doesn't start till two."

He tore open the letter and his eyes skipped from the familiar heading to the second paragraph.

"I don't know what it is. It's something that makes the leaves turn gold in autumn and green again in the spring. It makes the wind sweep a little sparrow skyward to see what men may never see. It is the time caught between today and tomorrow, the time that never comes and yet is always there just beyond your reach. . . ."

"What seems to be on her mind?" the girl on the couch was saying.

"Oh, nothing much." He smiled to himself. "The weather mostly."

"Isn't that nice." The girl leaned back and blew a cloud of smoke.

He went on reading. *"Maybe some day if I reach high enough, long enough, hard enough, I'll know. . . ."* He jumped down to the end. *". . . . and you shall tell me of all the wonders, just beyond the stars."*

"What's she like?" the girl asked.

"Like?" The boy stuffed the letter into his coat pocket. "She lives across the street from me at home. She's only 16. Let's go eat."

Here's another, admittedly out of the schoolboy orbit, since it involves a scene between a young veteran and his wife. But I wonder if, without the training of the thirty-odd themes he wrote before this one, or without the stimulus of the daily job to be done, our author ever would have penetrated his little domestic *impasse* so surely or described it with so steady a hand.

"Stuart—," she said.

I stopped taking the food out of the icebox and said, "What, Annie?"

"Stuart, let's sit down and talk a while before we start supper. We're not in any hurry."

"O.K. Annie," I said.

We went into the living room and sat down. I looked at her and she smiled, and we were silent a moment.

"What's the matter, Annie?"

"Nothing's the matter, Stuart."

"Well, what would you like to talk about?" I asked.

She smiled again, forcing herself a little. "Did you see any one today?" she asked.

"No, no one special," I said. "Just the usual people."

"Well, did you see any one interesting?" she persisted.

"No, I guess not. What do you mean, interesting?" I said.

She answered, "Well, just interesting," with a small vague movement of her arm. "Did you see that German teacher or that Mr. Thompson, for instance?"

"Yes, come to think of it, I saw them both," I said.

"Well, why didn't you say so?" she asked, sitting up straight.

"I would have, Annie, but I didn't think anything special about seeing them."

"Stuart, that's what I mean—if you would only tell me things."

"Well, Annie," I said, "It's just that usually nothing of any importance happens."

"I don't mean important things—just little things," she said; "I don't see you all day and I just like to know what you've been doing."

"Well, I'll try to remember from now on."

"Will you, Stuart?" She looked at me hard.

"Of course I will, Annie."

"I wish you would," she said.

We have one final slogan which we reserve as a kind of grand summation for the last week or so of the term. (I should have said long ago that this is a one-term course. Neither students nor faculty could stand the strain much longer. The second term is devoted to the short story. The class is divided into sections of about ten each, and each student writes a story and delivers it to the class for group criticism once every two weeks.) Our final slogan is: UNIFY BY A SINGLE IMPRESSION. Here the emphasis is on the theme as an artistic whole. Do all the parts fit, and do they work toward a single, powerful impression? Without further ado, let me give you one last example of a theme that achieves this about as well as any I remember. It is an exceptional performance, I admit, and you can imagine my delight as I pulled this one out of the daily grist:

When the bus reached the entrance of Margam Castle where we were billeted, all four of us were in good cheer from the half-and-half and shots of Dutch gin at the Talbot Arms and from the spirit of Christmas which prevailed in Wales in spite of the blackout and the shortages. There were a lot of other soldiers stumbling up the steep black path to the MP post at the main door, most of them drunk, but we four hung behind and stopped by the dark lake to sing "The First Noel" which sounded fine, even outdoors, because Larry Florcyk got the tenor descant right. Then we pushed on up the hill, following Bill's shaded flashlight, singing the Welsh football song we'd learned from Larry's girl, until we got out of breath.

When we reached the main door the MP said, "Youse guys is makin too —— much noise!" but we didn't pay any attention and went on into the great front hall with the vaulted ceiling. George Nakhnikian went "Boooom" in his big ringing bass and said, "Boy, listen to those acoustics! Let's try something." We did. We just stood there, in the middle of the hall, with our arms around each others' shoulders and we sang "All Through the Night" with the Welsh words—"Are Heed A-nos"—very softly and humming the second chorus. Our voices blended and the sound went up and bounced around against the stone, pretty as anything. Then we sang "I Love You As I Never Loved Before" with lots of schmaltz because we wanted to see how the tricky echoes at the end would sound. They sounded wonderful and Bill's lead was fine so we did "Down Mobile" and "Mandy Lee."

We knew we couldn't stay there much longer without a beef from somebody, probably Colonel Walker, so we decided to do just one more. I suggested "Mavourneen" because we were in form and I loved to do the baritone. For once we got it pitched right and started off soft enough. It was the finest thing we'd ever done and ever did do, even with Fred Johnson later on in Germany, after Larry got killed. When we got to the "Your poor slave is Barney O'Flynn" part we really let go, singing down each others' throats with tears in our eyes. The great stone arches were still ringing with the close harmony when we repeated the line again softly, as you're supposed to, and ended with Bill's lead going way up strong and clear and true. We stood there shoulder to shoulder without saying a word until the last reverberation died, then tiptoed slowly up the wide steps to check in with the CQ.

Since a central theme in one of the Conferences was creative writing, and since Mr. Sewall's ideas on the subject grew out of his experiences with a college course, we asked a committee, composed mainly of teachers in secondary schools (with one member who is both a teacher of writing in college and a poet) to consider the same topic; what follows is the committee's report. The members of this group, like Mr. Sewall, believe strongly in the discipline of frequent creative writing, although they differ from him in offering their students more specific directions for writing, indicating the form in which the student is to work. This may be because they were dealing with high school rather than with college students..

The appendix to this essay should be especially useful, for it offers a series of assignments which these talented teachers have found to work well with their classes, as well as examples of writing in response to the assignments. Some of these papers show what high school pupils can accomplish when they are encouraged to make use of their talents.

5

Creative Writing

MABEL MORRILL, *Rutland High School, Vermont, Chairman*

WALKER GIBSON, *New York University*

ALICE HOGAN, *Hillhouse High School, New Haven, Connecticut*

HART LEAVITT, *Phillips Academy, Andover, Massachusetts*

FRANCIS NEWSOM, *Brookline High School, Massachusetts*

CORINNE OLLI, *The Chapin School, New York City*

"I, too, dislike it", Marianne Moore wrote in the first line of the poem which she called *Poetry*.[1] When the Committee on the Teaching of Creative Writing began to prepare for this conference, we, too, disliked it—the term *creative writing*. Our dissatisfaction, we found, derived, not from intrinsic weakness or lack of validity in the term itself, but, rather, from the uncertainty and serious questioning which have, in recent years, accompanied its use. "Is not all writing creative writing?" asks a puzzled administrator sitting in on a discussion among teachers of creative writing. "Can we not find a more exact, a more truly descriptive term?" ask interested teachers. "What about 'imaginative writing' or 'personal writing'?" " 'Creative writing' (whatever that is)," remarks John Ciardi, obviously nettled, in a recent *Saturday Review* article. To return to Miss Moore, her first line

[1] Marianne Moore, *Collected Poems* (New York, The Macmillan Co., 1952).

79

continues, "There are things that are important beyond all this fiddle."[2] Cudgeling of brains and unsatisfactory casting about for an improvement in terminology brought the Committee to a similar conclusion. We believe that *creative writing* is more descriptive than any suggested substitute of the kind of writing for secondary school students with which we were to concern ourselves in this report.

What, then, do we mean by "creative writing"? In our schools, in English and in other classes, good and necessary instruction must be offered in writing that is not creative. Students learn forms and disciplines of writing that make for ease and competence in the varied day-to-day practices that depend upon verbal communication. Much of our writing in the secondary school is also a factor, together with many others, in the long, involved process through which education seeks to preserve man as the *thinking* animal. While creative writing contributes significantly to the latter aim, its first concern is with the literary forms which have, through their infinitely varied development, made literature an art.

DEFINING CREATIVE WRITING

Very early in the discussion of our problem, the Committee agreed that a definition of creative writing was necessary, as a point of departure and as a control. We accepted for brevity and comprehensiveness this statement: *Creative writing we define as an act of composition in which the student creates a controlled dramatic voice and an imagined world, without sacrificing the sense of logic and reality. The creation of this world is a process of making concrete the personal experience of the student in the literary form—prose or verse.*

With this basic definition to steer by, the Committee examined its experience in the teaching of creative writing, and attempted to put into words something of what happens, as seen from our differing backgrounds, when the student experiments with this kind of writing. The statements that follow are extensions and applications of the basic definition.

1. Creative writing is a mode of composition in which the student, aided by his imagination, shapes the raw material of his own

[2] *Ibid.*

thoughts, feelings, and experiences into some literary form. By so doing, he externalizes these thoughts, feelings, and experiences and is able to interpret and evaluate them against the background of his environment.

2. As we use the term here, creative writing is the expressing and the sharing by the writer of the meanings, the feelings, the emotions which have been aroused in him by his sensory contacts with the world. It is the result of a process in which the intellect, the imagination, and the emotions are engaged. The work produced, usually a story, a poem, an essay, a play, or perhaps merely a bit of any of these, expresses him who creates it. It is the result of the bringing together of the understanding of one's outer and one's inner world, the fusion of things and self. Every intelligent human being is capable of expressing this creativity in some way and to some degree. Whatever is felt on the painter's canvas, in the composer's concerto, upon the writer's page, has been created. The feeling is the thing.

3. Creative writing is the "controlled" and orderly literary presentation of "an imagined world" in that it reconstructs observed reality to heighten and illustrate personal conviction and feeling, and to offer individualistic reaction to experience in an artistic and dramatic form. Its artistic essence is mood, sincerity, and effectiveness. Its form is in some sense governed—at least in initial stages—by the accepted traditions of taste and media. Although it should embrace the perceptivity of analytical and explanatory style, it is to be distinguished by its embarkation on individualistic disregard of any previous pronouncements or attitudes on any given subject. In short, it is a magnified conception of moments of existence to give meaning or immortalization or emphasis to man's relationship to his world.

4. Creative writing for the high school student who is beginning its practice is his first attempt to isolate experience, to concentrate upon it, to explain to himself why he remembers it, to comprehend its significance. It is the recreation of experience so that significance comes through. To communicate, he learns to be attentive,

to concentrate upon all of the parts from which he is fashioning a whole. He is guided, subconsciously, by his reading in the form in which he is working, and, consciously and subconsciously, by the goal to be achieved—*his* expression of *his* experience extended by *his* concept of its significance. The importance to him of what he is doing sensitizes him; he becomes critical, dissatisfied, determined that the inevitable words shall somehow be quarried out of the stubborn rock of unexperienced self. In the hard work of trying to communicate, he realizes that, although all his material is there, inside himself, it is through bringing it out, seeking to expose its uniqueness (and, incidentally, putting it back inside himself concrete and alive) that it takes on any reality for other human beings. He has begun to learn that what is *given* is *not* what is *created;* that it is his responsibility as a creator to find, to recognize, and to use *his* symbols of significance.

TEACHING CREATIVE WRITING

If there are those who scoff nowadays at the idea of *teaching* creative writing, they must be a stubborn breed. Evidence that it can be taught has accumulated so rapidly and is so widely known that mention of it seems almost superfluous. For nearly as long as some of us veterans have been teaching, the Scholastic Magazines Writing Awards have been demonstrating that high school students can write creatively. The *Atlantic* School Contest provides a showcase for writing talent which the University of Pittsburgh considers important enough to warrant the granting of an annual scholarship. Other contests, national or regional in scope, are familiar to teachers of English. Young poets, many of them still at college or university, are now submitting to the *Atlantic* work in such quantity and of such excellence that the magazine has recently adopted the policy of publishing a highly selected portion of this work in two issues each year. Perhaps a few of these successful young writers have courted the muse in inspired solitude, but there are simply too many of them to make credible any theory of the flowering of isolated individual genius. No, there have been classes, just regular everyday English classes for the most part, with a scattering of hard-won specialized creative writing sections, in which just regular everyday English teachers have somehow made it possible for high-school-age boys and girls to learn the creative approach to writing. It has been done in the midst of life—school life, that is, with its myriad intrusions upon concentrated, sequential, and consequential effort. It has been done despite report card conferences, despite the delays attendant upon setting up the projector for the showing of literary background films, despite those solid blocks of material to be "covered" so that amplitude of covering may be demonstrated in semester exams, despite the inner grumblings (always of the teacher, of course) when fifteen minutes are sliced from the English period—inevitably on a writing day—for a basketball rally. It has been done in schools where the teacher is blessed with small sections and a total of eighty students, and in schools where the blessing is more prodigal, running to five or six sections daily with a minimum of thirty-five occupied desks. There is no magic formula, no secret ingredient. Creative writing is possible for any group of students if the teacher is convinced of its values and is game to try.

It is true, of course, that the atmosphere of the classroom in which this kind of writing is to be done is important, for creative writing is individual and personal, and students and teacher must be at ease and unselfconscious. Each pupil should feel important and respected as an individual; he must be able to share his doubts, his beliefs, his prejudices. The teacher should be one with the group, divested of the aura of perfectionist-judge, enthusiastic and actively encouraging at times; at other times withdrawing into the background, available for individual consultation. He may, as Carl Wonnberger proposes in *The English Journal*, try himself out on his own writing assignments.[3] A new awareness of the teacher involved in Eliot's "intolerable wrestle with words and meanings" would grow in a sympathetically shared experience. Respect for sincerity, impatience with sham and shallowness, recognition of the importance and dignity of the individual—all these belong in the atmosphere of the classroom in which creative writing is possible.

Perhaps in the simple word *sharing* lies the essence of the creative writing experience, if we remember that the great and simple things, like love, humility, and truthfulness, must always be learned through

[3] Carl G. Wonnberger, "They All Can Learn to Write," *The English Journal*, Vol. XLV, No. 8 (November, 1956) pp. 455, ff.

submitting to disciplines. "To believe that your impression holds good for others is to be released from the cramp and confinement of personality," [4] says Virginia Woolf. The successful sharing by the student writer of his experience and its meaning is, of course, the point of climax in the activities of the class which is experimenting with creative writing. Before he can *share*, he must learn to *seek*, within and without himself, and to examine attentively the effect upon himself of the coalescense of what is within and what is without. Writing of his work in the December, 1955, *English Journal*, Wilson J. Thornley, who teaches English and creative writing at the Ogden, Utah, high school, says, "All the activities of the entire course are focused on the problem of sharpening and training and exercising the ability to be aware of what is going on around us, and, being aware of it, to develop insight into it and tolerance and appreciation of it. The attention is concentrated on sensitizing the five channels through which human experience can be received: taste, touch, sight, smell, and hearing. And no matter how intense grows a side issue of form, structure, mechanics, vocabulary, etc., this realizing of life remains the chief occupation of the class." [5]

This committee believes that creative writing belongs *in* the English curriculum of the secondary school, not set apart from it and thus partially removed from the potential richness and variety of the over-all English classroom program. Indeed, there seems to be general professional agreement that, at least in secondary schools, creative writing acts as a vitalizing agent, while, at the same time, drawing foundation and background from all other aspects of the program. Investigation of how it is done reveals that there is no one infallible method of integrating creative writing with procedures accepted and necessary in the on-going work of teaching and learning English. For example, a teacher in a girls' private day school has this to say of her methods:

We have no creative writing course per se. . . . Every girl tries her hand at creative as well as other kinds of writing, on the principle that if there is value in imaginative writing for one, there is value for all. . . . Most of

[4] Quoted in Elizabeth Drew and John L. Sweeney, *Directions in Modern Poetry* (New York, W. W. Norton and Company, Inc., 1940) Ch. 1, "The Poet and His Audience," p. 32.

[5] Wilson R. Thornley, "The Case for Creative Writing," *The English Journal*, Vol. XLIV, No. 9 (December, 1955), pp. 528–529 ff.

our writing is done in conjunction with our reading. We read ballads in the ninth grade, for example, and then we try our hand at ballads of our own, on subjects drawn from school life or the morning paper. The same thing is true of almost every form of creative writing that we attempt, in verse and prose. Directly or indirectly, our creative efforts spring from our reading. For instance, in the eleventh grade, with a bow to Coleridge and his avowed purpose of creating a "willing suspension of disbelief," we attempt among other things a story of the supernatural. Spurning such timeworn props as graveyards, haunted houses, night shrieks, and the touch of a clammy hand, we try a disarmingly natural approach, with, we hope, an adumbration of sinister things to come. One such story was set in Rockefeller Center, of all places, and concerned the ghost of an elevator operator who had committed suicide. Another story opened with a gay prom scene at a boys' boarding school; it ended with the discovery of the body of the missing boy in the belfry, to which there was no access. The teacher can only try to persuade such a student that an honest effort to express something *she* thinks or feels about a subject will be valued, no matter what the result, that no one expects her to write like Emily Dickinson or even like the most articulate person in the class. . . .

Under the teacher's direction, a variety of simple exercises lead toward the writing of the short story. The assignment and working procedure for the short story are presented in the appendix to this report. Since we are here considering approaches to creative writing, a few of the exercises will be mentioned, with some examples of the results of one. This teacher uses: various exercises in observation—articles on a table, pupils passing through the room, things seen outside the window, a *Who's Who* of the division, to help in self-searching, in which each pupil writes one unusual thing about himself; the telling aloud of a humorous story or anecdote to pinpoint suspense; characterizing a person by look or gesture or revealing traits, with point of view illustrated as pupils place differing interpretations upon the same actions. This limited excerpt, lifted from the context of an entire unit, illustrates a point which the Committee believes is important: that very simple writing assignments can and do construct for the beginning writer a background and an attitude which lead directly toward writing in one of the creative forms. The illustrations which follow, from the *Who's Who* exercise, show concentration upon the single character as well as choice of appropriate, revealing detail.

Ever since I was old enough to create more petunias than were originally on the wallpaper in my bedroom, I have been fascinated by and engrossed in the study of painting and sketching. These mediums have always symbolized a means of escape from my troubles and problems. The tranquility of being apart from others and of working upon my canvas has a mysterious power over me when I am in a melancholy or a sulky mood. At the first stroke of my brush, I find myself in a magical world of fantasy.

Now sixteen, I have been an aqua-lung diver for over three years. I have explored, taken pictures, slept, salvaged, and almost died under the surface of Long Island Sound. . . .

"I wonder what makes this work." Oh, how many times I've said that and then, to answer that call of my curiosity, have proceeded to take *this* apart. Everything seems to go according to plan until I start to reconstruct the huge pile of gears, wires, and dials I have assembled. Then my mind goes blank. I sit in bewilderment for fifteen or twenty minutes, and then calmly pick up the pieces and carefully place them in the trash barrel. Leaving the basement, with the resolve never to take apart another thing, I stop suddenly, shyly eyeing a bright new piece of equipment, and saying to myself, "I wonder what makes *that* work."

In fairness, we could not ask our students simply to express themselves, for little is to be gained from the usual inexactness, generalization, ranting on pet theories, and general incoherence. They have to come to us to learn *how* and *what* and *why*. . . . The course in which this learning progresses is built on paralleling and interaction of, reading and writing. While a novel is being studied in class, for example, there are two creative writing assignments: first, a description of a scene from real life, close enough to the student so that he can revisit it as often as necessary to check the accuracy of his observation. The writing of this description is preceded by the submitting of an exact diagram, showing distances, measurements, and unusual features. When this diagram is clear to the teacher, the writing of the description begins. The second writing assignment during the study of a novel is a careful portrayal of ten minutes of action which includes several people, with a diagram again required to account for detail in action, and relative positions. Respect for the skill of the novelist in his management of setting, incident, and their interaction grows in the student as he sets himself to learn, through similarly exact assignments, as his class reading embraces the other literary forms. We hope that we have not belabored this point of approach to creative writing through regular English class work, but we suspect that some of the dubiousness and confusion of those who are suspicious of creative writing in the schools arises from lack of understanding of this very point. If there *is* an ivory-tower approach, the student hunts his elephant and builds his tower—with diagram—in his English class.

Since a "how to do it" section that would be of any real value would be much too long to include in the body of this report, the Committee has used an appendix for that purpose. In it are included specific suggestions, methods, and assignments, with illustrations of their results, for writing both prose and poetry. These are arranged from simplicity to complexity, thus providing sequences which the teacher may adapt to his own purposes. May we add that any teacher capable of including all the steps of these sequences in one year's work would be the sort of miracle that we should prefer not to see in action.

* * *

Creative writing forces a student to isolate and examine his own experiences, as against analyzing the experiences of characters in a book or newspaper, and as against expressing ideas and emotions which he has heard that other people sometimes express. Since it requires him to fit his experience in a communicable form, creative writing also leads a student, in his present highly self-centered life, to evaluate his own self-centers. This, over a period of months, may help in doing what many teachers, ironically sometimes, say is their great duty: to build character. If a student has to study his own actions as possible literary substance, he may discover moral meanings about himself, since literature is always based on moral values. Furthermore, in trying to develop a story, which is based on interaction of character, he will be led to study the actions of others who took part in his own experience. This could conceivably lead to better adjustment, not in the curricular sense, but in a personal sense. Boys and girls have only a vague sense that they act on their emotions, often to their own detriment, and others', too. To study their own actions as revealing emotion, which literature must do, may lead to the best kind of self-knowledge.

Through words, the writer finds his way into his own ideas, learning to make the interchanges between general and specific demanded by the thought process. When he moves freely and certainly among his own ideas, he opens the door to imagination, since imagination requires ease and virtuosity in associating ideas to produce new combinations which become new concepts. As suggested earlier, today imaginative power is choked off by pressures in the structure of modern society, yet imagination there must be if we are to be saved from the chaos with which our skills and our stupidities threaten us.

* * *

In 1954 Henry A. Murray, Professor of Clinical Psychology at Harvard, gave one of the series of remarkable addresses honoring the Bicentennial of Columbia University. His subject was "Versions of Man," and, in his conclusion, he had this to say of the importance of the imagination:

> The family and social systems which were . . . most encouraging to young and free imaginations were . . . eventually most strengthened by all kinds of practical, unifying, and inspiring innovations—tools and weapons, heroic sagas, rituals, moral principles, and religions. That the superior striking power, if not the continued existence, of an entire nation may hang on the unimpeded imaginations of a few theoretical scientists is today only too appallingly apparent.
>
> It is not so apparent, however, nor widely and sufficiently acknowledged that imagination is the fountain from which all inventive and regenerative currents flow. It is not squarely appreciated, for example, that our esteemed democratic system, for the preservation of which so many noble men have lived and died, was derived from mutations of ideas that once upon a time occurred in the head of John Locke and of Rousseau. With many such precedents in view, it can be predicted that if there is to be any beneficent response to the challenge posed by the now absolutely weaponed, blazing hatreds of the world, it will come from the spontaneous and unfettered imaginations of informed and profound minds that are granted hearing at the seats of government.[6]

May we not conclude that, for the individual and for society, our times confront us with a necessity which the schools will neglect to our peril, that the curriculum emphasizing the easy and mistaken "fundamentals" and "college requirements" no longer serves in a world that needs the light of imagination, and that we who teach English have a responsibility that we can at least adequately begin to meet by insisting upon a place for creative writing in our classrooms?

* * *

In the specialized class there should be a place for students who have shown aptitude for and interest in writing and also for those "best

[6] Henry A. Murray, "Versions of Man," *Man's Right to Knowledge*, 2nd Series (New York, Copyright Columbia University Press, Herbert Muschel, Publisher, 1955), pp. 41–42.

minds" that may not have shown specific writing talent but belong in the group because of the benefits of a course which disciplines the entire nervous system. Work in such a class is concentrated, for both student and teacher; hence it should be small, enrolling from ten to fifteen. Projects should grow out of intensive literature study in all forms. Careful instruction should be preferred over suggested imitation. There should be sympathetic personal criticism, given individually in all attempts. Work should be done according to fully explained assignments in progressive stages. The work should begin with simple portrayal of what is seen. From the start, there should be no illusion that creative writing is a "snap" course. Nor should there be any misunderstanding about the amount of reading required by the course, or the importance of that reading. The teacher should understand that the odds are against his turning out even a light sprinkle of eventually professional writers, but in this selected group, he does have the "carriers" of appreciation of literary tradition and innovation in this generation. As Mr. Gibson of the Committee says, writing on "What the Writer Teaches," in *College English*, the teacher's function "is to enlarge and refine the literary experience of the student, to make the student more aware of words. It seems obvious that a disciplined course in writing can contribute to such an awareness, and can provide an important part of the student's whole literary upbringing." [7]

But what of the many schools that are not yet ready to provide for the gifted in specialized classes? Surely the personal values that have proved themselves again and again in the creative English class should not be denied to secondary school youth in general. Can the unselected take it? Will it do them as much good as workbook drill and writing out the answers to the questions at the end of the short story? Carl Wonnberger says this of a "slow" class—students who were "defeated and deflated" by other English class experiences:

I was . . . determined that there would be no workbooks, no diagramming, and no "grammar." At first, results seemed disquieting, for I was used to quicker progress, but shortly after midyear this "slow" class of ninth graders amazed me by winning twenty-one state writing prizes including five first places in a contest which involved many older students.

[7] Walker Gibson, "What the Writer Teaches," *College English* (February, 1956), p. 298.

My embarrassment was complete when I realized that several of the winners were even then failing my course. Talent is where you find it, and it seems to be less a matter of original power than of dedication; almost anyone can learn to write well if writing comes to be the accepted thing in the social group.[8]

If we wish to make a real and consistent effort to put creative writing into typical, varying, unselected classes, how shall we go about it? For what they are worth, particularly for the teacher who wants to make a start, the Committee offers the following suggestions for a simple, manageable plan of work for a year:

Have an aim for the year, with most classes a simple aim, such as developing the ability to present material in the pattern that is reasonable and appropriate for it. Make each assignment a single step toward the achievement of this aim. Start with exposition, seeking order and clarity. Use précis, explanation of ideas from reading, substantiation of a point of view, summarizing of themes from literature being studied, working for sequence and emphasis. Limit scope of papers; keep them short; require revision. Move on to observation, stressing accuracy of detail in reporting. Make students observe, report, and omit all personal judgment. Again limit scope: one object, one very restricted area—a mantel, a tree in the yard, a person in one spot at one time. Use several observation assignments, keeping them short, requiring revision. The next step might be a transcript, as accurate as possible, of dialogue, overheard or participated in. This will need "trial runs" to foster the habit of really listening to what people really say. Characters involved must be clearly seen and reported factually. When observation and reporting can be handled with some success, move on to a simple narrative. (We are miles away from the short story, remember.) The narrative should be of a single incident, including not more than three characters, and be taken from experience, *observed, not remembered*. It may include dialogue, but that is not necessary. It will include position (important), movement, and time sequence. It must begin and end definitely, with specific sensory detail. Plan to get ten short papers from the class during the year, spacing them to fit reasonably into the over-all pattern of the class work. Tell students of the plan for the year's writing and encourage discussion of aims. Let them

[8] Wonnberger, *op. cit.*

read and discuss examples of the kind of writing they are attempting. Make time in class for at least one individual teacher-pupil conference on strengths and weaknesses in writing produced.

Every English teacher who encourages appreciation of literature is a potential teacher of creative writing. Every English teacher who appreciates and tries to understand his pupils as individuals is a potential teacher of creative writing. It is only a step to make the classroom the place where, as Dewey put it, experience becomes saturated with "the conscious meanings derived from communication and deliberate expression," so that man loses in large measure his fears of living. Dewey calls even the simplest of such human endeavors "art in germ," and he says that "even in its rudimentary forms, it contains the promise of that delightful perception which is esthetic experience." [9]

* * *

For these urgent reasons, then, this Committee believes and strongly recommends that the opportunity to write creatively be provided through the curriculum for all high school youth. It is true that the writers of day-after-tomorrow sit in our classrooms now; even more important, those who will *make* day-after-tomorrow, and live in it, sit in our classrooms now. Finally, we would remind all of us that we cannot avoid, nor should we wish to, being potential figures in a "divine conspiracy." For we never know, we never know, when that night may come, when, as the clock says 11:30 and we take from the pile the last paper we can possibly read tonight, we find, with wonder transcending fatigue, that this is the one, this is the one that speaks to us out of the dark in the mineshaft, and out of other and magical depths, to tell us that "If a light come in the mine . . . the rivers in the mine will run fast with the voice of many women; the walls will fall in, and it will be the end of the world . . . but when I walk through the shaft, in the dark, I can touch with my hands the leaves on the trees, and underneath . . . where the corn is green." [10]

[9] Joseph Ratner, ed., *Intelligence in the Modern World, John Dewey's Philosophy* (The Modern Library; New York, Random House, 1939), Ch. 19, "The Artistic-Esthetic in Experience," pp. 958 and 962.

[10] Emlyn Williams, *The Corn Is Green* (New York, Random House, 1938), p. 57.

Appendix

One of the most interesting and obvious conclusions of the Committee on the Teaching of Creative Writing is that the teaching of this kind is almost as personal as the writing itself. All of the committee members have been blessed with major or minor successes in their efforts to "teach" (for want of a better word) creative writing. Yet comparison of their methods and approaches, while indicating certain similarities, reveals that no two teachers will follow exactly the same procedures. Since the committee is particularly concerned to emphasize divergence of approach to the problem and challenge of making creative writing a vital and valid part of the secondary-school curriculum in English, it seemed that the kind of appendix which follows would be the most effective demonstration of no *one* royal road, but *many* paths, byways, secondary roads, and through-ways "of royal hope." In it, six teachers state in their own unedited words what they *do* in their classes to help young people learn to express themselves creatively. In some of the items, the teacher is discussing his method; in others, approach and assignment are presented as they are given to a class; in all cases, illustrations from student work, indicating varying degrees of success, are included.

LEARNING TO USE FRESH, VIVID, APPROPRIATE, FIGURATIVE LANGUAGE

In an attempt to awaken their eyes and minds to the things in life which they obviously do not see, I have experimented with photographs. I have used a series of portfolios of pictures which *Life* put out several years ago for this very teaching purpose, copies of the *Photography Annual* published by Popular Photography, Steichen's magnificent anthology *The Family of Man*, and a collection of my own.

In an attempt to combine accurate and sensitive seeing with good diction, I have used as one classroom exercise, a silent study of pictures, culminating in students' choosing single words, or phrases, or metaphors to describe a detail (facial expression, texture of an object, mood of a motion), or an aspect, or a fundamental unity of a picture.

I can easily write a book on what is revealed by this process in class, or as a homework project. I am sure, for example, that there is considerable shock value to a student who has used a fatuous cliché, in hearing right next to him a word or phrase which is original, sharp, colorful, and right. This is quite different from sending a boy downtown to describe the things that go on standing on the corner, for then there is no check. But in class, it is marvelously exhilarating for the teacher to be able to say, "But look at the picture in front of you! Isn't there anything else you can say besides, 'Boy, that's neat'?" Then comes the dirty work of this kind of assignment: sitting and waiting while a boy studies and tries to see more and to find the right words. Sometimes nothing happens, but now and then the forced intellectual march he has to make through the picture and his own bush-league vocabulary will produce something individual and new.

EXAMPLES

His unshaven face was lifted skyward, scanning the screaming rigging.

. . . at the moment she is "confined" to an old people's home where she lives contemptuously with a bunch of lunnitics [sic].

. . . his hands held the saucer and cigarette as if they were surgical instruments. The wrinkles in his brow were the worries of yesterday and today and tomorrow, and the sleepless nights of coronaries, and O.B.'s, the pains and sufferings that he felt as acutely as did his patients.

I remember how dark the room was, and how all the faces bobbed about in the gloom like brightly colored buoys on water.

Phillips Academy
Andover, Massachusetts

LEARNING THROUGH IMITATION OF A STYLE

Another device I have used is straight imitation of style. The purpose here, again, has been to arouse interest in the problems of language, and as Mozart and Beethoven did at first, the class writes in deliberate aping of a successful professional work. I think in this kind of exercise there is more-than-ordinary virtue, in that students are forced to work within the limits of a small mold, and they are required to observe very closely how, in the smallest details, a professional achieved his results. I think my students sometimes see, with some objectivity, not only the discrepancies between their work and the professionals', but also their own very near misses.

EXAMPLE

An imitation of Leacock's "A, B, and C, the Human Element in Mathematics."

Pearson's Breadwinner

When one has reached the ninth grade in school, he is quite familiar with a character named Julius Caesar. Every day the high school student translates a difficult Latin sentence only to find that Caesar is still sending a lieutenant to build a bridge across the Rhone river. The Latin student of today gets the impression that Mr. Caesar spent the major part of his life sending messengers to warn the Sequoni of war, or to ask the Helvetians why they were exchanging hostages amongst themselves. To break the monotony, Caesar is given a sidekick named Labienus. This character adds intrigue to Caesar's life.

Caesar, of course, never does any work. He amuses himself by ordering poor Labienus to face about the standards and harass a village or to carry some grain to the horses that are blocked in the Rhone river. All day Mr. Caesar is "dixiting" people to bustle about and do all kinds of senseless jobs for him.

Now we analyze humble, tortured Labienus, a mere ghost of a man. Labienus is a good-natured soul always working and carrying out Caesar's commands so that Henry Pearson can make a living. He leads a sheltered life in the dative case. Sometimes he is allowed to run in and out of the second periphrastic, a feat which Romans have long considered a great honor.

Let's be so rude as to peek in on a typical day in J. C.'s life. Caesar rises in the morning with his head simmering with orders for Labienus. The first order of course is his "cibum" as Mr. Pearson puts it. Analyzing the word we find that it is probably laurel leaves and olive oil sprinkled with some grain. (I believe that the reason Mr. Pearson never came right out and defined cibum was because he was ashamed of his hero's diet.) After stomaching this cibum, Caesar reaches unsteadily for his bottle of "Dative of Possessor" pills, a Roman Bromo-Seltzer. Caesar then struggles into his tunic and draws up a battle line or two.

Then Julius Caesar sends a very denunciatory letter to Orgetorix, his enemy. He signs this note with a forged seal of The Helvetian Gang. This gang is composed of a bloody bunch of mobsters who hang out on the east side of Rome. Orgetorix, being one who can never resist a battle, raids The Gang's hideout. When the results of the skirmish have reached Caesar's ears, he creeps off to his diary to write down a distorted version of how he captured Orgetorix and The Helvetian Gang singlehanded. This diary was later published as "Caesar's Gallic Wars."

For the remainder of the day, Caesar spends his time having Labienus carry out such orders as to allow the daughters of Ariovistus to shout that after they had thrown their spears they stuck weapons in the Germans' rear, so that the women and children, who had been called together in one place, would not be captured by the barbarians. This is one of Julius' typical orders and feeble-brained Labienus has to decipher this sort of command and carry it out.

Then comes a most tragic day. Labienus speaks back. Caesar has just given him one of his daily orders and Labby, because he has been studying up on his advanced Latin, says that he might not. Of course he uses the subjunctive. Caesar is so insulted that he almost jumps out of his conjugations. He immediately has Labienus put in jail for an accusative extent of time. As Labienus journeys to his imprisonment, a sequence of tenses, the leader of the Helvetian Gang throws a javelin at him. Faithful, gray-haired Labienus lies bleeding in the gutter all night. As the first arrows of dawn pierced the blackness, sobbing, broken-hearted and broken-headed Labienus ceases breathing. The end has come.

When Caesar received the news he sheds a tear at the realization that he will never have any amusement quite as enticing as sending Labienus on his eternal missions. Yes, now the Latin student finds that whenever Labienus is mentioned, he is used in the past tense. Now the intrigue is gone. Caesar spends his old age ordering "a certain lieutenant" or "one of the ambassadors" or "encouraging his men," but never will he give another order to his faithful Labienus.

Phillips Academy
Andover, Massachusetts

DESCRIPTION FROM OBSERVATION

I. *Assignment:* Write a sketch involving the description of a scene that evoked an emotion in you. Try to produce that same feeling in the reader by your subject and arrange your details accordingly.

EXAMPLE

Walpole St. Peter

It rose out of the flat fens, gray like the close sky and the miles of waving grass, surrounded by miles and miles of nothing but the windmills on the horizon. A crumbling wall circled the half-buried gravestones and the English daisies that ran riot over the time-softened hill. In the center, pocked with yellow-green moss, and niches put by centuries of English wind and English rain, softer and darker than the slate sky, Walpole St. Peter stood alone.

I stood ankle-deep in August grass and looked at the strong steeple, the delicate buttressing, and the high roof scattered with splintered shingles. There was more than a hush in the air. I pushed the silence back with my hands; I trampled it down. As I picked my way through grass that coiled about my ankles to smother my footsteps, the gravestones heaved their crooked patterns in the shadow of the church.

I, too, stood in the green-gray shadow, not caring whether I was looking at Perpendicular or Early English, not remembering the two lines in the guide book that had led us off our well-mapped route to see this "church of the marshlands." I felt only the pull of the mottled stone, and of the jagged reflections in the high leaded windows. I suddenly wanted to throw myself against the wall, to feel the stone with my whole body. I could not move for a moment. Then I stepped through the porch and in through the open doorway.

The church was deserted. The rows of pews were empty, and the notices on the guild table were out of date. The basket for foreign missions was scattered with only a few sixpences and an occasional shilling. The carved wood baptismal font was festooned with cobwebs. Every one of my footsteps sounded like a hammerstroke on the hard, cold stone, and echoed to the vaulted ceiling. Suddenly I was aware of another noise that echoed and echoed, a soft rhythmic whirring that paused, then started up again, punctuated by sharp stacatto slaps of something against stone. It was a pigeon high above, beating confused wings against unyielding walls.

I approached the altar, unwilling to enter the sanctuary, feeling even more a trespasser for being alone. I began to realize how unusually light the church was, why I did not know, until I looked again at the leaded windows. There was no colored glass, no soft glow of prisoned sunlight in the air to make it jewel-shadows on stone. Instead the unearthly simplicity of gray-white shafts filled the church. The door by the altar was open. A soft breeze rustled the new blue brocade behind the altar. Everything was bare but not empty, unkempt but not uncared for.

"The most beautiful parish church in England." It was a soft voice, hardly more than a whisper, but there was no need for him to speak loudly—he was standing behind me close enough to be my shadow.

I quickly withdrew the hand that had reached out with a tourist's reflex to touch the faded screen that stood by the altar. I half turned, startled and annoyed to be jarred from my reverie. I did not want to talk now. I wanted to recapture the feeling of loneliness and of bleak splendor.

Sustained point of view (first the distant view of the church, then the closer approach, finally the interior) and well-managed detail are here, but what is more, the whole piece has in it the substance of poetry; phrases like "time-softened hill"; "grass that coiled about my ankles"; sentences like "I pushed the silence back with my hands; I trampled it down" and "I felt only the pull of the mottled stone" succeed in communicating to us what this sensitive observer sees and feels. Here are some passages which might be read aloud to illustrate the intent of the assignment:

1. A description of a stable yard on a rainy day from "The Stout Gentleman" in Washington Irving's *Bracebridge Hall*, beginning "It was a rainy Sunday in the gloomy month of December. . . ."
2. The opening paragraph of Poe's "The Fall of the House of Usher."
3. The description of the "dirty water of Leith" from "The Manse" in *Memories and Portraits* by R. L. Stevenson.
4. The description of the "voice of the Pacific" from "The Old Pacific Capital" in *Across the Plains* by R. L. Stevenson.
5. The description of the farm and the orchard in Galsworthy's *The Apple Tree*, beginning with "How well he remembered it. . . ."
6. A description of spring in Chapter 22 of Blackmore's *Lorna Doone* beginning "Many a spring have I seen since then. . . ."
7. The passage in Conrad's The Lagoon beginning "The Malay only grunted and went on looking fixedly at the river."

The Chapin School
New York City

II. Take a scene from real life, to get an idea of relative distances and perspective, and to go back to for observation and details. Photographs or pictures will not do. The scene should be experienced and near at hand, for memory can scarcely fill in details.

Draw a diagram or rough sketch of the scene and mark with X five of the most important spots in it, with a circled X for the spot from which you are observing, and a doubly circled X for the center of interest. Label all parts which are not obvious. Mark actual distances on your diagram, from one point to another; and mark heights and sizes, since it is frequently advisable to state heights, sizes, and distances as if you had previously examined them close at hand. Such knowledge not only clarifies the facts, but it gives confidence in your ability to portray them. Fill in your sketch with notes on colors, materials, arrangements, details of how things are put together, relative placements, importances, or uses of the parts.

It is not necessary to have an unusual or attractive scene to describe. Often the usualness or commonplaceness of a setting better serves for observation. Stories do not always happen in the unusual places. Your aim should be for accuracy, clarity, compactness, and reality—not to thrill the reader with an amateurish pseudo painting. . . .

The ordinary is sufficient, if it can be observed factually. Often several people looking at the same thing . . . will notice different details. Each of the observers may be startled by the observations of the others regarding the significance of unobtrusive parts he may have seen but not considered important. You should teach yourself to see these things the first time; to observe and present the unusual in the usual, as well as the apparent which we all see.

Avoid

. . . Describe as if you were for the first time seeing and understanding what you present, with no former association with it, and no apparent contact at the moment. Do not use the impersonal pronoun *one*, as it detracts from the subject of the description, which must be followed assiduously. Do not repeat yourself by having to go back to details you left unfinished. . . . Avoid confusing digressions by finishing with a part at a time, for your subject cannot be followed properly except by logical, rather than haphazard, process. . . .

Do

Begin by introducing your whole scene first. Tell what and where it is, giving as clear and whole a picture as you can at the very beginning.

Characterize it immediately. An office may be a law office, a doctor's office, or one of many other kinds. A woodpile is not merely beyond the lawn. It may front on the lawn from beyond, or be at its farther edge. . . .

Keep your position always in mind as to left, right, above, below, behind, before. Make clear where you are without stating it. Everything first appears in relation to where you are. Select only those parts, details, characteristics of the scene necessary to give a complete sense of reality. Fit these parts separately into the word-picture in relation to the whole, to the center of interest, and to each other. . . . Everything finally appears in its relationship to every other thing about it. Compare your description with the diagram and ask yourself if it is as accurate, clear, and convincing as the diagram. . . .[1]

EXAMPLE

A Game Room [2]

From the bottom of the stairs in the middle of one of the longer walls the game room in the basement of 260 Clark Road, Brookline, extends approximately ten feet on either side and eleven and half feet across. Each of its four walls, whose panels resemble driftwood, has two aluminum half-moon light fixtures, so placed that they follow an even pattern around the room. In approximately the center of the coral-colored rubber-tiled floor, a cream-colored pole reaches six and a half feet to the sound-proofed ceiling. In the right corner of the opposite wall is a niche three and a half feet high and one and one half feet deep, containing a dark mahogany radio-phonograph combination over which is a two-door wooden cabinet of similar height. Seven and a half feet to its left is a closed door. Further left and hung on the wall is a picture map of Edinburgh, three feet high and slightly less in width, over a bamboo chair with plaid seat covers. A large maple table extending from its left to the far left corner of the room holds a large beige lamp whose shade depicts a farm scene in red, green, and yellow; a dark wood cigarette box seven inches long and shaped like a leaf. In the center of each of the two shorter walls at left and right is a narrow window two and a half feet high and five feet from the floor, with

[1] Adapted from *Writer's Technique: A Practical Guide to Creative Writing*, by Francis W. Newsom (New York, Coleman-Ross Company, Inc., 1954), pp. 9–12.
[2] This paper was written by Mildred Cooper, a Junior in Mr. Newsom's Creative Writing Class, Brookline High School.

wool plaid curtains partially hiding the three mud-spattered panes. Under the window at the right, and extending the full width of the room, is a bench finished exactly like the walls. Under the window at the left is a red leather love seat beneath a map of Japan which extends beyond the window a few feet toward the corner. In the immediate right corner of the nearby wall is a map of Scotland over a glass-topped nest of tables which holds on the topmost surface an oval glass ashtray five inches long; and nearby, this side of them, a large bamboo chair with blue flannel seat covers and plaid trim. To the immediate left and right of the stairs are twin doors, paneled like the walls, leading to a passageway and a washroom respectively. The immediate left corner of the wall is broken twice again by two doors.

Brookline High School
Brookline, Massachusetts

THE PERSONAL ESSAY IN WHICH THE NARRATIVE ELEMENT IS LIKELY TO BE DOMINANT

The writer's purpose is to isolate an experience that has impressed him so deeply that he frequently recalls it and/or finds that it has come unbidden into his consciousness to be relived; to become consciously aware of the emotional quality or qualities that accompany this recollection; and to search for the meaning which the experience has added to his understanding of and sensitivity to significances in the pattern of his life.

The "formula," written on the board, and used often in discussion, is Experience + Emotion + Meaning.

Preparatory class discussion and reading (usually by the teacher of the class) of examples of this sort of writing occupy approximately three class periods. The purpose of the discussion is to help the students account for remembering and forgetting, to give them a concept of the way millions of experiences drop into oblivion in the subconscious, and to make them aware that remembering has its reasons. Readiness to search in themselves for the meanings in their own lives of impressive experience is the final preparatory goal. (The teacher is aware of the arrival of this time of readiness when he sees before him young eyes growing reflective and turned inward quietly.)

Examples read to the class are from other student essays of this type, occasionally from adult writers, and sometimes specifically from a recent *Atlantic* which all members of the class have in their possession.

The procedure for writing is usually something like this, although it goes without saying that the teacher knows his group and will suit the procedure to their personalities and needs:

The first part of the work is done in class; many, of course, don't stop, but go on in their next study hall. In general, they work in class, with teacher conference available, until about half of the first draft is completed. Step one is choosing *the* experience; and one has to be a bit arbitrary, not allowing them to hesitate too long among three or four. Step two is the assembling of details, with emphasis on distinct sense impressions, time sequence, and arrangement of scene in space. Next comes a detailed outline. During the first or second period of class work, after the experience is selected, they are asked to write a brief statement of what the experience is and what they think they have found to be its meaning. These statements help the teacher to be directly helpful in the classroom conferences as the writing progresses. Assistance with the mechanics of writing is also possible as the classroom work progresses. After approximately three writing periods in class, the completion of the first draft is carried on as outside work. First drafts are returned with comments and suggestions; often after-school conferences are requested, and one hopes that one has time for them. The final draft is judged upon the success with which experience is recreated to bring its meaning as felt by the writer to the reader. These papers are likely to run, in length, anywhere from 800 to 2500 words.

EXAMPLE

From an essay in which a Vermont girl wrote of her first impressions of the Mojave Desert, her reaction to it as it became more familiar to her, and her sense of the spell of the desert. This is from the concluding paragraph.

. . . The sky was a pale, unhealthy hue, the sun at white heat, yet there was something about the desert—something irresistible, magnetic. What is it that draws men back to the desert if they have once seen it? That question no one can ever answer. Is it the dry, hot noon with the heat waves dancing like dervishes on crest and dune—is it the cool sunset with mountains close and friendly? Or is it the tiny 'dobe huts crouching on the face of the desert, the immutable Indian with his eternal Ford, and the lush greenness of irrigated fields beside brick-red roads? No—it is all of these and much more. If men return, it is for the feel of cottonwood shade after miles of dust, it is for the straggling desert town and Mexican sombreros, and the sunshades, and the corner lots of realty developments festooned in barbed wire and tin cans; for the sight of children going barefoot to school, and for the dawn on the Joshua trees and red stone mesas. There is the wind bowling the scudding clouds along the alley of the sky, and the tangleweed humped up against the fences. All this is implicit in the lure which calls the wanderer back to Mojave, as it is calling me.

Rutland High School
Rutland, Vermont

NARRATIVE OF THREE PEOPLE

After careful observation, reconstruct a scene in which three people—at least two of whom are mature—are engaged in some action in common. Have an action in which all three are in some manner concerned, and covering perhaps ten minutes of time. Use no names for any of them. Make clear the occasion, the place, and the purpose of what is being portrayed. The episode need not be concluded necessarily, but should stop at a fairly impressive point where the action can stand without a letdown feeling on the part of the reader. Use no conversation.

In avoiding names you will be forced to be much more careful in distinguishing between people and in learning how to be clear without too much repetition. In avoiding conversation you will be forced to concentrate on details of action.

Again, waste no time in introduction or description. Use only such descriptive bits as are necessary props to the story, and only in connection with the action. Begin with action and fit the people all into the action as you proceed.

To give perspective, depth, and reality, the sense of what each person is doing at each moment should be faithfully conveyed. Keep the balance of the picture as a whole. Never lose sight of any one person for a single moment. We must have a feeling of what the others are doing and where they are while *one* is being featured at the moment in particular. Instead of following the motions of any one person, we must be made to follow the blending and relative continuities of action by keeping all three in mind at once. We must trace the relatedness of movement constantly from one to the other. We must see who is carrying the interest and what the others are doing meanwhile. It is what each is doing every moment as it pertains to the actions of the others and to the development of the whole picture of action, that gives the sense of reality. Good narrative is synchronized action made evident as the story proceeds. It is concentrated development of the interreactions in the flow of something happening which emphasizes human touches. It is like action in slow motion, showing the smallest details of every movement of all three simultaneously, as far as language will permit. You can't deal separately with people in narrative, for any length of time, without losing the sense of drama and balance, unless you are dealing with the picture of action in the mind of one person alone. And even there, we are made to feel the consciousness of others in the background.

Clear narrative is also description of action. It should be realistic in every detail of motion and change, showing exactly what is accomplished and how. There should be no general statements. For instance, instead of saying, "She moved the chair," it is better far to show how she took hold of the chair, and where; what kind of chair it was; whether she needed or received any help; whether she lifted or pulled it, and with what results; and how and where it was finally placed. It is better to start to show how a thing is done in exact and minute detail than to leave an unclear or incomplete picture.

Again, there should be no holes in the action of good narrative. It should be logical and complete in connecting up any breaks occasioned by time, or changes in place or action, or in moving from one character to another. Most of all there should be no breaks in the simple accomplishment of actions. The narrator should take nothing for granted. He is there to tell what happened, and he must be sure that he portrays it all. His reader will see only what he is told, or be forced to fill in the gaps with unsatisfactory conclusions. Occasional details of background should be carefully connected with the action to give a sense of completeness.

It is important to draw a simple diagram of the exact scene where the action takes place, marking the spots where the characters are, the spots to which they move, and showing the relative distances and positions at all times. This sketch will save you from errors in explanation; it will enable you to be exact and ready in the details of portrayal, *and in the connecting links*.[3]

EXAMPLE

A Sabbath Eve [4]

The dining room is a study in white. The first person to enter its thirteen by fifteen foot area for the Sabbath Eve meal is a twenty-three-year-old, five-foot-ten-inch boy on crutches who approaches the archway from the reception hall at the right. Poised on his crutches, both feet on the floor, he pauses in the archway to survey the white cloth-covered table which has in its center a tray containing a brightly polished twisted brass candelabra with a white unlit Sabbath candle in each of the five stems, the two on each side formed by semicircles of brass, the lower of which is much wider than the upper and inner one, thus leaving the levels of the candles sloping downward from the center on either side. The table is set for three, with plate, silverware and napkin, identical but for the open prayer book, wine decanter, and silver wine cup with the hand-engraved Star of David upon it, which stand at the near side of the setting at the head of the table opposite; the gold-rimmed crystal wine cups, one of which stands beside each of the other two settings, and the white skull cap which lies beside the setting at the foot of the table. Setting his crutches a few steps ahead of him, the boy advances slowly to the foot of the table, swinging his body as he walks, and leaning slightly over his crutches, places his left hand on the back of the maple arm chair which stands before his place, draws it back about two feet from the table, walks around to its front, leans a crutch on each side of its back and, placing a hand on each of its broad arms, drops himself into its contoured seat. He then takes the crutches singly with his left hand and turning to his left, leans them against the wall in back of him to the right of the archway. As he turns back and reaches for the white skull cap lying beside his plate, his father, a middle-aged man in shirt sleeves and with a conservative hat on his head, enters the room from the kitchen through the open swinging door just in time

[3] *op. cit.*, pp. 15–17.

[4] This paper was written by Miriam Samuels, a Junior student in Mr. Newsom's Creative Writing Class at Brookline High School. It is not a final draft, although it is in the later stages of development.

to see the boy don the skull cap and draw his chair closer to the table with a bumping motion of his torso.

The father walks to the head of the table and takes his place there at a similar armchair during this process, and before he has drawn up his chair, the mother enters briskly from the kitchen, carrying two wooden matches in her left hand. The father and son look up at her as she crosses to her place at the far side of the table facing the candelabra, places one of the matches on the tray beside the candelabra, lifts her right foot and strikes the other match on the sole of her shoe and with the lit match in her left hand begins lighting the candles, one by one, from left to right. As she touches the flame to the first candle a shadow is cast on the face of her son, who sits with arms folded on the table watching reverently the age-old custom being re-enacted by his mother. She lights the second and third candles and the combined lights of the first three candles reveal the proud attentiveness of the father, who sits with his hands folded in his lap. Having lit the fourth and fifth candles she extinguishes the flame from the burning match with a quick snapping motion of her wrist, places the burnt match beside the unused one on the tray near the candelabra, and still standing, covers her face with her hands, bows her head slightly, and begins repeating the silent blessing of the candles, as the candlelight casts a radiant glow upon her. The father moves his hands to the table without shifting his gaze from her while the son unfolds his arms and crosses his hands, nodding his head briefly in thoughtful understanding. In a moment she has finished the blessing and as she uncovers her face and smiles first at her husband, then at her son, the traditional Sabbath greeting, "Shabbat Shalom" (A Sabbath of Peace), spoken by all three simultaneously seems to fill the air. She crosses now in back of her chair and as she draws it out with her left hand to sit down, her husband rises, pushing back his chair and lifting the wine decanter from before him with his right hand. His wife completes the act of seating herself and, pulling in her chair, places her hands on the table, one on each side of her plate and watches him as he removes the cover from the wine decanter with his left hand and fills his own gleaming silver goblet with the sweet purple liquid.

The son utters some pleasant remark during this process and is immediately silent again as his father replaces the cover in the decanter, and the decanter on the table, lifts the full wine goblet in his left hand, places his right hand on his right hip and begins to chant the Kiddush (traditional Sabbath blessing of the wine) alternately reading from the open prayer book before him and looking up to his wife and son. They remain smilingly silent until he has finished, then they utter the ceremonial Hebrew affirmation of his prayer, "Ahmain," as he sips the wine and fills their cups from his own, first reaching across the table to fill his wife's cup as it remains on the table and then filling his son's cup which is picked up and handed to him by his wife and which he receives with his left hand. He hands this second full cup to his wife, sets down his empty goblet and rises, as his wife returns the wine-filled cup to her son. Walking to his right around the table, he exits through the archway to wash in customary manner, leaving his wife and son, the former sipping her wine and the latter, having just touched his wine to his lips and pushed it aside, chatting happily with his mother. The father returns shortly to his place at the table, and, lifting a white embossed napkin with his left hand uncovers the oval-shaped dish of freshly baked white bread standing before him on the white cloth-covered table, and removes a slice of bread with his right hand. He breaks the bread in two, placing one half on his plate as his wife hands him a glass salt-shaker which she takes from the table near her and which reveals between her fingers, the white of the salt within. The father shakes salt on the half slice of bread still remaining in his hand. His son has stopped talking and resumed his cross-armed position as his father, still standing, begins the final blessing before the meal, thanking the Lord for the bread of the earth. His wife, remaining silent and somewhat reverent affirms his prayer with her son once again as the father concludes by tasting a piece broken from the bread, closing the prayer book, and drawing back his chair to sit down to the Sabbath meal. This is served from the kitchen by the mother, who rises, pushes back her chair, and leaves the dining room by the swinging door to the kitchen; and a young girl, who now enters from the kitchen.

The father receives the first bowl of hot chicken soup and as it is set before him, lifts his spoon with his right hand, dips the spoon in the bowl, and raises it to his lips cautiously testing the temperature. Finding it satisfactory, he continues to eat quietly as his son, receiving his portion at just that moment from the hands of his mother, who has re-entered, swallows too much of the hot soup at once and drops his spoon noisily into the bowl, grasping his throat with his left hand and crying for water. The mother, who is just about to reseat herself, remains standing to the right of her chair with her left hand on its back and glances at her son concernedly. Seeing, however, that he is merely in jest and has broken into a laugh, she erases the frown from her face and, together with her husband, joins him in gay laughter as she seats herself and lifts her spoon with her left hand to begin eating.

Brookline High School
Brookline, Massachusetts

CHARACTERIZATION—SHOWING INSTEAD OF TELLING

The distinction between those two procedures is hard to get across. As we know, the young in their attempts to characterize are given to generalizing: "She was a snob, and her haughty look made everyone dislike her." Maren Elwood's book, *Characters Make Your Story*, published by The Writer, Inc., illustrates very clearly the difference between *Telling* and *Showing*. She discusses ways of individualizing a character (I generally read aloud from her book) by his walk, his gestures, his facial expression, and of course by the way he speaks. One cannot say enough about the value of dialogue as a tool in writing the short story. It can supply information and bits of description; it can advance the action. Moreover, if skillfully handled, it can imply so much more than it says. What follows is a bit of dialogue from a story by a student. The dialogue not only characterizes the mother, but gives us some insight into Billy's attitude toward his mother, and suggests that Billy's vacations are not an unmitigated joy. Billy arrives home from boarding school and is met by his mother at Grand Central:

He gathered his things carefully, and shouldered his way through the thinning crowd, then up the ramp. Don't drop the clarinet; where is she, where is she? Oh, there, over there, there she is.

"Billy, darling! Not a trombone! I'm *so* glad to *see* you: too bad you failed your French, darling, it's *impossible* to get a taxi. Is *that* Mrs. Buxton over there with that awful little boy, shall we have lunch at the Oyster Bar, oh—you don't really like fish, that's right, what form *is* the Buxton boy in. Oh it is so good to see my *Bill*, haven't you grown, dear? Let's go to Longchamps, or would you rather L'Avion, the taxi. . . ."

"It's not a trombone, Ma, it's a clarinet, and the worst thing to play in the whole band, and besides. . . ."

"Well, how about Mario's then. Your voice is deeper, isn't it? We just have to get you a suit before we do anything else this afternoon, darling, and then we can go to the Translux before we meet Daddy for supper, the cook's left and I'm afraid that means you'll have to do your own room, too, so Mary can get her extra work done, I just can't ask her to do many meals, and. . . ."

He forced his words through hers, "I don't need a new suit, Ma. Gee, let's go home so I can take a bath or something."

"Well, of course I didn't know you'd have quite so many suit cases and the—that thing, too, and I suppose you'll have to take a bath if we are going to the theatre tonight, but what about lunch?"

"Lunch," he said dully, remembering those pistachio nuts he had bought in Providence—"Let's have it at home, huh?"

This student has allowed his characters to *show* what they are and has not resorted to *Telling* in this wise:

"Billy's well-meaning but scatterbrained mother met him at Grand Central and unloosed an incoherent flood of words—something about his bringing home a trombone (he tried to tell her that it was a clarinet, but she rarely stopped talking long enough to listen); about his failing French, about his having grown, about having lunch at L'Avion, and on and on."

The Chapin School
New York City

A PROCEDURE FOR TEACHING "POSITION" IN CREATIVE WRITING (POINT OF VIEW)

"Creative Writing we define as an act of composition in which a student creates a controlled dramatic voice. . . ." Why "dramatic"?

More and more in teaching young writers I have been thinking in terms of an analogy with the stage. When you begin a story or a poem, you are as if wandering on to a bare stage in an empty theatre, and you clutch the hand of a blindfold stranger—your reader. What are you going to tell him? You are his only source of information; what you see he sees, what you say is all he has to go on. *Position* therefore is everything at the beginning: you lead your blindfold stranger to a spot on the stage, and from there you point to this and that, the props and backdrops and actors with which you proceed to fill your scene. (Sometimes of course you deliberately leave your stage practically bare.) And you can't see anything from where you're standing! The main point, though, is that *you do not move around*, unless you have a darn good reason for doing so. Once having taken a position, made your X (as Mr. Newsom puts it), you force your blindfold acquaintance to change position only when you have to, and you should realize you're doing it if you do it.

A familiar position taken by the dramatic pose of the writer is, of course, inside the head of one of the actors. We see the stage from some particular person's "point of view"; we share his vision and are privy to his thoughts and attitudes. (Note that for the actual playwright this is pretty much impossible.) Again a simple rule of consistency applies: don't fly out of one person's head and into another's, carrying your panting reader with you, unless you're darn sure you know what you're doing.

Here are some sentences from a very short story about a hitchhiker, by a student who didn't know what he was doing. His problem I would define as a problem of position: a case of the reader being asked, unnecessarily, to take up too many points of vantage in succession. The story begins:

The small grey Chevvy pulled up to the side of the road and halted as the hitchhiker dropped his solicitous thumb and moved to the car.

"Going to Baker?"

The driver, decked out in blue denims, gave a nod and replied, "Sure am fellow, hop in back."

The stranger got in and found the back seat already taken by a large German police dog. His surprised grunt came just as the farmer's companion, apparently his wife, turned around and rasped, "Don't worry about him, son, he's pretty friendly. Get down, Boss."

The object of her order gave a perturbed gesture with his front paws and jumped to the floor as the new rider took over the back seat. He glanced at the backs of his two benefactors . . .

Our physical position here is "with" the hitchhiker: we watch as the car pulls up to the side of the road, and we follow the hitchhiker in to the back seat where we can observe the police dog and from which we can see the backs of the "Benefactors" in the front seat. But we are not "with" the hitchhiker in any way except physically: we are not privy to his thoughts and attitudes. He is referred to as "the stranger," "the new rider." We are outside everybody—maybe most of all the dog, who by a terrible lapse of elegant variation becomes "the object of her order." We proceed:

. . . the dog was resting, head on his paws, with his eyes fixed on the new rider. He was a massive beast, etc. etc. The stranger passed his eyes from the dog's rump along the line of his back to his head, noticing the canine gaze still upon him.

The gaze prompted a sudden thought, and . . .

ERROR!! After our position outside the hitchhiker has been reinforced by repetitions of "stranger" and "new rider," we are abruptly taken inside his head where we can hear a sudden thought being prompted. After this a conversation starts in the car, and a few sentences later we read:

"What happened, he ever get his money back?" came from the back seat.

ERROR! We have been catapulted over the upholstery into the front seat—an abrupt change in physical position this time—where we hear a question coming *from* the back seat. A paragraph or two later:

Jamie [that's the driver's wife] seemed intent on carrying on the interrogation for a second but the idea of some new plan faded from her mind and she turned full around to face the front and the unwinding road . . .

ERROR! First she "*seemed* intent"—that's all right and consistent with some of our earlier positions—but obviously when we know that an idea "faded from her mind," we have to be in a position to know that, and the only such position is inside Jamie herself. Here the switch in position has taken place inside a single sentence, between the first and second independent clauses.

There are of course great writers who can pull off this sort of thing, and do, where inconsistency of position becomes a kind of consistency of its own. Virginia Woolf is an example. But our students are not Woolfs, and our first job with a student like this one, it seems to me, is painstakingly to point out to him just what he has done. It is likely to be a revelation to him.

And then *position* is more than a physical spot on a sort of stage, and more than a vantage point inside or outside the mind of an actor. It also can be applied to the relation one assumes toward that poor character whose hand one holds—the reader. Do you hold him at arm's length?

A strong possibility has arisen that the Metropolitan Opera will take over the artistic administration of . . .

Or do you cuddle?

Remember that heat in October and November? Sure burned us! You should see the huge stock of suits and coats we *didn't* sell!

Do you ask him to join you in ecstasy?

> Beautiful beautiful music with such thrilling voices singing the beautiful beautiful arias . . .

Or do you speak so formally that you pretend he isn't there at all?

> Pursuant to the provisions of the amended Certificate of Incorporation, notice is hereby given that the Board of Directors . . .

These variations in position with respect to the reader are what we mean by *tone*, and the examples above were taken with no trouble at all from the newspaper. They illustrate, if illustration were necessary, what a barrage of tonal shifts the newspaper reader is asked to take in with his morning coffee.

Our students have to learn (returning now to our definition of creative writing) how to create a *controlled* dramatic voice, and this means a voice that can take up a position with respect to its reader *and hold it!* If you start with a formal relation at arm's length, don't cuddle in your second paragraph. The role you play toward your reader is not unlike the ones you adopt in conversations with actual people in your daily life. You don't speak alternately in a friendly and then a hostile manner when you talk to people—not if you're sane and in control of yourself. The moral of all this for a writer is: Control Yourself. Know where you are—and that means as well, Know who you are.

Amherst College
Amherst, Massachusetts

BEGINNINGS AND ENDINGS IN THE SHORT STORY

I. Paradoxically, a short story cannot really begin at the beginning, but must begin somewhere nearer the middle. One cannot pause too long at the door, but must walk boldly into the heart of a situation. That is not to say that the opening lines can afford to neglect the who, what, when, and where, either. And that is not all—a good beginning should contain the essence of the whole story, a fact which re-empha-sizes the need for knowing how your story is going to end before you begin it. The beginning should, in a sense, imply the ending.

EXAMPLE

Here are the beginning and ending of a story, *The Discovery*, which was written by a twelfth-grade student and won second place in the *Atlantic* contest of 1954.

Philip Dayne's breath caught ecstatically in his throat. It was the most beautiful little plane he had ever seen. As it rested on his outstretched palm, it felt so light that his grasp instinctively tightened when a breeze from the open door of the shop stirred the little propeller. He had wanted a plane like this more than anything else, and had put it at the top of his birthday list. But he had not received it; his grandfather had given him a very grown-up book instead. Philip gulped as he looked at the large peppermint-striped box on the counter. There were many, many little planes in there, exactly like the one he was holding, with their wings shimmering in the late afternoon light.

Suddenly a thought occurred to the little boy that made his heart knock wildly at his ribs. If he should take the plane, who would ever know it?

Philip takes the plane, even though his act gives him a "sick feeling in his stomach" and promises himself that he will bring the plane back tomorrow. He tries to do so, but loses courage. Meanwhile his guilt gnaws away at him, making him thoroughly miserable. A day or two later, an observant and sympathetic teacher advises Philip to "tell someone—the one you have done the wrong thing to." Philip realizes that he must first approach his austere grandfather, General Payne, who knew Philip so little that he had given him a "grown-up book." But the ordeal is not as painful as he thought it would be, for his grandfather is surprisingly kind and understanding. Later that evening, General Payne goes to Philip's room, thinking him asleep.

Suddenly Philip stirred in his sleep and dimly made out the form of his grandfather bending over him. Without quite realizing what he did, the child seized one of his grandfather's fingers.

"Grandfather, will you wait for me outside Shantwell's tomorrow when I take the plane back?" he whispered. . . .

Philip's grandfather could only nod in answer to the little boy's questions, not trusting himself to speak; and as he pressed the little hand in his, it almost hurt Philip. Then, turning as he left the room, to make sure his grandson was observing him, General Payne saluted the little row of tin soldiers guarding the door.

In this story, the toy plane which Philip wanted badly enough to steal is the catalytic agent which brings the boy and his grandfather together. Hence, the elements of the story, including its ending, are present in the opening paragraph. One might also point out in passing that the title of the story, The Discovery, implies that Philip not only learned a moral lesson, but discovered his grandfather, also.

The Chapin School
New York City

II. Conflict is the indispensable element of the short story. The beginning of the story must make the reader aware of the involvement of the central character in the conflict which, in the development, he will resolve or fail to resolve. Clarification and exposition of the conflict will unfold with the story, but the beginning must bring the impact of conflict by proposing the question which motivates the story. For the novice, the simplest method is to start with an incident which shows the central character under pressure from the conflict. *He* may or may not be aware at the start that he *is* involved in a conflict, but the reader must always sense that he is.

The ending disposes of the conflict appropriately. The reader understands, and is satisfied, that the central character has met the conflict as it would be natural for him to meet it, has opposed it with the weapons that it is possible for him to use. Whether the central character succeeds or fails, the reader should finish the story feeling that it had to be that way.

EXAMPLE

From "Just Once"
Atlantic Contest Prize Story, 1948–1949

Martha James woke up in the dark, restless and unhappy, as she had so many other nights lately. In the smothering June shadows she could see her bedroom window opened wide, but no breath of air stirred the ruffled curtains she had helped her mother make. Her back was hot and sticky as she listlessly rolled over against the cool wall trying to evade the hours of wakefulness that lay before her.

"What's the use, anyway?" thought Martha, pushing back the hair that clung damply to her neck. "I might as well stop pretending." All day she had pretended, in front of the kids at school and the sympathetic looks of her family, with a tight ache when she saw the other girls making plans for the dance.

They tried so hard not to hurt her or say things in front of her—good kids. "We've had fun together." There she was pretending again; oh, they had good times, but how many other nights had she lain here on this same bed thinking of them laughing at dances, going on dates? "Why, I've never even had a real date all my own," she reminded herself, though it hurt. "I always thought this time would be different." For four years she had comforted herself that *she* would be asked to the senior ball, just like the rest of them. Why kid herself? This time was no different—the girls always asked her places and trusted her; even Mr. Boedry, the cranky algebra teacher, liked her—and—and—and—"What about the boys?" she asked herself for the millionth time.

Even the next day, the day of the dance, Martha continues to hope— a little, but when the phone rings, it's the faculty adviser asking her to take tickets at the dance. Still, there's a chance. Maybe the boy who does the lights will notice how nice she looks and ask her to dance, but he remains absorbed in his spotlights. The climax comes when a bluff, blundering parent, there to look on at his popular daughter, sees Martha outside the gym door, and tells her heartily to get her young man and go in there "where she belongs."

"Where I belong," she repeated, the tears aching their way into her eyes. All at once she realized she was crying, picked up her jacket, and ran swiftly out the door and down the steps.

It was a beautiful night. The stars hung low and the warm evening air smelled sweet; the music was drifting out from the dance. Martha neither heard nor saw as she ran blindly home where she could be alone with all her hurt.

The house was dark, her folks were still playing bridge, and Martha let herself into the hall and stumbled up the stairs to her room. Slamming the door, she fell across the bed, her sobs choking her as if they would never stop. All the unhappiness which had built up within her during the last weeks came tumbling out . . .

Tomorrow, Martha would be her smiling, capable self; everything would seem rather unimportant and she'd be one of the gang again. She would grow up into a fine, a lovely woman, who perhaps could laugh at this some day. . . . But this, this was tonight, and Martha buried her head deeper in her pillow.

Rutland High School
Rutland, Vermont

III. Conflict in the short story is a developed uncertainty as to the course of action a character will or should take under pressure of events, and as to what will happen as a result of his decisions. It involves necessities to act, or impulses to act thrust upon one through other people, or through the ordinary or unusual events of living. The indecision or suspsense is generally complicated by what is newly to be expected as a result of growing events. There is no conflict without *expected action*. There is no conflict without the *necessity* which gives the impulse to act. . . .

In a short story, conflict is *arranged* in a plan of action, or plot, from a motivating incident, or realization of the impact of forces, through a climax, or determining incident, to a final outcome, or resolving of the elements of conflict. The motivating incident is the first indication of an issue involved between inharmonious or disagreeing elements of the story. From this point the action proceeds through devious uncertainties to a relatively important tensity of action where there is a seemingly conclusive decision for an outcome, or a vague feeling as to the final outcome; for certainly the reader must be prepared for the ending before it happens. The ending, or conclusion, is the final touch of revelation showing the outcome, its significance, and effects. There must be no more of the conflict of the original story at the conclusion.[5]

EXAMPLE

From "The Employment Office"
Atlantic Contest Third Place Story, 1955–1956

It was a green, ugly room. A pair of abstract paintings, looking to me like swirling linoleum wildly spotted with tigers' eyes, hung on the wall above one of the leather and chrome sofas. I sat in the corner near the desk, waiting to be called. Much too warm to search through the stacks of the *Ladies' Home Journal* and *Harper's Bazaar* for a possible copy of *Esquire* that would be full of colored cartoons. I sat quietly and sweated.

The room was rather dark, except in the few places where it was shot with sunlight that came from between the slats of the venetian blinds. I looked around at the other—I want to say "passengers" for some reason—applicants, I guess it is. There were about six of them ahead of me—not especially interesting. Now that I think of it, I can't even remember what

[5] Newsom, *op. cit.*, pp. 70–71.

any of them looked like. There was the man, of course, but I didn't notice him until a little later.

I want to tell you what was running through my head while I waited: that the paintings were horrible; that they might have been done by somebody's wife, the same one who subscribed to the *Ladies' Home Journal*. Maybe she'd picked out the lamps in the room too . . .

The sort of conflict suggested by the atmosphere of the room occurs. The girl who is telling the story is indignant at the cavalier treatment given by "the woman at the desk" to a Hungarian immigrant, a man who is seeking employment as a furniture designer. In the course of her emotional disturbance she is led to question her own attitudes and motives, to inquire into herself, to wonder to what extent she is honest in her generous impulses and to what extent self-indulgent. The story concludes:

Suddenly I feel very tired. All my life I've been in constant rebellion, but against what? What is my criterion for the love, the hate that is so sudden and unreasoning? Why not the woman at the employment office, instead of Mr. Schwarz? My world is too black and white, and arbitrarily so. What right have I to flatter myself as a champion of human dignity? I have no dignity, no courage, no love. I am weak and vain. Do I really hate authority, or is it just responsibility that I hate? I judge because I fear judgment myself. Am I indignant because I love Mr. Schwarz, because I love humanity? Or do I love only myself?

Quite a tender picture: a girl crying in school, a woman running up to a strange man and saying, "I love you, I love you!"

Turn out the light and go to sleep now. Tomorrow morning I'll have to get up at seven and go to work.

Brookline High School
Brookline, Massachusetts

THE SHORT STORY

A. *Writing exercises preliminary to the writing of a short story.*
   (The teacher would make selections from these appropriate to the class with which he is working.)

   1. Various exercises in observation. Articles on a table, pupils passing through the room, things seen outside the window, and so on.

2. In a *Who's Who* of the division, each pupil writes one unusual thing about himself. (This helps in self-searching.)
3. Tell aloud a humorous story or anecdote. Why did some stories succeed and some fail? (Suspense.)
4. Make up a tall tale about the naming of some town you find on the map. (This stimulates imagination.)
5. Write a paragraph of description, using all your senses in so doing. (This gives opportunity for observation and for the use of fresh and vivid phrasing.)
6. Characterize a person by look or gesture or revealing traits. (To show point of view, let other pupils describe the same person, with a different interpretation of his actions.)
7. Write out a statement of the significant truths illustrated in two or three stories which you have read. (This encourages reading beneath the surface.)
8. Make an exact recording of a piece of dialogue overheard. If it does not advance plot or reveal character, how can it be changed to do so?

B. *Final writing assignment: a short story.*
(This is a 3-day assignment.)

First assignment: Some of the themes suggested by the short stories you have read might easily be related to your own experience or to that of someone you have known closely. Select one such theme.

Write a paper in which you explain the situation or the problem which illustrates the theme you have chosen. Include in your paper the thoughts and the feelings of the principal person concerned in the situation. This person may be you, or someone you have known. You may use your imagination to change this person in any way to suit your story's purpose. Suggest what he is like, why he acts as he does, and so on. Tell how he solves his problem, giving the events that lead to its conclusion.

NOTE: A problem may be solved by the character's adjusting to his situation as well as by his conquering it.

Discussion period. Pupils meet in groups of five or six to discuss one another's choice of material. In each case they decide whether or not the story is believable, whether it actually illustrates the theme it purports to illustrate, and whether or not the characters involved seem to be real people. Pupils are encouraged to give suggestions freely, and often find at this conference that real incidents and real people have to be altered to make them *seem* real.

Second assignment: Decide upon the point of view you wish to establish, and whether you wish to tell your story in the first or third person. Then set your character in motion in the story. Include bits of dialogue, description, so that your story will not sound too *related*. Keep your attention focused upon *one* character, *one* situation, *one* conflict (which may be within the character himself) and move the story steadily forward to its conclusion.

Discussion period. Discuss the stories in the final group meeting, with the teacher moving from group to group, commenting whenever his comments will be helpful. This time pupils discuss the integration of character, theme, plot, setting, dialogue, and so on. They are concerned mostly, however, with whether or not the author has accomplished his purpose in the story. Again, criticisms and suggestions are welcomed, although authors are cautioned against making any changes in their stories with which they do not thoroughly agree, since these should be basically their own creations.

Third assignment: Revise and rewrite the story before submitting it to the teacher in its final form. Stories which, in the opinion of the group, have accomplished their purposes may be typed and later bound, with selected essays and poetry, written during the periods in which these forms are studied, into a volume which has been compiled and edited by the division.

EXAMPLES

In some cases pupils veered a little from the themes they said they had chosen, but when it was obvious that the themes had at least *suggested* the stories, this was deemed satisfactory. There was the usual number of stories of an exciting experience which turned out to be a dream; there were some rather weak sport-success stories, and a few science fiction tales. But most of these were weeded out in the discussion periods. I found that most of the successful stories were the personal-experience type, told in the first person. It must be remembered, that in a situation such as I have been describing (large public high school, big classes, heavy schedule), an English teacher must, of necessity, carry on a creative writing project such as this one in a somewhat incidental way. That is, he does not have the time to continue working for more finished stories with complex character development, but must be satisfied with the simplest of tales. The story which follows is typical of the better ones received.

Theme: It is often difficult for a child to accept the death of a parent. *Suggested* by the short story "A Mother in Manville" by Marjorie Kinnan Rawlings.

The Flashlight

In 1944 when I was five years old, my father was given a commission in the Army, and a few months later he went overseas. There were just the three of us—my mother, my father, and I—and before he went into the Army, we used to go on picnics together, to the shore in summer, to the country in fall or spring.

I remember the day before my father went away. It was October and we spent the whole day in the country. It was as warm as June. Trees glowed in yellow and scarlet; all the hillside flamed with color.

My father and I played ball for a while and wrestled, and after we had eaten, my father rolled his jacket into a pillow and lay with his head in my mother's lap. The sun and the exercise had made his dark face sort of sunburned and young, and his hair looked rough and curly, the way it did when he'd first get up in the morning, before he slicked it down after his shower. The sun just touched my mother's hair, which, I remember thinking, looked as yellow as the leaves in the tree above her. Even now sometimes, I can see my father and my mother as they looked to me that day.

Then all of a sudden, the way it is sometimes in October, it was dark, and my father had to get his flashlight from the glove compartment so that he could see to pack our things away in the car. "You drive, Helen," he said to my mother. "I just feel like riding tonight."

Well, I sat in the middle, swinging the flashlight along the darkened roadside, and watching the trees and bushes appear.

"When I was a kid I always wanted a flashlight," my father said. "But I never had one until I was grown. Then I got the best one I could find and it's still good." He cleared his throat as if he had a frog in it. "It's yours now, son," he said after a minute. "You're the man of the house now. I'm counting on you to take care of your mother for me."

I looked at my father and swallowed, hard. "But you'll come back, won't you, Daddy?" I said. Suddenly I did not want to flash the light any more, and the road was dark and scary and unfamiliar.

Instead of answering, my father caught my hand, and pressing the button on the flashlight, swung my hand about so that houses and signposts and places I knew well showed bright and clear again. "Look, Tommy," my father said, as if he knew what I was thinking. "The darkness hid those things so that you thought they had gone, but they were really there all the time as I will be, even when you don't see me here."

I wasn't sure what my father meant, so I looked at my mother and when I saw that she was crying, I knew that my father was talking to her too, and that if she understood, everything would be all right and I did not need to worry.

I'll never forget that night, riding with my father and mother—all of us in the car, so close and warm together.

But the next morning my father went away. Within two months he was missing in action and before the summer we had the telegram from Washington saying that he was dead.

I wouldn't believe it at first. All the time, getting ready to move from our house to an apartment in the town where my grandmother lived, I never cried except once, when I couldn't find the flashlight my father had given me. My mother would hug me to her and cry, and once she said in a kind of despairing tone, "Oh, Tommy, you're so *little*!" But she stopped when she saw how stiff I was in her arms. I couldn't tell her, but I could never make it real that my father was dead. Every time the phone rang, every time an old Nash stopped before the house, I'd expect it to be my father.

Then one day I found the flashlight in the bottom of a box where the packers had stored it when they moved us, and, I don't know why, but when I held the flashlight in my hand, I knew that my father was dead, and that I would never see him again. I threw myself on the bed then and cried and cried until I fell asleep at last, with the flashlight under my cheek.

When I awoke, my mother was leaning over me, and I threw my arms about her and cried again. Only now I felt better. Because I was six now, and though I couldn't have explained their meaning, I knew what my father's words to me that day had meant. At least, I understood that I had to realize that my father was never coming back, before I could know, as I knew that minute, that he had never really been away from us at all.

James Hillhouse High School
New Haven, Connecticut

FIVE-FINGER EXERCISES IN PREPARATION FOR WRITING POETRY

It is hoped that they prepared for more sharp and vivid writing of all kinds.

A. Practice in simile, metaphor, and personification. Becoming accustomed to these figures in reading, becoming aware of them in speech. An assignment or two in which examples heard and read are brought to class for exchange and comment. Writing one's own, first from a given list of subjects from which choices may be made, then selecting one's own subjects.

EXAMPLE

Street lights gaze at themselves in wet pavements and imagine they are stars.

A fog is the ragged mantle of a tired day.

Candlelight—a rising and falling cadence of light.

Lumber in snow—frosted wafers.

Trees in the wind—skeletons standing proudly in the weather of their choice.

A country road is like life; it is generally true that one cannot see what lies beyond at any great distance.

She had been crushed under the thumb of circumstances.

B. Experimenting with very simple poetic form. Hokku and cinquain are used for forms that are both simple and exact. At first, they are given a "start" to carry on to completion, if they want to. Some use it, but others start on their own.

Hokku

The Purging

God gives rebirth to
Nature each spring; our souls' comes
With absolution.

Together

His smile, my stifled
Sigh, a silent thought . . . a step
Toward paradise.

Conduct

Ah, youth, What guides it?
Its undertakings' password—
"What's in it for me?"

The River

Green is the river,
Rapidly flowing like life,
Singing and sighing.

Upping [5]

The swan swims gently
And the peaceful lake reflects.
Nymphs' tranquility.

Cinquains [6]

Upward

Pine cones
Stand bristling high
with silver teeth to make
tree-peaks that fill with azure sky
and sun.

[5] Suggested by the old British custom of choosing annually the most beautiful swans for the Royal Lake.
[6] Experiments by twelfth-grade students, suggested by *The Hollow Reed*, by Mary J. J. Wrinn (New York, Harper & Brothers, 1935).

Old Friend

Full moon,
Why do you nod
So knowingly as I
Now roam and try to find one lost,
Myself?

Light—Dark

Night moth,
Renouncing dark,
Seeking disaster's flame,
All wispy whirr of winged life ends with
One puff.

Out

No room
In class for those
Who dare to share. Exams,
It seems, are personal, not joint
Affairs.

The Chapin School
New York City

HAVING FUN WITH LIMERICKS AND EPITAPHS

Assignment: Have fun writing verse. Try some limericks and epitaphs.

Limericks: Bring your favorite limericks to class to read aloud. The teacher reads other limericks from *The Complete Limerick Book*, by Langford Reed (New York, G. P. Putnam's Sons, 1925).

There was a young man of the Clyde
Who went to a funeral and cried
When asked who was dead,
He stammered and said,
"I don't know—I just came for the ride."

There was a young woman named Bright
Whose speed was much faster than light.

> She set out one day,
> In a relative way,
> And returned on the previous night.
> (With apologies to Professor Einstein)

The essential qualities of a good limerick are: (1) a good last line. (2) ingenuity of rhyme. (3) plot. (see page 24 of *The Complete Limerick Book*)

EXAMPLES

> There was an old dragon in jail
> Who mournfully wept on his tail;
> Said he, "When I'm tired,
> I often get fired
> And conflagrate when I exhale."

> There was a wee mouse from Ceylon,
> Who was born without any tail on.
> "The one thing to do,"
> Squeaked he as he grew,
> "Is to find some old tail I can nail on."

> A lady in far Timbuktu
> Is ingenious with the lasso
> She can rope in a zoo,
> Or a gentleman too,
> Which is handy to know how to do.

Epitaphs: Write a humorous epitaph for yourself or one of your friends (with his permission!). Let it reflect some trait of character or some idiosyncrasy of its subject. Do not write more than a quatrain. Use rhyme.

EXAMPLES

> Her body dead,
> We hope her soul will be
> More punctual
> Than ever she.

> Here lies my body beneath the grass.
> My life was spent in science class
> Dissecting earthworms and anthropod
> Only to meet them under the sod.

Here lies her
Gone and departing
She failed English Grammar
And died broken hearting.

The Chapin School
New York City

FREE VERSE

Free verse is known for its singing quality in rhythmic appeal without meter, or without any regularity of meter; for its emotional force; its graphic power in concrete images and figurative suggestions; its insight into the significance of what is seen or heard; and its impact and singleness of impression.

From the following subjects choose one about which you have strong convictions or feelings:

a. An unkindness or injustice.
b. A disappointment.
c. A moment of personal rebellion.
d. A moment of war or history, brought home to you.
e. A moment of indecision.
f. A realization of wasted time.
g. An experience that might have been avoided.
h. A rainy day.
i. A person whose wisdom, or story, or influence has impressed you.

After reading Amy Lowell's *Lilacs* or *Patterns*, Carl Sandburg's *Grass* or *Fog*, Stephen Crane's *I Saw a Man*, Edgar Lee Masters' *Ann Rutledge*, call up from your memory an exact picture suggested by the subject you have chosen. State this experience in brief rhythmical phrases and sentences, showing the image in your mind, the significance, thoughts, and feelings attached to it, the concrete details, the figurative comparisons you might now make in trying to explain it vividly. Use alliterative words. No rhymes are necessary, or—for this exercise—advisable, since you should strive for completely natural and direct emotion. Never for an instant lose sight of the experience itself. Strive for one mood, one impression. Build your whole thought into an explanation of one thing—no matter how many examples you may use. Arrange your statements into lines of poetry by grouping ideas together in phrases and sentences or even mere parts of sentences that you wish emphasized or set off. The lines, although constantly varying in length according to the phrases emphasized, should never be long if you wish to gain the best musical effect, and ordinarily, single-word lines—although they appear to great advantage in *Lilacs*—might tend to appear forced or artificial. Every line should be an effusion in itself, a complete unit of emotion, a satisfying stroke of pictorial detail, a rhythmic pulsation in the life of the greater effect. In free verse you cannot afford to be less than dramatic, or breathlessly swift and natural. You may offer bits of wisdom unhampered by considerations of form. Vividness, freedom of imagination, realism, colorful imagery have nothing to hinder them. You may write at any length. And if you can add vision, insight, and drama in the purely natural emotional form, you should have good poetry.[7]

EXAMPLE

Conformity[8]

Conform!
I see two strong, brutal hands, clenched fists, shooting forth to pound in
    that wretched thought.
Conform!
I feel my soft dress, once flowing free about my bounding legs, held fast
    in rough, harsh hands.
I look up.
"They have no faces!—" I begin to shout.
The words are held fast in my throat, even as my dress is now tightly
    fastened about me.
I try to walk, but I am as a stone.
The blue river beckons to me.
I stumble down the green-carpeted hill and gather the river's reflections
    to me.
It is not I!

7 Newsom, *op. cit.,* pp. 41–43.
8 Written by Barbara Firger in her Junior year.

I have lost my identity in this mad whirl and my features are fled.
They have erased them with a single word—
Conform!
They snatch me back from the stream and, pulling, lead me.
I fall, for I cannot see.
I have no eyes.
Even now, I am forgetting the freedom of my green haven and its rippling,
cerulean stream.
I feel a cold wind, then, none at all.
The ground no longer slopes.
It is all flat and barren.
I smell no blossoms, feel no stones.
I yearn to stumble, to know some challenge:
To scale a spiny rock;
To be thrown and tossed about by a rushing waterfall—
Cool, delicious danger!
I breathe, but do not live!
They seat me on a chair.
Its back is straight.
It does not yield.
It pushes me all together, cramping me with its straight, conforming arms.
I try to yell.
Memory! You deceive me!
I Have No Mouth Or Mind!
My lifeless head begins to nod.
I do not hear what they say,
But it is as if an evil power were within my head, forcing me, as it were,
to sit in everlasting damnation of affirmation of all they say.
I try to shake my head to say, "NO!"
It does not move.
They have pierced my soft, young neck on either side with staid, steel
rivets; (it moves not!) they have hinged it, back and front; attached a
string of discarded men's minds to manoeuvre mine—or my lack of one.
Can I never break loose?
I turn to God.
But have they shut Him out, too?
Wait!—It comes rushing back, now, to me—
"Our Father——"
I hear a crash of thunder.
I burst my shackles!
They try to stop me but they cannot touch my freedom.

As I run, my dress falls again about my ankles, loose and free.
A dim light pierces the iron-barred sky of Conformity's Hell.
Once more, I fall upon my green carpet.
I kiss the cool, blue stream.

Brookline High School
Brookline, Massachusetts

WRITING SONNETS

I. Read, memorize, and write with scansion the following sonnets, in order to fix the meter in your mind, and to learn to think naturally in the sonnet form: Shakespeare's "When in disgrace with fortune and men's eyes," Keats' *When I Have Fears that I May Cease to Be*, Milton's sonnet, *On His Blindness*, Lizette Reese's *Tears*. State in one sentence for each, the thought of the octet, or first eight lines; in a separate sentence for each, the thought of the sestet, or last six lines. Now read Wordsworth's *The World Is Too Much with Us*. Notice that the sonnet always has fourteen iambic pentameter lines, with divisions of thought between octet and sestet clearly marked; and with a definite rhyme-scheme which differs somewhat in the above sonnets. We are here chiefly concerned with the Shakespearean sonnet, with its three regular quatrains and its end couplet, the rhyme pattern being *a,b,a,b/c,d,c,d,/e,f,e,f,/g,g*.

Notice that the sonnet (which is a form nearly all poets from early Elizabethan times have used) is deeply emotional, is very personal, direct, and sincere, and is a powerful medium for figurative language; also, that its form, which began as a love poem, can be accommodated to almost any great subject of emotional importance.

Choose one of the following subjects for writing a Shakespearean sonnet:

a. Any sound which has fascinated or inspired you.
b. Any single thing in nature, such as a flower, bird, or tree, which aroused your feeling.
c. Any images that have teased the imagination, such as clouds, rocks, or leaves.
d. Any scene which has a small enough center of interest to be described.

e. Any great moment of your experience which has helped you to gain a new feeling regarding life or things.

State in a single sentence what you would like to say in the fourteen lines as a whole. Then state in a single sentence the idea you wish to convey in the octet. This part may be almost entirely descriptive. For your sestet, which should also be stated in a single sentence, you may express a reaction to, or an effect grown out of the thought of the octet. There should be a distinct division of thought between the octet and sestet, without losing the unity of the whole. Cause and effect, condition and conclusion, picture and significance, experience and reaction give an ample working plan. Your octet should be written by quatrains, one at a time until it is entirely suitable. In the octet you must describe, you must grasp the significant details; you must enter into the feeling of what you see or hear and express its newness to you, the essence of what it seems to convey to you, the details of what is there, the conception of what it means. Portray only what you distinctly see or hear or feel at the moment. In the third quatrain, which is the beginning of your sestet, be just as descriptive of your reaction or conclusion. The couplet may summarize your conclusion or your idea as a whole. It should hold a compact clarity that outshines the rest of the sonnet.

Avoid taking too large a subject or trying to say too much. Avoid letting rhymes trick you into saying what you do not mean. Avoid unnatural language and statements which look good but are not sincere. Remember the sonnet is you at your best, and in your most sincere and thoughtful mood. It is strictly personal. Avoid getting lost in your couplet at the end. Remember that these two lines may repeat, emphasize, or strengthen the idea of the third quatrain or re-express what you stated in your summary sentence for the sonnet as a whole. Avoid abstractness. Remember that the sonnet is very much visual and very figurative. The visual element pictures what is looked upon actually and what is called to mind as pictured previously. The figurative element is built upon the concreteness of the pictures presented.[9]

9 Newsom, *op. cit.*, pp. 37–39.

EXAMPLE

Caesar [10]

Atlantic Contest Prize Poem, 1954–1955

I long to know this man and I explore
Suetonius for words he might have said,
Search Plutarch for accounts of what he wore,
Ask Shakespeare if Rome wept when he was dead;
I listen to Respighi: through the pines
Along the Via Appia, I see
His mighty legions stretched in endless lines—
The fear of Gaul, the boast of Italy.
But what are words and deeds and battles fought
If nowhere in these fragments do I find
The truth of what he dreamt and felt and thought
And hid from all the world within his mind?
One cannot see a man through others' eyes;
Who would explain a Caesar only lies.

General Grant at Appomattox [11]

Alas! the battle's done, the Brother's War
Is buried with the ashes of its dead.
Nothing is left but triumph's awful chore—
The yielding words of Lee which must be said.
How straight he stands, his pride a golden sun!
A swift salute, a nod, then face to face
Divided North and South must talk as one
Of fertile lands now left a barren space.
I see him bend to loose his scabbard belt
With brimming eyes and lips a parted line;
And knowing awe that triumph never felt,
I bid him stop, for this could not be mine.

[10] This poem was written by Joan Moffit, a Junior in Mr. Newsom's Creative Writing Class, Brookline High School. It was awarded the University of Pittsburgh Scholarship. It is reprinted with permission of *The Atlantic*.
[11] This dramatic monologue in sonnet form was written by Elaine Sallop in her Senior year.

My battle's won, and I, the victor, stand,
Yet who is here to shake his mighty hand!

Brookline High School
Brookline, Massachusetts

II. Generally we do not attempt the sonnet form until the twelfth grade. By then we have read the sonnets of Shakespeare, Milton, Wordsworth, Keats, Robinson, Millay and others. From the eighth grade on, we have tried other forms of verse: ballads, lyrics, rhymed couplets, blank verse. We have also had other reading and writing experiences designed to make us aware of the connotative power of words, of the appeal of sensory detail, of fresh metaphors and similes, of images and symbols, and of word music. (There are many excellent suggestions for exercises designed to prepare the student for writing verse in Wrinn's *The Hollow Reed*.) It is perhaps unnecessary to point out that the English sonnet is easier than the Italian form because the rhyme scheme is more flexible and the three quatrains allow more "room" for developing an idea.

Assignment: Write an English sonnet. Note the following:

1. The rhyme scheme is *a,b,a,b/c,d,c,d/e,f,e,f/g,g* and the meter is iambic pentameter. Run-on lines are permissible if you keep to the rhyme scheme.

2. The subject (see list that follows) should not be too slight or too large for the narrow confines of the sonnet—a big order! The first three quatrains develop the idea or supply the details and facts if you will—generally quatrain by quatrain. The couplet at the end sums up your point of view about the details presented in the quatrains. The last two lines can also contain the unexpected, reversing or contradicting what seems to be indicated in the quatrains.

3. Choose one of the subjects below and then write out in prose what you plan to say in the first twelve lines and what conclusion you reach or what point of view you take in the final couplet. After your prose version has been approved, write your sonnet. Remember that poetry although rooted in fact, does not make literal statements; it suggests through imagery and connotative words.

Portraits: some member of your family, or someone outside of school, whom you know well; one of your ancestors whom you may know through a portrait or family legend.

Qualities: cheerfulness, courage, serenity, pride, charm.

Animals: your pets or any animal you have observed closely.

Objects: a music box, a crystal chandelier, a grandfather's clock, a silver christening mug, an heirloom, or anything glimpsed in an antique shop.

Places: some natural landscape or part of a landscape; a view from a window or rooftop, a favorite room.

EXAMPLES

Two sonnets by students follow. The first is by a girl who spent part of each year in Florida; the second by one who spent week ends and summers on a farm.

The Everglades

Enormous, wet, stretch out the Everglades,
And white and yellow waterlilies bloom
Surprisingly among the saw-grass blades
That flourish from the muck. Where headlands loom
Above the marsh, the twisted banyans grow
Providing perches for the cool egret
Or red-necked buzzard who looks out below
Untiringly for death, without regret.
Here death and life go on as once they did
Across the whole of Earth, in fetid heat
And sunny steaming silence; here, amid
The grasses, cycles changelessly repeat.
    When man intrudes, he finds an ancient pace;
    Fourscore and ten means little in this place.

The student has viewed a scene familiar to her not only with a discriminating eye, but with a thoughtful inward eye as well. Note especially "sunny, steaming silence." Perhaps having to write this sonnet made her "see" the Everglades for the first time.

Country Morning

As the sun rising with his light fingers
Tempers the cool and spicy air of night,
The graceful doe, browsing, no longer lingers,
But hastens to the thicket in her flight.
And the rabbits with their mien bewitching,
Steal into the fields and gardens near,
And quickly hop about, their noses twitching,
To find the freshest herbs and clover spear.
The waking cocks crow longer, more demanding,
The cattle bawl and crowd up near the gate.
The foals on unsure knobby legs are standing
Beside their mothers, shining and sedate.
Lastly awakes the farmer with a yawn,
Rising to feed his stock and damn the dawn.

Here there is concrete, rather humorous description, with a somewhat unexpected ending.

The Chapin School
New York City

Bibliography

Selected and annotated by the Committee as being of particular value to the teacher of creative writing in secondary school.

ARNSTEIN, Flora J., *Adventures into Poetry* (Stanford, Calif., Stanford University Press, 1951).

A revealing and engrossing book drawn from the author's experience with six- to twelve-year-olds. Establishing the right atmosphere for appreciating and writing poetry is the keynote. Inspiration for the teacher of any and all age levels, with much delightful children's poetry included.

CONNOLLY, Francis, *A Rhetoric Case Book* (New York, Harcourt, Brace & Co., 1959).

Merits careful study by teachers because of its detailed treatment of both objective and subjective writing: definition, exposition, argument, description, narration, the short story, the informal essay. Each section is provided with unhackneyed, illuminating examples drawn from literature, past and present. These passages are analyzed and specific writing assignments suggested, which can be adapted by the individual teacher to suit his needs. The section on description is particularly good. It includes: organizing details to create a single impression; maintaining a point of view and attitude; arranging vivid details in climactic order; blending narration and description.

GRAVES, Robert, and HODGE, Alan, *The Reader over Your Shoulder; a Handbook for Writers of English Prose* (New York, The Macmillan Co., 1943).

An elaborate and possibly oversophisticated analysis of prose style, with close examinations of many passages from contemporary writers. Exciting to any teacher concerned about the muddiness of language, but probably only indirectly applicable to practical secondary classroom practice.

HAMILTON, Anne, *How to Revise Your Own Poems* (Los Angeles, Abbey San Encino Press, 1936).

———, *How to Revise Your Own Stories* (Boston, The Writer, Inc., 1938).

Although intended for professional writers, these books are useful to the teacher because of their specific approach to problems of technique. The author uses the question-and-answer method in both volumes. In *How to Revise Your Own Poems*, for instance, she answers clearly questions like "Does a poet have to be grammatical?" "Why did you blue-pencil all those lovely adjectives?" "What exactly is connotation?" In *How to Revise Your Own Stories*, she directs the attention of the story writer to important aspects of story structure by such questions as "How much have I told the reader in the first sentence, the first paragraph, the first page?" "What is the decisive moment in my story?" Both books are as practical as their titles suggest.

HOGREFFE, Pearl, *The Process of Creative Writing* (New York, Harper & Brothers, 1956).

Divided into two parts, the book deals first with narrative (from the moment of experience to the developed short story) and secondly with personalized exposition. It emphasizes the ideas that creative writing is the stuff of experience, that writing and reading are very closely related, and that the various types of writing often overlap. To illustrate her ideas, the author has sprinkled her book liberally with examples of student and professional writing, with questions and assignments, and with suggestions for finding material on which to write.

KEMPTON, Kenneth Payson, *Short Stories for Study* (Cambridge, Mass., Harvard University Press, 1953).

Although intended primarily as a manual on short-story writing, this book is invaluable for the pointers it gives on how to read a short story, an art which the teacher must master in order to be effective in the classroom. The discussion of the important aspects of short-story technique (point of view, content, persons, places, plot as idea) is given point and clarity by the inclusion of stories by Jessamyn West, Sloan Wilson, W. D. Edmonds, Aldous Huxley, and others. Each story is specifically analyzed, so that both positive and negative qualities emerge. Its informal, lively tone makes for good reading.

MUNSON, Gorham, *The Writer's Workshop Companion* (New York, Farrar, Straus and Cudahy, Inc., 1951).

A companion to *The Written Word*, published in 1949, this book emphasizes all the aspects of becoming a professional writer, but it could very well be used by the high school teacher and pupil interested in writing. It contains many quotations from various writers and many examples of fiction and nonfiction (for the most part excerpts, rather than complete selections), which are illustrative of the points made and the advice given in the book about the technical side of writing.

NEWSOM, Francis W., *Writer's Technique: A Practical Guide to Creative Writing* (New York, Coleman-Ross Company, Inc., 1954).

The book, addressed to the student writer, was developed from the author's experience with the teaching of creative writing to selected classes of high-school juniors and seniors at Brookline (Massachusetts) High School, and is the textbook used in those classes. Its special strength lies in firm guidance in detailed observation and accurate, factual reporting of what is observed as the foundation for all creative writing.

O'FAOLAIN, Sean, *The Short Story* (New York, The Devin-Adair Co., 1951).

This book is a collection of short stories by masters in the profession, including Henry James, de Maupassant, Chekov, Hemingway, Frank O'Connor, and Elizabeth Bowen, but it is much more than that, for the stories are used to illustrate the principles expounded by the author in chapters devoted to such subjects as construction and language, subject, and conventions of the short story.

ORVIS, Mary Burchard, *The Art of Writing Fiction* (Englewood Cliffs, N.J., Prentice-Hall, Inc., 1948).

This book seeks to help beginning writers by directing them away from the imitative and the sterile into the creative and the sincere. It emphasizes insight into experience as first in importance, and skill and technique, though necessary, as secondary. By quoting extensively from the "best" writers of the day, the author points out the subjects best suited for narration and the devices available to achieve the desired effects.

SANDERS, Gerald, *A Poetry Primer* (English Pamphlet Series; New York, Rinehart & Company, Inc., 1935, reprinted 1956).

A useful, inexpensive short account of technical fundamentals.

WHARTON, Edith, *The Writing of Fiction* (New York, Charles Scribner's Sons, 1925).

It is always a pleasure to reread a book that reflects the intelligence, the cultivation, and the fastidiousness of its author as clearly as this one does. The section entitled "Telling a Short Story" is well worth careful reading, not only for the soundness of the advice it offers on matters of technique, but also for the quality of its style.

WOOD, Clement, ed., *Wood's Unabridged Rhyming Dictionary* (Cleveland, The World Publishing Company).

———, *Complete Rhyming Dictionary* (Garden City, N.Y., Garden City Books).

Practical tools for the creative-writing classroom.

WRINN, Mary J. J., *The Hollow Reed* (New York and London, Harper & Brothers, 1935).

". . . it was at the request of young persons for definite training in the craft of poetry that this book was conceived." A thorough treatment of the forms and terminology of poetry, with many suggested approaches to writing. Abundance and variety of exercises are particularly useful for the beginner. Ample illustrative material.

SELECTED PERTINENT ARTICLES

McFEELY, Richard H., "The Place of Creative Writing in the Academic Program," *Bulletin* of the Columbia Scholastic Press, Advisers Association, Vol. 13, No. 3 (January, 1957).

O'FAOLAIN, Sean, "Looking Back at Writing," *The Atlantic* (December, 1956).

ORWELL, George, "Politics and the English Language," *New Republic* (1946).

Much reprinted in anthologies. A tough-minded and entertaining attack on the obscure absurdities of expository prose in our time.

From *The English Journal:*

REDFORD, Grant H., "Of Teachers, Students, and 'Creative Writing'" (December, 1953).

HENRY, George H., "Only Spirit Can Measure Spirit" (April, 1954).

THORNLEY, Wilson R., "The Case for Creative Writing" (December, 1955).

WONNBERGER, Carl G., "They All Can Learn to Write" (November, 1956).

The next four essays deal with the type of writing most taught in our schools, expository writing. Here the emphasis is on getting the student to say exactly what he means; the materials are not books about writing, but the student's own ideas. The teacher's function is to stay with the paper until it is exact. The student learns when he gets the right words in the right order to say what he means to say. Nothing less should satisfy the teacher.

Edwin Sauer and G. C. Waterston discuss the paragraph, and show how they talk out the problems with the class, put the individual's writing to the group, and work hard on revision. Harold Martin demonstrates how a class discussion based on defining and clarifying terms can be the key to the kind of thinking that makes for good writing. Arthur Mizener concentrates on the clear single sentence. If a student were to write a sentence a day and put it to the syntactical tests Mr. Mizener suggests, he would learn to say what he means without ambiguity.

All four teachers agree that a tough approach to writing is necessary, that writing can never be made easy, and that the student must use his mind as well as he can. The quality of the writing is a measure of how well the student is thinking; the demand is that he do his best, not that he merely write.

6

The Co-operative Correction
of Paragraphs

EDWIN H. SAUER, *Walnut Hills High School, Cincinnati, Ohio*

In the whole academic year there is no hour quite so dark for the teacher of English as that in which he takes the first look at the results of the student's initial assignment in paragraph writing. This, as Emily Dickinson observed about some other harrowing experience, is:

> . . . the hour of lead
> Remembered if outlived
> As freezing persons recollect the snow—
> First chill, then stupor, then
> The letting go.

One is tempted to abandon composition in the course—at least for a while—and go back to the handbooks and drill exercises to teach the parts of the sentence and the forms of verbs. The possibility of getting across to an entire class the notion of a paragraph as a structural unit, a rounded development of an idea, seems so remote that one is inclined to risk not trying. Maybe a sense of paragraphing will filter through from their reading, we say to ourselves, as we add a few extra essays to their reading list. Maybe they can learn to write good paragraphs by not writing any.

But of course they can't. Some few students, unusually sensitive to the rhythms of rhetoric, may improve their writing skill demonstrably as a result of subconscious imitation of prose pieces they have read, but for the others—if they are to acquire the simple techniques of exposition and persuasion—there must be the agony, the exhaustion, and the desperation which accompany *all* efforts to put thought into prose, but especially the first.

The first papers of the year always give evidence of student distress, all right, but of the wrong sort. The kinds of exhaustion and desperation which accompany this beginning exercise make themselves apparent in the tortuous constructions, the multiple tautologies, and the flagrant solecisms which are found on nearly every paper. Faced with such immensities of disorder, what does the teacher do next? To point out all lapses in unity and coherence, to specify all slips in clarity and logic, and to mark all errors in usage, grammar, sentence structure, and diction is a task of such frightening proportions that the teacher begins to cringe—sometimes literally. Is there another way out? Can we, in some other way, though with these same pieces of composition, work to the same effect?

I think so—for the first few pieces of writing at least—with a co-operative method of correction, which I use somewhat as follows: In the first few theme assignments I never ask for more than one paragraph—of perhaps five or six sentences. "The solid paragraph of five or six sentences, if properly written, raises for the students all the problems of a long essay," said Mr. Arthur Mizener to this conference last year, and there are advantages for both student and teacher. In this initial paragraph the student is free to write on any subject of interest to him, though he is limited to composition of an expository or persuasive nature—no narrative or descriptive paragraphs.

When the papers come in, I read all of them through carefully and then from a class of, say, thirty students select about twelve or fifteen paragraphs which I consider representative; generally I choose an equal number of good, mediocre, and poor pieces, which are then reproduced by duplicating machine so that every member of the class has a copy of each of the selected paragraphs. Then, together, in class, we go to work on them, a paragraph at a time.

The students read the paragraph silently, and when they have finished, I question them about its meaning. Are they able to say without hesitation what the paragraph is about? Can the thought of the paragraph be expressed in a single sentence? If so, is there one sentence already in it which seems to convey the central idea around which the paragraph is built? Are all other sentences closely related to the central thought? If not, which ones are out of line? This for them is a very revealing exercise as they see, in specimens of their own work, the difficulty for students other than the author to know what the paragraph is trying to say. The paragraphs are always presented to the class anonymously of course, but I have known the author of a paragraph under discussion to become so distressed with the inability of the class to penetrate his meaning that he has blurted out, "Now this is what I meant," giving us then a clear and straightforward statement, which he recognized at once as the topic sentence he ought to have written.

Thus we are stimulated into a consideration of the whole problem of unity in a paragraph, and the discoveries which we make about a particular piece of work will be (1) that the unity of the paragraph is substantially good and needs no significant changes, or (2) that the deletion of one or more irrelevant sentences will greatly improve matters, or (3) that the material is so unrelated that nothing less than a complete rewriting is called for.

If our finding is of the first or second nature, we go on to consider the order of the paragraph. Are the sentences in the right place? Does the second one follow from the first, the third from the second, and so on to the end? Is there a smooth transition from one sentence to the next—a natural flowing line of development? If not, what, first of all, are the possibilities of rearrangement? What words, phrases, or clauses could be suggested to improve the ease of passage from one sentence to another? Thus, without even introducing the terms, the teacher leads the class into a sense of paragraph coherence and standard transitional devices.

Next we look at the grammar, spelling, sentence structure, diction; in short, the mechanics of the paragraph. Obvious errors are spotted at once and corrected. More complex matters—parallelism, dangling modifiers, vague reference—will probably be discovered by perceptive students, but I sometimes have to direct their attention to these faults through leading questions. We are ruthless about sentence fragments and comma faults, insisting that though there may sometimes be a stylistic excuse for a fragment, early exercises in composition demand that it be marked as intentional. Whatever in this whole area of mechanics any student objects to, he must oppose authoritatively —that is, he must specify in terms of established conventions why he would make a particular correction.

The student should have from the beginning of any course in high school English a friendly orientation to grammar, for the *fear* of grammatical error is likely not only to cause his greatest discomfort in writing but also to falsify or obscure his thought. I think that the student should know that the worst language faults of our day are not the errors of bad grammar, incorrect usage, faulty diction, slang, and vulgarity, painful as these are to the sensitive ear, but rather the offenses of jargon, gobbledygook, tautology, euphemisms, clichés, and dangling, squinting, and misplaced modifiers. The student's fear of grammar will cease to damage his composition work if he can be brought to see grammar for what it is—at best, a description of the language, and thus negative and analytic, and of secondary importance to a writer of good prose, whose approach to language must always be positive and constructive. The student will have to recognize that there is scarcely a principle or rule which for the sake of clarity and precision he will not at one time or another have to be willing to abandon or compromise.

This is not of course to recommend language carelessness to him. He cannot ignore that definitely established language conventions exist, and he must see the real necessity for order in language. Without the conventions of grammar, sentence structure, punctuation, capitalization, and the mechanics of English in general, we would have language chaos, and communication of an exact and honest nature would cease. But it is the word *conventions* that we ought to insist upon. Today's student of composition must learn that it is highly inaccurate to speak of the "rules" of grammar, if by the word *rules* we mean something fixed, unchanging, and immutable, like the rules or laws of mathematics; for language does not operate according to such rules. The proper approach for today's student of composition is, it seems to me, the historical one, the understanding that a really living language constantly undergoes change; that many of the forms and constructions which we approve today were once considered most improper; that correctness is finally determined by use, and that the fundamental law in operation here is that the conventions of language mechanics exist solely to facilitate communication, and not the other way around. Today's student of composition should know what is in the grammar textbooks, but, more important, he should have his ears in public places, listening to the way the people of his time are establishing meaningful verbal contact with one another. Then he will be able to relax a bit, and the fear of using "incorrect" English will no longer do violence to the easy expression of his thought.

After mechanics we are ready in our co-operative scheme to talk about the *logic* of the piece—the accuracy or inaccuracy of the views presented, the quality of truth and the general validity which the paragraph contains. If the paragraph is persuasive in character, we are especially careful here to evaluate the soundness of the argument. We examine critically the assertions of the author; we analyze his proposition and test his definitions. Above all, we inquire into the reasonableness of what he has said. Is his conviction acceptable to us? And, if not, what are our recommendations? Can the paragraph, with a few sentences, be "saved"? Or is its "logic" so questionable that nothing less than a complete rethinking of the proposition is required?

If we feel secure in proceeding, we go on to talk about the "rhetoric" of the paragraph. How can we improve it stylistically? How can we make it more exact and economical, more forceful and effective, more fluent and graceful? Here we experiment with sentence variety and attack the jargon, gobbledygook, tautology, and general awkwardness. We help the student who has written, "It has very seldom been the case that our vicinity has had so much snow in the winter months of January and February" to write, "We have seldom had so much snow in January and February." "While still engaged in the effort to pursue the values of the elementary school curriculum, I acquired the decision to someday embark on a program of university instruction" is likely to become "When I was still in grade school, I decided to go to college," and "After we had imbibed a sufficient quantity of liquid refreshment, we were desirous of partaking of solid sustenance" might possibly come out "We had had so much Pepsi Cola that we thought we had better eat some chow." Affectation and pretension get rough treatment, irresponsible abstractions are expunged or made concrete, triteness is massacred. Again I get a splendid opportunity to insist that the really serious language faults of our time are more likely to be heard in high places than in low—faults which would probably never have been deplored by old-school grammarians and language purists, the faults of pomposity rather than of innocence. The gardener who says to his employer, "I ain't hardly got no room for them tulip bulbs" will be understood, and in such a way his problem can be faced head on—you help to find room or you don't plant them. But I ask my students what they would do with this statement from an actual business letter: "Gentlemen: In re your communication as to the expediency of our continued controls of merchandisable materials, may we state that, pursuant to many requests from patrons, we are endeavoring to expedite delivery of said materials along the line of equitable distribution." The writer of that horror means, I take it, that the order will be filled as soon as possible, but I can't be sure. Citing another example of this kind of language irresponsibility, I sometimes ask the very diligent of my students to unravel for me this sentence from a textbook in psychology: "The basic patterns of behavior in this area illustrate failure of adjustment in the preadolescent period of emotional tension, where the compulsions of articulation predominant in our competitive culture produce a dichotomy of purpose."

This form of outrage, as Sir Arthur Quiller-Couch warned us a long time ago in his immensely useful book *On the Art of Writing*, is jargon, and a dreadful kind of writing it is. Says Sir Arthur: "To write jargon is to be perpetually shuffling around in the fog and cottonwool of abstract terms . . . to beat the air because it is easier than to flesh your sword in the thing. The first virtue, the touchstone of masculine style, is its use of the active verb and the concrete noun. When you write in the active voice, 'They gave him a silver teapot,' you write like a man. When you write, 'He was made the recipient of a silver teapot,' you write jargon." In an essay titled "Politics and the English Language," George Orwell, perhaps even more effectively, illustrates this practice. He quotes first the familiar passage from *Ecclesiastes:* "I returned and saw under the sun, that the race is not to the swift, nor the battle to the strong, neither yet bread to the wise, nor yet riches to men of understanding, nor yet favour to men of skill; but time and chance happeneth to them all."

In jargon, says Orwell, this would come out as follows: "Objective considerations of contemporary phenomena compel the conclusion that success or failure in competitive activities exhibits no tendency to be commensurate with innate capacity, but that a considerable element of the unpredictable must always be taken into account."

Students learn soon to detect this kind of pompousness and, better still, to avoid it in their own writing. Coming upon jargon in paragraphs studied under the co-operative method of correction, they suggest at once a straightforward and unpretentious diction which *says* honestly what it *means* honestly.

Improvement of the rhetoric of the paragraph is nearly the last step in the co-operative method, and, as you might expect, students by this time have come out with something quite different from what they started with. Let me illustrate. When I performed this exercise last fall with a group of high school juniors, one of the original paragraphs read as follows:

In choosing a college after completion of high school it is necessary to first consider entrance requirements. While considering this, decide whether a coeducational, religious, or military school is most desirable. Of course the field of study which you wish to pursue must be considered. If a specific field is of interest, the facilities of the school in this field should be ascertained. In connection with the facilities, endowments must be considered. If there are few endowments, either by alumni or interested organizations or families, there will be less equipment available. Also if the endowments are few there is less chance of attracting better teachers. The faculty should always be considered because it determines indirectly the quality of the education you receive. Another matter to be considered is whether it is a small or large college and its location. Of course of greater importance is whether or not it is an accredited school, because if it is not, your degree will mean much less. Last but not least, cost must be considered. This will include tuition, living expenses, supplies, and other essentials. The number of available scholarships in your field should be considered.

We were agreed after we read this paragraph that it is seriously defective in a number of ways, its major fault being that its author has crowded too much into it; there is sufficient material here for an entire theme, with the various "considerations" serving for development into small paragraphs themselves. The crowding produces a deadly repetition which is made even more objectionable by the eight uses of "considered." The paragraph has no "shape"; there is apparently no order to the arrangement of these factors; there are several shifts in person; and the ending is abrupt, giving us neither summary nor conclusion. The class was not sure that the paragraph was worth working with, but decided to try to reconstruct it anyhow, largely, I suppose, because the challenge was so great.

Tackling mechanics first, getting rid of the shifts in person, and adding a conclusion, we came up with this version.

In choosing a college after completion of high school, one must first consider entrance requirements. While considering these, one should decide whether or not he wants to attend a coeducational, religious, or military school. Of course one must consider the field of study he wishes to pursue. If a specific field is of interest, the facilities of this school should be ascertained. In connection with the facilities endowments must be considered. If there are few endowments, either from alumni or interested organizations or families, less equipment will be available. When the endowments are few, there is less chance of attracting competent teachers. One should always consider the faculty because this determines indirectly the quality of the education one receives. Other matters to be considered are the size and location of the college. Whether or not the school is accredited determines the value of the degree. Finally, the cost of tuition, living expenses, supplies, and other essentials must be considered, along with the possibilities of a scholarship if necessary. Attention to all these matters will result in a wise choice of college, which, in turn, will benefit one's later life.

We could see at once that we were still some distance from a good paragraph, so on we trudged. A few slips in logic next caught our eye. Choosing a college is probably best accomplished *before* one leaves high school. The division of colleges into "coeducational, religious, or military" not only does not exhaust the possibilities but also does not set up distinctly separate categories. The faculty of a college will determine the quality of an education directly rather than indirectly, and we could not feel very confident that "attention to all these matters" would automatically result in a wise choice of college, as the conclusion we had just added seemed to assert. These were minor difficulties, however, as we proceeded to attack the big problems of order, sentence variety, coherence, and vocabulary.

But there was just too much to do, and effective oral discussion and remedy would have taken too much time. Plainly the thing to do at this point was to let each student go to work on the paragraph himself, reshaping the material as a written assignment. Next day, therefore, we had about thirty versions to consider, each of which was a marked improvement over the original. Here is the one which the class selected as best.

When one begins to think about choosing a college, he should be careful to evaluate the schools in terms of his own particular interests and needs. He should decide, first of all, whether he wants to go to a private or state-supported institution, and if he prefers the former, there are other considerations: whether or not it is denominational, coeducational, or limited in the kind of curriculum it offers, many private schools being only liberal arts colleges. Where one goes will undoubtedly be affected by the facilities of the school in a person's field of interest, and since the quality of both faculty and equipment is often determined by the size of endowments, the prospective student will try to learn how the college receives its support. Very few people will give a second thought to a school which is not accredited, but this matter should certainly not be overlooked. Size and location are important, but these are problems of individual taste and judgment. Finally, the cost of tuition, living expenses, supplies, and other essentials must be given some thought, along with the possibilities of a scholarship grant if necessary. Only when he has considered each of these subjects carefully is the student ready to make a wise choice of college.

The writer here might seem much more gifted in composition ability than the author of the original version. But this is not true. The author of this revised and improved version and the author of the original are the same person! Obviously in a few days' time he had learned something about the construction of paragraphs.

Here is another piece of writing from the first assignment.

Several factors have contributed to the use of musical interests of the past decade. The most notable being in the technical branch. Radio has been (and is being) widely exploited as a means of providing musical entertainment, for nearly everywhere you go, there is a radio. Also in this field is the phonograph, which has been improved greatly in the past few years. Probably the development which has most influenced the serious listener of music is the long-playing record. Before this invention, listening to records was hampered by the interruptions occurring when a record must be turned over, or a different record started. An ever-increasing number of musicals have been produced in Hollywood recently, and Broadway is never without its hit musical shows such as *Kismet* and *Pajama Game.* Even the harsh medium of television has been used to present musical plays and operas in the past year. Those are the major reasons for the increase of interest in music.

Attacking this paragraph co-operatively, students agreed that though it was generally poor, it was not altogether hopeless. In the paragraph as a whole a thought was available to them, although the first, and, presumably, the topic sentence was meaningless. They realized at once that the major failure here is that of vocabulary rather than of thought: "the use of musical *interests*," "radio has been *exploited*," "the *harsh* medium of television." Nevertheless, the class approved the unity of the piece and saw also that the problem of coherence was solved somewhat automatically by the means of development which the topic sentence demanded, that is, naming the "contributing factors." Students then observed at once the sentence fragment and the unnecessary punctuation, went on to attest the general correctness of what the author says, though noticing that he had omitted important musical activities, and then made their suggestions for improved rhetoric. This is what resulted from the oral reconstruction.

Interest in music has been growing rapidly during the past decade, largely because of improved methods of presentation and reproduction. Radio has been providing universal musical entertainment, for radios are everywhere. Another contributing factor, the phonograph, has been made consistently better in the past few years. The serious listener gladly welcomed the development of the long-playing record, because, before this invention, listening to records was hampered by the interruptions occurring when a record had to be turned over or a different record started. An ever-increasing number of both light and serious musicals have been produced in Hollywood recently, and Broadway is never without its hit musical shows, such as *Kismet* and *Pajama Game.* For audiences of more serious tastes there are always many concerts and recitals. Even the highly-commercialized medium of television has been used to present musical plays and operas during the past year. All of these activities have greatly increased the pleasure of listening to music in America.

Though this new paragraph represents a marked advance over the original, my students were still not satisfied with it, and for the very best reason of all. They felt that it was "jerky," and when I pressed them to explain what they meant, they said that, upon reading it, one could tell that it had not been written by one person but by a number of persons. In short, they had learned for themselves that though the discussion and correction of paragraphs can be a co-operative enterprise, the successful writing of them cannot. A paragraph must be written out of the experience, intelligence, and sensibility of one human being, for no group of people can do his thinking for him or go on to order his thought in the firm structural outlines of a good paragraph. The re-formed paragraphs which they came up with always dissatisfied them finally; for they were learning the lesson basic to an understanding of what good prose is, the organic relation of thought and language. "Thought and speech are inseparable from each other; matter and expression are parts of one: style is a thinking out into language," John Henry Newman told us in *The Idea of a University*. My juniors learned this practically, out of their own experience.

Here is a paragraph which they rejected as being virtually meaningless, too confused in its thinking for rewriting.

In this argument the author is referring to federal scholarships. These scholarships would be given to qualified high school graduates, according to need for college training. Since there is lack of space, the author will only attempt to mention the main points. First of all, many of the present scholarships are negligible. They average only two hundred and seventeen dollars apiece. Obviously that amount is not going to help a person who can't afford to spend any money for college. Also, we must give equal opportunities to the smartest people for their benefit and also for ours. For every smart person in college there is one person who hasn't got the resources to attend college. Some people who are not as smart as these people are in college because their parents make enough money. If colleges are forced to admit students on a basis of wealth rather than on academic standards, then an intellectual aristocracy will result. This situation only increases the serious shortage of technicians and scientists necessary in our turbulent world. The best thing that the United States can do is to set up a program of federal scholarships and thereby improve the American academic standards.

Here, on the other hand, is one which students were inclined to leave almost as the author wrote it.

Short-wave listening is an entertaining and educational hobby. It is usually practiced by a prospective "ham," or radio amateur, who is learning Morse code and radio procedure in order to obtain a license. Furthermore, he probably also listens to talking "hams" to learn their various styles of patter, for it is interesting to note the different accents and phraseology of "hams" from many sections of the country. Radio amateurs do not constitute all of short-wave radio, however. To the layman it is a thrilling experience to tune in commercial stations from the other side of the world. The simpler receiver can "pull in" the BBC and usually will be able to get Mexico or Venezuela. Of course many times the reception will be in a foreign language, but most countries have English broadcasts beamed at the United States at one time or another. An average set can receive the English propaganda broadcasts from Moscow, which are very interesting and sometimes amusingly ridiculous. With a little effort one can pick up countries as far away as Australia or Japan. Short-wave truly brings the world to your ears.

There are weaknesses here, but the students could see the rounded development of an idea stated clearly and comprehensively in the opening sentence. They observed the use of details and examples, the coherent means whereby the paragraph moves, with a fair degree of smoothness, from point to point, and the sense of style which brings the paragraph to a natural and at the same time artful conclusion. It was a fairly easy task to travel onward from their approval of this paragraph and their rejection of the preceding one to a rudimentary though fairly precise notion of what skill in composition is. To clinch the matter, we did similar co-operative laboratory work on paragraphs from a few pieces of effective modern writing, expository paragraphs not by literary stylists but simply by successful professional writers like John Gunther, Elmer Davis, and Corey Ford. Students had access to a pocket-book selection of modern expository essays, and from them we took paragraphs which we broke down for evidence of the very characteristics of good organization and construction seldom found in the student work. The comparison did not discourage my juniors, however, but rather made them want to try for the same kind of effectiveness. A good paragraph was no longer a mystery.

They were ready then for the next assignment in theme writing, and when the results came in this time, the hour for the teacher was not nearly so dark.

7

The Teaching of English Composition

G. C. WATERSTON, *Brooks School, North Andover, Massachusetts*

The suggestions which I am going to make this afternoon about the teaching of English composition may strike you at first as too narrow in scope. So I would like to say at once that I am aware of some of the limitations of the method I shall outline and I am going to state them briefly in a moment or two. I also hope to be able to show, as I go on, that it is quite possible to produce great things from little things and I shall suggest that a restrictive method does not necessarily lead to restricted results.

Since time is limited I am going to talk about some aspects of English composition only, beginning with those which concern expository writing, but going on to show that concentration on this kind of writing does not at all exclude *creativity* in the common or garden sense of the term. Since we are all teachers here, I am going to be even more selective and abstract those elements of English prose writing which I consider most suitable for sheer teaching in the narrow sense. I am going to leave unspoken some of my most earnest sentiments about all sorts of indispensable classroom factors—factors such as encouragement, inspiration, and a general friendly rapport with the students without which I am quite convinced most teaching would be sterile. I know you are all convinced of this too, and therefore there is no point in my wasting these few minutes preaching to the already converted. I hope you will believe, as I talk about teaching from the head rather than from the heart, that I am nonetheless very far from thinking that we can do without the urgency, the vitality, and the enthusiasm which produce good art—and if English prose composition is not an art then what is it?—but these elements, though they can be *communicated* by good teachers, cannot, in the sense I am thinking of, be taught. Indeed, if it were not for the fact that all art is dependent upon form and structure of some sort I sometimes wonder if any of the arts could be taught at all.

Once you have persuaded your students that form and structure are necessary—a strangely difficult point to make clear—I think it does not matter very much what *particular* form you choose for their first essays. I think it also follows that it does not very much matter where you begin so long as you start with something definite and familiar and stick to it until it is understood and developed as far as it will go. Within these limits the choice can be quite arbitrary.

I happen to have acquired most of my experience in grades ten through twelve, though I have taught classes of varying degrees of ability in all grades from the eighth upwards. As a result, what I have to say will concern the teaching of pupils who have, in general, been exposed to one kind of structure, namely sentence structure. At least they understand (and if they don't I go over it again with them) that a sentence consists of three parts: subject, verb, and predicate. These constitute a rough structural representation of the process of cause and effect going on in the world we observe with our senses, and they also constitute a rough scheme of what goes on inside us when we organize that world in our minds. Many of the pitfalls, both formal and informal, in sentence structure are familiar to students at this level through their study of grammar. Furthermore, they know that of the three parts of the sentence, each is capable of almost infinite modification, by adjectives, adverbs, clauses, and the rest, so that every sentence can be made to branch out and flower like a fruit tree. Thus each student who has made some study of grammar can be made to see that out of a simple basic structure there can grow an almost infinite variety.

Now grammar has no other purpose but to lead into rhetoric and logic. If complex sentences can be made to grow in power and beauty out of the single simple structure of cause and effect expressed as subject, verb, and predicate, there are also structures of structures—which we call compositions—and which are governed by similar principles. A theme should consist of a sequence of ideas of a very elementary nature which bear upon one another in the same way that the parts of a sentence do, and which, like the parts of a sentence, are capable of modification and amplification to an almost infinite degree.

In order to illustrate this point I have found it convenient to start my classes writing themes which are syllogistic in structure. This is purely arbitrary and I always explain to my classes, as I hasten to explain to you, that this is by no means the only way to write a theme. The point is that it is *a* way of writing a theme that has an *easily recognizable structure* and which therefore is *teachable* to beginners.

Nevertheless, one must be careful not to overteach it and drift too far into the rigors of formal logic. While I am on this point, I must make one of several digressions which I am going to permit myself to say that I think grammar itself is often overtaught and that it is often confused with the rules of correct usage. We sometimes obscure the basic structural elements with the profusion of "do's" and "don'ts" which we inject into them. The College Board does not approve of our saying "For he's a jolly good fellow, which nobody can deny," since this makes use of an unrelated "which," and I am sure it would censure Macbeth for saying "Lay on Macduff! And damned be him who first cries hold enough!" Such points have their importance in the general scheme of things, but they seem to me to be subordinate to principles of general sentence structure which ought to be in the forefront of our minds. By the same token I do not wish you to think that I would recommend the introduction of a full-blown course in logic at the tenth-grade level except to introduce the student to the pattern of logical structure. I maintain that anyone can recognize the structure of a syllogism and see what it is intended to do. For a beginner in composition looking for a handy framework for his ideas this is almost as much as he needs to know. To be sure, formal, informal, and semantic fallacies run through every kind of syllogistic thinking and writing, but it is easy to keep the general consciousness of this fact alive in the student's mind. It is not necessary to labor the point at this stage. As I stand here I do not think I know, myself, what a syllogism in the mood of Barbara is and I certainly do not teach it to my classes. For my purposes the syllogism is nothing but a formal framework for a theme. If there are any logicians in the house and if this seems shocking to them I can only apologize. To return.

In practice I follow more or less the following procedure: after quite a cursory explanation of what a syllogism is, or ought to be, some fun with logical fallacies and absurd syllogisms and a little bit of practice in diagramming syllogisms on the board—certainly not more than three class periods in all—I take a few subjects of the sort usually assigned to debating teams. I start with relatively simple propositions such as, "Work and pleasure are never identical," or "The study of foreign languages should be abolished," or "The school should be run by and for the students," and move on to more complex topics such as "War is a biological necessity," or "Materialism is the Achilles' heel of our society." Needless to say if this happens to be a class which has been nurtured on themes such as "Small Boat Sailing" or "Why I Like the the Summer Vacation," these subjects usually appall it to start with. I therefore begin with a general discussion of the topic in which anybody may join and everybody usually does, though I often find myself contributing most of the leading ideas. Whenever a point is raised or a strong argument comes up I make a note of it on the board in full view of the class. Eventually there is a sufficient body of ideas so that everyone feels that there is something to write about. The advantage of the initial debate is that it sometimes generates a certain amount of heat, and strong feelings one way or the other help to develop the incentive to prove oneself right on paper.

The ideas on the board appear in the order in which they have been suggested; in other words they form a sort of compost heap—rotting, chaotic, but fertile. I find it important to remind the class that the random meanderings of a "bull session" are formless and without structure and that the language is also informal and probably unsuitable to the final theme. The problem, therefore, is not (as schoolboys usually think) "to find something to write about" but to give coherence to a more or less chaotic flood of ideas.

When there is enough on the board, I invite someone to invent a very simple syllogism, however outrageous in its bald implications, into which the ideas might be fitted. Of course a great many of the ones suggested have to be discarded, either because they cannot be made to include enough of the ideas or because they lead to conclusions which everyone feels are false. In the end something workable is invented. On the Work and Pleasure theme, for example, a boy suggested the following and planned his theme around it:

> Only creative, original work is pleasure.
> Menial tasks are not original or creative.
> Therefore menial tasks are not pleasurable.

As soon as a satisfactory syllogism has been discovered by each boy or by the class as a whole, I assign a theme calling for five paragraphs: a general introduction which states the topic and defines some of the important terms (a process which must be taught and which I shall describe later), a development of the major premise, a development of the minor premise (preferably in this order), a development of the conclusion of the syllogism, and a general conclusion or summary.

The results of these early exercises are always stiff and discouragingly clumsy.

At this point one is usually tempted to give the whole thing up as a bad job. However, experience has convinced me that the experiment is worth pursuing to a more advanced stage.

In case this stubbornness demands an explanation I should like to digress again for a moment and revert to a few of the ideas which I hinted at in the beginning of this talk. Structure—structure of any sort—is the thing which nearly all my pupils, when I first get them, completely ignore. They ignore it to the point of having only the very vaguest idea of what the teacher means by the term. They are puzzled and dismayed when they are criticized for failing to impose some sort of structure on their thoughts, and, as a rule, they have not the very faintest idea of how to set about achieving and manipulating a formal structure. Often they are irked by a defect for which, though they receive abundant criticism, yet they can foresee no remedy. Provided, therefore, they are constantly forewarned that a syllogistic structure is by no means the only sort of coherence which can be given to a piece of writing, they can usually be persuaded to be thankful for small mercies in that here at least there is something they can get their teeth into and work at until they achieve some degree of mastery.

So, in the early stages, I do not let myself be too dismayed by the poverty and the stiffness with which the average boy handles this medium and I am rather careful not to discourage the pupils by too severe a criticism. Anyone who achieves anything remotely resembling a syllogism gets some sort of credit in terms of grades.

After three or four practice themes of this kind on relatively simple topics, we go on to the next step.

If, at this point, we approach a more complicated topic such as, "War is a biological necessity," it often happens that, after the subject has been discussed and while syllogisms are being called for to cover the notes on the board, someone will come forward with an atrocious sentiment such as:

To reduce the population is biologically necessary.
War reduces the population.
Therefore war is biologically necessary.

"But," someone will hasten to point out, "War is not the only factor that reduces the population, and what do we mean when we say that the reduction of the population is *biologically* necessary?" At this juncture I usually ask whether the major and minor premises of a syllogism are ever incontrovertibly true, or whether, rather, this truth is not a merely relative matter, dependent upon assumptions which are fixed only in appearance, but which in reality cry out for infinitely careful and balanced modification and redefinition, just as the subject, verb, and predicate of a sentence are capable of infinite modification and therefore of relatively greater precision. I go on to show that the theme as a whole is nothing more nor less than a process of pushing modification to the ultimate extreme which the prescribed length of the theme permits, and that the aim of this kind of expository theme should be to give the right proportion, order, and emphasis to the greatest number of factors affecting the original syllogism.

Several new elements of this kind of writing now emerge. First of all, from the mass of ideas (on the board or on scratch paper) the writer must make up his mind what his final conclusion is to be.

Then he would do well to write his introduction. If I have not already done so, I call for a short exercise in which only the introduction and the conclusion are actually developed on paper and the intermediate syllogistic paragraphs are written in as bare propositions. This makes it easier for the writer to go in a straight line of reasoning from point to point and impresses upon him the fact that a well-written introduction and conclusion may give cogency to an otherwise mediocre argument. We shall see later that, under some conditions, the argument may be allowed to wither away completely. Next he must devise a raw basic syllogism into which he thinks he can conveniently group the greatest number of important modifying factors. Lastly he must have some idea of the relative importance in terms of proportion and emphasis which he wants to give to these ideas so that they may hang together naturally.

To assist the movement of the argument, it is vital to consider the small connective words in the language, words such as *yet, to be sure, however, furthermore, but,* and the rest. As an oral exercise I often have boys recite a list of such connectives alone, leaving silent spaces between them and making suitable forensic gestures and altering their tone of voice to suggest that an entire speech is being made. If you have a couple of good actors in the class this can be an amusing piece of mimicry. It illustrates the point that a sort of sense can be achieved with connectives alone and that connectives are vital if the words of a theme are to be made to crackle *toward* their target instead of meandering away from it.

Now, or possibly earlier, is the time to explain that the basic syllogism which the student has struggled so hard to achieve should not be apparent on the surface of the theme at all. It should not knock the reader's eye out, indeed he should not be conscious of it. It should be a concealed weapon, not a club. It can be concealed by a flow of words so contrived that they appear inevitable and facile because of the latent structure, and in consequence carry conviction and give clarity and coherence. To the extent that boys at this stage are capable of style I tell them that clarity is the essential ingredient. This should be the clarity of a perfect pane of glass which does not in any way call attention to itself but simply serves as a medium so transparent that it reveals the underlying thought.

A theme of this kind now becomes an immensely more complicated structure in which the interaction of every part counts. Even the affective elements, metaphors, imagery, epithets and the emotive values of the words must be subtly articulated. It becomes, in fact, a work of art, a unit in which the parts should, if the ideal were to be attained, be indistinguishable except to the trained eye.

This is difficult advice to follow but I have found, and I think that some of my pupils might agree, that with a basic pattern of some sort they gain confidence and have more incentive to write well.

From time to time we all have difficulty in finding suitable subjects for themes. I know I do. A theme is always just another exercise to our pupils; and because it is just a practice run, it is difficult for anyone to get wildly excited about the subject. To some extent, however, themes suggest themselves in class. Have you ever had any of your pupils complain that Conrad's *Lord Jim* is an unnecessarily confusing book because "Any writer who uses so many flashbacks and so many narrators is bound to be confusing"? There is some truth in the contention, as Conrad would have been the first to admit, but as a premise it cries aloud for all sorts of modifications, and the modifications lend themselves to a theme of the sort we have been considering.

It was an unsuccessful experiment with this very topic which led me to believe that a syllogistic structure might help my students to write more coherent book reports in which, instead of the usual insipid plot summary, they would take a central argument about the book in question and group the details around it. I usually have to contribute this central idea myself. For example, after a boy has read *A Farewell to Arms,* I usually suggest that he read also *The Old Man and the Sea* and the short story "The Undefeated" from *Men without Women.* I then propose a syllogism which would run something like this:

One of the characteristics of a great writer is that he suggests that the human spirit can survive mere physical disaster.
Hemingway suggests that the human spirit can survive mere disaster.
Therefore Hemingway possesses one of the characteristics of a great writer.

Such a framework gives the student ample opportunity to comment on the salient points of Hemingway's style—its toughness, its precision, its concern for brute fact and terse dialogue—and yet to show that it is the genius of Hemingway to open perspectives which transcend these facts. To show how he does this demands detailed knowledge of the books.

So now I come to the last step which the boys must be called upon to make. Basically this step confronts them with one of the most ancient of human paradoxes, the fact that the human mind is equipped not only to perpetrate its own generalizations but to enumerate and evaluate the sense data which give rise to these generalizations. It would be rash to say that it can do these two operations simultaneously, but the speed with which the mind executes this sort of shuttle service is to all intents and purposes instantaneous. Deduction and induction ebb and flow perpetually. If this is true of the mind it should be true of the written word.

I have mentioned earlier the necessity for definition of terms in the introductory part of the theme, but the process of definition is very seldom properly understood and is one of the most difficult which confronts the student. If, as some wit once said, it is true that a syllogism proceeds from preconceived opinions to foregone conclusions, then an argument of this sort is fully convincing only if something is done to justify the preconception. Thus the process of defining is often found to be very much akin to the process of introducing supporting evidence—that is, after all, one way of defining. Now, as soon as you begin to introduce supporting evidence you have to abandon the deductive method, at least for the time being. You inject inductive arguments into the syllogistic structure. Since this involves the description of sense data, it may well turn out that a piece of expository writing will involve long passages of description or even of narration. In extreme cases the descriptive elements may absorb the entire composition so that the implied syllogism is suppressed just as any climax may be suppressed for more telling effect. As a result the syllogistic method which I have just outlined opens the doors to a much wider perspective. To be complete, a theme which has a syllogistic structure must include supporting passages of which the structure is inductive. A very practiced writer may then abandon the explicit argument or reduce it to the smallest possible proportions.

You will see that I am considering definition and description as if they were one and the same thing. It would probably be truer to

say that description is *one kind* of definition, but I like to identify the
two because I find that students at the levels we are considering have
very little idea about defining other than to rush straight for the
nearest Webster's dictionary. How many themes do you get that
start with the words "According to Webster——"?

Now the trouble with this is that what the reader needs to know
about the writer and, above all, what the writer needs to know about
himself is how he, the writer, is going to use the terms in question.
Webster has nothing to do with it. The writer must reveal his own
mind a little bit and show that he recognizes within himself, rightly
or wrongly, certain assumptions, and that he is honest enough and
aware enough of himself to make those assumptions explicit instead
of following them blindly and expecting the reader to do so. He
should be able to bring his assumptions to the surface instead of har-
boring them somewhere in his subconscious. He should bring the
evidence for these assumptions to the sensuous mind of his reader.
There may be many ways of defining but they all amount to acts of
honest introspection. To rely on Noah Webster is an act of cowardice
in this context. . .

Boys who started off their school year struggling with a theme of
which the premises are:

Only creative original work is pleasure.
Menial tasks are not original or creative.

can easily see from this example that, for the purposes of their theme,
definition need not and should not be the narrow dictionary task
which they usually imagine. It may be the open sesame to a whole
new field of the mind and "definition by evidence" may become the
most creative part of a composition and may by its power eliminate
altogether the necessity for subsequent deductive arguments by presenting the assumptions so vividly in terms of their living causes that
the conclusion can be left unspoken.

How many of us teach an approach to poetry at the same time as
we teach English composition? Most of us, I suspect. It is one of the
baffling things about most English courses that they are supposed to
cover a little of everything. If you start with the sonnet, as is so often
the practice, may I suggest that your syllogism also helps to open
this door? Run through the corpus of Shakespeare's sonnets and you

will find that at least half a dozen of them have a "When . . . when
. . . then" structure, and where this structure is not explicit it is often
implied. It is very easy to show that we have here a syllogistic structure and that the sonnet form is made to its measure. The major
premise and the minor premise fall into the first two quatrains, which
are so closely allied in thought that, in many sonnets, the rhyme
scheme is contrived to weld these two parts together into an octave.
Then comes the pause or waist of the sonnet (a kind of intellectual
caesura) as the poem gathers itself together for the movement into
the concluding quatrain followed by the clinching couplet, where
again the rhyme scheme may be devised to link both into closer relationship as a sestet.

Before I lapse into silence, then, let me give you one example to
show the emotional and imaginative scope of which our allegedly
restrictive syllogism is capable:

> When I consider every thing that grows
> Holds in perfection but a little moment,
> That this huge stage presenteth nought but shows
> Whereon the stars in secret influence comment;
>
> When I perceive that men as plants increase,
> Cheer'd and checked even by the self-same sky,
> Vaunt in their youthful sap, at height decrease,
> And wear their brave state out of memory;
>
> Then the conceit of this inconstant stay
> Sets you most rich in youth before my sight,
> Where wasteful Time debateth with Decay,
> To change your day of youth to sullied night;
>
> And all in war with Time for love of you,
> As he takes from you, I engraft you new.[1]

[1] William Shakespeare, *Sonnet XV*.

8

Writing and Thinking

HAROLD C. MARTIN, *Harvard University*

At the second Yale Conference on the Teaching of English, in 1956, two gifted teachers described and, by implication, argued the superiority of diametrically opposed procedures in the teaching of composition. Although each, I have little doubt, would have admitted virtues in the proposal advanced by the other, the two programs, as I read them in the report of that Conference, do represent very different assumptions about the purpose of such teaching and therefore about the intellectual and emotional needs of students. The first to speak, Mr. Waterston, of the Brooks School at Andover, showed very impressively how a basic logical structure, the syllogism, could be used to discipline students' habits of exposition and to direct their scrutiny and appreciation of works of literature. The second, Professor Sewall, of Yale, gave equally convincing evidence that daily writing of almost any kind could produce equivalent results if that writing was supported by occasional instruction in principles of rhetoric and by a few discerning comments on each piece of writing presented. It is true, of course, that Mr. Waterston was speaking about teaching composition to students several years younger than Professor Sewall dealt with, and a case can be made—if you want to make it—for subscribing to both methods but insisting that what works best for the fourteen-year-old works less well, or not at all, for the young man of twenty, and that the twenty-year-old student responds healthily to a procedure which would neither satisfy nor help the downy-cheeked boy. There is, in fact, corroboration for such a resolution in that wise book by Alfred North Whitehead, *The Aims of Education*.[1] In his chapter on the "rhythm of education," Whitehead argues that, in his use of language, the high school student is avid of fáct and order, that he has an almost biological need for categorization and for the accumulation of minutiae; as he comes out of the shell of adolescence, Whitehead suggests, his desires and nervous capacities change: he wishes, and needs, to explore widely, to stretch his mind on the rack of the improbable, the mysterious, the cosmic. What I can remember from years of teaching junior high school and high school English and what I daily observe about the undergraduate and graduate students I now teach leads me to accept Whitehead's hypotheses about cyclic rhythms in education as among the most valuable generalizations in modern pedagogy. It might seem, therefore, that I am committed this morning to accept what was ably said two years ago and retire, or to propose a kind of Hegelian transformation of Whitehead's cyclic theory, describing the opposing sides of the cycle as thesis and antithesis and coming up with a synthesis of my own, a sort of "higher" compositional formula which is a result of the merging of the two others I have mentioned.

Obviously I do not plan to retire. And I must confess that I do not see how a meaningful synthesis of the Waterston-Sewall polarities can be reached without sacrificing the principal values of each. What I shall do instead is propose a particular function for the teaching of composition and argue that, for the last year or two of high school and for the first years, at least, of college, it is best served by scrupulous attention to the rigors of ordered thinking—to logic, if you will.

The particular function of the teaching of composition in these years, I believe, is that of stabilizing the student's world rather than that of reproducing, or expressing his sensations in it. The very young man, the very young woman, has begun a romance with the universe, and he is certainly entitled to it; at the same time, he has to finance the romance while it goes on and if it ends successfully, to capitalize it later. To change the figure, though he leap like Antaeus, he gets his strength for leaping from his contacts with the ground. Explicitly, then, the teaching of composition should work in these years, I believe,

---

[1] Alfred North Whitehead, *The Aims of Education* (New York, The Macmillan Co., 1949).

as a constant check against excess and as a constant consolidator of experience.

To fulfill that function, the teaching of composition must be anything but passive. The assignment of writing exercises in the fashion of an inventory-taking at the corner grocery—now an argument, now a description, now a character sketch, now a definition; second shelf, peas, beans, two bags of precis, four plot-summaries, an anecdote, and ten cans of hash—such a procedure is both tedious and sterile. Whatever comes out of it is largely incidental to the apparent intention of the assignment; whatever goes into it is a tribute to students' capacity to rise above assignments, whether out of love for teacher, fear of the parental rod, or just simple self-respect. What I have in mind is something very different from that.

For the energetic and groping mind, writing should be, first of all, a matter of inquiry—of inquiry in the sense both of reminiscence and of exploration. By exploration, I mean the looking into corners, the peering under shelf paper, the ransacking of all the bureau drawers of possibility in a given subject of speculation. By reminiscence, I mean not that languid simmering in the tepid bath of one's own half-remembered sensations of pleasure and of pain, but the earnest and remorseless investigation of one's whole response to the subject of speculation. After inquiry, and growing out of it, will come expression, communication, rhetoric. The two, I hear you saying, are inseparable: the form is the content, and the content, the form. That seems to me, even in literary criticism, either a half-truth or a misleading statement, at best; but I need not argue the point here, for we are dealing, as teachers of composition, not with the work of art but with the artist himself, even if in embryo. What concerns us is the best—or, at least, a good—means of directing that embryonic artist, that remaker of experience into words and forms suitable only to his perception of the experience.

Now the immediate consequence of putting inquiry ahead of expression and of pressing the student unrelentingly to push against the barriers of his own thought is almost always a considerable degree of frustration for the writer and a considerable amount of turgid prose for the reader. At the teacher's insistence the student struggles blindly against enemies he does not recognize and for the achievement of a fleece which has been described to him as golden but which he has probably never had more than a glimpse of. If he is clever, he will cheat by aping the manners and language of those he thinks privy to the wisdom he is after; and the teacher's first responsibility, once he has started the knight-errant out on his quest, is to keep him from being clever. His next duty is to pick the fallen warrior up after each tumble, brush him off, tell him he almost got the dragon that time, and remind him of what he set out to do in the first place. The difference between romance and fact, a harsh difference, is that the dragons keep coming to life or growing new heads and that the fleece captured today is only cotton wool by tomorrow morning. There isn't any "happily ever after" in writing; there is only a growing skill in the use of the weapons of penetration and of defense and the confidence of knowing that what you have done once you can do again.

Like abstraction, metaphor is often the convenient shield for loose thinking, baseless claims, and vain expostulation. Before this audience, at least, I shall need to get down to cases. How is such an inquiry to be initiated? What subjects serve its purposes? What are the weapons of penetration and defense? The answer can best be given, I think, in the form of illustrations supported by commentary.

A class session begins from one of the *Meditations* of John Donne. The teacher calls attention to a part of one sentence concerning human activity during the ascendency of the Dogstar. Then he asks a question:

"Johnson, what do you make of that statement?"

"It's nonsense—superstition."

"The two are the same, nonsense and superstition?"

"Well, yes, roughly the same."

"All superstition is nonsense and all nonsense is superstition?"

"Well, I'm not sure about the second, but all superstition is nonsense, I think that's true."

"But not all nonsense is superstition?"

"No, maybe not."

"The words are not synonymous, then? If not, then how do you relate them?"

"Nonsense is bigger than superstition. Superstition is a kind of nonsense."

"So. We will put the word *nonsense* up here and draw a diagonal down to the word *superstition*. Now, what are some other kinds of nonsense."

(Silence)

"Will someone else name other kinds of nonsense?"

(Silence)

"Johnson, we need your help again. You used the word: what does *nonsense* mean?"

"It's anything that doesn't make sense."

"Not a very useful definition since I assume that we all know what *non* means. Can you provide something more helpful?"

"Anything that goes against reason."

"Good enough. What other things 'go against reason'?"

"Magic, for instance."

"Then magic and superstition are alike in kind, just as Baldwins and Greenings are alike in both being apples?"

"Yes."

Now a second student enters the conversation.

"No. Magic is what superstitious people believe in, so they can't be the same in kind."

"You'd like to change Johnson's word *thing* to *belief*, apparently: superstition is a belief contrary to reason. Is that your definition?"

"Yes."

"How, then, do you account for Donne's saying what he says in this sentence? Is he deliberately professing to believe what his reason tells him isn't true?"

"Probably not what *his* reason tells him isn't true, but what *mine* does."

"That is, Donne was superstitious because he believed what your reason tells you is not true?"

"It isn't just me. The facts show he was wrong."

"What facts?"

"All of them—astronomy. Everyone knows that astrology is false."

"How does everyone know it?"

"That's what we've been taught by the people who are supposed to know."

"And if they turn out to be wrong?"

"Then I suppose a hundred years from now someone would call me superstitious."

"Am I to understand that a man is never thought superstitious in his own time?"

"Oh, sure, we have a hired man on our farm who won't light a match during a thunderstorm. I think he's superstitious."

"Why?"

"Because he seems to think that lighting a match attracts lightning. He may not really believe it, because other people light matches just to bother him, but he won't do it himself. He says he won't take a chance on it."

"Would you call this a belief?"

"No. I'd say it was a sort of attitude."

"What kind of attitude?"

"Being afraid. Without knowing what he's really afraid of."

"A superstition, then can be a belief contrary to reason or an attitude of fearfulness without known cause, one or the other or both?"

"Both."

"Is it enough that a belief should be irrational for it to be superstitious—the belief that the earth was flat, for instance, in the fifteenth century?"

"Oh, I see. You mean, superstition is irrational belief *based on* some attitude."

"Is that what you mean? If so, on the attitude of fearfulness? and, if so, would you say, Johnson, that Donne is superstitious?"

"Maybe not. If he wasn't afraid, then I suppose he wasn't superstitious—about that, anyway. Maybe he was just saying what everyone accepted without thinking about it."

At this point, let me stop for some comment. What has gone on so far may take, not the three minutes I have used, but ten or twenty, of course. And such a procedure is sure to enlist not two or three but ten or a dozen students, and it is sure to run off on tangents unless the instructor remains completely in control. What is the purpose? Surely not to arrive at a definition, for that could be done more efficiently and more simply by reference to a dictionary. One purpose, quite obviously, is to make definition seem important, to make it become not the process of "looking up the word in a dictionary" but that of thinking the matter through. A second, and less obvious one, perhaps, is to suggest a method. The dialogue is a dramatic rehearsal of an activity of mind, an activity in which one part of the mind—the impulsive, the suggestive—is represented by the students' quick answers, and another part—the resistive and reflective—is represented by the teacher's interrogative objections and summations.

Now even in this simple stage of inquiry, two important lessons in writing can be taught. The first concerns emphasis and control of interest; the second concerns the strategy of development. If, at the end of the dialogue, you put the definition on the board and ask students what would follow in an essay which began with the definition, you direct their attention toward a deductive process leading from the initial proposition to its applications and consequences. If, on the other hand, you begin where the dialogue began—with the statement, "In the middle of one of his meditations on sickness and the order of nature, Donne speaks of the influence of the Dogstar"—if you begin with

that kind of sentence, you direct the students' attention not to demonstration but to inquiry, to a speculation whose effectiveness will derive
from its being a stylized enactment of the mental process itself. Moreover, the dialectical method already used orally will provide him with
the apparatus for conducting that speculation. Naturally he will not
use the alternation of question and answer; instead he will convert the
answers into proposals and the questions into objections and counter-
proposals. Instead of running on without direction, he can use the apparatus that lay under the dialogue—that of definition, for the most
part: class and subclass; genus and differentiae.

What you do not want, of course, is a bare-bone reduction to that
apparatus, for the point is to make apparatus serve the writing, not
writing serve apparatus. This, for example, is the kind of perversion
you must anticipate:

In the middle of one of his meditations on sickness and the order of nature,
Donne speaks of the influence of the Dogstar. This might suggest that he
was superstitious, but what is superstition? Is it the same as nonsense? No,
it is a belief in something that isn't true. There are two kinds of belief in
something that isn't true. Some people believe because that is what everyone else believes. This is not superstition. Other people believe something
because they are afraid of what they don't know. This second kind is
superstitious. Donne believed in the Dogstar because everyone else believed
in it in his time. But he may have been afraid of what it could do to him
also. So he may or may not have been superstitious.

Now bad as that little essay is, I prefer it to this one:

In the middle of one of his meditations on sickness and the order of nature,
Donne speaks of the influence of the Dogstar. Such ideas were current in
his time, and when people call them superstitious they are just showing that
they have an advantage that Donne didn't have. No one should refer to
another man's belief as superstitious because everyone has some reason
for thinking the way he does. Donne's reason for thinking that the Dogstar
could influence lives was the belief in astrology in his time. Now that we
have astronomy, we no longer believe in the influence of the stars. If we
did, we would be superstitious, but not Donne because that was the belief
in his time, as I said above. If we are afraid of anything, we may be superstitious ourselves without knowing it.

My guess, if I had no other evidence, would be that the mind of the
second writer is better than that of the first, but it is certainly less well

used. That is to say, without the apparatus, the first writer would almost certainly write worse; with it, the second writer might very well bring order out of chaos and even make effective use of the wasted last sentence.

In the middle of one of his meditations on sickness and the order of nature, Donne speaks of the influence of the Dogstar. In a man as reasonable and thoughtful as Donne, this allusion strikes us as strangely superstitious. But it is important to realize that faith in astrology was common in Donne's time and that his remark would seem to any of his readers entirely sensible and even factual. We have good reason now to know that stars do not influence human destiny and that his statement is, therefore, false. But a statement may be false without being superstitious. If what men believe on the basis of the best evidence they have available turns out to be wrong, they can justly be accused of error. We can accuse them of superstition, however, only if their belief is the result of fear and runs contrary to the evidence they have. It is fear, especially fear of the unknown, that is the distinguishing characteristic of superstition, and if we look closely at the matters about which we have little solid knowledge today we may discover that our own beliefs are often characterized not by what we know but by what we don't know at all and are afraid may be true.

Here we have three paragraphs written at the conclusion of the dialogue I have recounted. With them in duplicated form for the next class meeting, we can take another step. By one means or another, these paragraphs should now be used to show (1) that a dialectical activity of mind can provide a ready scheme for writing, (2) that it "leads" its reader most effectively if it is not entirely bare, (3) that its happiest termination is in a question about relevance: "What means this to thee and me?" The first and third paragraphs follow the dialectical process; the second and third raise the question of relevance; the first is bone bare, the second disordered, the third perhaps somewhat prolix. What comes next? Obviously, the process of inquiry demands an extension of the possibility raised at the end of paragraphs two and three. Where will you look? At all the stuff about the thirteenth floor, black cats, and the waning of the moon? Whose speculation is this anyway? Are *you* frightened by a cracked mirror or salt spilled at table? If not, by what?

One place to look, then, is at the fears you really do have. But there are so many and the causes are so various that the search looks uninviting. Where else to look? The definition provides two leads: *fear* of the *unknown*. If fears are too complex to give you a start, try the unknowns. What was unknown to Donne? Not the stars certainly, and not the human events which he was describing, but the relationship. What about the relationship? How was it different from other relationships toward which he paid no such attention?—between eating too much and getting a stomach-ache, for instance. It will take only a few questions to elicit the useful answer—that the relationship between the Dogstar and men's lives is a mysterious one. The influence of the Dogstar is not to be doubted: tradition says that it exists; religious and secular literature, including that of medicine, use it as an assumption; and one has oneself seen otherwise inexplicable happenings during its ascendancy. But how it exists, no man knows. The body of knowledge is there, it is accepted, but its workings are beyond analysis. That is why the influence inspires fear. What relationships in your own life, then, do you accept even though you know of no rational means of explaining them?

You now have the student where you want him: he is completely at sea. Or, better, if he is sensitive, he is at the edge of the abyss. How can you get him to look down; how to venture along the edge while he looks; how to shine the flashlight of his scrutiny into the blackness of his own mind? You don't want him to jump in, and you don't want him to back away or turn around. You must, therefore, take him by the hand. More questions: how is it that, if one ignorant man is a menace to wise policy, a multitude of ignorant men make wise policy a certainty (a superstition of democracy)? If overpopulation is already a problem in underdeveloped countries, why is it desirable to raise the standard of living in them (a humanitarian superstition)? If intelligence is innate and constant, why is universal education desirable (an educational superstition)? If the objects of personal affection change with the years, and sometimes with the wind, why is marriage a recommendable or sacred institution (a social superstition)?

The questions are, of course, hackneyed to you, but they may not be to young men and women who have unquestioningly received the noble teachings that marriage is the bedrock of social order, that it is our great duty to our fellow men to provide a refrigerator and a guaranteed supply of Shredded Wheat for every household, that every boy and girl should go to school until he is seventeen, that decisions demo-

cratically arrived at have the added sanction of Heaven. Your purpose
—let me make this clear—is not to throw the student into the abyss on
whose edge he stands, but to get him to look into it; you must, therefore, be as stern with the fellow who jumps as with the one who shud-
ders and draws back: cynicism and cowardice are Siamese twins.

You will already have noticed that I put these questions in hypo-
thetical form, making each interrogative depend upon a preceding
"if." They may be put in propositional form, of course, but the hypo-
thetical structure has particular merit because it gives the student two
points of attack. He is almost certain to challenge at one or the other:
either he will say, "I don't accept the premise," or he will say, "I don't
think the implied proposition follows from it." Either way, you have
him, for now he has taken on himself the obligation to defend his dis-
sent. So you make another step forward.

He has tried a definition; he has challenged a statement and got himself involved in an argument. How is he to go about it? If left alone,
he'll try the old debating technique: shut your eyes and ears to everything except what is useful to your side of the argument and what you
can readily refute that favors the other side; dress it up as slick as a
greased pig, and let fly. The teacher's duty, at this juncture, is to head
the student off before he gets started. First, you ask if any reasonable
men believe the proposition to be true, then if any reasonable men, in
addition to the student, are known to believe it untrue. The answer can
only be "Yes." So you ask, "How could equally reasonable men come
to opposite conclusions?" Now at this point there is sure to be a burr-
headed Arthur, the dimwit of the class, who answers, "Because they
had different opinions." That's a chance to go back to definition, if
you're looking for one; if not, you ask the same question over again,
using Arthur's weasel-word: "How could equally reasonable men
have opposite opinions about it?"

Before going ahead, I want to go back for a few minutes. The process I have described so far takes, in my own classes, about six weeks:
six weeks means six meetings, and six meetings means six hours—six
hours of instruction, perhaps twenty hours of assigned reading, and
two or three essays. The first essay, you will remember, started students off in search of a definition, a search intended to give them practice in exploring relatively safe terrain—a sort of rough country hike
with the eye out for boulders, ditches and potholes, swamps and

barbed-wire fences. And to help the student make this trip, we gave him some homely rules of thumb in the form of a dialectical movement —spurt then reconnoitre. The second piece of writing should involve new difficulties. Instead of a definition, a statement that *x* is *y*, we present him with some very different statements: because there is an *x*, there's a *y;* although there is an *x*, there's a *y;* whenever there is an *x*, there's a *y;* if there is an *x*, there *ought* to be a *y;* no *x*, no *y;* when there's no *x*, there's always a *y;* Hurrah for *x*, and down with *y!* who ever said there was any *x* in the first place? And we ask him what differences he finds between these statements. Let him use whatever means he will, he is bound to come up with useful distinctions from which you can proceed. The one I generally lead him to choose of his own free will is a distinction between these groups: sentences which simply make an assertion, sentences which ask a question, sentences which put emphasis on obligation—on what *ought* to be—and sentences which express approval. Does he see the differences clearly? Let him prove it. Give him a few words (pleasure, work, money) and tell him to make as many sentences as he can without using any other nouns though he may inflect the ones he has and he may supply verbs, modifiers, and connectives at will. From such a little exercise, the student can quickly see two things: (1) that his arrangement and inflections alter according to his *intention;* (2) that some forms raise problems of comprehension much more difficult than others. What, you may ask him, is the difference between "Work brings pleasure as well as money" and "Work brings money as well as pleasure"? A nice question, for it leads him to recognize that a statement can rest on an unstated assumption—in the first, the assumption that most people think of money as the reward of work, in the second that they think of pleasure as the reward of work. Now the second assumption seems so unlikely as to raise another question: Does anyone really think that pleasure *is* the normally expected reward of work? If no one does, then it is obvious that the sentence "Work brings money as well as pleasure" should offend. Does it? Not particularly. Why not? Well, because some people may think that we *ought* to work for the pleasure it gives, not for the money. That's the answer you want, and you pounce on it. The sense of *oughtness*—it can be produced from more than one of the sentences he might have written with those three words, by the way—the sense of *oughtness* raises, in explicit language, the need for coming to a decision about what should and what should not be, about value. When the student sees that the need for decision is there, you ask him whether or not there is any decision connected with another of his sentences, for instance, with "Work brings money and pleasure." There is, indeed. Is it of the same kind? Not quite. Why not? Perhaps he would like to explore what is involved in making decisions about a single sentence. He would like to—or, at least, he agrees to do so. To make this job of dissection fairly easy, you need to give the student a complicated sentence, one which he can break into several parts. Here is an example:

Browning's finest poem, "Soliloquy in a Spanish Cloister," completes the cycle of dramatic monologues properly by focusing attention on the necessary triumph of simple-hearted goodness over sophisticated evil in the everyday affairs of men.

The sentence, as you see, does not have to be a true one; ideally, it should be a mixture of truth, falsehood, and ambiguity; of simple proposition, assumption, implication, ethical statement, and anything else you want to throw in. The question for the student is this: What are the places in the sentence at which decisions must be made; and what will you have to do in order to make them?

This work on the nature of statement I put between definition and proof for reasons of convenience, but the order is not of first importance. However you go about it, the aim is to lead the student to recognize that making statements implies making decisions, that a single sentence may contain several decisions, some of them not apparent even to the maker, at least, not at the moment of the making. Insofar as possible, the aim is to make the student feel that responsibility for statement is a matter of intellectual alertness rather than one of virtue.

But there's no sense in making him alert unless you can help him to do something about what he learns to see. So we turn back to the question which we left hanging and proceed to the final step of this termlong wrestling match with the simplicities of logic as they affect exposition. That question was: "How could equally reasonable men have opposite opinions about something?" Handled thoughtfully, the range of answers to that question can take all the time—and patience—you want to give it, because each answer raises a half-dozen questions. For the purpose of this talk, I limit myself to one answer: "They have different opinions because they don't see the same thing even though they think they do." How can this be? Well, for one thing, like the blind men with the elephant, each sees only part. More than that, his seeing it is affected by expectation and by experience and by habit. The facts that each man talks about are, then, not entirely the same; the facts are inside their heads, and outside their heads lies the raw material from which facts are made. Decisions, then, must take both worlds into consideration—the affective and intellectual world of the mind and the existential world of trees, the smell of smoke, the sound of waterfall, and smiling faces. The questions you pose to students about the inner world of mind and the outer world of matter are the same for both: What data do you have for study? What means do you have for studying it? Are comparisons possible or meaningful? Can the truth or validity of a statement concerning these data be decided beyond question, only in a tentative way, or not at all? The purpose of this line of questioning, rehearsed again and again as it must be, is to make students aware of what they are examining, to get them to look at it with lively eyes, and to give them some simple instruction in using their minds to look with. They must learn to see both *through* and *with* the eye if they are to write well.

Although this sharply abbreviated account of one approach to expository writing may seem, from the form I have given it here, to be largely an oral battle of wits, that is not really the whole story. Writing goes with it, hand in glove—short pieces, sometimes only a sentence or two, often more than once in a class hour; long pieces, written as homework, in which the student finds his way through some small problem alone. The structure of definition helps him to get focus and to control direction; a procedure for the analysis and classification of statements helps him to lay out in proper perspective the various responsibilities any piece of writing entails; the methods of testing data and statements for truth and validity teaches the strategy of exposition, the deployment of resources. The topics for writing need not be, *should* not be, ponderous or sententious. Just quickly, let me suggest some topics for short essays. Here's one based on a single word: "St. Paul says, 'prove all things; hold fast to that which is good'; a proverb says, 'The exception proves the rule.' Discuss 'prove.'" And here is a neat one: "What's the difference between 'outside' and 'inside'?" If you like doublets, have students try their wits on "peace and quiet," "wear and tear," "high and mighty," "good and old." When they're eager for bigger pasture, try pairs of contradictory proverbs: "Honesty is the best policy" with "Virtue is its own reward"; "The wise man sleeps with one eye open" with "Sound slumber is the sign of a safe conscience"; "Waste not, want not" with "Penny-wise, pound-foolish." And, of course, if you run out of neat little mazes like these, you can always let students grapple with the universe, provided that they agree to use your grappling irons.

I have deliberately made this procedure for building a course in composition on logical analysis sound as though it were conducted by small-arms fire across a hasty barricade of classroom chairs. In practice, the give-and-take is good fun, just as any exercise involving contest is good fun. Of course, it must be more than good fun, and I assure you that it is. Once a student gets some feeling for the differences among statements, he will have a conscience about flinging them about with abandon; once he has elementary notions of evidence in his mind, he will feel a prickling in his thumb at the approach of those fire-breathing forest-dragons Irrelevance, Non Sequitur, Ambiguity, Vagueness, and blind old A Priori.

Frequently I hear teachers wonder aloud if such a course does not stifle imagination, cut off the creative bud before it flowers, dam up the freshets of the mind. In short, they wonder if it may not be just a bit dull. The answer—for their wondering is really a rhetorical question, of course—is, of course, "Yes." Such a course may be dull; so may any other. All that dullness needs for service is dull people, on either side of the desk. And all that excitement needs is lively ones, on *both* sides. I will say that the kind of course I have attempted to describe—or, perhaps, to illustrate more than to describe—is hard; hard for teachers, that is. It is not a whit harder for students than the free-writing program which Professor Sewall described, for the simple reason that both put the strain of self-examination on the student. The only argument I have for preferring my method over Professor Sewall's—beside the fact that I thoroughly enjoy using it—is the one from which I began. A course in exposition based on logical analysis can serve a very particular and important function in the education of the sixteen- to twenty-year-old in the same way a tether serves a bull calf: it gives him plenty of room to exercise and graze but it brings him up short when he gets a belly-full of locoweed.

9

The Craft of Composition

ARTHUR MIZENER, *Cornell University*

I must confess to considerable embarrassment at standing up before this group to talk about teaching composition. There is, of course, nothing headier than an opportunity to tell other people how to run their business, and the teaching of English composition is—alas —not exclusively the secondary school teacher's business or entirely unknown to the college teacher; still, I think you will agree with me that most of the real work is done in the secondary schools. As a college teacher of composition, I hear just enough of the complaints made by those who expect us to produce a miracle in a single composition course to know how you must feel when people who don't have to face the job at the secondary school level come along to tell you how to teach composition. I think it must always be a mistake to tell people how to run a business you haven't worked at yourself, and my only real excuse for making that mistake today is that I believe we are all— secondary school and college teachers alike—distressed enough about the state of English composition to welcome a chance to talk the whole matter out.

It will be healthy, I imagine, to begin by admitting that as teachers we probably have less success in composition courses than anywhere else. We are all acutely aware of the causes for our failure that lie outside our control. We are aware that the practice of our colleagues, both in their own work and in their grading of students, sometimes sets a bad example: even the social scientists are showing signs of suspecting that social scientists have some bad compositional habits. We are aware of how newspapers, slick magazines, advertising, television, and radio force on our students habits of inaccuracy and vagueness, and the nauseating jargon of a cheap set of values. So powerful is this influence that I know at least one large insurance company that has hired an English instructor to teach its agents how to write letters; the agents' letters had become so incoherent that the head office could no longer determine what they were trying to say. As teachers we are convinced that the effect of these forces is doubled by the influence of homes where parents talk too much like television commercials and Chesterfield ads. We see that evidence of these influences everywhere in student life, in their casual conversation, their newspapers, their classroom recitations, and their writing.

I do not doubt the reality of these influences, and we can probably agree that an educational system, like a government, cannot be much better than the society which it serves. Nevertheless, there is that area between "no better" and "not much better" within which we can operate, and if we are to operate there successfully, we had better concentrate on the causes for our failure that do lie within our control rather than on those that do not. Let us remember that there is a natural impulse in people to express themselves well and ask ourselves why we do not manage to make more of it. If school and college newspapers discourage us, we all have experiences which do not. A couple of months ago, Harrison Salisbury lectured on Russia at Cornell. As we were coming out of Baily Hall after his lecture we were confronted by Ithaca's lone Rolls Royce, standing isolated, spectacular and chauffeured at the entrance to the hall. An undergraduate near me remarked, with a fine affectation of surprise and interest, "Look! A capitalist demonstration!" We ought to be able to teach students like that a great deal about composition, yet much of the time we do not and I believe that some of the reasons we do not are faults in us.

We do not, for one thing, take enough interest in actual writing, so that all of us some of the time and some of us all of the time are looking for excuses to teach our students the symbolism of D. H. Lawrence's short stories, or some such thing, instead of composition. This impulse leads us to stress very heavily the relation between reading ability and writing ability and to deceive ourselves into thinking that if we teach our students to analyze short stories and essays they will learn more or less automatically to write. Of course there is a relation between reading and writing; some interest in language is certainly involved in all reading, so that anyone who reads a great deal on his own initiative will probably have a feel for the written language; probably, too, teaching people to read well—which is something different from teaching them to analyze Hemingway or Faulkner—will in the long run make them better writers. But only in the long run and only in certain respects. There is a corollary argument here which we hear a great deal, that students write well only when they are interested in what they are talking about. If this argument means they cannot write without some knowledge or understanding of their subject, of course it is true. But it is equally true of all learning, not simply of composition: no one can speak intelligently on a subject of which he has no knowledge or understanding. But if this argument means that composition courses must limit students' writing to those subjects in which they profess an interest before coming into class, and that they are not to be asked to write about anything but sports, women's fashions, or the problems of dating, then I think it is not only generally vicious but even in the narrow sense mistaken; at least my experience is that students writing on such subjects imitate sports and fashion writers. Few sports writers write well and when they do it is in a highly specialized, seriocomic, rococo vein. I suppose the fashion writer's style must be nearly the worst there is.

It seems to me evident that we should ask students to write on a serious subject about which accurate information is obtainable and ask them to write as little about it as they need to in order to say only what they have thought about carefully. That little will not be much, but that is an advantage for the student on other grounds which I will come to in a moment. It has one obvious merit for the teacher. With the best will in the world most teachers have not time to assign and *read* enough writing to give students the practice they need. The only college course I have ever heard of that did so is the course at Yale which used to be called Daily Themes. I do not know if Professor Nangle still teaches that course, but when I shared an office with him over in Pierson College, he did. I saw what killing work the course was for him, but I also saw something of the astonishing results he produced. He once put the secret of this course to me very clearly. When I knew it, the course required each student to hand in a typewritten page of work every day for a term. "They all start out," Professor Nangle said once, "being fine writers. But about the third or fourth week they begin to get desperate and to write on 'Shaving in the Morning.' That's when they really begin to write."

Most teachers are in no position to assign the amount of work Professor Nangle did. But if we ask students to write only three or four serious and careful sentences, then we can ask them to do so with considerable frequency. I doubt if we can exhaust the advantages of such training in less than a half term. After that we must assign longer compositions, but I think the assignments should be lengthened very gradually. The solid paragraph of five or six sentences, if properly written, raises for the students all the problems of a long essay, and I suspect that in a term's course the climactic essay should not be longer than three or four solid paragraphs.

The important reasons for planning a composition course in this way are not, of course, the practical necessities of the teacher's situation; they are the advantages for the students, and I would like now to turn to the questions of what we should be teaching in a composition course and how we should be teaching it.

We are all aware that in teaching composition we are teaching an art, and we all suspect that in teaching the practice of an art, we cannot succeed by teaching a set of rules, and cannot quite succeed, either, without doing so. This dilemma is itself partly a compositional one, however, a problem in diction. The things we ought not to teach are rules in the ordinary sense: "All main clauses joined by *and, but, for, or, nor,* or *yet* should be separated by a comma"; "pronouns always refer to the immediately preceding noun or pronoun." There are two serious objections to rules in this sense. The first is that they are not true. For instance, anyone can think of short sentences of two main clauses joined by a conjunction in which there is no real need for a comma. If participles should never dangle, why do we not object to sentences like, (1) "Considering all the circumstances, Mr. Dulles is to be congratulated on his decision"? Since *to* is only a sign of the infinitive and not an integral part of it, an infinitive can be split only by putting something between two of its syllables. To say so is not pedantry or hairsplitting, because we get into an endless muddle if students do not recognize that "come" is an infinitive in both "You ought to come" and "You must come." The problems of the reference of pronouns in English are not going to be solved by any rule of thumb and we oughtn't to pretend they are. What becomes of the rule of thumb in a statement like, (2) "John began to attack Harry cautiously; then he became more aggressive and began hitting him with both hands; finally he knocked him out."

But there is an even more serious objection to such rules than the objection that they are not true. A dependence on rules, even if they be true, creates a false relation between the writer and what he is writing. What we need to make students conscious of is the established patterns of the English language, its customs and habits. To distinguish them from the kind of rules I have just been discussing, I will call these patterns conventions. Apart from some—but not all—aspects of diction, they are almost all matters of syntax. A student who is made conscious of them is being made conscious of the resources of his instrument, of its immense flexibility and its occasional stubborn defects—for example, its lack of an indefinite personal pronoun and its lack of a possessive form of the relative pronoun *which*. He will look on language as something *of which* the ways can be understood, not as something which is comprehended by a set of rules. I find it hard to believe that a student who is capable of any interest at all cannot be interested in the madcap ways of language, and I would like now to consider some of the ways of language which it is particularly important for him to be conscious of and some of the means by which we can perhaps make him so.

Just to make sure that what I am trying to do here is quite clear, let me take as a random example a common syntactical problem of which we are all in a way aware but which we do not seem to succeed in conveying to our students. This is the problem raised by the causal effect of a phrase at the beginning of a sentence. We had an illustration of this problem created for us by the last College Board examination and I think it will illustrate my point. Most of you will be familiar with the "fix-it" examination used by the College Board. The passage in the last one I am interested in reads as follows:

(3) Louis was consumed with a desire, or lust, for power. Utterly unscrupulous in his methods, superstition rather than religion was his forte. It was the belief and conviction of Louis that money, or filthy lucre as it is better called, could buy any man or any saint.

There are, to be sure, a number of problems of composition raised by this passage and I hope to return to some of them. For the moment, however, let us look at the so-called dangling modifier in the second sentence. It is the unhappy fact that a simple concern for its dangling is more likely than not to get a reviser in trouble. The simplest and most frequent revision such a concern produces is something like, (3a) "Being utterly unscrupulous in his methods, Louis took superstition rather than religion as his forte." There are, I take it, two possible ways to read this sentence. You can assume that, like many newspaper writers, its author is simply throwing two unrelated ideas together in the same sentence by putting one of them in a participial phrase. That way, as we all know, madness lies, for English is profoundly dependent on syntax for meaning, and if we habitually flout the conventional associations of certain syntactical patterns with certain meaning patterns, we shall destroy that dialect of the tribe which we are told it is part of our duty to preserve. The other way of reading this sentence is to assume its author means the sentence to say what this syntactical pattern usually says; that is, that (3b) "*because* Louis was utterly unscrupulous, he was superstitious rather than religious." But when this suggestion, inherent in the "being" phrase which precedes its subject, is thus brought out in the open, its absurdity is clear. No one could mean to say that unscrupulousness causes superstition. Nor does it cause a lust for power, as is suggested by another revision: (3c) "Being utterly unscrupulous in his methods, Louis was consumed with a lust for power."

How firmly entrenched in English syntax the causal implication of this "being" phrase really is shows clearly when it is used in a meaningful way, as in the revision, (3d) "Consumed with a lust for power, Louis was utterly unscrupulous in his methods." Because of the meaning enforced by this syntactical pattern, we can even make a kind of sense out of (3e) "Utterly unscrupulous in his methods, Louis believed that money could buy any man," though to be sure the emphases of this sentence are awkward and we would be happier if the meaning which lurks in this revision were more clearly focussed: (3f) "Utterly unscrupulous himself, Louis was convinced that every man had his price." The force of this syntactical pattern is perhaps most strikingly suggested by the fact that we shall even find ourselves struggling toward a meaning—if a fairly silly one—if the reviser writes, (3g) "Being superstitious rather than religious, Louis was utterly unscrupulous in his methods."

The moral here is that any two clauses which are syntactically related have a relation of meaning which is determined by the very nature of English syntax. It is these convictions, not rules, which we ought to teach our students, for they are the whole point of syntax, and syntax is almost the whole point of written English. Consider, for example, one more, quite different revision of the passage about Louis' unscrupulousness. (4) "Louis was consumed with a desire for power and he was utterly unscrupulous in his methods." Here we take the methods in question to be, at least mainly, his methods of obtaining power. Partly we do so because we feel something like "of obtaining it" follows "methods"; mainly, however, we do so because we read "and" as a consequence. I guess the theoretician's way of describing this situation is to talk about "the causal *and*"; but however we talk about it, our job is to make students conscious of the meaning which is suggested by this relation between two independent clauses.

Not all participial phrases are causal, of course. The convention which establishes their meaning in any particular instance depends on their place in the pattern of the sentence. For instance, the student who writes, (5) "In *Quentin Durward* Scott portrayed Louis as a liar and cheat, employing only men drawn from obscurity," is in bad trouble of a kind which frequently arises when a sentence trails off into a participial construction. Our first inclination is, I suppose, to believe in the comma here and to think that Scott was employing the obscure men. But our good sense probably tells us the sentence cannot mean that Scott was a painter who employed a group of obscure journeymen to help him execute an equestrian portrait of "The Universal Spider." The comma must then be a mistake and "employing" must be meant to connect with "Louis." But if it does, then the participial phrase can only mean that (5a) "Louis lied and cheated while he was employing obscure men," which I suspect we shall suspect is not what the author of the sentence means at all. The truth seems to be that our author mistakenly imagines this trailing participial phrase to mean the same thing as a co-ordinated verb and thinks his sentence says that the character in *Quentin Durward* (5b) "lied and cheated, and habitually employed obscure and insignificant men."

I hope this illustration of what the teaching of syntax involves has not exhausted your patience. I promise you I shall not canvass at such length any further illustrations, though I am frank to admit that I would like to, if only because such problems seem to me endlessly fascinating. What I would like to do now is to suggest to you some of the important syntactical patterns which are, in my experience, frequently mishandled by beginning writers.

Probably we would all agree that the most important of these patterns is what we call parallelism—not simply the parallelism called for by correlatives but structural parallelism. Because English relies very extensively on the order of the words in the sentence to establish their relations, the order of any sentence will carry over into the one that follows it if we give that order half a chance. By doing so, it will keep the meaning clear, even though the sentences in question flout some of the minor conventions of syntax.

A good example of this power is sentence 2: "John began to attack Harry cautiously; then he became more aggressive and began hitting him with both hands; finally he knocked him out." Here parallelism keeps the meaning clear even though the pronouns are somewhat confusing. Maintaining structural parallelism of this sort is closely connected with the task of keeping the real subject the grammatical subject of the sentence, of avoiding, that is, the mistaken elegance of unnecessary shifts of subject. The avoidance of such shifts is in turn a means of avoiding the circumlocutious passive constructions which are responsible for so many misplaced modifiers. This familiar complex of troubles is neatly illustrated by a sentence from an old College Board examination which read:

(6) Although fresh from the flattering of her courtiers, no flattery around the council table was tolerated by Queen Elizabeth; she was plain of speech with her councilors, and plainness of speech was what in return she expected from them.

There can hardly be any doubt that the real subject of the first independent clause is "Queen Elizabeth"; if it is made the grammatical subject, this first clause is brought into parallel with the second, and the reader is not misled by it into thinking this sentence is going to tell him something about flattery instead of something about Queen Elizabeth. If Queen Elizabeth is also put at the beginning of the third independent clause, most of the difficulties of this sentence disappear, for we then have:

(6a) Although fresh from the flattering of her courtiers, Queen Elizabeth tolerated no flattery around the council board; she was plain of speech with her councilors and she expected plainness of speech in return from them.

There are some minor flaws in the sentence still, but the major defects have been repaired by making the real subject of each independent clause its grammatical subject and placing each at the beginning of its clause, thus bringing the three clauses into parallelism. All this, again, is so because the English language associates certain patterns of meaning with certain patterns of syntax and therefore the minds of readers of English automatically anticipate certain relations of meaning the minute they encounter certain syntactical patterns. Most students can be made to recognize that this is so if it is pointed out to them in connection with specific sentences, particularly if they have themselves written the sentences. To recognize the right syntactical pattern when we see it, however, does not automatically guarantee that we will produce it when we need it. Mixed up in this process somehow is the student's ability to understand precisely what he wants to say. This is a next question and is not our business today. But I think it is safe to say that when a student is made to realize what sentences do say, will he, nill he, he will be more likely to ask himself if he means to say what he has said.

Closely related to the effect of the unnecessary shift of subject is the effect of passive constructions in sentences where the agent is clearly the important consideration; for example, (7) "From her father was inherited Elizabeth's hearty manner." Clearly this sentence means to say, (7a) "Elizabeth inherited from her father her hearty manner," and it might better have said so. Or, (8) "The power of the House of Burgundy was broken by Louis XI which had threatened France for almost a century," a sentence which certainly means to say (8a) "Louis XI broke the power of the House of Burgundy, which had threatened France for almost a century." I sometimes wonder if the artificial and affected style of the military and business communications hasn't something to do with the increasing use of this passive—"It is ordered that you. . . ."

In any event, the affectation of the passive leads to the meaningless use of the "it is . . . that" formula. This formula has a real use in English. For example, (9) "It is uncontrollable anger, not plain stupidity, that leads John to do these foolish things." Here the construction focusses our attention on the important distinction between anger and stupidity. But the ordinary use of "it is . . . that" is at best a meaningless waste of words; for example, (10) "It was from Ann Boleyn that there was derived the sensuous part of Elizabeth's nature" is only a confusing way of saying, (10a) "Elizabeth derived the sensuous part of her nature from Ann Boleyn."

There are perhaps two other matters of syntax which, if my experience goes for anything, are seldom understood by students: the relations of the various past tenses and the customary order for subordinate clauses. I suppose the best thing we can do at this late date with the past perfect subjunctive is to advise our students to avoid all occasions which require it, and certainly to do so if an infinitive is involved. We all remember Thurber's comedy about the man who tried to write a note which came out (11) "We would have liked to have been able to have found you at home." But we probably cannot avoid the simple past perfect. For instance, students will more often than not write, (12) "Louis XI completed the task which *was* begun centuries before, the task of uniting France." It is not really very difficult to make them understand that this subordinate clause is trying to describe an action which occurred before the time of the main clause and that if the main clause is in the past tense, the subordinate clause cannot be, but must be in a tense that asserts a time before that of the past tense, in short, that it must be in the past perfect tense: (12a) "Louis XI completed the task which *had been* begun centuries before, the task of uniting France." Students see this point when it is explained to them; as nearly as I can make out, it seldom is.

A failure to understand the habitual order of clauses in English leads to what are usually called split constructions, the separating by a qualifying clause of the elements in the sentence which convention leads us to expect will never be separated. The temptation to split constructions is often very great. For instance, take the sentence I quoted in my last paragraph. Suppose it had been written, as it well might have been, (13) "Louis XI completed the task, which had been begun centuries before his time, of uniting France." The expectation of the reader trained in English is that "task of uniting" will not be split apart in this way. It is possible to reduce the split to (13a) "Louis XI completed the

task, begun centuries before, of uniting France." This is a less obtrusive split but still a split. Nonetheless, it is perhaps the best that can be
done with the sentence. But most really obtrusive splits are unnecessary. The commonest kind splits subject and verb; for example, (14)
"Louis XI, although he was not a good king, was a very clever man."
There is no excuse for a sentence like this one, since it is perfectly easy
to write, (14a) "Although Louis XI was not a good king, he was a
clever man." If Louis' cleverness seems more important to the writer
than his badness as a king, he can write, (14b) "Louis XI was a very
clever man, although not a good king"; if the writer's faith in cleverness is less sure, he can write (14c) "Louis XI was not a good king, but
he was very clever," or even (14d) "If Louis XI was not a good king,
he was very clever." If, on the other hand, the writer holds to the let-
who-will-be-clever view of Louis' cleverness, he can write, (14e)
"Louis XI was a very clever man but he was not a good king." Whatever the author's exact shade of meaning, however, the split construction will not express it.

I wish there were time today to discuss the problems of diction and
coherence which arise in students' writing. They are almost as important as the problems of syntax, but they cannot, I believe, be dealt with
effectively until the student has some grasp of syntax. It is obvious that
words have their meaning in context and until they are at work in sentences we do not really know whether they constitute effective or ineffective diction. Consequently there is a danger in all vocabulary
work which is carried on apart from work with actual sentences. I
picked up the other day, for example, a vocabulary manual which was
teaching students the dictionary meaning of *umbrageous;* it is appalling to consider the temptations that lie in wait for the high school
senior who has that word kicking about in his head. It is only in context that we can discover the effects of mixing "levels of English" in
general and know whether any particular instance of such mixture is a
virtue, as it is in Henry James, or a vice, as it is in the "long-time-no-
see" school of letter-writers.

Much the same kind of thing can be said about coherence. We do
not know whether any group of sentences coheres until we know the
precise force of each sentence, and the common fault of throwing in
transition words without considering whether they point to the rela-

tion which really exists between the sentences can be explained to students only after they understand the force of the sentences taken separately. For example, (15) "Marquand is not unqualifiedly critical of the American businessman; on the other hand, he does criticize Charley Gray and Harry Pulham, but he makes us sympathize with them too." This sentence comes close to providing that rare and wonderful occasion when the colon is in order. (15a) "Marquand is not unqualifiedly critical of the American businessman: he does criticize Charley Gray and Harry Pulham, but he makes us sympathize with them too." But until the student understands both clauses and the syntactical pattern which makes them nearly equivalent, he will hardly see how completely misleading that transitional phrase, "on the other hand," is, or how it suggests that having said Marquand is not wholly critical, the sentence sets off from the semicolon exactly as if it were about to take back what it has just said by asserting something like, (15b) "on the other hand, he *does* criticize Charley Gray and Harry Pulham and criticize them severely."

Once we have given the student some confidence that he understands how the syntax of the ordinary English constructions works, we can move on to paragraphs and to essays of several paragraphs, where in the natural course of things questions of diction and coherence will arise.

The range and flexibility of English syntax is so great that it allows for the expression of far more shades of meaning than most of us, to say nothing of our students, have to express. We cannot hope to make a student aware of all these possibilities, or to teach him the virtuosity which can control them, but I think we can hope to give him a knowledge of the commonest and most important of them and an understanding of how they suggest the particular relations of meaning they do suggest; this understanding seems to me the thing we need to teach him first. That conviction is what leads me to believe we ought to begin any course in composition with the sentence and to begin with frequent but very brief writing assignments. This procedure has the corollary advantage of being the easiest way to interest students in the game of composition, to make him take pleasure in the craft of composition.

These may seem like modest goals; they certainly assume that we cannot in a single course make finished expository writers out of sows' ears. I suspect, however, that these goals suggest something that with hard work we can actually accomplish and something that will at least start a student on the road to a modest, clear, and unostentatious prose.

The final essay in this section deals, as its title indicates, with some general problems of writing—and of the teacher of writing. Beginning with a plea for support of the effort to reduce the burden of paper work by making clear to laymen the importance of careful teaching of composition and the impossibility of that kind of teaching with too many or too large classes in English, it goes on to suggest not only a philosophy for the teaching of writing, but also ways and means by which that philosophy may be carried into action. The editors believe that these suggestions from a committee of experienced teachers will be helpful to many others.

Of special importance is the stress on clear thinking—by the teacher as he prepares assignments and by the pupil as he executes them. Errors in mechanics, unhappy as they are, are less important than errors in thinking which permit ambiguity and jargon to come between the reader and the idea struggling for expression.

10

Some General Remarks on Writing

FLOYD RINKER, *Newton High School, Massachusetts,*
  Chairman
ALICE BROWER, *Mount Vernon High School, New York*
CHRISTOPHER ADAMS, *Darien High School, Connecticut*
HARDY FINCH, *Greenwich High School, Connecticut*
MARIE HENRY, *Needham High School, Massachusetts*
CROSBY REDMAN, *Great Neck High School, New York*

A teacher of English may speculate on why he teaches; further, he may wonder why he teaches English, especially when he is compelled to read compositions from many classes and examinations of the essay type. He may have seen the teacher of mathematics checking in a matter of minutes the work of two or three divisions. He knows, perhaps, the mechanical progress through written work in language courses. He marvels at the speed with which an instructor reads the results of the machine-corrected tests, commonly given in science. He wishes for the *joie de vivre* that must result from a rubber stamp that says "Approved" or "Accepted" for the bulky report; but these stamps are for departments that emphasize the project and permit the copying of copious amounts of predigested matter from periodicals, encyclopedias, and other books of reference. He looks with envy on his colleague in speech, whose briefcase is used to carry a thermos and little else. He does not think of teachers in other departments, with "homework" that can be accomplished during class time, or of his fellow-workers in physical education with a schedule that makes even a flexing of the muscles an optional task.

The teacher of English teaches because he has chosen teaching as his field, and he teaches English because only here can he know the satisfactions and joys which teaching can bring. Envious of the freedom, the leisure, and the limited responsibility of staff members in other areas, the English teacher, nevertheless, accepts his situation. He accepts it, perhaps, too readily. Have you ever known a true teacher of English who would be content to free his days and lessen his devotion by accepting an assignment in some other subject? The answer is all too obvious, as experience tells us.

The case being so, we want to recommend, in this introduction to our considerations, your active support of the resolutions approved by the School and College Conference in English, 1947 and 1948. Only by making eminently clear both to school committeemen and administrators and to the community in which we work the excessive demands upon the teachers of English and, even more important, the highly specialized yet broadly humanistic nature of their endeavors, can we hope to achieve some emancipation for ourselves and respect and dignity for our profession. The teacher of English is, in the truest sense of the word, the specialist in the teaching profession.

Will you learn and will you repeat when you believe the occasion opportune these resolutions accepted by the School and College Conference?

1. The number of pupils in an English class in a public high school should not exceed twenty-five. However, twenty pupils should be recognized as the ideal number. The smaller number makes possible almost daily individual participation and assistance.

2. The number of classes assigned to a teacher of English should not exceed four sections meeting five times per week, or five sections meeting four times per week. The number of lesson preparations daily should not exceed two, if preparation is to be adequate and if presentation is to be effective.

3. In addition to the daily recitation periods, at least two additional periods should be provided weekly for conferences with individual

pupils or for remedial work with small groups. In the larger high schools teachers of English might well be freed from study-room responsibilities, this time to be used for conferences with pupils as needed.

4. Visual and auditory teaching aids, as well as facilities for mimeographing, should be available.

5. Library facilities should be provided. If possible, a permanent librarian should be in charge.

6. In the allocation of funds for textbooks, allowance should be made for the necessarily higher per capita usage of books in English classes.

7. Adequate pupil-hour allowances should be credited to teachers in charge of school publications, literary clubs, and other extracurricular activities, frequently assigned to teachers of English under the erroneous assumption that only they can supervise such enterprises.

8. The assumption that any teacher can properly teach English must be rejected.

The goal of this Committee has been to show some practical applications in the teaching of written composition, rather than to attempt to demonstrate all of the facets, purposes, and practices which characterize English teaching. We have therefore limited our remarks to problems which, however important, are but a fraction of the larger task.

In planning the work for a class, the teacher must make assignments in written work. The manner in which this is done and carried out will determine the degree of success and, also, the time the teacher must have for correction. Most often the writing is exposition. In a subject required of everyone, training in composition should be concerned with writing experiences most useful to the student and to the adult. Creative writing—lyric poetry, narrative verse and prose, realistic dialogue, atmospheric descriptions—is, it must be remembered, more meaningful to boys and girls with special interests and talents. No denial of the importance of free writing is implied; no diminishment of the teacher's just estimate of its worth is warranted; no forgetting of the teacher's personal joy in the art of writing is condoned. What I am saying you know from your own experiences in the classroom: creative writing is for the special moment or for the special class.

Exposition is universal expression. Directions and explanations, lecture notes, term papers and examinations, reports and announcements, prepared speeches, minutes of meetings, book reviews, newspaper writing, and letters comprise nearly all the writing an average man will attempt in a lifetime and a very large percentage of all he will read. Exposition is equally important to all, the nonacademic as well as the college preparatory students. It is no surprise, then, that effective teachers stress expository writing and that here the most rewarding results are obtained.

Best subjects for writing are based on experiences and interests of the class. The topics should be familiar, but original in approach and geared to the intelligence of the class in such a way that both the bright and the pedestrian student are challenged. For instance, have each pupil in the class select a topic from a group of controversial subjects and prepare a logical argument defending the side he chooses. Topics might include voting age, compulsory automobile insurance, recruiting of amateur athletes by colleges, TV commercials, school fraternities, honor systems, male supremacy, the right of censorship, and coed colleges.

The preparation for the assignment must stress the relation between writing and thinking, between writing and the reading of appropriate materials, between writing and the class discussion. It is the teacher's responsibility to clarify the methods involved in these three processes and so secure in the written compositions an extension of the speaking and thinking done in the class. A day or two spent in the preparation of a sample question may turn out to be the year's most profitable experience. Among other things, such as instruction in punctuation, sentence structure, grammatical relations, and word power, here is the right moment to teach the outline as an aid to the finished composition. Let the teacher outline one topic on the blackboard. This device should demonstrate the logic of using the outline and of writing it before, not after, the composition. Ideally, the composition is outlined in the student's head and the teacher should work for the attainment of this specialized mental process. To require a written outline for every composition or to overemphasize the importance of outlining is poor teaching and consummate folly.

The writing of the assignment may be done as homework or, and in many cases this procedure is preferred, it may be done in class. If you have planned it for class time, the students should have spent time outside of class in prevision, thinking what they wanted to say, making notes, and possibly writing first drafts. The students should be ready to apply what they know about the value of an effective introduction and a sound conclusion. If the assignments are finished at home, the students must accept full responsibility for revision and proofreading, both of which are rendered more effective by a reading aloud of one's work. Neatness is important and students ought to have a pride in the appearance of their manuscripts; these considerations, however, should not outweigh the more important concerns of subject matter, organization, and style.

If the composition is done in class, the teacher who walks about the room checking the students' work and answering questions in problems in writing is practicing precorrection. Only on examinations does the teacher become the unbending judge of accomplishment. On other occasions he is instructor and tutor, and his mission is ideally one of helpfulness. He longs for the success of his students and he measures his own accomplishment in teaching by their growth and progress. When the "C" student begins to write "B" papers, both the student and the teacher should rejoice. When the "B" student passes in "C" papers, the teacher needs to be actively concerned and discover if he himself has contributed to the student's failure.

The correction of the assignment is something more than a grade or the liberal use of red ink. Symbols of correction should be standardized for the school and reduced to a simple and practical list. Rarely is the teacher justified in marking every single error. For students who have difficulty with composition skill, the teacher usually must limit the number and variety of errors he will mark. There is a need of reiterating in class the criteria for passing, for success, and for honors. Students when writing their compositions and when looking at their corrected papers need to be conscious of the emphases that are being considered as well as the standards the teacher has set. Compositions are ill-read and graded if the concern is only with neat handwriting and a small number of errors in mechanics. Of equal weight must be richness of subject matter and variety of expression in a clear and logical development. The question of a single versus a double or triple grade is not too important. The device of one grade over another does emphasize comparative values in thought and style, but there remains in the minds of teacher and student the question, What is the paper really worth? Marginal notes of explanation and encouragement are called for, and the teacher's final written comment, which always should be done in a thoughtful and helpful manner, is the supreme test of his ability as a critic and guide.

The assignment is not finished with its correction. The next step is discussion in class. Errors common in the papers must be brought to the students' attention by the teacher's remarks, by blackboard illustrations, or by use of the opaque projector. Reading of sample papers in class by the teacher, the student writer, or by a fellow student is an excellent exercise, though a teacher careful to guard against embarrassments is wise to have the writer's consent or to conceal any identity of the work.

"Please see me" or "Confer, please" is often the only way to handle some problematic phase. The teacher, in conference on the assignment, can say things difficult to write, give tutorial help, or discuss problems revealed in the student's composition. In the teacher-student conference on English composition many schools have been getting the best of their guidance programs.

If a student's work is discarded at this point, the teacher and student are burning their bridges behind them. Corrected compositions can be used in many ways. For easy access they should be placed in a folder, but not as contents of a dead file. Ideally students' folders should be kept in the classroom, a cumulative record of one or more years' work, for the use of the student and the teacher and for conference with parents or school authorities. In some school systems, English teachers have set times for examining the folders. A record of this work is made in the written comments on the folder covers. Students are trained to use their folders as workbooks; they correct their mistakes or rewrite compositions when required; they keep lists of Never-Again Errors, Words Misspelled, Correct Punctuation, New Words, Books Read, and Books to Read. In a final analysis, the student's folder is the concrete record of his growth and success in English.

Obviously, the paper load of the teacher of English is heavy. In planning assignments he must consider his own tasks. With prompt return of corrected papers the ideal, some staggering of assignments in various sections is sensible. Reading papers at different hours and in different places seems to lessen the monotony and to increase reader efficiency. Correcting a set of papers for particular errors in style or in mechanics, or reading a set with concentration solely on content or reasoning, is sometimes prudent. There are excellent arguments in favor or writing for practice. No teacher should be criticised for the occasional return of a set of papers without correction or grade. Sometimes, but not frequently, students may be called upon to correct their own or each other's compositions. Once or twice a year, an exchange with a fellow teacher will be refreshing, quite often revealing. For fun and excitement, and as a challenge to more objectivity in marking, I like to have a class pass in typewritten papers without heading or to have them conceal identity by copying the original work of classmates. Correcting sheets usually can be classified as mechanical devices for busy work, though advertised as efficient timesavers for the harassed teacher.

Appendix

SUBJECTS FOR WRITTEN COMPOSITION

1. Write a paragraph on how to write a good paragraph.

2. Describe a person of your choice in suitable surroundings and in incongruous surroundings.

3. Write a review of a film.

4. The wheel—man's greatest invention.

5. The influence of pocket books on mass reading habits.

6. A letter to an architect who is to design a new school.

7. A defense of wasting time.

8. Write an experience of your own three times: sympathetically, antagonistically, objectively.

9. The best editorials I have read.

10. These are the things I love.

11. Anyone can cook today!

12. I never laughed so hard!

13. What is she like?

14. If I were my parents.

15. Observing people in spring (autumn, summer, winter).

16. Our favorite dish.

17. My Credo

18. Do It Yourself

19. Problems:
    a. To perceive, analyze, and describe a picture placed before the class ("The King"—Rouault).
    b. To resolve two opposing points of view:
    "Man is born free"—Rousseau
    "Man is not born free"—Huxley
    c. To analyze the false thinking in an advertisement, particularly a visual advertisement.
    d. To analyze the psychological impact of "anticipation, participation, and reminiscence." (The candidate may make a choice or not. He should give examples.)

20. In this series take up the problem of how to do something very simple—but how to do it perfectly, with complete accuracy and efficiency. The idea is to discuss a commonplace action with scrupulous clarity and precision, the interest or humor of the article coming from this detailed, scientific examination of something taken for granted.

> How to Open a Door
> How to Thread a Needle
> How to Pour a Glass of Milk
> How to Sit Down
> How to Draw a Straight Line
> How to Steal Candy from a Baby
> How to Shoot Fish in a Rainbarrel

21. A great poet once sat, "blind," in the midst of a wood at midnight:

> I cannot see what flowers are at my feet,
>   Nor what soft incense hangs upon the boughs,

But embalmed darkness, guess each sweet
   Wherewith the seasonable month endows
The grass, the thicket, and the fruit-tree wild;
   White hawthorn, and the pastoral eglantine;
      Fast-fading violets covered up in leaves;
         And mid-May's eldest child,
The coming musk-rose, full of dewy wine,
The murmurous haunt of flies on summer eves.

Darkling I listen; . . . .
   While thou art pouring forth thy soul abroad
      In such an ecstacy!

Ode to a Nightingale–Keats

Let me hear you say something about the four senses. Write briefly about each, divorced from the other.

a. Don't write about the ear, but about hearing: a symphony, jazz, animal sounds, the song of silence.
b. Not about the nose, but perfumes, sweet odors, acrid smokes, and pungent smells.
c. Touch: heat and cold, the fanning wind, something "Palpable as a globed fruit" (*Ars Poetica*–MacLeish).
d. The taste of foods and drink: a lollipop, wormwood!

Write of sensations—experience the senses, one by one—separately—alone!

22. *Hamlet* Essay: Write a full-length, completely developed essay discussing through close analysis "Hamlet as a Tragic Hero" or, to put it another way, "The Factors Which Make *Hamlet* a Tragedy." Be sure to use the following, in detail where necessary:

a. The play, through direct quotation and reference.
b. The book or books you have read about *Hamlet*, through direct quotation and reference.
c. Notes taken in class.
d. Aristotle's concept of the tragic hero (*Poetics*).
e. A. C. Bradley's "The Substance of Shakespearean Tragedy."

The essay must show that:

a. You have read and understood Hamlet thoroughly.
b. You have read and understood materials (books, essays, etc.) about *Hamlet*.

Choose *one* of the following statements as a starting point. *Copy* the statement, placing it at the beginning of your essay. If none of the statements fits your particular interpretation, write one of your own or find another from your reading; place this statement at the beginning of your essay.

a. Hamlet's tragedy is that of a man "who, though not outstandingly virtuous and just, yet falls into misfortune not through vice or depravity but through some 'tragic flaw'."
b. Hamlet's tragedy is that of a civilized man in a barbaric world.
c. Hamlet's tragedy is that of a disillusioned idealist.
d. Hamlet's tragedy is that he "possesses to a fatal extent *idealism regarding human nature*."
e. Hamlet's tragedy is that "Character is Fate."
f. Hamlet's tragedy is that he is too civilized to be a Laertes, too emotionally involved to be a Horatio, and too melancholy to be a Fortinbras.
g. Hamlet's tragedy is that of a man caught essentially by his deep religious convictions.
h. Hamlet's tragedy is that of a chronic melancholiac.
i. Hamlet's tragedy is that he suffers from a psychosis; his case is pathological; i.e. he suffers from the Oedipus complex.
j. Hamlet's tragedy is that ————. (Finish the statement with a quotation of your own choice or your own words.)

Once you have chosen a statement, stick to it, follow it, develop it, and be sure to come to a sound conclusion.

25. Plan for Autobiographical Sketch: Your study of biography should suggest the purpose of life-writing. Gamaliel Bradford's essays give you examples of one man's way of achieving these purposes. Even within the smaller scope to which you must limit your autobiographical sketch, you will find that you are able to apply many of Bradford's successful methods for sketching human life. With this in mind, you will want to review the techniques employed by Bradford: the emphasis upon essential character traits; the careful selection of details; the summary form for dry but necessary facts; the quick profiling of other persons involved in the life; the dramatization of a meaningful action or statement; the unfolding, in so far as he is able, of the very complexities and contradictions of which the human being is comprised.

Suggested approach to this composition:

a. Choose a theme (a specific subject) denoting the part of your life you wish to treat. For example:

> The Day that Changed My Life
> My Home is an Anchor
> I Hate School
> Weekends in My Life
> I Have Lived a Long Time
> My Life and World Affairs
> Brothers and Sisters, I Have Some
> The Extrovert
> Life in This Town
> The Last Time I Saw Topeka

Remember that your *real subject* is *yourself*. Because your space is limited, you are selecting some specific part of your life. Choose the attitude, situation (time, place, and events), or human relationship that best reveals you.

b. Collect all the details that come to your mind and select the best ones for your purpose.

c. Plan your composition in a topic or sentence outline carried out to three degrees.

d. Select as your main method for development the one that best suits your topic: exposition, description, narration, or argument.

e. Write your first draft.

f. Check that you have kept to the theme. Replace weak words and re-work awkward sentences before you write the final draft.

QUOTATIONS FOR COMPOSITION WORK

1. Books are for a scholar's idle times.

The American Scholar—Emerson

2. I disapprove of what you say, but I will defend to the death your right to say it.

To Helvetius—Voltaire

3. All men are created equal.

The Declaration of Independence—Jefferson

4. Man's Yesterday may ne'er be like his morrow;
Naught may endure but Mutability.

Mutability—Shelley

5. No man lives without jostling and being jostled; in all ways he has to elbow himself through the world, giving and receiving offense.

Sir Walter Scott—Carlyle

6. No man, for any considerable period, can wear one face to himself, and another to the multitude, without finally getting bewildered as to which may be the true.

The Scarlet Letter—Hawthorne

Bibliography

ALTICK, Richard D., *Preface to Critical Reading* (New York, Henry Holt & Co., Inc., 1946).

BEARDSLEY, Monroe C., *Practical Logic* (Englewood Cliffs, N.J., Prentice-Hall, Inc., 1950).

BODMER, Frederick, *The Loom of Language* (New York, W. W. Norton & Company, Inc., 1944).

BIRK, Newman B. and Genevieve, *Understanding and Using English* (New York, The Odyssey Press, Inc., 1949).

CONNOLLY, Francis, *A Rhetoric Case Book* (New York, Harcourt, Brace & Co., 1953).

DAVIDSON, Donald, *American Composition and Rhetoric* (New York, Charles Scribner's Sons, 1953).

FOWLER, H. W., *A Dictionary of Modern English Usage* (New York, Oxford University Press, 1954).

FRIES, Charles Carpenter, *The Structure of English* (New York, Harcourt, Brace & Co., 1952).

LEE, Irving J., *The Language of Wisdom and Folly* (New York, Harper and Brothers, 1949).

PERRIN, Porter G., *Writer's Guide and Index* (Chicago, Scott, Foresman & Company, 1942).

THOMAS, Joseph M., MANCHESTER, Frederick A., and SCOTT, Franklin W., *Composition for College Students* (New York, The Macmillan Co., 1948).

WYKOFF, George S., and SHAW, Harry, *The Harper Handbook of College Composition* (New York, Harper and Brothers, 1952).

III

THE TEACHING

OF LITERATURE

The eight essays of our final group are on the teaching of literature. We suspect that reading is often better taught in secondary schools than is writing, perhaps because it lends itself better to large classes. And while there are students who dislike reading, they are surely less numerous than those who do not like to write.

A major fault in teaching literature, to which these essays address themselves, is overconcern with what happens in the book, rather than with why it happens. If we had to generalize about the essays that follow, we could say that they are all, in various ways, asking, why is the piece put together as it is? and then suggesting some answers to this question. The works they have chosen to discuss are among those most often taught in the high schools.

These essays have another quality in common: they are all concerned with how the student should read. To help him develop an understanding, not merely of the facts and the order in which they occur, but of their significance is clearly, to all these teachers, the real aim of the high school course in literature.

———————◆—◆◆◆—◆———————

11

The Teaching of the Novel:
Huckleberry Finn

CLEANTH BROOKS, *Yale University*

I am to talk to you about the intensive reading of literature, and I have taken for my text Mark Twain's *Huckleberry Finn*. The book may seem to you a strange choice. Hawthorne's *Scarlet Letter*, for instance, would obviously offer so much more to intensive reading and so much more easily. In *The Scarlet Letter* certain objects and incidents have an evident symbolic force and it would be easy to select many passages which would support and justify close examination, so convolved is the meaning and so rich are the layers of significance.

But I felt that to choose *The Scarlet Letter* would be to level my gun at a sitting duck. The target is too easy. If I am to make a convincing case for this kind of examination, I must show its applicability to all sorts of works, not merely to special instances of allegory and symbolism. Does a novel like *Huckleberry Finn* require close reading? Can our appreciation of it even profit from such a reading? We think of *Huckleberry Finn* as a big, loose-jointed novel, full of exaggeration, full of melodramatic scenes of colorful violence. But does this novel have the requisite closeness of grain, the fineness of texture, the attention to the detail of the pattern that go with the arrangement of more subtle effects? I think that it does, but I hope that this answer is not obvious, for mine is something of an *a fortiori* argument. If I can make my case for such a reading of *Huckleberry Finn*, I would hope that you would regard the argument proved for all those novels which, in closeness of texture, are on the hither side of *Huckleberry Finn*.

In emphasizing the richness and coherence of this book, as I shall do, I do not forget the fact that it is loose-jointed and even slapdash. Incidentally, I think that one will do well to meet with perfect candor the student who is alert to, and troubled by, these issues. I find some of the coincidences preposterous, and certain episodes unconvincing. I doubt capitally that Huck Finn would dress himself up as a girl in order to spy out the land and get information, and granting that he would do so, it is difficult to think that when he became uneasy at the questioning he would do what he is made to tell us he does: "I had to do something with my hands; so I took up a needle off of the table and went to threading it." Huck would not have done this and the author's motive in forcing him to do so is transparent: Mark Twain is arranging matters so that Mrs. Judith Loftus, with whom Huck is talking, will be able to score her point about women holding the needle still and poking the thread at it, whereas men hold the thread still and fetch the needle up to it. The novel is not a tightly constructed symbolist work and that point had better be conceded at the beginning.

Again, in indicating the possibilities of an intensive reading of *Huckleberry Finn*, I do not mean to slight more extensive treatments. Indeed, I must ask you to allow me to take a great deal for granted. For example, I assume that anyone teaching this novel will undertake to see that the class understands the larger elements of plot and the twin themes of Jim's search for freedom and Huck's moral development. Huck's moral development is, of course, something that is not sought after consciously by Huck. The boy, like Jim, is searching for freedom too, first and immediately from his father's drunken tyranny, and secondly from the constricting refinements of genteel society. How Huck's joining forces with the other fugitive, Jim, contributes to his moral development is obviously the theme of the book. I do not see how anyone could teach this novel without constant reference to it. But what I am going to say in this necessarily brief paper must take that emphasis for granted. Again, some of the larger problems that have to do with the plot must come into consideration of any teaching of *Huckleberry Finn*, but I can do no more than mention them here.

For example, there is the function of the river in providing the constantly changing highway down which our two fugitives flee. There is the generally picaresque character of the action as our hero meets with charlatans and knaves, the good, the strong, and the pathetically weak. Again there is the melodramatic cast of the narrative, with scenes of violent action and coincidence, some of them wildly improbable.

With the larger elements of the book such as these I will have to deal merely by implication or not at all. I am asking you to remember through the course of this paper that I am deliberately and perforce leaving out any consideration of these all-important topics. If I seem pedantic in this insistence I hope that I can earn your pardon. But I have become accustomed in the last fifteen years to have readers, because I have written principally on poetry, say that I am not in the least interested in fiction, or because I have written extensively on verbal nuance, say that I refuse to admit the importance of plot. So you must bear with me if I insist upon pointing out that what I am to talk about in this paper is only part of what I should expect any teacher to deal with in actually teaching this work.

We may agree then that Huck's moral development is a central element of the book. The student must be brought to see it, but there are ways and ways of accomplishing this. If we do it clumsily, the student will miss something very important in the book. Managing it ineptly, we may even distort the book. Let me illustrate. Mr. Lionel Trilling in his attractive introduction to the Rinehart edition of *Huckleberry Finn* seems to me to risk just such a distortion. He refers to Huck and Jim on the raft as constituting a "community of saints." Now I think that I see what Mr. Trilling means. Huck and Jim lack the kind of pride which distorts the vision and which dries up human sympathies. But it would certainly embarrass Huck to be thought a saint, and the student, on this point, is himself much closer to Huck Finn than he is to Lionel Trilling. The phrase "community of saints" will simply confuse the student. In any case, Huck's progress down the Mississippi on his raft is something more than a Pilgrim's Progress from the city of destruction to the heavenly city—even if we translate it to such terms as a progress from the parochialism of the small slaveholding community to a wholehearted belief in the community of man. And even if Huck's voyage did in summary constitute such a progress, we still would have to vindicate it in detail. For it is the concrete detail of the story that renders it a work of art. It is this that brings us back to the book again and again as to something that is ultimately inexhaustible. No bare bones of a moral allegory protrude from this story. Such, then, would be one justification for the intensive reading of certain passages—to help the student to see in the very handling of the concrete detail of the story some of the specific workings out of the moral development that occurs in Huck.

But not only does Huck himself develop, as the novel goes on. He is the means through which the author's own moral judgments are mediated. For it is Huck who tells the story, and it is what Huck says and sometimes what Huck in his naiveté fails to say that gives us the author's vision. The quality of Huck's vision is then all important. It is the matter which T. S. Eliot stresses in his introduction to the novel. He writes: "Huck has not imagination, in the sense in which Tom [Sawyer] has it: he has, instead, vision. He sees the real world; and he does not judge it—he allows it to judge itself."

Eliot's observation is central. From the quality of Huck's vision we can work outward to Huck's moral development. What Huck sees helps determine his moral development, and what he sees in turn measures that development for us. But the quality of Huck's vision also gives us our necessary point of reference for examining the sights and scenes and happenings that make up the novel; for, since Huck tells the story, his consciousness is its organizing principle. The way in which Huck sees, then, relates to both the formal properties of the novel *and* to the theme of moral development.

The quality of Huck's vision is central, but how shall we go about making the student share in it? We cannot simply tell him about it. We shall have to suggest it to him concretely and dramatically. Something like an intensive reading seems to be in order. For only some such mode of reading can furnish the student with the concrete particulars that he will require.

This kind of examination can, of course, be applied to any part of the novel. But I shall limit myself to one section of the novel, that beginning with the Grangerford episode and ending with Huck's visit to the circus. It is a very rich section, giving us in addition, the arrival on the raft of the Duke of Bilgewater and the rightful King of France, the murder of Boggs, and the attempt to lynch Colonel

Sherburn. But I shall have time to discuss only a selection from this wealth of description and incident.

The Grangerfords, with their highfalutin' manners, their special code of honor, and their interminable feud, are worked out in the broadest caricature. One knows something of Mark Twain's abiding hatred of violence and his unease with romantic pretensions, particularly those of the Southern gentleman. Yet as Huck sees this family they come to life immediately, the three big men with guns, the two young women with "quilts around them and their hair down their backs," and "the sweetest old gray-headed lady" that Huck ever saw. We are convinced that Huck means what he says a little later: "I liked all that family, dead ones and all." The two young ladies singing "The Last Link is Broken" or playing "The Battle of Prague" on their little tin-pan piano; the young gentlemen turning from the sideboard, raising their glasses of bitters and bowing to their elders with "Our duty to you, sir, and madam"; the dead Emmaline's crayoned pictures with their lugubrious titles: "Shall I never see thee more alas" and—this time to the dead bird—"I shall never hear thy sweet chirrup more, alas" and, this time with the heroine clasping a black-bordered letter, "And art thou gone yes thou art gone alas"—all these details make the impossible Grangerfords come alive, though they must have been for Mark Twain a kind of horrible object lesson of the baleful influence of Sir Walter Scott upon the antebellum South. It is not that Huck makes allowances for them or sentimentalizes them: his gaze is in its innocence cleansing but also fortifying. Poor Emmaline's pictures and poetry constitute incidentally the most devastating commentary upon Edgar Allan Poe ever written, for Emmaline is a very precocious young female Poe. Yet even Emmaline, as mediated through Huck's vision of her, manages to be something more than ridiculous. Perhaps Mark Twain here has outwitted himself. The Grangerfords, as Huck sees them, put on flesh and blood, persuade us of their reality, and even seduce us along with Huck to acknowledge a certain charm in their quixotic mode of living. If their feud is absurd, it is horribly so, not preposterously so. For they are not content with romantic folderol. They shoot to kill. This deadly private war is evoked with immediacy and terror as Huck actually witnesses the death of the Grangerford boy and his cousin: "When I got down out of the tree I crept down along the river bank

a piece and found the two bodies laying on the edge of the water.
. . . I cried a little while when I was covering up Buck's face for
he was mighty good to me."

The horror and meaningless bloodshed and the sense of waste in
the destruction of this household need no moralizing comment. It
never occurs to Huck to make such a comment. But the presentation
of the state of affairs through Huck's fascinated yet innocent eyes
does something more. The Grangerfords have the virtues of their
defects. They are ardent in their kindness and sympathy as well as in
their feudalistic violence. It is noteworthy that the bourgeois refinements that irk Huck so much at the Widow Douglas's do not seem
to trouble him at the Grangerfords. Perhaps the atmosphere of these
homespun aristocrats is less constricting to Huck, the born vagabond.

A little later, after the bloody ending of the Grangerford episode,
Huck is again on the raft and the two preposterous vagabonds, to be
known as the duke and the king, have now come aboard. These
charlatans are soon planning the first of their theatrical ventures. It
is to be the balcony scene from *Romeo and Juliet*. Huck tells about it
in this way: "So the duke he told him all about who Romeo was and
who Juliet was, and said he was used to being Romeo, so the king
could be Juliet." To the old man's objection that he can hardly be
cast as a young girl, the duke answers airily that "these country jakes
won't even think of that. Besides, you know, you'll be in costume
and that makes all the difference in the world."

The cream of the jest, it seems to me, is that whether or not the
country jakes will know the difference, *Romeo and Juliet* is not in
the least remote from this valley of the great river: the situation that
Shakespeare treats in *Romeo and Juliet* has just materialized on the
other bank. For what are the Grangerfords and the Sheperdsons if
not the Capulets and the Montagues. Indeed, Huck himself has been
involved in carrying the message from Miss Sophia, the Grangerford
Juliet, to young Harney Sheperdson, the Kentucky Romeo. If Huck
sees the connection he does not say anything about it. And perhaps
the duke "in telling him all about who Romeo was" gave Huck a
drastically foreshortened account. But whether Huck realizes that
the absurdly remote Shakespearean story to be enacted for the edification of the one-horse Arkansas town bears upon the tragic story
which he has just witnessed, the student ought to realize it. For this

is simply one of many similar counterpointings. The storybook romance of Tom Sawyer's boyish fantasies or of Emmaline Grangerford's lugubrious poems or of the duke and the king's tatterdemalion theatricals is constantly being put to shame by the actuality that Huck encounters almost daily.

Toward storybook romances, Huck is diligently receptive! Here he trudges dutifully after Tom Sawyer's instruction. He tried to instruct Jim in the ways of kings and chivalry, from King Solomon to the Saxon heptarchies and after. But it never occurs to Huck to consider as romantic the scenes of danger, excitement, and death that he actually encounters.

The teasing mixture of good and bad which makes up the world—the mixture of qualities in the concretion of reality—these are things which are rendered for us through Huck's vision in the Grangerford episode. They are rendered perhaps even more vividly in the events which Huck reports in the chapter entitled "An Arkansas Difficulty." The two charlatans who have now come aboard the raft plan to put on their performance of a Shakespeare revival at a little river town which is, in Huck's words, "pretty well down the state of Arkansas." Huck goes strolling around the town which is mostly "old, shackeldy, dried up frame concerns that hadn't ever been painted" and listens to the village loafers, when to their jubilation old Boggs the drunkard comes in "for his little old monthly drunk." The villagers assure Huck that Boggs is harmless though Boggs rides in with the proper vaunt and threat in the best river tradition. We have already heard it from the buckskin-coated raftsmen to whose raft Huck had swum out in an earlier chapter. Boggs declares that he is on the warpath, and promises that the price of coffins is going to rise. He even challenges Huck, riding up to him with the questions "Whar'd you come f'om, boy? You prepared to die?" Huck is scared, even though someone assures him that Boggs is really "the best natured old fool in Arkansas," but Huck is not so scared that he does not take in clearly the events that follow. Boggs in his drunken fury blackguards Colonel Sherburn, a proud-looking man about fifty-five, until Sherburn, at the end of his patience, quietly tells Boggs that he will shoot him if he is still in town by one o'clock. There follows, you will remember, Bogg's persistence in his cursing, the decision to call his daughter who can sometimes calm him, Bogg's own dawning fear as one o'clock nears and he begins to sober, and finally the implacable Colonel's stepping out with his pistol, bringing the barrel "down slow and steady to a level" and firing.

At least up until this point one's sympathy has to be with Sherburn. Boggs is a nuisance and worse. He reflects morally the squalor of the town already rendered physically so powerfully in Huck's description of the slovenly houses and muddy streets and rooting pigs. Boggs epitomizes at the least the bad manners of the back country, with its noisy boasting and its cowardly bullying.

Colonel Sherburn's cool deliberation, his keeping his word so meticulously, his shooting to kill, swing our sympathies the other way. Whether or not they swing Huck's also, Huck does not say. Again, he simply renders to us vividly what happens: ". . . they tore open his shirt first and I seen where one of the bullets went in. He made about a dozen long gasps, his breast lifting the Bible up"—someone had placed a Bible on his breast—"and letting it down again when he breathed it out—and after that he layed still; he was dead. Then they pulled his daughter away from him, screaming and crying, and took her off. She was about sixteen, and very sweet and gentle-looking, but awful pale and scared."

This is superb as reporting; it is so superb as to render commentary superfluous. Dramatically, of course, it is right that it never occurs to Huck to make any commentary here. He is sufficiently caught up in the excitement that he simply goes on telling us what happened next and then next. Somebody remarks that Sherburn ought to be lynched for what he has done and in a moment Huck is part of a yelling mob that snatches down "every clothesline they come to to do the hanging with." The mob makes its way, with the boy Huck swept along by it, to the fence that surrounds Sherburn's yard.

"Just then Sherburn steps out onto the roof of his little front porch with a double barreled gun in his hand, and takes his stand perfectly ca'm and deliberate, not saying a word. The racket stopped and the wave sucked back." Then Sherburn stares them down, overawing them in a stillness that becomes, as Huck calls it, "awful creepy and uncomfortable." And Sherburn finally proceeds to taunt them with their cowardice, pointing out the absurdity of "*you* lynching anybody." And after a further tongue lashing in which he points out that "the pitifulest thing out is a mob," he actually orders them to

leave, and they do. Huck remarks, and presumably here he speaks for
the others in the crowd, "I could 'a' stayed if I wanted to but I didn't
want to."

Our sympathies surely this time are with Colonel Sherburn. He is
a brave man, the mob is poor-spirited and contemptible. Yet the
Colonel is the same man who a few minutes earlier had shot down a
man in cold blood and he is now armed, not with a pistol but with a
double barreled shotgun, presumably because, after shooting Boggs,
he had contemptuously "tossed his pistol onto the ground," before
he turned on his heel and walked off.

It is a complicated world that Huck sees as he drifts down the
river. Huck is the apparently simple observer, but he does not sim-
plify what he sees. He renders it in its full moral complexity. If the
student can be brought to see this fact, he will be far on the way to
an understanding of Huck's character, of his importance as the focus
of narration, and of many other things necessary to an appreciation
of the novel.

Huck could have stayed and faced out Colonel Sherburn if he
had wanted to, but like the others in the crowd about him he didn't
want to. Indeed, for a moment, Huck is a part of the mob—at least to
the extent that he shares the fear and abashment that the members of
the mob feel as they look into Colonel Sherburn's cold glinting eyes.
Huck is not in the least self-conscious about this or inhibited by a
false pride. He simply puts himself in the mobster's place. But Huck
does not let the murder and the collapse of the lynching bee prey
upon his spirits. His next sentence indicates that when he decided
not to want to stay around Colonel Sherburn's, he went off to the
circus. He slips under the tent, and since it is a "real bully circus," he
soon loses himself in that experience.

This is the scene, you will remember, in which Huck, in his innocence, is completely taken in by the bareback performer who pretends to be a drunken townsman. The obstreperous drunken man
insists upon riding the circus horse, cannot be persuaded to go away
quietly, is finally allowed to ride, and after precariously hanging on
to the horse for a hair-raising first few minutes, suddenly stands up-
right, throws off his tousled clothes, and reveals himself in all the
glory of circus spangles. Huck lives through every moment of this
with changing feelings. When the apparently drunken man tries to

cling to the rearing horse, Huck says "it warn't funny to me though; I was all of a tremble to see his danger." And later, when the rider reveals himself in his gaudy professional costume, Huck feels sheepish to have been "taken in so" and commiserates with the ringmaster, now "the sickest ringmaster you ever saw." But Huck is not quite so naïve as at first glance may appear. The figure of the drunken man carries for Huck a heavy emotional charge. There is the vivid scene, earlier in the novel, in which Huck's father, when insanely drunk, tries to kill him. A little earlier on this very day, he has seen the fire-eating Boggs, whose fury turns out to be only Dutch courage, reduced suddenly from the heel-clacking half-alligator, half-horse desperado, to the wheezing man dying with a bullet in his chest. And so now this apparently drunken man whose neck is in imminent danger of being broken, finds in Huck a most sympathetic observer. In the section of the novel about which I have been talking, Huck moves steadily through a world of violence. It is a world in which there are human beings who are either brave men, like Colonel Sherburn, or the best natured old fool you ever saw, like Boggs, or perhaps they are what Colonel Grangerford might be said to be: both at the same time. These men are killing or being killed and they are doing so because they are drunk with some conception of pride or honor or are indeed quite literally drunk, in addition, with corn whiskey. This world is terrifying most of all because these men are not without virtue. Indeed they are most of them in some sense "good" men. Even Boggs is evidently a weak and foolish man rather than an evil man.

It is a world of violence, then; it is also a world in which things are not what they seem. Everyone has noticed how wary of human beings Huck is. He approaches every stranger cautiously. He rarely tells the truth about himself. One motive for his caution is the protection of Jim, but the wariness is also part of his character. A realization of the unpredictable nature of the world in which Huck lives and of its almost casual violence can help account for this. It is a world of boasters and charlatans and liars, and two of the most notable of them are Huck's own companions on the raft.

Through these episodes that I have been discussing, Huck's role has been primarily that of the detached spectator. Even at the Grangerford's, Huck has been guest and stranger. It is a point of honor for the Grangerfords that they should not involve Huck in their blood feud. And though when Huck hears that Buck has left for the war, he sets out to find him, it does not occur to Huck to bring his own gun. Instead, he says: "I clumb up into the forks of a cottonwood . . . and watched." Indeed, one can say that throughout this whole novel, Huckleberry Finn avoids involvement as much as he can. He has a zest for life, but he is perfectly willing to indulge it in merely observing life. Even his commitment to Jim is one which he tries more than once to repudiate before the claims of humanity make it impossible for him to betray Jim. If we realize how deep rooted is Huck's instinct to avoid all such commitments, we shall feel an enhanced respect for his moral triumph over himself. Because Huck is temperamentally the spectator, sensitive, honest, uncommitted, uninvolved, and uncorrupted, he can be the excellent observer that he is.

But the quality of Huck's vision, I must repeat, is something that cannot be taken for granted. The student must grasp it imaginatively —must participate in it rather than simply be told about it. I see no way to accomplish this except by having him consider the concrete particulars of Huck's experience. Something like an intensive reading is necessary though it need not deal with the episodes from which I have taken my examples. Other passages would do as well. But whatever the passages, the student must come to see what Eliot means in the comment that I have quoted earlier: "[Huck] sees the real world; and he does not judge it—he allows it to judge itself."

Huck's characteristic role of spectator determines the nature and process of his moral growth. Huck begins by holding the Abolitionists in horror, and, a matter that has usually escaped observation, Huck ends as he began. Huck, far from feeling a moral shock at Tom's behavior in reference to the freeing of Jim, seems almost relieved to find that Tom is not an Abolitionist. As Huck puts it: "I couldn't ever understand before, until that minute and that talk, how he *could* help a body set a nigger free with his bringing-up." Huck's own resolve to help the slave Jim escape comes as the result of concrete judgments and experiences. His enlarging sympathies are precisely that. It is the concrete experiences that shift Huck's ideas, not the power of an idea which changes his sentiments. This again is what we should expect in a world in which the relationships are all highly personal and concrete, in which the Mr. Phelps, who is holding Jim in confinement as a runaway slave, comes in to Jim every morning to read the Bible to him and pray with him. Huck's actions and attitudes constitute a mute but penetrating criticism of the ideas and customs of the society about him. But they are the criticism of the detached and uncommitted observer. The child was not taken in by the emperor's new clothes. He saw and said that the emperor was naked. This is the quality of Huck's innocent gaze. Huck is the vagabond, not the reformer.

Huck is then not the doctrinaire Abolitionist. He would scarcely qualify even as a devoted believer in democracy if one uses the term in the large and quasi-religious sense in which we tend to use it today. Huck likes individual human beings. He has a powerful dramatic sympathy. He projects himself into the plight of others. He can feel pity for even those scoundrels, the duke and the king, as he sees them clad in their tar and feathers, being ridden out of town on a rail. But Huck is tough-minded rather than tender-minded; he has few illusions about man's capacity for depravity. In the chapter appropriately titled "The Orneriness of Kings," Huck assures the sceptical Jim that the royalty on the raft is not too bad: "I don't say ourn is lambs, because they ain't when you come down to the cold facts, but they ain't nothing to *that* old ram [Henry VIII], anyway. All I say is, kings is kings, and you got to make allowances. Take them all around, they're a mighty ornery lot." For Huck the spectacle of human history is almost as bleak as it was for his creator, Mark Twain, himself.

But I do not mean to suggest that there is in Huck bitterness or despair. That would be to miss the point entirely. The qualities that I would stress in Huck are those of the born artist. Huck's interest in human beings, his dramatic sympathy, his concern for the concrete and the particular—these are the interests and powers of the artist. They accord well with other features of Huck's character that we have already observed: his lack of commitment, his detachment, his willingness to be pure observer, his resistance to the pressures of his society—in short his uncorrupted perceptivity. Small wonder that Huck Finn embodies the finest imaginative qualities of his creator. Indeed, Huck as an artistic intelligence actually surpasses his creator, for some of the traits of Samuel Clemens get in the way of the artist—his bitterness, his rage against man's follies, his verbosity, his commentary, his preconceptions and prejudices concerning science, religion, and politics.

Is the argument here too finespun to take up with the student? Perhaps it is. Yet it is almost worth venturing, and with some classes the teacher will be forced to venture it. For a class that is led to reflect upon the artistry of the novel at all soon comes upon this problem: here the author is deliberately limiting himself to the perceptions and intelligence and language of an almost illiterate boy. The author gains thereby, to be sure, a certain verisimilitude, a certain flavor; but can these advantages outweigh the apparent losses—particularly in view of the fact that authors do constantly succeed in tales that they tell in their own persons. How then can limitation be a source of positive gain?

I should suggest an answer by asking the student to think of Huck as a lens—a lens that organizes the picture, giving it a certain depth and focus. But if the student protested that this analogy was unfair, since a lens is a positive thing, a complex and complicating thing, then I should suggest another analogy, that of the snow glasses made by primitive men such as the Eskimos. Those snow glasses—a shield of bone pierced by a tiny slit—are apparently sheer limitation. (The student can test the principle by pushing a pin through a bit of card board and seeing for himself how this primitive lens works.) The eye is forced to peer out at its world through a tiny aperture, but the glare is shut out, and the Eskimo hunter sees as he could not otherwise. Mark Twain, forcing himself to see the world through Huck Finn has apparently seriously limited his view, but the shimmering light of a hundred subjective impressions—abstractions, generalizations, and prejudgings—is cut out, and he sees a world with an almost pristine freshness and with a terrible accuracy. It is that kind of vision which this book accords to us.

12

Teaching the Novel:
Great Expectations

PAUL PICKREL, *Yale University*

I had my only firsthand experience with the teaching of fiction in the secondary school back in the days when I still sat on the other side of the teacher's desk, in a country high school a thousand miles and almost as many years from here. Doubtless things have improved immeasurably since then, but in those days teaching a novel was something like turning a felled tree into cordwood. First the teacher sawed it up into lengths of convenient size for consumption—these were assignments. Then each day's supply was hauled into the classroom and painstakingly scrutinized for knots and other irregularities—for hard words, figures of speech, allusions classical and Biblical, freaks of syntax or of rhetoric. Possibly some heat and light were generated; at any rate the process ended when that day's allotment had been reduced to a fine, powdery ash, uniformly dry in texture and uniformly gray in color.

In spite of my description, a good deal of the teaching of fiction that went on in that country high school was both necessary and useful, and when I think of the limitations that prevailed—our limitations, our teachers', our community's—I seriously doubt that I could do the job any better than it was done. Our teachers were pretty good at helping us to grasp the "plain sense" of the text, and that is a fundamentally necessary accomplishment. To be sure, the emphasis was often peculiarly reversed, so that we were left with the impression that a novel existed to provide a forbidding collection of linguistic oddities to be categorized and labeled, with little or no notion of what function these oddities performed or what place they had in the novel. We knew, for instance, that the difference between a metaphor and a simile was a matter of grave importance, and that failure to master the difference would end in disgrace on a test, but it never entered our consciousness that a metaphor or simile might have some relation to the meaning of the book. Yet our ability to deal with language was increased in a measure; we did learn to recognize some of its more elementary wiles and strategies. That was a help.

At least one teacher could take us a step further than comprehending the "plain sense" of the text; she had the ability to help us to participate in the book, to enter into its imaginary world, so that the people and the places took on reality; in her class we laughed at the funny characters and dared with the courageous and scorned the petty. This kind of thing is now, I gather, rather frowned upon; it is labeled "appreciation" and is suspected of being meretricious and sentimental. But teaching, at least in a secondary school, is not exactly the same thing as literary criticism. The teacher I now recall was no critic, but she was a good reader, a good reader aloud to us, and a good reader in the sense that she was willing to immerse herself in the book and let it speak to her.

We students stood on the brink of the dark valley of adulthood; already we were beginning to recognize that it contained mysteries that we knew little of. We were anxious to be cued into the world of adult emotion; many of the adults we knew in those days of the great depression were themselves fumbling and uncertain, their chief claim to being adult—their ability to make a living—having ended, for some of them, forever. So it meant something to us to have a teacher who could help us to participate in a book like *A Tale of Two Cities,* who could make us feel that a man like Sidney Carton could rise above the waste and uncertainty of his life and do a "far, far better thing."

What I find curiously lacking when I look back upon my experience in high school classes in literature is any suggestion that a novel does anything more than tell a story, that it has, to use the most slippery of words, *meaning*. It simply never occurred to me that the whole complex of character and action and symbol that make up a novel might be rendered intellectually intelligible. There is a stage beyond comprehending the plain sense of the text, a stage beyond participating imaginatively within the world of the novel; there is a stage where we contemplate the book, see it as a whole, and recognize in its structure some kind of "meaning." We, in high school, never reached that stage.

Whether the secondary school teacher should attempt to bring his students to this point is at least open to question. But I have little doubt that he will be a great deal better teacher if he has brought *himself* to this point, because it will give a direction and aim and selectivity to his teaching of the linguistic detail, and it will give him confidence when he attempts to help his students to participate imaginatively in the world of the work.

How a teacher goes about seeing a novel as a whole doubtless varies with individuals. I start by trying to see what is at stake in the book—who loses, who wins, what they lose or win, whose side the author is on, and how I know which side he is on. You may object that this is merely to say that I start with the conflict and that not all novels contain a conflict. I am inclined to think that all of them do, though the conflict need not be between characters, between a hero and a villain. Often it is not. It may be between two attitudes toward life, or between the individual sensibility struggling for integrity and the randomness of experience, or between appearance and reality, and so on. The very act of writing a novel establishes a kind of conflict, for it is an attempt to save something—some person or event or attitude or insight—from the general destructiveness that we see in the world around us. So perhaps it is enough to say that we can start our contemplation of the novel with the very simple question: what is this book trying to save?

In a novel like *Great Expectations* the answer to that question is not very difficult, at least until we try to put it into words. The best I can do is to say that what Dickens is trying to save in *Great Expectations* is the poetic view of experience. I think that is what all his novels are trying to do, but in order to make it anything more than a formula of words we must look at the novel for a little while.

Great Expectations is in the first place a fantasy. It is a fantasy of a sort that many children have; perhaps all children have it, and certainly all lonely children, all children who feel too little wanted or appreciated, who feel the powerlessness of childhood. Nor is it a fantasy limited to children; anyone who buys a chance on a Cadillac or a sweepstakes ticket shares it, and probably it plays a larger part in the fantasy life of adults than most of us would care to admit. It is a fantasy of sudden translation or sudden transformation, the fantasy of arrival at a point where yearning is magically fulfilled, commonly expressed in such phrases as "when I get rich" or "when my ship comes in." It is a fantasy of a beneficent if unpredictable universe that will someday shower us with gold without any effort or indeed any merit on our part.

Pip, the main character and the narrator in *Great Expectations*, is a little boy at the beginning of the novel. He is an orphan who has been "brought up by hand" by his much older sister, the harsh and loveless Mrs. Joe Gargery. In the normal course of events he will be apprenticed to his brother-in-law, the blacksmith Joe Gargery; he will learn blacksmithing, and he will live out his days working beside Joe at the forge, perhaps someday marrying Biddy, an unkempt little girl who helps her old grandmother run a miserable evening school for the children of the village.

But two powerful, fantastic figures come into Pip's life and change its course. One is Magwitch, the criminal. He erupts in the first chapter, when Pip is out in a graveyard on the marshes one cold Christmas Eve. Magwitch is a convict escaped from the prison ship, the Hulks, "the wicked Noah's ark." He is in leg irons, cold, hungry, desperate. He is everything that a weak and passive child fears in the adult world: its capacity for wickedness, the brutality of its emotions, its strength and violence and consummate egoism, the threat of being utterly outcast and utterly alone. Magwitch demands that Pip steal food for him from Mrs. Joe Gargery's larder and a file for his leg irons from Joe's forge, and in terror of his life Pip does both. That is apparently the end of the incident, but the first encounter with the convict on the marshes that cold winter twilight leaves a slimy trail across Pip's life—a trail of prisons and criminals and crime—until years later when Magwitch erupts again.

The other fantastic figure in Pip's world is Miss Havisham, a rich old woman who represents the promise of adulthood as much as Magwitch represents its threat. At first glance, this is an extraordinary role for her to play, for her whole life has been sacrificed to memorializing the frustration of her own hopes, in commemorating the moment when the man who was supposed to marry her failed to show up for the wedding. Her clocks stand stopped at that hour, she has never since seen the light of day, she sits in her ruined wedding dress, one ruined white satin slipper still in her hand, the ruined wedding feast spread in the room across the hall, the only guests coming unbidden from behind the plaster. The very name of her once fine house is a mockery: it is "Satis House"—"enough house"—so called in boast by the ancestor who built it because he vainly supposed that whoever had such a house could never want for more, although Miss Havisham, the last of her family, has lived out her years there in testimony to the corrosion of all great expectations, whether based upon the love of man or the seeming certitude of stone.

The reason Miss Havisham can represent the promise of adulthood, in spite of her own ruin, comes partly from the fact that she is rich and partly because she is not alone. She has an adopted daughter, Estella, a little girl as beautiful and coldly distant as the star whose name she bears. Like many people who have made one great self-denying gesture, Miss Havisham is abandonedly self-indulgent, giving a free reign to her whims and self-pity. Adopting Estella was an act of indulgence on her part: bored and foolish, she keeps the child as a plaything, and rears her on a principle of vengeance, carefully cultivating Estella's beauty so that she can grow up to break the hearts of men.

Out of her impatience to see what effect Estella will have on a representative of the male sex, Miss Havisham sends down word that she wants a little boy to come and play in her rooms, and the boy who lives at the blacksmith's, Pip, is the one hit upon. When he appears at Satis House Miss Havisham has reason to congratulate herself: Pip is hopelessly smitten by Estella's beauty; in the presence of her superior manners he realizes the crudity of his own upbringing and the vast difference that stretches between Joe Gargery's forge and the polite world. He and Estella play a card game called "Beggar Your Neighbor," and while Miss Havisham croaks out in the background, "Beggar him, beggar him," Estella proceeds to do just that.

Pip dares not speak of Magwitch to anyone, and he cannot tell the truth about what happens at Miss Havisham's. When pressed for details he lies outrageously: Miss Havisham and Estella belong too much to the world of fantasy to be shared with his companions in everyday reality. In their dark, candlelit rooms, they are fairy godmother and the beautiful princess of a fairy tale, and the thick-fingered, badly dressed, ill-mannered boy from the forge must defend them against any suggestion that they might belong to the daylight world.

A few years pass. Pip is apprentice to Joe Gargery, and Miss Havisham pays his premium as an apprentice, in this way rewarding him for past services, and indicating that his relationship with Satis House is at an end. He was good enough for Estella to practice heartbreak on when she was a child, but now Estella is being trained for bigger game.

Cut off from the figures who have nourished his fantasy, no longer content with the humble expectations Joe Gargery had foreseen for his 'prentice days—those larks they were going to have together—Pip sees in the very landscape of the village a token of his lost hopes: he sees himself like the lowly marshes, while Estella is more distant than ever.

Then comes the most fantastic stroke of all. Suddenly from London the lawyer, Mr. Jaggers, appears at Joe's with the information that Pip has expectations—great expectations—after all. An anonymous benefactor has decided to lavish luxury and education on the boy, to turn him into a "gentleman." The translation that will put Pip on an equal footing with Estella is to take place; the shower of gold begins to fall. Someone—can it be anyone other than the fairy godmother?—has waved a wand; surely the boy from the forge is destined for the glittering princess.

The story is, then, a fairy tale, with a terrible ogre, Magwitch, a wildly eccentric fairy godmother, an exquisite princess, and a sudden magical transformation. But it is not only a fairy tale, for it is set in a moral universe. One beauty of the life of fantasy, and one reason some of us devote so much time to it, is that it is free from considerations of good and evil. In fantasy we kill off our friends and relatives with impunity; we grow rich without effort; we bestow lavish presents without impoverishing ourselves; we live in immense houses without concern for the servant problem. The moral universe is quite different from that: there our acts have consequences, our choices matter, our privileges entail responsibilities.

Now, just as Dickens defines the world of fantasy by two characters, or groups of characters, Magwitch on the one hand, and Miss Havisham and Estella on the other, so he defines the moral universe by two groups of characters, one group centered on Pip's brother-in-law, the blacksmith Joe Gargery, and the other centered on the London lawyer, Mr. Jaggers, who brings Pip word of his great expectations. Or perhaps that is not quite accurate: Dickens uses Joe and Mr. Jaggers not to define the moral universe—that is done by the plot—but rather to personify or embody two different attitudes toward it.

Joe lives by truth to feeling and Mr. Jaggers lives by truth to fact. Joe characteristically looks at a situation as a whole and relates himself to it as his heart bids him. Mr. Jaggers characteristically breaks the situation down into "evidence" and disposes of the evidence in whatever way his mind tells him is appropriate. Joe holds a poetic or symbolic view of experience; Mr. Jaggers holds an analytical. If Joe, for example, had come across Christina Rosetti's line, "My heart is like a singing bird," he would have known just what she meant, because he would have recognized its truth to feeling; but if Mr. Jaggers had come across the line he would have asked with a snort, "Tell me, Miss Rossetti, precisely what color are the feathers on your heart?" because the evidence that the chief organ of the circulatory system in fact resembles a singing fowl is extremely meagre.

At the bottom the difference between the two men lies in a difference in their sense of how things are related in the universe and, consequently, in their sense of how an individual can relate himself to them. This comes out most strikingly when we look at the way the two men have behaved in roughly parallel situations. Before the novel opens each man has come across a mother and baby, and each man has responded to the situation in a highly characteristic manner. Joe Gargery came across Pip and his older sister, who was attempting to bring the baby up singlehanded. Joe wanted to help the child, and he did so by embracing the situation as a whole. Though the sister was a termagant with little in her nature to bring the idea of matrimony to a man's mind, Joe married her and so became a kind of father to the baby. Mr. Jaggers, on the other hand, came across a young woman with a baby girl, and his method of dealing with the situation was to separate them. The child he put out for adoption where she would never know who her mother was, and the mother he took into his own house, not on terms of affection but as a servant kept in place by terror. The situations are not strictly parallel, because the future Mrs. Joe Gargery was only a shrew, whereas Mr. Jaggers' future servant was actually a criminal and her baby daughter the child of another criminal, but there is enough similarity to indicate the moral points of view of the two men.

Another way that the difference is dramatized is in the way the two men relate themselves to Pip. Joe's relationship is based upon feeling for the boy, and he allows nothing to cloud the purity of that feeling. This is brilliantly dramatized in the scene where Miss Havisham insists on paying Pip's premium as an apprentice. Joe had never expected such a premium, of course; he expected to take Pip as an apprentice because he loved him. So when Miss Havisham summons them to Satis House, Joe addresses all his remarks to Pip; the money he cannot decline, but he flatly refuses to turn a relationship based on love into a commercial transaction. In speaking to Miss Havisham only through Pip he asserts that nothing she does on this occasion can change their love. Mr. Jaggers, on the other hand, never tires of telling Pip that in their relationship he is acting purely as a businessman. Mr. Jaggers does not approve of the unknown benefactor's scheme and says so; he has no confidence that Pip will profit by his expectations and says so; he is simply carrying out instructions.

Life for Joe is a perpetual marrying and giving in marriage. He constantly gives his heart and accepts the mixed consequences of his generosity. Mr. Jaggers is the purest bachelor, the completely disassociated man. For him the world is a dungheap with an occasional jewel in it. The shrewd man rescues the jewels when he can; otherwise he tries to stay at a distance from the dungheap, and when he must touch it, as a criminal lawyer like Mr. Jaggers frequently must, he will constantly wash his hands with strong soap, as Mr. Jaggers does after each interview.

There are several curious things Dickens does with the characters of Joe and Mr. Jaggers. For one thing, they are both men, and for another they are both good men. More recent English novelists who have tried to defend the poetic view of experience ordinarily use a woman to embody it, and ordinarily make her superior to those who represent another view. Virginia Woolf, for instance, in *To the Lighthouse* uses Mrs. Ramsay for this purpose, and Mrs. Ramsay is in every way a more appealing character than her analytical philosopher-husband. E. M. Forster usually gives us a middle-aged woman who defends the wisdom of the heart, the wisdom that "connects" person with person, or race with race. She is clearly a better person than the callous males whose wisdom only divides.

But Dickens uses men to embody both the poetic and the analytic view of experience. Perhaps by the time he wrote *Great Expectations* he no longer had much confidence in women as an embodiment of the poetic view; at least there are only two rather minor female characters in the whole book who are not cold and heartless. But, whatever the reason, by using male characters to embody both views, Dickens avoided the danger of allowing a question of truth to become a question of sex.

And it is testimony to Dickens' fairness that Mr. Jaggers is so powerful a character and so good a man. Some readers have not thought so well of him, but he seems to me to be admirable—honest, trustworthy, devoted to duty. In the end his way of looking at experience is mistaken, but he remains a good as well as a brilliant man, and in one wonderful scene he drops a hint that he knows his own mistake.

Another testimony to Dickens' fairness is the fact that he does not allow these two characters to stand alone, but surrounds them with other characters who serve the purpose of modifying the argument. Around Joe are grouped Mrs. Joe, Uncle Pumblechook, and a few other residents of the village, and they are all dreadful people. They show that the poetic view of experience, so noble when held by one of nature's noblemen like Joe, can easily go a little askew and become the blackest of all tyrannies, the tyranny of the heart. Love with the slightest sign of a price tag is emotional blackmail, and Mrs. Joe is an accomplished emotional blackmailer, a tyrant of the affections. She believes that her act of generosity in taking care of little Pip entitles her to a lifetime of adulation, and whenever the adulation grows faint she issues a cutting reminder of her due. Beside such sharp trafficking in emotions Mr. Jaggers' reliance on facts seems honest and dignified.

Mr. Jaggers does not stand alone on his side of the argument either, for he has a clerk, one Wemmick, who manages to combine the analytical view of experience with the poetic. At the office Wemmick is as closemouthed, as adamant for facts, as Mr. Jaggers himself. His constant advice is to accumulate "portable property." But when we see him at home we discover that his property is anything but portable: he has a little house, a tiny Gothic castle surrounded by a moat. He has an Aged Parent, his deaf old father, whom he somewhat lightly calls "the A.P." but whom he cherishes. He has a pig, and a cannon he shoots off, and a ladyfriend, Miss Skiffins. He is as much married to life as Joe Gargery himself—outside the office.

Probably a student of nineteenth-century thought would call Wemmick the Victorian compromise at the level of whimsey. He is also the most modern man in the book, living part of his life in accordance with one view of experience and part of it in accordance with another.

Behind *Great Expectations* and behind most of nineteenth-century and twentieth-century literature lies a fact that was becoming increasingly apparent throughout Dickens' lifetime and is even more apparent today: the fact that in practical matters the analytic approach to problems is vastly more successful than the poetic. Science and technology provide the outstanding examples of the triumph of analysis, but it is difficult to think of any field of human endeavor in which the introduction of analytic techniques has not had a remarkable effect; it has even influenced those undertakings in which traditionally a sense of wholeness has been sought—philosophy, poetry, religion.

Often it seems that what I have called the poetic view of life—the feeling that things somehow hang together and make sense, that we can somehow relate ourselves as a whole to experience—often it seems that the only argument in favor of that view of life is our profound need of it. But Dickens saw a stronger argument, and in *Great Expectations* he advances it as a novelist ought to advance his arguments —by the plot.

The plot of *Great Expectations* is a good one; it holds the reader's interest; it is full of surprises and odd turns; its complexities all come out neatly in the end. But more than that, it is a symbolic representation of Dickens' vision of the moral universe, and the chief characteristic of that vision is that good and evil, what we most desire and what we most loathe, are inextricably intertwined, involved with one another in such a way that no human hand can sort them out.

The plot is resolved through the discovery of a series of surprising relationships, and each of these is a relationship between something loathsome and something desirable. The first of these is the discovery that Pip does not owe his geat expectations to the fairy godmother, Miss Havisham, but to the ogre, Magwitch. Magwitch has been transported to Australia; there he has prospered as a sheep rancher, and he has decided to use his wealth to make a gentleman of the little boy who stole the food and file for him on the marshes long ago. Pip's rise in the world has not been an act of magic; it has actually been a reward for theft, for what he has regarded as the most shameful deed of his life.

The second great discovery is that Estella, whom Pip has wasted his life in loving, is far from being a princess; she is in fact the illegitimate daughter of Magwitch by the criminal who now serves as Mr. Jaggers' servant. Miss Havisham is no fairy godmother; she is a foolish old meddler.

Life is not, Dickens is showing us symbolically by the plot, a dungheap in which one can find an occasional jewel to pluck out, as Mr. Jaggers supposes. It is an old, old growth; the fairest flower and the most noxious weed have their roots in the same ancient soil. Joe Gargery's view of experience is right because he has grasped this fact—not intellectually, for Joe is no intellectual, but by accepting in love the complexity of the moral universe. In Lear's phrase, he has taken upon himself the mystery of things.

Pip himself represents an impure mixture of the easiest parts of both Joe's and Mr. Jaggers' attitudes toward experience.

Actually it is not altogether fair to compare Pip with Joe and Mr. Jaggers: they are unchanging, fixed points of reference in the book —so much so that they seem never to age. But Pip changes. When first we meet him he is an innocent little boy. When last we see him he is a man in early middle age, much chastened by experience. The book is essentially an account of Pip's moral education, and in order to understand the nature of that education we must see Pip's attitude toward experience clearly—in itself, and in relation to Joe's and Mr. Jaggers'.

Joe and Mr. Jaggers have this in common: they are both in some sense moral realists. To be sure, they differ as fundamentally as two men can about what should be dignified with the label of reality, but they are realists in that both accept the consequences of their own views. For Joe this means that, if to follow the demand of his heart, to love and cherish little Pip involves marrying a shrew, then he is ready to pay the price, and he never whines of it afterward. When Joe realizes that the larks that he and Pip were to share are never going to happen, when he realizes that there is no longer any place for him in Pip's life after Pip has gone to London, he recognizes the situation for what it is; his love takes on a tragic cast, but it remains love. Mr. Jaggers is equally steadfast in facing the worst that his own attitude toward life entails: he is a man isolated, cut off from other human beings—respected and feared but unloved. But Mr. Jaggers can face the worst, unflinching, and recognize it for what it is.

Pip differs from both men. He is not a realist; he is a fantasist. He supposes that he can have the best of both views and the unfavorable consequences of neither. He embraces isolation, as Mr. Jaggers does, but he embraces it selectively—or, in other words, he becomes a terrible snob. He cuts himself off from his own past—he neglects Joe, he does not go back to the forge, he is ashamed of his blacksmith's arm among the languid or vicious young bloods whose society he cultivates in London. He isolates himself from those who love him, but he does not accept the natural consequence of his action, which is lovelessness. Love is as necessary to Pip as to Joe Gargery, but Pip wants it on his own terms, the terms of fantasy. He can only love the fairy-tale princess, the coldly glittering distant star, Estella.

Now Pip is not entirely to be blamed in all this. His early life *was* fantastic; his contacts with creatures like Magwitch and Miss Havisham could only encourage the habit of fantasy in him; and then in adolescence to have his wildest dreams realized, to be suddenly transformed from a humble village apprentice to a young Londoner with great expectations—what result could all this have except to make the boy suppose that the world is indeed whatever his fancy would like it to be? How could he avoid supposing that he was one singularly excused by the gods from facing consequences?

Dickens understood the life of the fantasist because he had lived it, and no one who is familiar with the recent scholarship dealing with Dickens' life can doubt that *Great Expectations* is a kind of symbolic autobiography. *David Copperfield* is closer to the facts of Dickens' life, but *Great Expectations* is closer to its spirit. For Dickens, as for Pip, life had "come true" to an extent that even his wild fantasy could hardly have suggested in childhood. As a boy Dickens knew poverty and limitation and social disgrace—his father in debtors' prison, his own experience in the blacking factory. He knew what it was to be "cut off from all the luxury of the world." But he was extraordinarily successful, extraordinarily young, and with the possible exception of Mark Twain, there has probably never been another writer to know such fame in his own lifetime. The world was at his feet, yet he was afflicted with a passion for a woman who almost certainly did not return his feeling and probably found him simply distasteful. It is useless to speculate how close Estella in *Great Expectations* is to the woman Dickens loved in the last years of his tempestuous, fame-soaked, unfulfilled life; the point is simply that in writing the novel Dickens is not "talking down"; in creating Joe Gargery and Joe Gargery's attitude toward life, he was struggling to save something he needed as much as we do.

The novel ends with Pip and Estella reunited at the gate of the ruined Satis House. As you probably know, Dickens originally had them simply meet and part, presumably forever; but his friend Bulwer Lytton prevailed upon him to supply the "happier" ending. Some readers have deplored the alteration; to me it seems not to matter, for by this point Estella has been so thoroughly discredited as a creature of fantasy and Pip so thoroughly discredited as a fantasist that they are hardly the same people they once were; they are at most a middle-aged couple who have failed.

The healing touch at the end of the novel is not the reunion of Pip and Estella, but Pip's return to the forge. By the time he goes back, his sister, Mrs. Joe Gargery, has long since died, and the ageless Joe has married Biddy, the girl whom Pip might once have married had he been free of the myth of his own life. They have a child, a little boy, and they have named him Pip. "And there was I again!" the old Pip cries to himself. Another generation has come along; another branch of that ancient vine, the human race, has sprung forth. Its roots are in the tangled dark, as ours are; they will have to learn to live with that fact, as we must; but perhaps, acknowledging the dark, they will do a better job of seeking the light.

In the century since his career was at its zenith, there have been many Dickenses. There was, for instance, Dickens the defender of hearth and home. That Dickens is not very popular today, partly because of the sentimentality that marks the more domestic aspect of his work, and partly because increased knowledge of his private life gives the role a doubtful appropriateness. Then there was Dickens the reformer, the social thinker, the radical. As recently as twenty years ago he was something of a favorite of the Marxist critics, who saw him as very nearly one of their own. Dickens certainly did take a marked interest in the social problems of his time, and he attacked injustice where he found it and as he saw it, bitterly and brilliantly. He was also profoundly conservative; he loved the old England before the railroads, and was the last great chronicler of the stagecoach, the country inn, the roast beef of Old England. As for any program of reform he might have envisioned, as George Orwell has pointed out, it hardly amounted to more than this: that we should all behave better, as indeed we should.

The Dickens I have tried to sketch tonight is a kind of symbolist poet, a man with a sweeping vision of the fundamental relatedness that underlies the surface fragmentation of human life, a man with the insight to see the moral and psychological consequence of that vision, and a man with the power of imagination to set it forth in a vivid, wildly fantastic, yet deeply controlled narrative.

13

How Should We Teach Novels? Report of the Committee on Intensive Reading

MARION SHERIDAN, *Hillhouse High School, New Haven,*
Chairman
WALTER BONNER, *New Bedford High School, Massachu-*
setts
GLADYS MANSIR, *Staples High School, Westport, Con-*
necticut
JOSEPH MERSAND, *Jamaica High School, New York*
HAROLD OWEN, *Proctor Academy, Andover, New*
Hampshire
ARLINE ZEHNDER, *Bronxville High School, New York*

When you think of the intensive reading of a novel, think also of extensive reading, of writing, of listening, and of language. Reading a novel will be facilitated by a rich background gained from life, language study, and experiences with broad, independent, and deep reading. Likewise, the intensive study of the novel should aid the student in listening, in understanding language, in writing, in reading independently, and in interpreting life. The close reading of a novel is not an entire or exclusive program but a part, inseparable from life, language, writing, and extensive reading. Each phase is dependent upon the other phases.

In the light of some stereotyped judgments about the teaching of English, it is dangerous to focus on close reading. English teachers are perennially warned against being dissectors or dessicators of literature. Attention to parts, sometimes really minute parts, may be attention to the pieces of Humpty Dumpty. "And all the king's horses and all the king's men couldn't put Humpty Dumpty together again." Close reading may make students nearsighted, unable to stand off and view the whole from a distance. They may see one or two windows in the Yale Hall of Graduate Studies or one stained glass window in a cathedral but remain unaware of mass and form. The intensive study of literature, often of novels, has been indicated as an unnatural way to read, an unfailing way to bore students, a certain way to create an incurable distaste for English and for reading.

It is somewhat dangerous to consider the teaching of a novel. *The Teaching of English,* issued by the Incorporated Masters in Secondary Schools in England and published by the Cambridge University Press in 1952, reports that because of the difficulties resulting from length and the fact that pages are of varying degrees of interest and children of varying degrees of ability, some teachers "incline to the view that the novel is not a suitable form of literature for class study . . . ." [1]

Even critics have veered away from the novel. William Van O'Connor in "The Novel in Our Time," in *Forms of Fiction,* wrote, "More critics have applied themselves to the study of poetic forms than to the forms of the novel, possibly because the novel, for whatever reasons, is more difficult for the critical mind to assimilate." [2]

The novel, however, is important. Its basic appeal has been enjoyment, an appeal which must not be underrated. With students the length of the novel may be an asset, for it gives a chance to live with the people of the novel long enough to have them make an impression. Wordsworth's short poems had not obtained for him his deserts, said Matthew Arnold. They lacked impact. Arnold therefore selected and rearranged them to provide a sustained effect. A sustained effect is an integral part of a novel.

[1] p. 88.
[2] *Essays Collected in Honor of Joseph Warren Beach,* William Van O'Connor, ed. (Minneapolis, The University of Minnesota Press, 1948), p. 3.

The novel has influenced judgments of life. Lionel Trilling wrote of this in "Manners, Morals, and the Novel," when he said: "For our time the most effective agent of the moral imagination has been the novel of the last two hundred years. . . . Its greatness and its practical usefulness lay in its unremitting work of involving the reader himself in the moral life, inviting him to put his own motives under examination. . . . There never was a time when its particular activity was so much needed, was of so much practical, political, and social use. . . ." [3]

In teaching this important art form intensively, the qualities of the teacher are of the utmost importance. In spite of some practices that suggest that anyone speaking English on any level may teach English, not everyone can teach a novel. The teacher must be enthusiastic. Many teachers transferred from other departments are not enthusiastic. Even some teachers who have majored in English have not recognized the importance of enthusiasm. It may make possible an atmosphere of excitement, often desirable. The enthusiasm should lead to sharing: teacher, artist, student. Needless to say, the teacher must be sincere.

The teacher must know the novel at hand and novels as a genre. He must be able to make apt and penetrating references to a wide range of literature. Through them he is teaching future lessons. Such references should not be forced or self-conscious, nor should they be affected for what has been called prestige. They should be natural, introduced to interpret, to guide students skillfully to see reality and to distinguish it from illusion. Such teaching, subtle teaching, should lead the student from one novel to another and to other phases of literature. The teacher must be alert to seize what the committee calls "teachable moments." Student comments, often quiet ones, may serve as wedges to open doors, as springboards from which to leap.

A novel is a part of a year's work. How long should such study take? There is no one answer. Books, classes, occasions vary. Too much time has been spent; too little. The aim should be to reduce the time as far as is consistent with "reading" the novel. If a novel may be read in an afternoon, it is wisdom to question spending six to eight weeks in class on the book. It may or may not require further con-

[3] *Ibid*, pp. 159–160.

centration. A novel chosen for intensive reading should offer something that will repay close reading.

In a year possibly only one novel may be chosen for intensive reading. Even with so-called homogeneous grouping, students in the reading group will vary in abilities and interests. Regardless of these individual differences, a group should have a common experience with a novel. As the New York City course of study suggests, our cultural life is centrifugal. At times our study should be centripetal, working in the direction of unifying. There is much to be said for a common literary heritage as a force to bind diverse people together through understanding, and even to provide a sense of security; one means is reading a book in common. The rich experience of really reading a novel, of penetrating the work of an artist and of penetrating life to unsuspected depths may provide a pattern for the understanding of other novels, varied in pattern as novels are.

Granted there is to be a novel, the question is "Which novel?" The choice is difficult. It may be made by the teacher; it is better if it can be made by the group with their teacher. Whether the novel was written a hundred years ago or today is comparatively unimportant. What is important is what the novel has to communicate. The needs of the class, their tastes, their experience, and the accessibility of the books will influence the choice. There is not one indispensable novel, either *Silas Marner* or *The House of the Seven Gables*, although Lionel Trilling states "that all prose fiction is a variation on the theme of *Don Quixote*." Any edition with good type, all editions—with leather covers and marble end papers, with stiff covers and with paper covers—are possibilities. New copies are preferable to worn and soiled ones. If possible a copy of the novel should be the private property of the student, his own to enjoy like any valued possession, to mark up, to share.

The novel, difficult enough to justify class study, must not be so difficult that it will frustrate. As Edgar Dale pointed out in "The Problem of Readability," [4] "High interest in a story will cause the reader to override difficulties." The novel for intensive reading should be one that can be enhanced or realized through analysis, discussion, and reflection. It is desirable to use a complete novel. The report

[4] *The News Letter*, The Bureau of Educational Research, Ohio State University, Vol. XIX, No. 5 (February, 1954).

from England suggested that abridged editions are preferable to simplified versions. The only excuse for abridged editions may be for students unlikely ever to read the original. Many believe that if the novel is to be cut, the teacher himself should abridge to suit his particular class.

Novels are usually read each year of the secondary school course. Sometimes it is overlooked that the novel read intensively in the senior year may be the last fiction studied by a student, even if he is going to college.

The recent trend has been to teach short novels. To be sure, *Silas Marner* and *The Scarlet Letter* are short. Thackeray's *Henry Esmond*, *The Newcomes*, and *Vanity Fair*; Blackmore's *Lorna Doone*; Austen's *Pride and Prejudice*; and Scott's *Quentin Durward, Ivanhoe*, and *The Talisman* have been succeeded by *The Red Badge of Courage, Ethan Frome, The Rover, My Antonia*, and *Goodbye, Mr. Chips*. Students appropriated *The Old Man and the Sea* without consulting teachers.

Short compact novels lend themselves to intensive reading. They provide a complete experience. Longer novels, however, are also in use, among them *Mutiny on the Bounty, Green Mansions, The Mayor of Casterbridge, The Return of the Native, Arrowsmith, Drums, The Yearling, The Forsyte Saga*, and *Giants in the Earth*.

We are asking that high school students—working outside of school perhaps, working in school with other subjects, busy with demanding extracurricular activities of all kinds—should sit down to read a comparatively long book and to see it as a whole. The novel chosen must also compete successfully with a confusing number of entertainment features—movies, radio programs, and TV—which students may have to sacrifice. Those media, however, should not be overlooked as a motivating force for reading.

So that students will get the full experience of reading a novel, strangely enough it is urgent to say that the study must focus on the novel. Often not the novel but the periphery has been the center of interest to the exclusion of the novel itself. Surveys of literature or studies of the history of literature or the biography of the author and accounts of his time have too often ignored or obscured the novel. The student is to experience the novel; he is to get into it as far as he can, even to becoming an actor in the events of the story.

In some great novels, however, there is no direct identification of the reader with the characters. Furthermore, with all kinds of novels the student should learn to get outside the story far enough to be able to look at the author's presentation objectively. The reader or moviegoer who is sufficiently detached to say "This is only a movie," at the same time that he is breaking out into a sweat as a train hurtles down upon the heroine, has reached a stage of maturity. So has the reader or dreamer who can say as his nightmare becomes unbearable, "This is a dream. Wake up!"

The novel may or may not be part of an idea-centered or theme-centered unit. The endeavor to link the central idea with that of other works of literature or with phases of life should not distort what the novelist has to say, nor should it limit the full experience that the novel has to offer. The student should read without an a priori conclusion. The desirability of better race relations may be presented in a novel, but it may not exhaust the content of the novel.

Another danger may come from focusing on the novel as a type of literature. What does it profit a student to recite all the tags of incentive moment, climax, plot of a novel but not to know the novel, not to have seen or felt its inner life? Concentration on the characteristics of the type may result in generalities and pat definitions, in an identification of externals, distracting the student from the experience the novel should bring.

A teacher does not teach a student to read a novel by having him read two or three chapters a day, by having him retell what he has read, by emphasizing fact, incidents, and plot. The plot is a skeleton, only bones, not a living thing.

Sometimes there may be oversimplification in defining the way to teach a novel. A recent article opposed teaching *Ethan Frome* as a literary work and favored teaching it to teach the concepts and values of family relationships. The author defined the teaching of *Ethan Frome* as a literary work as dealing with reading comprehension, structure of the plot, details of characterization, literary style, characteristics of the novel in general as exemplified in *Ethan Frome*, and biographical material on the author. The writer opposed such study, for the teacher might never come to grips with "matters at least equally significant for boys and girls who on graduation will be getting jobs and getting married."

It is possible to present *Ethan Frome* by neither of those alternatives. A study of the novel as a literary work may be defined in other terms. A literary approach is objectionable if it means identification of cold, lifeless, formal, isolated elements. Interesting as family relationships are, they are not the sole consideration in the teaching of *Ethan Frome*.

Reading the novel means a full comprehension of what Edith Wharton presents, how she presents her vision, and why. A good novel is more than the sum of its parts, more than an addition of chapters. It is an idea presented in action. The way of the novelist, as of the artist, is by indirection. He gives one thing in order to give another. The study of the novel works toward an understanding of his conception. The novel is fiction, not nonfictional prose. The novelist gives concrete particulars; the reader has to draw conclusions. The novel has some kind of pattern, some form. In teaching the novel, the teacher must work toward the student's appreciation of a work of art; toward an understanding that the artist selected what he wished to present, even though the novel may be loosely constructed.

The novelist selected a story, decided through whose eyes the reader is to see that story, decided on the order in which the reader is to learn of motives and outcomes. Edith Wharton in an introduction went into detail about her reasons for writing *Ethan Frome* as she did, but the novel is more important than that introduction.

Novels give insight into characters, and most teen-agers are interested in people. So are adults. Pearl Buck expressed this idea by saying, "I can think of no novel which is enduring from past to present which is not about people, rather than a comic or tragic situation or an adventure. In short, a novel stands or falls, even for the moment, not by whether it is timely, or exciting, or well written, or by any other thing except by the reality of its people." [5]

At Bread Loaf there was a story that Robert Frost was greeted on a Vermont road by a farmer friend with the casual greeting: "How are ye today?" Mr. Frost paused to think. "How am I? On what level are you asking, my friend?" The intensive reading of a novel is on many levels of understanding. From an apparently simple question may develop a discussion ranging from obvious fact to profundi-

[5] "Fiction and the Front Page," *The Yale Review* (Spring, 1936), pp. 481–482.

ties; the said and the unsaid; the recognition—or detection—and understanding of implications.

The novel should be studied on these levels, vertically. It should also be studied horizontally.

The approach is important. The teacher may ask his students to move with him into a strange country or with strange people or with those of different age groups. The locality may be interesting, as it would be in starting *Moby Dick* with students in New Bedford. Short stories, such as "The Cask of Amontillado," have provided an approach. Material in current newspapers and magazines, in radio and TV programs may be used to bridge the gap. At one time the life of the Collier brothers gave the opening for the teaching of *Silas Marner*. Klaus Fuchs was being tried in the Old Bailey when another class was reading *A Tale of Two Cities*. Excerpts from motion pictures, prepared for school use by Teaching Film Custodians and a committee of the National Council of Teachers of English, may help in getting started. Among the films are *Washington Square*, based on Henry James's novelette; *Meet the Forsytes*, based on *The Forsyte Saga;* and *Kipling's India*, based on *Kim*.

It is often valuable to have the students read the novel as a whole and as quickly as possible. There are usually logical divisions of the book that can be discussed, if they are read by all. Students can be urged to forge ahead independently. What can they grasp of the broad brush strokes of the author? What is the pattern? What is the author trying to do?

Paradoxically, when the aim is to go beyond the facts, incidents, and plot, the next step may be a short-answer objective test. The test may stimulate close reading and establish facts, incidents, plot, and the identity of the characters. It may anticipate significant points in the novel which will take on meaning in rereading. The importance of facts must not be underrated. Students may have colossal ignorance about facts that are basic to the understanding of the book. Sometimes it is strange how disembodied and nebulous the high school reader's grasp of place as well as time can be. Attention to facts has been criticized and rightly so—if the reading of the novel stops there. Too much high school teaching of fiction may have been a recital of facts and of what happened. Noting facts or episodes are on the lowest level of reading a novel, sometimes termed the primitive level. Establishing them merely gets the reading off to a good start.

The study must go on from plot or narrative level to structure, concerned with the arrangement and relationships of the episodes and scenes and with details of action.

To give an awareness of levels, it has been suggested that you ask a class to list for ten minutes all the possible answers to this one question: "Where am I now?" Then have the answers read aloud. Such answers have ranged from the obvious: "Third seat, in the second row, English class, Westport High School" to "In trouble, in a world of dreams, in a conscious state." The range is from a personal, limited horizon, with thought of physical self in space, with a subjective point of view; to a wider, more objective horizon, with self placed in business, social, and political groups in larger space areas, with limitless abstractions and ideas.

On succeeding days such questions as "What time is it now?" "Who am I?" should be asked. After these discussions the slowest will become surprisingly aware of levels in thought. They can begin to see the difference between fact and abstraction, between self-centered concepts and social consciousness.

Perhaps the basic technique in teaching is the thought question with the emphasis on questions asking "Why?" Why is a certain incident important in the story? Why is there this particular ending? If another were substituted, what changes would have to be made? Why is a certain color emphasized?

A series of questions that proved valuable in bringing Hemingway's *The Old Man and the Sea* to life led from the simple to the complex, from the whole to a part, from the plot to the theme. A few examples of the questions are, "How do you explain his calling the marlin 'friend'?" "In what way could you call the fishing trip successful?" "Why do you suppose Hemingway called this story *The Old Man and the Sea* instead of *The Old Man against the Sea?*"

Oral reading of special passages, proportionately few, may create a mood. Serenity and nobility are implicit in the closing of *The Rover*. The lines may well be read aloud and then perhaps used as a basis for amplification as to why the ending is fitting.

There may be some dramatizations, as of David Copperfield in the inn. The relationship of the incident to the novel needs to be brought out.

In the study of structure the position of the narrator is fundamental. The reader must know who the narrator is, where the story asks him to be, and why he is there; he must anticipate what will result. A story may be told by a central character, in the first person, or by a minor character. It may be told by one outside the action, merely an eyewitness. The narrator may be an all-observant omniscient outsider, as is the narrator in Hemingway's *The Old Man and the Sea*. The point of view may shift from one narrator to another as in *Treasure Island* and *Ethan Frome*. It is always profitable to ask why the narrator was chosen, and why the shift in point of view, if there is one.

Time order must be noted. *Moby Dick* is in chronological order. In *The Rover* the story jumps in point of time. Time is not given directly in dates, but indirectly by signs, for example, by the size of the English razor, captured in far-off seas and honed down over the years.

Characterization is involved in the point of view and in time shifts. More often characterization is indirect rather than direct. It is conveyed to an alert reader through actions, words, and the effect of one person upon another.

In a work of art details are likely to be significant. Sense impressions of light, color, sound, and feeling, as in the scene in the chimney in *The Return of the Native*, are parts of the whole.

When the study gets to the use and arrangement of words, it is concerned with style. Among specific devices are irony and imagery, including figures of speech and symbolism. Irony involves a second look, a further implication, an unexpected outcome. There is irony in *The Great Gatsby*, even in the title. There is irony in the pickle dish, an object, in *Ethan Frome*, and in the wild sleigh ride, an incident. There is irony in the character of the Rover, the kind and noble member of the Brotherhood of the Coast. Irony gives depth and complexity. It involves sequential consideration, a before-and-after situation, requiring an understanding of more than the immediate detail. The coffin which Queequeg builds, for instance, ironically becomes the instrument which saves Ishmael's life. Irony may be a slight shift in meaning or a complete paradox. Understanding irony leads to understanding the author's tone.

Imagery, a broad term including *metaphor, simile, synecdoche, metonymy, onomatopeia,* is not for decoration but for communication. The mere ability to spot metonymy at twenty paces on Monday morning may not help a student to evaluate the effect striven for by an author. The metaphor, a most important figure, is the use of one kind of experience to describe another. Superficially, metaphor seems more subtle or elusive than a simple statement, but it is likely to be natural and direct. Children use metaphor unconsciously. The examination of metaphors is not an attempt to collect figures of speech like rare insects but to help an inexperienced reader see as the author sees. A simile reveals the whole direction of Ethan's thought: "he sat in fascinated contemplation of the way in which her hands went up and down above the strip of stuff, just as he had seen a pair of birds make short perpendicular flights over a nest they were building." [6]

Symbols, sometimes defined as metaphors from which the first term has been omitted, are ubiquitous in advertising, in neon lights, in television. They are not uncommon in novels. Hardy, for example, uses a provocative symbol in *Jude the Obscure,* by reference to Samson and Delilah. When Jude entered an obscure public-house, ". . . the sight of the picture of Samson and Delilah on the wall caused him to recognize the place as that he had visited with Arabella on that first Sunday evening of their courtship." [7]

Teaching must go far, but it must not go too far or too fast. It may be well in an intensive study of structure and style in a novel to keep in mind the words of Delmore Schwartz at a meeting of the School and College Conference on English:

They were outside, and one student said to me in a way which was both pathetic and touching: "Isn't *Moby Dick* really about whaling?" He had heard all sorts of interpretations of it, many of them very good, about its religious meanings and so on. Now, as I was saying before, the student will be able under instruction to ascend from primitive reading to an understanding of the style, structure, simple irony, and other matters.

[6] Edith Wharton, *Ethan Frome* (New York, Charles Scribner's Sons, 1939), p. 93.
[7] Thomas Hardy, *Jude the Obscure* (The Modern Library; New York, Random House), p. 79. See also p. 48.

My main proposal, which I advance with a good many misgivings, is that the ascent from primitive understanding to the other matters in much too rapid. The primitive understanding to the other matter is much too rapid. The primitive reading is entirely ignored. You are plunged into the most extraordinary matters of myth and structure and irony and attitude by the good students and meanwhile the ordinary, intelligent student—and I think that the number of intelligent students is usually underestimated—is left pretty far behind. If you've seen courses in fiction particularly, I've encountered students who will use the method of the New Criticism in a way which shows just how bad it can become. They will read fiction as if fiction were lyric poetry. They will count the number of images; they will come forward with the most ingenious interpretations of recurrence of symbols. They will actually become creative: that is to say they will create their own poem out of a serious story. They will—this is my experience especially at Kenyon College—they will refuse to believe that in a story something really happens.[8]

The intensive study of a novel—inseparable from listening, writing, extensive reading, and language—should present a novel as a whole. From the reading a pattern or form should emerge, even an imperfect one. And great novels may be imperfect in structure. Somerset Maugham called *Moby Dick* "a great, a very great book" because "no creature of fiction" approaches Captain Ahab in stature.[9] Mr. Maugham also stated that ". . . it would be stupid to assert that his [Melville's novel, *Moby Dick*] is well constructed." [10]

Intensive study should discover for the reader the vision the novelist has chosen to present. The reasons for the actions of the characters and for the arrangement of scenes should lead to an understanding of the richness of the novel as a sustained presentation of human beings and human life. So should penetration into the economical and skillful choice and arrangement of words in irony, imagery, and symbols. The novel seldom fails to reach thoughtful readers emotionally and to give at least a glimpse of beauty.

Ethical values are to be found in novels, as Lionel Trilling sug-

[8] Delmore Schwartz, "The New Criticism and the Newest Medium," paper delivered at the Annual Midwinter Meeting, School and College Conference on English, February 19 and 20, 1954, p. 28.

[9] W. Somerset Maugham, "Introduction," Herman Melville, *Moby Dick* (Philadelphia, The John C. Winston Company, 1949), p. xxviii.

[10] *Ibid.*, p. xxvii.

gested.[11] Through questions they may be made explicit. They must not, however, be wrenched out of their place in the whole. Often they should be left implicit. Like the grass in Sandburg's poem they might say, "Let me work." [12]

Finally, novels do tell a story in which something happens. They are to be read for enjoyment. Helen Haines, for example, in *What's in a Novel*, stated that in reading fiction "pleasure is the motive that underlies all others." [13] Somerset Maugham wrote, "I cannot repeat too often that a novel is to be read not for instruction or edification but for intelligent enjoyment, and if you find you cannot get this from it you had far better not read it at all." [14]

T. S. Eliot may believe that "the novel is a form which will no longer serve," a form that "ended with Flaubert and with James." [15] There are still many, however, who find pleasure in reading novels for the rich experience they offer, in guiding students to read them intensively, and in observing the enjoyment of students and their consequent growth in appreciation and human understanding.

Bibliography

ADLER, Mortimer, *How to Read a Book* (New York, Simon and Schuster, Inc., 1940).

BEACH, Joseph, *The Twentieth-Century Novel* (New York, Appleton-Century-Crofts, Inc., 1932).

BENTLEY, Phyllis, *Some Observations on the Art of Narrative* (New York, The Macmillan Co., 1947).

BOAS, Ralph P., and SMITH, Edwin E., *Enjoyment of Literature* (New York, Harcourt, Brace & Co., o.p.).

[11] Refer to Note 3.

[12] "Grass," *Complete Poems* (New York, Harcourt, Brace & Co.).

[13] Helen E. Haines, *What's in a Novel* (New York, Columbia University Press, 1942), p. 7.

[14] Maugham, *op. cit.*, p. xxvi.

[15] T. S. Eliot, "Ulysses, Order, and Myth," *Forms of Modern Fiction, Essays Collected in Honor of Joseph Warren Beach*, William Van O'Connor, ed. (Minneapolis, University of Minnesota Press, 1948), p. 123.

BOWEN, Elizabeth, "Notes on Writing a Novel," *Collected Impressions* (New York, Longmans Green & Co., Inc., 1950).

BROOKS, Cleanth, and WARREN, Robert Penn, *Understanding Fiction* (New York, Appleton-Century-Crofts, Inc., 1948).

BROOKS, Cleanth, PURSER, John, and WARREN, Robert Penn, *An Approach to Literature* (New York, Appleton-Century-Crofts, Inc., 1952).

DREW, Elizabeth, *The Enjoyment of Literature* (New York, W. W. Norton and Company, Inc., 1935).

FORSTER, E. M., *Aspects of the Novel* (New York, Harcourt, Brace & Co., 1942).

GEROULD, Gordon H., *How to Read Fiction* (Princeton, N.J., Princeton University Press, 1937).

HOOK, J. N., *The Teaching of High School English* (New York, The Ronald Press Company, 1959).

LENROW, Elbert, *Reader's Guide to Prose Fiction* (New York, Appleton-Century-Crofts, Inc., 1940, o.p.)

MIRRIELEES, Lucia, *Teaching Composition and Literature* (Harcourt, Brace & Co., 1952).

MUIR, Edwin, *The Structure of the Novel* (Pennsylvania: Dufour Editions, 1954).

RICHARDS, I. A., *How to Read a Page* (New York, W. W. Norton & Company, Inc., 1942).

ROSENBLATT, Louise, *Literature as Exploration* (Progressive Education Association Publications; New York, Appleton-Century-Crofts, Inc., 1938).

SHERIDAN, Marion C., "Literature: Freighter, Fighter, and Star-Steerer," *The English Journal* (October, 1944).

SMITH, Dora V., ed., *The English Language Arts* (National Council of Teachers of English Curriculum Series; New York, Appleton-Century-Crofts, Inc., 1952).

WHARTON, Edith, *The Writing of Fiction* (New York, Charles Scribner's Sons, 1925).

WOLFE, Thomas, *The Story of a Novel* (New York, Charles Scribner's Sons, 1936).

14

The Teaching of Poetry

LOUIS L. MARTZ, *Yale University*

Despite the outcries that we frequently hear about the decline of literary values in our culture, I believe that teachers today are in a better position to develop an active appreciation of poetry in their students than were the teachers of twenty or thirty years ago. I say this because we are now in a position to reap the advantages of one of those great revolutions in poetry which seem to overtake the course of literature once every hundred years or so. Now for nearly half a century the poets of our era have been making constant headway in a campaign to convince their readers that fine poetry can derive from the roots of common life—that poetry does not dwell apart in some rarefied realm called Beauty, but actually lives and breathes among us, so that every man is, potentially, a poet, whether he knows it or not. This may seem a surprising argument, since so much of modern poetry has been accused of obscurity—and some of it *is* difficult, some of it cannot be adequately apprehended without a long process of reading and rereading, with a tenacious affection for poetry that most readers do not possess. But I am not speaking now of this more difficult poetry, as represented in Eliot's *Waste Land* or Pound's *Cantos*, or Yeats's *Byzantium*, or in many of the poems of Dylan Thomas. I am speaking of a much larger body of poetry that would include a great deal of writing by these very poets: the sort of poetry by which, I think, the young student of today can most easily and effectively be convinced of the value of poetry for him.

I am thinking of the poetry that could be used to answer one of the best students I ever had, in a large course where we were teaching poetry to engineering and scientific students. There was, some years back, in one of those classes, a brilliant engineer who used to punctuate every one of my earnest elucidations of poetry with an upraised hand and the query: "So what?" So what? He was very polite, very sincere, but he demanded an answer. And the answer I'm going to suggest today is one that, I am happy to report, worked; he became a devotee of modern poetry and even bought some volumes of his own.

The process, as I recall it, consisted in bringing to the fore all the poems in the book (and as many more as I had time to read aloud or mimeograph)—all the poems that began with some incident or situation that might occur to anyone who ever had a thought: poems like Frost's *Stopping by Woods on a Snowy Evening* or *After Apple-Picking*, Housman's *To an Athlete Dying Young*:

> The time you won your town the race
> We chaired you through the market-place. . . .

some little poem by Emily Dickinson that makes the universe flow in upon Amherst:

> I heard a fly buzz when I died. . . .

or

> Because I could not stop for Death,
> He kindly stopped for me. . . .

It might be Ezra Pound's version of an old Chinese poem where *The River-Merchant's Wife* longs for her absent husband; or some small but monumental poem by William Carlos Williams, such as the one called *This is Just to Say*:

> I have eaten
> the plums
> that were in
> the icebox
>
> and which
> you were probably
> saving
> for breakfast

> Forgive me
> they were delicious
> so sweet
> and so cold[1]

Poetry? Yes, it is poetry, I would argue, at perhaps its most rudimentary level: vivid words set in a rhythmic cadence, their meaning emphasized and developed by subtle pauses, creating in us as we read the sense of a moment of existence set apart for contemplation, like a picture in an album, by which we come to feel, understand, and value some aspect of our being, some tendency of human nature. Poetry, one might argue, for the purpose in hand, is a collection of such snapshots of our existence; and we linger over a volume of poetry for much the same reason that we leaf over and peruse a collection of snapshots: because they tell us something about ourselves. They remind us of things we have passed by, of experiences we have once had, and have lost, through a failure of memory, or through a lack of proper appreciation for the moment when it happened. Or, if it is another man's collection, it tells us (as cummings' poem) of *somewhere I have never travelled*, some place, perhaps, such as Frost's *Desert Places*, which we should not much like to see, but for which, at the very least, we ought to learn the possible location in our minds. I can never think of any better reason to justify the reading of poetry than our own insatiable curiosity about other human beings, and about ourselves.

Poetry tends to satisfy this "human interest" in a special way, beyond anything a photograph could do, for poetry works by placing us intimately inside the mind of some speaker; it allows us the privilege of following his thoughts from the inside. Thus in Frost's poem we have this speaker caught at the very moment of his stopping by woods on a snowy evening. This speaker is not necessarily the poet himself, but is no doubt some part of the poet selected and dramatized for this occasion. We follow the speaker's mind throughout the very process of its pondering:

> Whose woods these are I think I know.
> His house is in the village though;
> He will not see me stopping here
> To watch his woods fill up with snow.

[1] *Selected Poems of William Carlos Williams* (The New Classics Series; New York, New Directions, 1949). Copyright 1949 by William Carlos Williams. Reprinted by permission of New Directions.

My little horse must think it queer
To stop without a farmhouse near
Between the woods and frozen lake
The darkest evening of the year.

He gives his harness bells a shake
To ask if there is some mistake.
The only other sound's the sweep
Of easy wind and downy flake.

The woods are lovely, dark and deep.
But I have promises to keep,
And miles to go before I sleep,
And miles to go before I sleep.[2]

Why should the speaker be so embarrassed at the thought that he might be seen while stopping here? He is furtively glad that the owner of the woods is not there to see him. Why does he imagine that the horse must think it queer? Clearly the speaker feels that he is doing something unusual—something he, a busy man, does not usually pause to do: he is giving himself a chance to ponder his longing for some rest —some sort of rest that has the quiet attractiveness of woods filling up with snow, on a cold evening, the darkest of the year. Despite the frozen lake, the scene is not harsh—it is easy, downy, lovely, dark, and deep—a place where, for the moment, he feels a longing to abide. But he has his responsibilities to life; he has made promises, and so he knows it is not yet the time for rest. He has, as he so doubly and mysteriously puts it:

. . . miles to go before I sleep,
And miles to go before I sleep.

Is the repetition simply an expression of extreme weariness, or do we think of two kinds of sleep here?—the literal sleep of the coming night in bed, and a longer kind of sleep which will be his ultimate rest? I think the repeated line forces us to extend the literal sleep into the realm of the symbolic. Is it then "a poem about death?" Not exactly so, but rather a poem about a certain weary state of mind that all of us can recognize: "I'm so tired I could die." Here, then, we have a symbolic scene that shows a human being snapped at a moment when he catches

[2] From *New Hampshire* by Robert Frost, Copyright, 1923, by Henry Holt and Company, Inc. Copyright, 1951, by Robert Frost. By permission of the publishers.

a glimpse of needs and possibilities beyond those of his daily routine.

Of course, at this point, some student always seems to have heard of the remark Frost once made about the ending of this poem: "I might confess the trade secret that I wrote the third line of the last stanza of *Stopping by Woods* in such a way as to call for another stanza when I didn't want another stanza and didn't have another stanza in me, but with great presence of mind and a sense of what a good boy I was I instantly struck the line out and made my exit with a repeat end." Interesting—but it tells us very little, except that poets often love to pull the bench out from under the critic just as he sits down to play. Why didn't the poet want another stanza? and why didn't he have another stanza in him? We can only suggest that it must have been because the poem is so beautifully finished with that famous exit. Notice the power of the interlocking rhyme scheme: *a,a,b,a* for the first three stanzas, with the rhyme of line three in every stanza forming the major rhyme of the following stanza. Thus in stanza one *here* grows into the *queer*, *near*, *year* of the next; whereas *lake* grows into *shake*, *mistake*, and *flake*; and then, with a somber almost chanting finality, the poem draws to a focus and ends with the fourfold rhyme; *deep*, *keep*, *sleep*, *sleep*. The poem is firmly tied together and bound off at the end by the subtle, half-realized impact of the rhymes. Thus, as always in a good rhyming poem, the rhymes serve a valuable function in helping the words of the poem cohere into a meaningful whole. Here we have also an effect of strong emphasis upon each rhyming word, which makes us linger on that word and grasp its implications more forcefully.

Rhythm also serves a similar purpose, on the whole; rhythm ties the common words of the poem more closely together than they usually are found in common speech; rhythm helps the words to cohere in a special form that gradually lifts these words out of the flux and routine of the ordinary. Thus both the versification and the rhyming are here essential in making this poem an artifact, an object created in words, set apart, firmly and finally organized, for our contemplation. By rhythm I do not mean simply meter—iambic tetrameter; by rhythm I mean that continuous excitement that always occurs in a good poem when we feel the tension between the basic pattern of the verse and our actual timing, accent, and tone of voice as we read it. Our natural emphases, our natural pauses, guided by meaning, are continually

straining away from the strict pattern, but never far away. The good
poet too, has promises to keep—promises that he makes in adopting a
certain stanza structure; we expect him to keep it, and he does. But at
the same time both poet and reader have a large measure of freedom;
no two readers will ever read this poem in precisely the same way, nor
will the same reader ever read this poem twice in the same way, for
the simple reason that, by the time he has got around to reading it the
second time, he is no longer quite the same as he was. If I should read
this poem for you now again, I should be either more tired or more
exhilarated than I was; thus every reading of a poem is a unique experience, both in rhythm and in total meaning, despite the "sameness" of
the stanza form. Stanza forms are only the bones of a poem—upon
which our reading puts the flesh.

Let us see how this holds for the next poem on your sheets—Mac-
Leish's *You, Andrew Marvell*.[3] Let's forget about the enigmatic title
for a while, and look directly at the opening situation—again an experience that anyone can have. Here it is the experience of lying face
downward in the sun, somewhere in North America, apparently; and
being caught suddenly by a sense of the great turning of the earth—
which the speaker here puts in the common terms of the movement of
darkness up the curving face of this earth. In the brightness of noonday
it seems incredible that night should already be falling (or "rising") on
the other side, but he imagines, with wonder, how it must be so:

> And here face down beneath the sun
> And here upon earth's noonward height
> To feel the always coming on
> The always rising of the night
>
> To feel creep up the curving east
> The earthy chill of dusk and slow
> Upon those under lands the vast
> And ever climbing shadow grow

And now as we watch the movement of his mind we can see it starting
over in Persia, and moving toward himself, as the shadow moves over
Baghdad, Arabia, Palmyra in Syria, Lebanon on the shore of the Medi-
terranean, then over across the islands of Crete and Sicily, and then

[3] Archibald MacLeish, *Collected Poems, 1917–1952* (Boston, Houghton Mifflin
Co., 1952).

out between Spain and Africa, and across the Atlantic toward himself, on Jones Beach or Hammonassett. A neat trick, this following of the movement of darkness, but as we read the poem over again and again, we notice that some of the names he chooses to dwell upon are rather strange. Why should the first be Ecbatan, no longer the capital of Persia, but once the great capital of the Median and the Parthian empires? Why Kermanshah, no longer a place of great importance, but once a great trading city of the ancient world, when the caravans had to come through it over the westward pass in order to go from Persia to Baghdad, once too the capital of an empire—that stretched from Persia across Africa to the Atlantic? And why Palmyra, which is not even a city now, but was once the queen city of the Roman East? Clearly more is going on here than the movement of one day's time. The poet is making us cast our minds back over the whole movement of recorded history in the Western world; he is asking us to follow, roughly, its path from the ancient cultures of the Near East to the more modern cultures of Rome and Spain—and America. The darkness of this one day will only "deepen on Palmyra's street/The wheel rut in the ruined stone." Notice the vigor of the imagery. The wheel rut in the stone pavement suggests the movement of thousands upon thousands of ancient wheels upon the pavements of that glorious city —now a mere collection of Arabian hovels, the encyclopedia tells us. And this is true of many other details in this poem, the more we press them. There is something eerie about the darkness in the third stanza; a sort of flood is overcoming this scene, where even the mountains undergo a change, and all is empty, withered, with few travellers now; and not, we suppose, simply because it is late in the evening, but also because the flower of this great culture has long since passed. So the words pick up meaning as we read and reread: "And Spain go under" means more than the shadow of this night, if we think of the one-time greatness of the Spanish Empire. So we gain a profound sense of the inevitable movement of all time, the inevitable movement of oblivion, toward this speaker in America. We can see too how right it is that this poem should have no punctuation at all—but one inevitable movement; we see too how rightly the poem begins in the middle of a thought and ends, not with an ending, but with the three dots that indicate something more to follow. So too the rightness of the title, or the dedication, to the seventeenth-century poet who also wrote a famous meditation on time, Marvell's poem, *To his Coy Mistress*, which contains the lines:

> But at my back I always hear
> Time's winged chariot hurrying near;
> And yonder all before us lie
> Deserts of vast eternity.

You, Andrew Marvell, must also have felt something of this, the poet seems to be saying; you will understand what I mean here and now, face down beneath the sun:

> And here face down beneath the sun
> And here upon earth's noonward height
> To feel the always coming on
> The always rising of the night
>
> To feel creep up the curving east
> The earthy chill of dusk and slow
> Upon those under lands the vast
> And ever climbing shadow grow
>
> And strange at Ecbatan the trees
> Take leaf by leaf the evening strange
> The flooding dark about their knees
> The mountains over Persia change
>
> And now at Kermanshah the gate
> Dark empty and the withered grass
> And through the twilight now the late
> Few travelers in the westward pass
>
> And Baghdad darken and the bridge
> Across the silent river gone
> And through Arabia the edge
> Of evening widen and steal on
>
> And deepen on Palmyra's street
> The wheel rut in the ruined stone
> And Lebanon fade out and Crete
> High through the clouds and overblown
>
> And over Sicily the air
> Still flashing with the landward gulls
> And loom and slowly disappear
> The sails above the shadowy hulls

> And Spain go under and the shore
> Of Africa the gilded sand
> And evening vanish and no more
> The low pale light across that land
>
> Nor now the long light on the sea
>
> And here face downward in the sun
> To feel how swift how secretly
> The shadow of the night comes on . . .

I have taken these examples from poetry of the twentieth century, not because I think it is better than, say, the poetry of the nineteenth century, but because recent poetry seems, strategically, to provide one of the best ways of convincing our students that poetry has a meaning for them. Modern poetry speaks their language, slangy and colloquial as modern poets often are; modern poems use the imagery that we see about us: Williams even puts a soda-fountain menu into one of his poems. Poetry of today speaks to the students of today with an immediacy that older poetry can seldom match: but this is only a strategy for a beginning. After we have made our point with the moderns, we must go on to show that older poets have also written their brief interior dramas of the mind, however strange and remote their ways of speaking may now appear.

We may turn to John Keats, sick to death of the poetry of the eighteenth century ("They sway'd about upon a rocking horse," he said, "And thought it Pegasus."), and especially tired of Alexander Pope, whose translation of Homer *was* the true Homer of that century. Now he comes upon another translation of Homer which was as far from Pope's as he could get: the colloquial, free, racy, and daring version of that robust Elizabethan, George Chapman. Keats feels the power of Homer for the first time through the fresh and vigorous accents of Chapman. There is, Keats tells us here, a difference between hearing *about* poetry, and actually experiencing it as something that speaks directly to us:

> Much have I travell'd in the realms of gold,
>   And many goodly states and kingdoms seen;
>   Round many western islands have I been
> Which bards in fealty to Apollo hold.
> Oft of one wide expanse had I been told

> That deep-brow'd Homer ruled as his demesne;
>   Yet did I never breathe its pure serene
> Till I heard Chapman speak out loud and bold:

Notice here how Keats is deliberately using stately language, far re-moved from common speech, and thus makes the realm of poetry seem something remote—something too august and awe-inspiring to be quite grasped by a poor ordinary mortal. But then he hears a poet speak in a voice he can understand: and the experience is like the dis-covery of a new world, a new ocean of being. Suddenly the language and the rhythm of his sonnet undergo a subtle change. The words be-come simpler, more direct, more spontaneous in their action, while the lines are no longer so solemnly end-stopped; they now flow on with a breathless excitement, moving on inevitably into the one climactic word of astonishment that begins the last line: *Silent*.

> Then felt I like some watcher of the skies
>   When a new planet swims into his ken;
> Or like stout Cortez when with eagle eyes
>   He star'd at the Pacific—and all his men
> Look'd at each other with a wild surmise—
>   Silent, upon a peak in Darien.

Now there is, as people point out, a slight error in historical fact here: Keats seems to be confusing Cortez with Balboa. But in spite of this the allusion to Cortez makes, I think, for a greater poem than it would be if Keats had, more correctly, used the name of Balboa. Cor-tez is the greater man, the more notable conqueror: Cortez is the best representative of all the Spanish conquerors who travelled in those realms of Spanish gold; and so he fits in better with the basic imagery that unifies this sonnet. Keats, we note, has opened with a general, and only half-realized allusion to the golden realms of the Spanish Indies ("western islands"); and now at the end, with a dramatic close-up, he puts us there at the moment of discovery, and the general realm of gold is localized, focussed, upon the scene in Darien, the old name for Panama, from which so many loads of gold were shipped. So the whole poem is bound together with this central image of a realm of immense value. Thus Keats is able to create for us a drama of interior discovery, akin to that other discovery of Cortez-Balboa.

Let us turn now to a much older poem, this time a narrative poem.[4] I think we can show that here too we are really working inside the mind of a speaker. In a narrative poem we have the impact of some external event upon the mind of a hidden speaker: we have a narrator, however cleverly he may be concealed; and the meaning of the event for this narrator may be gathered from his selection and arrangement of details, as well as from any interspersed comments that he may give us. Let's look for a while at this "grand old ballad of Sir Patrick Spence" as Coleridge called it, and ask some questions. What is the attitude toward the King, implied in the first stanza?

> The king sits in Dumferling toune,
>   Drinking the blude-reid wine:
> "O whar will I get guid sailor,
>   To sail this schip of mine?"

The king, we might gather, is not only somewhat self-indulgent, as he sits and drinks, but he is not in very close contact, it appears, with the affairs of his realm; anyone, you would think, might know about Sir Patrick Spence. But the king is good at writing a broad letter, and signing it with a flourish, as we might imagine, and sending it with someone else's legs to this great sailor, who, as we might expect, is down to earth, active; the letter comes to him while he is walking on the sand, near his job. Why does he laugh? Because the idea of going out on a voyage at such a season of the year is ridiculous—until the thought hits him, with a double-take, that the letter is addressed to *him*, and that, whatever he may think, he really does have to go: it is the King's command. "The teir blinded his ee." He knows it is a sentence of death for him and his men; and his following outcry is a measure of his anguish at this folly. It would be too much for us to scent a plot on his life by the "eldern knicht," though some freshman always argues that point. No, I think the King's command comes only from ignorance and willfulness, and the "knicht," like Sir Patrick, is only doing his duty, come what may. Sir Patrick obeys, feigning a good cheer, though his sailors share his knowledge that disaster looms ahead—and this makes the king's folly seem even more outrageous. But the sailors go; he is, we note, their "master deir," and as Patrick obeys the king, so they obey their master, though apparently with more affection.

---

[4] See Appendix, "Sir Patrick Spence."

And now, having shown the situation skillfully, the narrator brings his attitude out into the open, with the common man's scorn for the idle rich, out of touch with reality; when Sir Patrick sails the nobles to their doom, the narrator has little sympathy to spend on them:

> O our Scots nobles wer richt laith
> To weet thair cork-heild schoone;
> Bot lang owre a' the play wer playd,
> Thair hats they swam aboone.

> O lang, lang may thair ladies sit,
> Wi thair fans into their hand,
> Or eir they se Sir Patrick Spence
> Cum sailing to the land.

> O lang, lang may the ladies stand,
> Wi thair gold kems in their hair
> Waiting for thair ain deir lords,
> For they'll se thame na mair.

> Haf owre, haf owre to Aberdour,
> It's fiftie fadom deip,
> And thair lies guid Sir Patrick Spence,
> Wi the Scots lords at his feit.

In death their positions are reversed: Spence is a good man because he has done his duty in the face of death, willingly, and in full knowledge of the facts; as for the lords, they merely drowned, and anyone can do that.

Here, then, is a poem of perfect artistry, and yet a poem in close touch with common life; we might call it a bit of inspired reporting about a famous shipwreck, developed by careful arrangement and selection of detail, in order to focus our minds on the most significant aspect of the disaster: the character of Patrick, and the virtues that he demonstrates. Here is obviously a drama in miniature, with five voices: King, knight, Sir Patrick, the sailors, and surrounding all, embracing all, interpreting all—the voice of the narrator who guides the ballad to its climax and at the close applauds the hero with one word that binds the whole poem together: "guid." Sir Patrick, we see, is not simply the "guid sailor," the able seaman and able navigator that the king has asked for: he is a *good man*, the best of them all.

One step more, and we enter the realm of drama, properly so called, where the voice of the narrator is completely pared away, except where he may seem to intervene now and then through some character who may appear to be his spokesman. But in the greatest drama, as in Shakespearean drama, it is dangerous to take anyone as the author's spokesman. The central point of view emerges from the total interaction of every aspect of the play, just as in these shorter poems the meaning resides in the interaction of every element—image, statement, rhythm, rhyme—every element which goes to make up the whole poem. Every utterance that we can call poetry, then, is a drama, small or large, whether it occurs within the mind of a single speaker, or whether it occurs through several speakers operating within the voice of a single narrator; or whether the narrator disappears, and all we hear are the intersecting voices of the several characters in dramatic conflict. We ought to make this clear, I think, for the sake of the student who says, every year, "I like Shakespeare, but I don't like poetry." If, somehow, we could convince him that all poems, however small, are miniature dramas, if we could train him to hear the voice of the speaker in every poetic drama, whether it be written by Robert Frost or by Shakespeare, we would, I believe, have won a large part of the battle for poetry.

Perhaps we could best show the relation between Shakespeare's poetical dramas and the smaller poetical dramas of Frost and Keats by making the students feel how every great speech in Shakespeare is really a short poem set within the fabric of the whole enormous poem that we call *Macbeth*, or *Hamlet*, or *Julius Caesar*. Isn't that really the justification for the old practice of memorizing the dagger speech, or the mercy speech, or "To be or not to be?" Because these great speeches are really short poems in themselves, interior dramas taking place within the mind of the given speaker? This is particularly clear in *Hamlet*, where the main action of the play is that which occurs within the mind of that highly introspective hero; the main action of that play, as I would see it, consists in the hero's effort to drag himself upward out of the desperate state of mind revealed to us in his first soliloquy.[5] There, with a dramatic inwardness, he reveals that his whole being has been shattered by the shock of finding evil so close to himself. Coming home from college, an idealistic young man, he finds wickedness in the person of his own mother, who has shown herself to

[5] See Appendix, The First Soliloquy, from *Hamlet*.

be, as he says, *common*—forgetful of her duty to his father, unfaithful in her professions of love, and indeed a criminal and sinner in the eyes of the Church, through her breaking of the Church's law against marriage with a husband's brother. Try as he may, Hamlet's mind cannot escape from this discovery of corruption in his own mother. Notice how the drama of this speech arises primarily from the speaker's attempts to draw away from that recognition of evil—first, by a vague longing for death, then by a furious denunciation of the whole world as a garden of weeds. But he cannot evade what lies at the center of his mind: the evil, from which he is descended, and by which, he feels, he is himself corrupted:

> That it should come to this!
> But two months dead: nay, not so much, not two:

and his mind veers off again to dwell upon the virtues of his father, but that thought only makes his mother's character seem worse:

> Heaven and earth!
> Must I remember?

Yes, he must; and it drives him to desperation:

> why, she would hang on him,
> As if increase of appetite had grown
> By what it fed on; and yet, within a month,
> Let me not think on't: Frailty, thy name is woman!

Notice how he is holding back the key word the reveals all her frailty; but now he comes closer to it:

> A little month: or ere those shoes were old
> With which she follow'd my poor father's body,
> Like Niobe, all tears; why she, even she,—

He cannot bring himself to say the word:

> O God! a beast, that wants discourse of reason,
> Would have mourned longer,—*married*

The word is out at last:

> married with mine uncle,
> My father's brother, but no more like my father
> Than I to Hercules: within a month

> Ere yet the salt of most unrighteous tears
> Had left the flushing in her galled eyes,
> She married.

And now, with a sound "like the hissing of snakes," he brings himself to utter it all:

> O! most wicked speed, to post
> With such dexterity to incestuous sheets.

Here, then, is a perfect short poem, set within the fabric of this great long poem, *Hamlet*. It is of course immensely greater than any other poem I have read here, but it does not lie beyond the realm that contains those shorter and lesser dramatic poems of Keats, MacLeish, Frost, or Williams. The realm of poetry, as Keats says, is broad indeed: it is large enough to include everything from Hamlet's taste of evil to William Carlos Williams's taste of those forbidden plums in the icebox.

Appendix

Sir Patrick Spence

> The king sits in Dumferling toune,
>   Drinking the blude-reid wine:
> "Oh whar will I get guid sailor,
>   To sail this schip of mine?"
>
> Up and spak an eldern knicht,
>   Sat at the kings richt kne:
> "Sir Patrick Spence is the best sailor
>   That sails upon the se."
>
> The king has written a braid letter,
>   And signed it wi his hand,
> And sent it to Sir Patrick Spence,
>   Was walking on the sand.
>
> The first line that Sir Patrick red,
>   A loud lauch lauchèd he;

The next line that Sir Patrick red,
  The teir blinded his ee.

"O wha is this has don this deid,
  This ill deid don to me,
To send me out this time o' the yeir,
  To sail upon the se!

"Mak hast, mak haste, my mirry men all
  Our guid schip sailes the morne:"
"O say na sae, my master deir,
  For I feir a deadlie storme.

"Late, late yestreen I saw the new moone,
  Wi the auld moone in hir arme,
And I feir, I feir, my deir master,
  That we will cum to harme."

O our Scots nobles wer richt laith
  To weet thair cork-heild schoone;
Bot lang owre a' the play wer playd,
  Thair hats they swam aboone.

O lang, lang may thair ladies sit,
  Wi thair fans into their hand,
Or eir they se Sir Patrick Spence
  Cum sailing to the land.

O lang, lang may the ladies stand,
  Wi thair gold kems in their hair
Waiting for thair ain deir lords,
  For they'll se thame na mair.

Haf owre, haf owre to Aberdour,
  It's fiftie fadom deip,
And thair lies guid Sir Patrick Spence,
  Wi the Scots lords at his feit.

Anonymous

The First Soliloquy
from
Hamlet

O! that this too too solid flesh would melt,
Thaw and resolve itself into a dew;

Or that the Everlasting had not fix'd
His canon 'gainst self-slaughter! O God! O God!
How weary, stale, flat, and unprofitable
Seem to me all the uses of this world.
Fie on't! O fie! 'tis an unweeded garden,
That grows to seed; things rank and gross in nature
Possess it merely. That it should come to this!
But two months dead: nay, not so much, not two:
So excellent a king; that was, to this,
Hyperion to a satyr; so loving to my mother
That he might not beteem the winds of heaven
Visit her face too roughly. Heaven and earth!
Must I remember? why, she would hang on him,
As if increase of appetite had grown
By what it fed on; and yet, within a month,
Let me not think on't: Frailty, thy name is woman!
A little month; or ere those shoes were old
With which she follow'd my poor father's body,
Like Niobe, all tears; why she, even she,—
O God! a beast, that wants discourse of reason,
Would have mourn'd longer,—married with mine uncle,
My father's brother, but no more like my father
Than I to Hercules: within a month,
Ere yet the salt of most unrighteous tears
Had left the flushing in her galled eyes,
She married. O! most wicked speed, to post
With such dexterity to incestuous sheets.
It is not nor it cannot come to good;
But break, my heart, for I must hold my tongue!

Shakespeare

15

Modern Criticism of *The Ancient Mariner*

FREDERICK A. POTTLE, *Yale University*

The drastic revaluation which has overtaken Romantic poetry in our time has dealt kindly with *The Ancient Mariner*. As E. M. W. Tillyard has said, people disagree as to what the poem means, but all agree in thinking it admirable.[1] The praise comes from practitioners of poetry as well as from academic critics: Mr. Robert Penn Warren has made it the subject of the most elaborate and learned critique it has ever received. It may be that it is now attracting a higher degree of sophisticated approval than at any earlier period of its history.

If this is so, it must seem rather surprising, for the poem employs many devices that are out of favor with advanced criticism. Modern poetry is suspicious of such pronounced rhythms, such regular metrical patterns and rhyme schemes as the poem employs; they are now considered more appropriate for humorous or satirical poetry (for example, Mr. Eliot's *Book of Practical Cats*) than for a deeply serious composition. Good modern poetry repudiates archaisms such as "eftsoons," and inversions such as "vespers nine," and expletives such as "did stand." It does not eschew elements of violence and horror, but it

[1] "Coleridge: *The Rime of the Ancient Mariner*," *Five Poems, 1470–1870; An Elementary Essay on the Background of English Literature* (New York, The Macmillan Co., 1948), p. 66.

does try to dispense with supernatural happenings. One would not expect a poem containing such devices as a ship without planking, a dicing skeleton, and dead men setting the sails of a vessel, to be credited with more than entertainment value by our present-day critics. The modern preference in serious literature is strongly in favor not only of possible happenings but even of happenings *probable* within the range of average human experience. Graham Greene attaches the apologetic label of "entertainments" to a group of his own novels, not because they are thin in characterization or jovial in tone, but simply because the plots are "exciting," that is, contain an improbable number of coincidences. And for that matter, we need not restrict to the present the uneasiness which serious readers feel about the supernatural machinery in *The Ancient Mariner*. Charles Lamb, in admitting that the poem "totally possessed" him "for many days," testified to his continued resistance: "I dislike all the miraculous parts of it." [2]

Twenty-five years ago the New Humanists were attacking its morality. "It is impossible," said Irving Babbitt, "to extract any serious ethical purport from *The Ancient Mariner*—except perhaps a warning as to the fate of the innocent bystander; unless indeed one holds that it is fitting that, for having sympathized with the man who shot an albatross, 'four times fifty living men' should perish in torments unspeakable." [3] And though our present-day critics show no such uneasiness, it must be admitted that the incidents of the plot *are* shocking if taken as a literal statement of Christian belief. The act of wantonly shooting a bird—even an albatross—is not admirable, but no responsible Christian casuist would say that it deserved the punishment meted out to the Mariner; especially, no Christian casuist would maintain that two hundred other men who had merely approved the act after it was done ought to suffer death by thirst under a hot and copper sky. We can go further: granting that the Mariner *had* committed a sin deserving such awful punishment, no orthodox Christian casuist would have assured him that he could obtain absolution by blessing a parcel of water snakes—and blessing them unawares.

We must grant, I think, that the elements of the poem which I have cited are not plus values—or at least are not obvious plus values

[2] Letter to William Wordsworth, postmark 30 January 1801, *The Works of Charles and Mary Lamb*, E. V. Lucas, ed., Vol. IV (New York, G. P. Putnam's Sons, 1905), p. 209.

[3] *On Being Creative, and Other Essays* (Boston, Houghton Mifflin Co., 1932), p. 119.

—for serious modern readers who read the poem merely as narrative. They must ask themselves, as I used to ask myself, "Why does this poem produce so powerful an effect on me? Why do I not immediately dismiss it as I do a detective story or a yarn in a pulp magazine? Why do I approve the effect and keep on studying it? Why am I not cloyed, let down, disgusted?"

There have been explanations: let us begin by considering some traditional ones. It has been maintained that the poem establishes its reputation simply by a massive overplus of aesthetic value. Coleridge was one of the greatest verbal and metrical artists in English literary history. I do not need to remind you who have taught the poem of the elaborate variations he made in the ballad stanza by expansion and internal rhyme, or of the dramatic structuring by which he places the word "albatross" in the last or next to the last line of Parts I, II, IV, and VI, in the third stanza from the end of Part V, and puts in the last line of Part III the word "cross-bow," which has been associated with "albatross" in the last lines of Part I, and echoed in "cross" at the end of Part II. Adopting Matthew Arnold's separation of aesthetic from moral value, we may say that in *The Ancient Mariner* a wonderful "felicity and perfection of diction and manner" more than compensates for some lack in "truth and seriousness of substance and manner." [4]

Or, we may say that the poet wins us by imaginative sleight of hand. This appears to be Coleridge's own explanation. Discussing the plans which he and Wordsworth made for the *Lyrical Ballads*, he says that they agreed to attempt two sorts of poems. "In the one, the incidents and agents were to be, in part at least, supernatural; and the excellence aimed at was to consist in the interesting of the affections by the dramatic truth of such emotions, as would naturally accompany such situations, supposing them real. . . . It was agreed, that my endeavours should be directed to persons and characters supernatural, or at least romantic; yet so as to transfer from our inward nature a human interest and a semblance of truth sufficient to procure for these shadows of imagination that willing suspension of disbelief for the moment, which constitutes poetic faith." [5] As the magician, by making us watch his right hand, renders us quite oblivious to what

[4] "Byron," *Essays in Criticism*, Second Series (New York, The Macmillan Co., 1930), p. 132.

[5] *Biographia Literaria*, Ch. XIV, 1st and 2nd paragraphs.

he is doing with his left, so the poet gets us to accept incredible events by keeping our eyes on credible ones. The incredible events are never explained or argued about, they just *are*. The concomitants are all of the homely, familiar world. Trivial, sharply realized details, felt instantly to be authentic, pitch us directly into incredible ones:

> We listened and looked sideways up!
> Fear at my heart, as at a cup,
> My life-blood seemed to sip!
> The stars were dim, and thick the night,
> The steersman's face by his lamp gleamed white;
> From the sails the dew did drip—
> Till clomb above the eastern bar
> The horned Moon, with one bright star
> Within the nether tip.

(203–211)

No ordinary Gothic would have found a place for the blanched face of the steersman or the dew dripping from the sails; but nothing could more effectively sap our defenses against the horror of that moon with its impossible star. The causal relation of events is accepted as adequate because the Mariner accepts it as adequate. The morality does not shock us, because, though Coleridge has given it an avowedly Christian basis, he has presented the story dramatically through the lips of a medieval, superstitious, and possibly deranged old man. It is, after all, not unlike a story from the Old Testament recording the exceeding fierce wrath of the Lord; for example, how he smote the men of Bethshemesh because, through no malice at all, they had looked into the ark; "even he smote of the people fifty thousand and threescore and ten men: and the people lamented." [6] The poem runs the gamut of genuine guilt and remorse, suffering and consolation, hate and forgiveness, grief and joy. Since the emotions are so true to universal human experience, we accept the events that are advanced as their cause.

Coleridge himself would certainly have insisted that the illusion or sleight of hand was employed for the sake of the truth of the emotions; John Livingston Lowes and other distinguished critics have reversed this, and have insisted that the truth of the emotions exists for the sake of the illusion. "The function of the ethical background of *The Ancient Mariner*," says Lowes, "is to give the illusion of in-

[6] I Sam. 6:19.

evitable sequence to (the poem's) superb inconsequence." Poetry—
at least this kind of poetry—is a charmed area, walled off from reality
like Kubla's park of fertile ground. "Its world," Lowes continues "is,
in essence, the world of a dream. Its inconsequence is the dream's
irrelevance, and by a miracle of art we are possessed, as we read, with
that sense of an intimate logic, consecutive and irresistible and more
real than reality, which is the dream's supreme illusion. . . . The
events in a dream do not produce each other, but they seem to. And
that is the sole requirement of the action of the poem." [7] This is what
I may call the naïve or old-fashioned dream theory. It seems extraordinary now that any critic writing as late at 1927 should have taken
the position that dreams are (or may be) delightful but are ultimately
meaningless.

The specifically modern explanations, of which I shall present two,
rest upon a theory of symbols. As applied to a poem like *The Ancient
Mariner*, this means that an imaginative narrative may, and probably
does, have different *levels* of meaning. Besides the *literal* meaning of
the plot or fable—the meaning accessible to everyday practical habits
of thought—the imaginative narrative may be surcharged with *symbolic* meaning. *Moby Dick* is undeniably a story about practical
whaling—indeed, it is an encyclopedia of cetology—but the great
white whale is more than any literal, historical whale. I shall leave it
to others to say *what* he symbolizes, but a symbol he certainly is. And
he is not a mere allegory. The difference between symbol and simple
allegory, as Coleridge himself insisted over and over, is fundamental.
In simple allegories the poet thinks out an extended "literal" meaning
and then deliberately *translates* it into another meaning, the second
meaning corresponding more or less point by point to the first. The
"meaning" of the House of Temperance in Book II of *The Faerie
Queene* is simply the human body: mouth, teeth, stomach, lungs,
heart, and much more. Symbols are direct movements of man's emotional life into concrete verbal representations: they may be endlessly
allegorized (every exploration of their "meaning" is an allegorization), but the allegorical meanings are derived, they are not constitu-
tive. When symbols are being properly "understood," they are not
being allegorized or explained at all. Symbols constitute a richer,
fuller affective language than the language of rational discourse.

The extended analysis of *The Ancient Mariner* in Maud Bodkin's

[7] *The Road to Xanadu* (Boston, Houghton Mifflin Co., 1930), pp. 300, 303.

Archetypal Patterns in Poetry applies to literary criticism the theories of the famous Swiss depth-psychologist, Carl Gustav Jung. Jung, who started as the favorite pupil of Freud, took over from Freud the concept of the Unconscious Mind. I assume that in a gathering like this I do not need to spend much time explaining this famous concept. In essence it asserts that the mental activity of which we are conscious constitutes only a tiny portion of our actual mental operations. The mind is like an iceberg floating in the sea: most of it is submerged. The language of reason—the language which is analytic and logical—pertains solely to the mind's conscious portion. By far the greater part of our mental activity is affective or emotional. The unconscious mind has needs, urges, and it seeks to gratify them. If it cannot obtain "real" gratifications, it seeks "imaginary" ones by pushing symbolic representations of them up into the conscious. Dreams provide the most obvious illustration of this activity. Most of our dreams are mere confused reworkings of the problems that occupied our conscious minds before we dropped off to sleep, but many are symbolic incursions of our unconscious.

Jung's particular theory—the point on which he parts company most decisively with Freud—concerns what he calls archetypes and the Group Unconscious. He insists that a part of the unconscious is common to all men, and that some symbols are not merely private, they are primordial and universal. We are not exactly born with certain images in our brains, but we are born with a brain structure that inevitably precipitates our experience into certain images. The archetypes are not confined to isolated images either, but may extend into patterns of considerable complexity. We do not have to explain the world-wide occurrence of the Oedipus myth or the Orestes myth as due to cultural dissemination: these myths are archetypes, and human minds were capable of inventing them independently at different times and in different cultures. A poet can surcharge his poem by making an archetype the basis of his plot, or by bringing in smaller archetypes at its crucial points, its pivots or bearings.

According to Miss Bodkin, Coleridge does both. His plot is a modification of the extended archetype which Jung calls The Night Journey Under the Sea, of which the most famous example is the Book of Jonah. Abstractly stated, it is a myth of Rebirth and Regeneration. This pattern is reinforced by other archetypes: wind and storm which symbolize creative force, stagnant calm which sym-

bolizes dull inertia, slime from the depths which represents our disgust and guilt-feelings about matters of our experience that we fear, the
color red which is primordially associated with guilt and punishment,
the Wandering Jew who is the symbol *par excellence* of refusal or
violation of fellowship. All these symbols carry great emotional
charge, and in *The Ancient Mariner* they are exploited with deep
artistic awareness of their tendency. The power of *The Ancient
Mariner*, Miss Bodkin would say, derives from its use of an archetypal
pattern as plot, and its building into the fabric at strategic points of
so many more congruent primordial symbols. Her own allegorization is coolly psychological. She always uses the word *guilt*, never
the word *sin*. For her the poem symbolizes no rare and spectacular
crime, but matter of universal, everyday experience. At its symbolic
level it is "about" frustration, depression, our horror of and revolt
from elements in our experience that we consider primitive and
sinister, our regeneration through acceptance of the disturbing elements. She reads the poem, in short, as a sort of symbol of psychoanalysis.

Mr. Robert Penn Warren has advanced a theory of symbolism
without psychoanalysis: that is, he does not think it necessary for
literary criticism to decide whether there is such a thing as the Group
Unconscious, or whether our common symbols are inherited or cul-
turally transmitted. That they exist and that they give multiple meanings to poems he has no doubt. He divides them into two classes:
necessary and *congruent*. His "necessary" symbols are identical with
Miss Bodkin's archetypes; in fact, in citing the wind in *The Ancient
Mariner* as an example, he acknowledges having taken it from her. A
"necessary" symbol is one that is established in universal human experience; a "congruent" symbol is one, like Yeats's Byzantium, which
the poet himself has discovered to be pertinent and fertile, but which
he must "validate" for us. The two explanations, *primary* and *secondary*, which Mr. Warren advances, again illustrate the distinction.
In his primary meaning, Miss Bodkin's psychological entities all
appear, but with theological significance. The poem, in this sense,
presents a sacramental view of nature: every object in the universe
is the outward visible sign of an inward spiritual force. Coleridge
himself states this view in *The Eolian Harp:*

> O! the one Life within us and abroad,
> Which meets all motion and becomes its soul,

A light in sound, a sound-like power in light,
Rhythm in all thought, and joyance everywhere.

The shooting of the albatross is a symbolic representation of Original Sin, the mysterious perversity of man's will. To symbolize the Fall adequately, the act *must* be unmotivated. The mariners share in the crime by themselves treating the universe with wanton detachment, violating its sacramental quality. The bird had been a pious bird of good omen, it had sought and received hospitality, but they justify its slaughter on merely practical grounds. Deliverance comes for the sailor when he recognizes the sacramental nature of things: when he loves the slimy things of the deep and blesses them. *The Ancient Mariner* in this view is no mere symbol of psychoanalysis: it is, more profoundly than the literalists realize, a parable of sin, retribution, absolution, and redemption.

Having pushed through this interpretation with learning and eloquence, Mr. Warren then points out that large areas of the poem which appear to carry symbolic change do not seem to be directly relevant to the theme of the One Life and the bias of man's will. In these he sees a secondary meaning, advanced in part by what he has called congruent symbols. As the primary meaning was theological, this is philosophical or aesthetic. The symbols of this meaning are the sun and the moon, with their concomitants wind, storm, fog, and mist. He points out that, by and large, the good events of the poem take place in moonlight or luminous mist; the evil ones in the glare of the sun. At this level the poem embodies the Romantic revolt from eighteenth-century rationalism. The sun symbolizes the analytic reason, what Coleridge followed Kant in calling the *Understanding*. The moon symbolizes the higher reason or Imagination. The mind starts in the sunlight of ordinary experience; a creative storm, which seems hostile because it breaks the ordinary routine, drives it to the misty, luminous state of the Imagination; the mind revolts against the Imagination, murders it symbolically, and drives again into the hard, clear light of the Understanding, now stagnant and sterile; it is restored again in the moonlight, and so on. The primary and secondary themes are fused at several points: the albatross is associated with mist, moonlight, and creative wind; the angelic troop with wind and moon; the Hermit is both priest of God and priest of nature.

That these readings of the poem are controversial is obvious, but it has seemed to me better to present them fairly and with some degree of fullness than to argue with their authors on points that I find less than convincing. How much of them you can use in secondary school teaching I do not know. Archetypes and the Group Unconscious would perhaps be strong stuff for adolescents. The prime danger of all such approaches, of course, is that, unless very carefully managed, they turn a class in literature into one in speculative psychology. It is very easy to shift attention from the poem as poem to its genesis, that is, to the events in the mind of the author which caused him to write it. Mr. Warren's explanations run no such danger, but they are likely to stir up resistance by their very ingenuity. It is a characteristic of all such approaches that they seem much more convincing in the bulk than in detail. I myself believe that I can present both Bodkin and Warren to college classes without lapsing into mere geneticism or ridiculously precise allegorization. The value of both theories, in the final analysis, is that they warn us that words used in poetry have more meanings than can be found in our ordinary dictionaries. The attempts here reviewed, largely pioneer work, to draft the extended dictionaries which poetry needs, are to be applauded rather than derided.

Bibliography

BODKIN, Maud, *Archetypal Patterns in Poetry: Psychological Studies of Imagination* (New York, The Oxford University Press, 1948).

Miss Bodkin's book is described fairly and at length in the fifth chapter of *The Armed Vision*, by Stanley Edgar Hyman (New York, Vintage Books, Inc., 1955).

WARREN, Robert Penn, "A Poem of Pure Imagination: An Experiment in Reading," *The Rime of the Ancient Mariner*, by Samuel Taylor Coleridge (New York, Reynal & Company, Inc., 1946).

Since the first 58 pages of the volume consist of a text of *The Ancient Mariner*, with line drawings by Alexander Calder, libraries usually catalogue it under Coleridge. Calder's grotesque and explicit male nudes probably make the book inappropriate for school libraries.

16

Some General Remarks on Poetry: Report of the Committee on the Teaching of Poetry

HAROLD H. OWEN, JR., *Phillips Academy, Andover, Massachusetts, Chairman*

EUPHA BONHAM, *Bennington High School, Vermont*

GERTRUDE BRANON, *Spaulding High School, Barre, Vermont*

FRANCES HUESTON, *Deering High School, Portland, Maine*

NORMAN PAQUETTE, *Stevens High School, Claremont, New Hampshire*

When our committee first began to examine this problem of the teaching of poetry, the temptation to say too much about poetry and not enough about teaching it was almost too great for us to resist. So many good poets, and so many more critics, have offered us so many excellent definitions, that we spent much time in exchanging our favorite definitions, and capping each other's quotes —one of the occupational hazards of the addicted poetry lover.

With considerable regret, we relegated many of the established and wonderful definitions of poetry to the appendix. We soon found that it was not easy to keep them there; in the process of asking ourselves what it was we did to teach poetry to our classes, we were forced to try to define the nature of the subject; we agreed that the attraction of poetry to a large extent consisted of its emotional appeal, and yet to say that to teach poetry was to teach the student to respond emotionally was obviously not very helpful. What is an emotional response, and to what does the student respond? How can we make him a more efficient responder?

In the course of preparing our answers to these questions, we were trying to avoid both the Scylla of subjectivity and Charybdis of technical terminology. We have probably not steered entirely clear of either; but we have, finally, made an assessment of our problem, and some specifications which are rather explicit. There are many of you who will doubtless take issue with some of what we say; so much the better, if in the heat of disagreement you are forced to take stock of your own thinking, and re-evaluate your own methods.

It was not for some time that we asked ourselves if the time and energy devoted to teaching poetry were worthwhile. Our investigations showed us very quickly that poetry is not a fast-moving commodity in the world of contemporary letters. Few magazines buy it any longer; of the relatively few books of poetry that are published, fewer make any money for the publisher, or poet.

Information like this would seem discouraging to a group of people trying to say something useful about the teaching of poetry, if it were not for a rather recent and phenomenal rise in the number of poetry *recordings* sold; two young women, graduates of Hunter College, started Caedmon recordings on a capital of some $2,500 and have sold a total of over one million dollars' worth of recordings to date. The poets represented include Dylan Thomas, Ogden Nash, the Sitwells, e e cummings—and the range covers the field of poetry, from Homer in the original Greek to the most modern poet to be labelled "obscure." [1]

We had, then a number of facts about the position of poetry today to reconcile. Apparently few people *read* poetry; at least few pub-

[1] Samuel Grafton, "They've Sold a Million Dollars' Worth of Other People's Poetry," *Good Housekeeping*, Vol. 142, No. 2 (February, 1956), pp. 70–71 ff.

lishers consider it a sound investment. Of the people who do, many consider much poetry written today obscure and difficult. At the same time, many people obviously enjoyed *hearing* poetry.

The conclusions we reached supported our individual feelings about the important elements in teaching poetry. Because of its very nature, most poetry must be read aloud, and read well. There is a place in the classroom for a library of recordings, by the poets themselves, if possible, and by competent readers at any rate. Obviously there should be some student reading of poems, and training in such oral reading. Poetry, like music, is an experience in listening, and one of our jobs is to make attentive listeners out of students.

Pitch, intonation, volume, and speed are some of the qualities which help a poem to become meaningful when read aloud; tone and attitude are revealed in the expression in the reader's voice; irony and subtle shades of meaning are more easily perceived.

Whenever possible, the student should be able to follow with his eyes the poem being read aloud; he should have a copy before him. For oral reading does not solve his real problem, which is to read the next poem more successfully by himself.

We are dealing, to a large extent, with a generation which is not so much illiterate as alliterate; not so much anti-intellectual as nonintellectual. We are dealing with what has become a group of passive readers, who are exposed to, influenced by, and often corrupted by, the language they face daily, with, too often, no concept of the effects wrought upon themselves, or the means by which these effects are engineered. Besieged by advertisements, surrounded by the kind of jargon A. P. Herbert calls "jungle english," [2] stupefied by endless radio and TV exhortations, they do not know what they face; they sit like vegetables in front of their sets, or magazines, and absorb what is offered, good or bad, with only rudimentary notions of which is which.

Our attempt to make poetry readers out of these students must begin with awakening them to the endless power and implications of language. Too often the student reaction to the news that he is about to begin a unit of poetry is like his feelings about the dentist's chair: he expects the process to be painful, but rather hopes that some good will come of it. And seldom does he wish to return.

[2] *What a World!* (Garden City, N.Y., Doubleday & Company, Inc., 1936).

Our first aim will be to convince the student that poetry is no special language in itself, removed from the main currents of his own language, but that it is language functioning at its highest efficiency; language whose matter and manner are developments of the speech he uses, listens to, and reads every day.

A poem, like any structure in language, is a psychological experience: words cause reactions in the reader's mind. As a result much poetry is largely a subjective or personal experience. The same poem may be read by two individuals; both will understand it equally well, but because of their natural individual differences their experiences derived from the poem may be quite different.

Our next aim will be to make the student a participant in the experience of the poem, to make him an *aggressive reader*, one who brings all his faculties to bear on the poem, and who uses his past experience to make the next poem yield more easily.

The teacher must also be an aggressive reader, familiar with the material, trained and enthusiastic. Books like Elizabeth Drew's *Discovering Poetry*, Brooks and Warren's *Understanding Poetry*, Laurence Perrine's *Sound and Sense* will prove invaluable, both for their suggested approach and their variety of exercises and questions. Our professional magazines like *The English Leaflet*, *The English Journal*, and the *Explicator* will suggest both methods of teaching poetry and close analyses of familiar poems. A dictionary, a handbook of mythology, a reference book like Bartlett's, a book like Benét's *The Reader's Encyclopedia* will provide the teacher with information useful to her class and exciting to herself.

The work done in the study of semantics in the last several decades is too important to the teacher of poetry not to be mentioned here. The various books by I. A. Richards serve as basic studies; the chapters which pertain to poetry in Wellek and Warren's *Theory of Literature* are highly useful; Hayakawa's *Language in Thought and Action* is readable and useful for the classroom teacher. The dedicated teacher of any language skill should devote some time to any of such books.

As for the poem: it seems a truism that one teaches best what one likes best. Yet it seems that too often the teacher works only within an anthology someone else has prepared; that while he works with the masterpieces of poetry in our language, he too often starts with what is archaic, Elizabethan, or Victorian.

We are not saying that these poems are not worth teaching, or not essential. We are saying, though, that by the nature of poetry, these poems are likely to be difficult, obscure, or to require a highly trained reader—which is to say the same thing, actually. Save these poems until the reader is sufficiently skilled to cope with them. Choose poems which will yield easily to the reader whose skill is yet undeveloped. Choose poems whose narrative vein is strong, or whose rhythm is pronounced and exciting. Read it aloud, first, and afterwards; after any examination, try to put the poem back together, and leave it whole.

We question the value of having poetry taught only as a separate entity, in a unit by itself. This setting apart tends in itself to call attention to a difference between prose and poetry which does not exist. Offer a poem to a class whenever the time seems opportune, whenever the poem says something related to the project under way, in theme, in manner; the poem presented could be the culmination of one of the great themes of human existence traced through an essay, a story, or a novel; the poem could be presented as one more example of irony, after close reading of prose where irony was a major device. It might then be effective to present Browning's *My Last Duchess*.

It may be effective to prepare a project in which an editorial, a feature story, and a sports article are compared with the poems, *A Song of the Shirt*, *Porphyria's Lover*, and *Casey at the Bat*.

With relative availability of paperback anthologies like *The Pocket Book of Verse*, Untermeyer's *Concise Treasury*, or Oscar Williams' several collections, it should be an easy matter to have copies of anthologies available in some quantity in the classroom.

A last suggestion, before we examine the specific teaching problems: the committee recommends strongly that some memorization be assigned, so that the student builds up a storehouse of poetry in his own mind, partly of his own choice.

SOUND

Poetry lovers are certainly not born, they are made; the making begins when the child has his discriminations in sound and tone made for him by his contacts with adults, and the music of the world around him. The awareness of the sounds of words precedes his recognition of word meanings; he takes his meanings, in fact, from the tone and inflection of adult language.

Later, perhaps he will be one of the lucky bright-eyes who hears from a *Hiawatha Primer* the poetry of Longfellow:

> By the shores of Gitche Gumee
> By the shining Big-Sea Water
> Stood the wigwam of Nokomis,
> Daughter of the Moon, Nokomis.
> Dark behind it rose the forest,
> Rose the black and gloomy pine-trees,
> Rose the firs with cones upon them . . .

What is it about this poetry that is good for the poetry-lover-in-the-making? What is it he'll get from memorizing and hearing and repeating that he'll not likely get from such sentences as "*John has a dog,*" "*Mary has a dog,*" "*See the dog*"?

If the child before school age, and in early school age, through memorization and ear acquaintances, becomes attached to beautiful patterns, not of word meanings, but of word-sound relationships, he has a sense of discrimination in the sounds of prose and poetry, though he may not know it as such.

"There are a lot of things you can do if you want to enjoy poetry more," says Thomas Riggs, Jr., in his short discussion "What Good are Poems?" "The first thing to do is read some poems; find some you like (you don't have to understand them right away); say them to yourself until they are a part of your thought. Do not try to force a meaning out of them in a hurry; their meanings won't yield to force. Memorize a few, until the music of their meaning is a part of your experience. Real poems can be enjoyed before you fully understand them, like real people. And like real people, they improve on acquaintance." [3]

There is an intimacy in the relationship between sound and sense in poetry that we do not often find in prose. They reinforce and substantiate each other in ways which are often special to poetry. Although there are many quite technical terms to label special situa-

[3] *The Wonderful World of Books,* (Mentor Books; New York, New American Library of World Literature, 1952).

tions, we shall not dwell explicitly on the many poetic terms available. Too often the teaching of poetry becomes a process of collecting metrical terms, the names of sound relationships, and the assimilation by the student of the names of several dozen figures of speech, so that the student ends up with a monstrous collection of technical jargon and collects rare examples with no awareness of what they contribute in meaning. For the moment, let us examine Pope's precept:

> 'Tis not enough no harshness gives offense;
> The sound must seem an echo to the sense.

One of the ways by which sound supports sense is by rhythm. The impulse toward rhythm is rooted deep in the experiences of the human race. The beating of the heart, the rhythm of breathing, the changing of day into night, and the cycle of the seasons, have all influenced the actions of man since he first existed. Increases and decreases in rhythm signal changes in emotion, as the rapidly beating heart signals danger, or increased tension. In expressing any intense emotion, such as pain, or grief, the voice tends to fall into a regular beat. The chant of primitive man invoking rain has pattern, as the cheerleader has who urges the spectators to greater efforts as the team draws nearer the goal line. One of the basic characteristics of poetry is rhythm, and hence is a natural expression for all of us. Under the influence of rhythm, we become more susceptible to ideas, attitudes, feelings, and images in a poem. The anonymous ballad writer of old knew well the power rhythm played in capturing his audience, as well as making the poem easier to remember and transmit. And since all poetry is written to be listened to, we recreate the poetic experience more validly when we read a poem musically well, aloud.

The different rhythms stimulate different feelings. In *The Destruction of Sennacherib* the poet wishes to stress the wild and turbulent charge of the Assyrian Cavalry; the rhythm is admirably suited to portray the onrush and swoop of these warriors on the defenseless village below.

To make the student aware of the power of rhythm, the teacher has only to point out those aspects of his existence, his body, his routine, which are marked by rhythm; the beat of a horse, the hypnotic swing of "rock and roll," the changes in speed of musical pieces as the rhythm changes—we only have to point out the appropriateness of the swift movement of *Ghost Riders in the Sky*, or have the rhythm pounded out of *The Highwayman*, to have the student sense the relative importance of the beat in *Lochinvar*, and the appropriateness of the conversational beat of the iambics in most sonnets.

Serving to bind the poem together, and to reinforce the sense, are the devices of alliteration, assonance, consonance, and rhyme. The labels are useful, of course; the danger in their use is that we become preoccupied with identifying them, only for the sake of identifying them. We must ask at all times for the purpose behind the use; for the relationship between sound and sense, for the manner in which sound and rhythm add meaning to the words themselves. The metrical analysis of a poem is seldom valuable as an end in itself, and how valuable it is to the understanding and enjoyment of a poem is very debatable. Let us say that such metrical analysis as helps the student to read the poem aloud intelligently, by making full use of the rhythm as well as the key words and phrases, is worthwhile.

FIGURATIVE LANGUAGE

Much of what we have traditionally accepted as great poetry is too difficult for our young readers. For one reason, the barrier of vocabulary is formidable, in the case of poems whose words have meanings which have shifted in the intervening years. For another, many poems have been written for an audience which was familiar with, for instance, the host of Biblical references and allusions to classical mythology. For many students the complicated syntax poses a problem.

By far the most difficult hurdle for the inexperienced reader to overcome is the figurative language which is the material of poetry.

We are dealing with language operating at its most efficient, at its most precise, at its most affective. We are dealing with language which ". . . reveals itself in the balance or reconcilement of opposite or discordant qualities; of sameness, with difference; of the general, with the concrete; the idea, with the image; the individual, with the representative; the sense of novelty, and freshness, with old and familiar objects; a more than usual state of emotion, with a more than usual sense of order.[4]

Coleridge's statement has within it the essence of what is important about poetry *that we can teach*, and thereby make of our students readers of poetry who bring the same critical perception and understanding, the same awareness of the good, the bad, and the mediocre, that they bring to their examination of a hot rod, or of the new clothes—"party-mannered separates for the sugar and spice set."

The material of poetry is words in order; the method of poetry is figurative language. All language is figurative, to a degree; since the user and the listener are conditioned by their former encounters with a word to each new encounter with it, every word is operating in several ways at once. We can isolate some of these ways, and teach their recognition.

At the first level of language, to start a classification which is of course arbitrary to some extent, is the level of information. Word points to object, or at least to the idea in the mind of the hearer of the object. *Red* means, denotatively, a bright color, a certain vibration on the spectrum, which is itself a reaction in the perceiver's mind.

The next level of language involves those affective qualities about words which make them the powerful and extraordinary tools of communication they are, which we have called the connotative qualities. Connotatively, *red* suggests to the hearer, according to the context in which it is used, and the experience of the hearer, such associations as blood, or murder, or sunset, or Communist. The exact denotation of *fog* is an atmospheric condition occurring when water vapor is visible; its suggestive, or connotative, use recalls sadness, gloom, or mental confusion. One reason for our stand against paraphrasing is that poetry rewritten as prose frequently loses all its connotative meanings, so that the flat prose statement sheds its significance and appropriateness and becomes a communication of something quite different from the poem—no longer, in fact, a poem at all.

We might call connotation the cargo that a word carries in addition to, or at times, in place of, its referential meaning as a label. To make the difference in connotative value of words clear, it is sometimes useful to present words which have roughly the same denota-

4 Samuel Taylor Coleridge, *Biographia Literaria* (New York, E. P. Dutton & Co., 1947), pp. 151–152.

tion, but which vary greatly in connotative power. We are all familiar with Russell's conjugation of value judgments:

> *I* am firm;
> *You* are obstinate;
> But *he* is a pig-headed fool.[5]

We can repeat this technique, with some enjoyment, on many of the value words we habitually use: *loyal, obedient, slavish; famous, well-known, notorious; generous, liberal, spendthrift,* and so on. The list may be increased to five words, going from approval to neutrality to condemnation; you may present a list of five words, to be put in correct order of degree of connotation. You may ask for words which have increasingly romantic connotations: *boat, ship, frigate, galleon.*

As part of the introductory work on figurative language, you might ask for brief paragraphs in which the student describes a scene, an object, a person, an inning in baseball, in three ways: favorably, objectively, unfavorably. Is your favorite baseball player slim, thin, or skinny? And so on.

The study of figurative language should start early. By figurative language we mean that aspect of speech which attempts more than the literal pointing out of things, and includes connotation, imagery, metaphor, symbol, and allusion. Slang is essentially figurative, the "poor man's metaphor" involves not only comparisons, but connotations, and American slang, especially teen-age slang, is full of vivid, expressive figures of speech. Make them aware first of the figurative character of their own speech. The stodgy person whom we call *dull* they call a *square;* a *real gone square* is a *cube*—square from any angle.

The sports page, the periodical advertisements, and the commercials on radio and TV are profitable fields for the teacher to explore. Sports write-ups are primarily based on metaphor: the student, accustomed to the device in the sports pages, has no trouble deciphering the write-up; advertisements rely heavily on the connotative powers of words. Can you imagine, for instance, a perfume being sold as "Evening in Brooklyn"? What are the romantic connotations of words to which Detroit seems so attracted, so that one does not simply advertise a special Cadillac, but a Cadillac Eldorado?

[5] Quoted in Felix Cohen, "The Reconstruction of Hidden Value Judgments," *Essays,* Leonard F. Dean, ed. (New York, Harcourt, Brace & Co., 1955), p. 27.

The first poem encountered should follow in some measure preliminary work in class on figurative language. It should probably be in language still current, about a contemporary situation, and deal with a story. If you choose, for instance, *Richard Cory*, you may note the transition from the word *gentleman* to the specifics which define it—Coleridge's reconcilement of the general with the concrete. What are the connotations, we ask, of the words *clean-favored, imperially, slim, quietly, human, glittered*, and so on? What, you ask, would be the effect of substituting other words (a convenient blackboard device) for ones in the poem: Why not *skinny* for *slim?* Answers will undoubtedly give opportunity for a discussion of rhythm and rhyme, as well as word choice.[6]

The teacher must make every effort to help the student feel all the possible values of words. Defining by context, discussing connotations, making use of the dictionary, and discussing etymologies will all help the student to overcome the barrier of language.

Metaphor as this committee uses it has a most general meaning. It is an all-inclusive term applying to many types of figurative language. Not only do we find figures blending into each other, but we believe it is important not to haggle over classifications. The important thing is to understand both the literal and the implied meanings. And again, our attention should be first focused on language in everyday use. Have the student notice the phrases in his own daily experience:

This jolly Pet Milk fruit cake kissed with raisins. . . .

The corn is as high as an elephant's eye. . . .

More choose THOR—the tools that build the cars. . . .

Midsummernight's scheme: Take your gal . . . Take your Luckies. Take a spin to the driving range. . . .

The big M . . . the Big Mercury . . . a magnificent value in the Ford family of fine cars. . . .

Flower-fresh salads made with cling peaches and cottage cheese.

Sentimental socks, latest fad to hit the campus, designed by a man's best girl to fit his personality. . . .

[6] Laurence Perrine, *Sound and Sense,* (New York, Harcourt, Brace & Co., 1956), p. 36.

KenFlex vinyl tile "colorful as a peacock". . . .

Our house blew away like a cardboard box. . . .

The English Language Arts points out that "consideration by the reader or hearer will lead to an understanding of values in pictorial words and figurative language in general. Since metaphor (in the broad sense) permeates all language, examination of his own figurative language will help the student to understand how language uses the old to express the new meaning. He will discover that comparison (expressed or implied) makes a greater demand on the reader than does a literal expression. He may understand a little better the power of poetic writing." [7]

The student who has not become acquainted with the vividness of his everyday language, the interplay of metaphor with the literal, will have difficulty with poetry at any level of schooling.

Metaphor describes a new experience in terms of the old; it describes an experience in terms taken from another field of experience.

The scientists at Alamogordo, New Mexico, had a new experience to describe in 1945. They did what everyone does when faced with a new experience: they described the new in terms of the familiar: they said, "A cloud shaped like a mushroom arose in the sky." [8]

Metaphor says that something is *like* something else, in some ways.

1. There is an open book on my desk. (*Literal*)
   His life is like an open book. (*Metaphoric*)
   (His life is like an open book in some ways. What ways?)

2. Large waves rolled up against the shore. (*Literal*)
   A wave of laughter rolled up from the audience. (*Metaphoric*)
   (The laughter of the audience was like a wave in some ways. What ways?)

And the step from the metaphor to symbol is one of degree, in which the comparison loses one part:

1. My dog was glad to see me. (*Literal*)
   The dirty dog stole my wallet. (*Metaphoric*)
   Every dog has his day. (*Symbolic*)

[7] Dora V. Smith, ed. (National Council of Teachers of English Curriculum Series; New York, Appleton-Century-Crofts, Inc., 1952), pp. 400–401.

[8] *Living Language, Grade 12*, J. C. Blumenthal, ed. (New York, Harcourt, Brace & Co., 1953).

It may be useful, when analyzing metaphor, to make two lists, using one to show the characteristics of the thing compared, the other to enumerate the qualities of the comparison used. Such a device will show not only the effectiveness of the metaphor, but the point at which, like all metaphors, it breaks down.

It is useful to use the terms developed by I. A. Richards when talking about metaphor. He labelled the part of the metaphor used to carry the meaning as the *vehicle*, and the implications, the qualities which applied both to thing compared and to comparison used, as the *tenor*.

Thus in the metaphor mentioned earlier, "his life was like an open book," the "open book" is the vehicle, and the frankness, obviousness, lack of dissimulation implied is the tenor.

Do not, we repeat, let your teaching of poetry become a process of collecting labels. Too often the student is rewarded and applauded if he can define caesura, tell us that Pope wrote in the heroic couplet, and produce a glib definition of antithesis, but be unable to explain how lines like

> The hungry judges soon the paper sign,
> And wretches hang that jurymen may dine [9]

get their force.

It would be foolish to worry about definitions of devices in a given quotation that has both elements of personification and metaphor. In Millay's *Renascence*, we find:

> The grass, a-tiptoe at my ear,
> Whispering to me I could hear;
> I felt the rain's cool finger-tips
> Brushed tenderly across my lips.[10]

We would not try to visualize the rain in human form, even though it has elements of personification: the poet gives it fingers; nor would we so visualize the grass, though it whispers. Laurence Perrine, author of *Sound and Sense*, would identify this figure as a submetaphor, one in which the figurative term is always a human being.

As Perrine says, personifications vary as to the degree to which they

[9] *The Rape of the Lock*, Canto 3, ll. 21–22.
[10] *Renascence and Other Poems* (New York, Harper & Brothers, 1925).

expect the reader to visualize the figurative part of the comparison. Shakespeare's description of the dawn gives us a comparison between the sky's colors and the cloak of a person, but the image—the sense impression formed in the reader's mind—may or may not be of a person walking:

> But look, the morn, in russet mantle clad,
> Walks o'er the dew of yon high eastward hill.

Economy of language, the soul of poetry, is demonstrated nowhere so well as in metaphor. With a metaphor, the poet can say compactly what would take paragraphs of prose to explain concretely. By way of metaphor the poet may in a few words suggest truths about life that would be difficult, or impossible, to say in prose. Witness the passage from Milton's *Paradise Lost:*

> The mind is its own place, and in itself
> Can make a Heaven of Hell, a Hell of Heaven.

In both these examples our comparison makes use of antithesis to further the tension of the lines.

Apostrophe is another means of making language come alive; the poet addresses some person absent or dead, as if he were present; or some abstraction, or nonanimate thing, as if it were capable of hearing. The use of this figure gives life to Whitman's *Out of the Cradle Endlessly Rocking.* Addressing the bird who has lost his mate, he says:

> Is it indeed toward your mate you sing? or is it really to me?
> For I, that was a child, my tongue's use sleeping,
>   now I have heard you,
> Now in a moment I know what I am for, I awake.

What better example than this boy's awakening through the song of the bird could the poet give what we really want our boys and girls to experience as we give them the poet in his own words? We should not waste time, of which we have so little, studying for hours what Poe did with his personal life, nor what romantic period he fits into, nor a lot of other biographical or historical data that few people are interested enough to dig up, unless such information helps us directly to understand the poem itself.

Do not overlook those poems which function as complete metaphors, in which the student must make a translation for himself; a whole poem may function symbolically, or allegorically, as Frost's *The Road Not Taken*, or Whitman's *O Captain, My Captain*.

As an individual word may, through special use in a poem, become a symbol, so may a whole poem; *Crossing the Bar* by Tennyson is symbolic of the end of life; note especially the symbolic uses of the sea as death, and the bar which is the barrier between life and death.

We have suggested that an inability to cope with figurative language may make reading poems impossible for the student. The language of *allusion*, as we mentioned earlier, is one such barrier, since it presupposes a knowledge of Bible, mythology, and earlier literature which our students too often do not possess.

We recommend that the study of mythology, and certain Old Testament stories be introduced early, preferably by the time the student is in the ninth grade.

High school students like to agree on definitions and to argue about examples. Let them formulate a definition for allusion such as this: an allusion is a reference by the author to some person, place, thing, or situation in the Bible, in history, in mythology, or in literature. Then send them to their newspapers and magazines, to find pictures and explanations of the various kinds of allusions. Advertisements are especially fruitful. In the *New York Herald Tribune* some time ago a full-page ad for *Newsweek* portrayed a wooden horse, with soldiers scattered here and there, with the caption, "Is Red Peace Offensive a Trojan Horse?" *The New York Times* this year ran a Best & Co. ad: "Party-Mannered Separates For The Sugar-and-Spice Set."

Have each member of the class find such examples, and write on them the definition that applies. Capitalize on this activity by having your classes collect those figures of speech they find in their reading, well in advance of your poetry unit.

Finally introduce them to that gold mine of William Rose Benét's *The Reader's Encyclopedia*. This is one of the most valuable books for the teacher and reader of poetry that has been published in this century.

The senior living in New England who comes across these lines from the "Invocation" of *John Brown's Body* will need to look up "Garden of the Gods":

And you are the clipped velvet of the lawns
Where Shropshire grows from Massachusetts sods,
The grey Maine rocks—and the war-painted dawns
That break above the Garden of the Gods.[11]

And this is what he will be rewarded with: "Garden of the Gods. A region of about 500 acres near Colorado Springs, U.S., where there are many strange formations of red and white sandstones."

It may be Tennyson's lines:

Dark faces against that rosy flame
The mild eyed melancholy Lotos-eaters came.

Our reader will find: "Lotos-eaters. In Homeric legend, a people who ate of the lotos tree, the effect of which was to make them forget their friends and homes, and to lose all desire of returning to their native country, their only wish being to live in idleness in Lotus-Land. Odyssey IX."

Perhaps it will be Chaucer's *Prologue* our students are reading:

Whan Zephirus eek with his sweete breeth
Inspired hath in every holt and heeth
The tendre croppes. . . .

And they'll find this: "Zephyr. The west wind in classical mythology, son of Aeolus and Aurora, and lover of Flora: hence, any soft, gentle wind."

". . . The teaching of rhetoric today," say Louis Zahner and others in *Language in General Education*, "like the teaching of grammar, suffers from a barren formalism inherited from the ancients without the living spirit which once created and dwelt in the form. Such teaching centers upon a few arbitrary elements in language and views the living language from these previously chosen standpoints. . . . The elements that are studied, such as figures of speech, are studied from a formally verbal and confining standpoint with more regard to the empty classification and definition than to the living use of the thing studied to express the full range of meanings in a fluid and organic language." [12]

[11] (New York, Rinehart & Company, Inc., 1928).
[12] (Progressive Education Association Publication; New York, D. Appleton-Century Company, Inc., 1939), pp. 74–75.

THEME

Though the student may get a total impression of a poem without understanding the specific meanings of all the words, the reverse is likely to occur, especially in poems where the tone of the speaker is important. Too often irony is missed completely by the unskilled reader; too often tone and attitude go unnoticed, because the student simply does not know how to spot them.

Our progression in the study of words goes from the simplest use of language to the most complex. At the onset we consider the denotations of words. To what objects or facts do they point? Next we consider the connotations. What additional meanings, implications, emotional content have they acquired? What image, we ask next, do they project in the reader's mind, specifically of sense? What colors, sounds, tactile impressions are we aware of? What figurative language is present? What comparisons are stated or implied? What is the purpose of devices like metaphor, simile, personification, allusion?

The poem itself is a whole experience. When we have made an attempt to establish word meanings in a poem, we attack the poem as a whole. Certain points in certain poems are critical, and may be brought into focus by asking a series of questions.

Who is speaking? In some poems, like certain ones of Hardy, the separation between speaker and poet is small, less important. In others, like Browning's *My Last Duchess*, it is wide: unless the student understands the personality of the speaker, he is lost from the beginning.

To whom is the speaker talking? About what? How does he feel about his subject? How do we know how he feels? How does the author of the poem expect the reader to feel about the subject? What language, connotative or figurative, reveals his attitude toward both subject and reader? What does he expect of his audience, in terms of attitude, in terms of understanding his tropes and allusions?

What is going on in the poem? What is the apparent meaning of the lines? What is the actual meaning? Poetry, says Cleanth Brooks, is the language of paradox; [13] the discrepancy between what is said and what is meant establishes the tension which makes poetry rich.

When there is an apparent contradiction between what is said and meant, we call it paradox: when Pope says

[13] *The Well-Wrought Urn* (New York, Reynal & Company, Inc., 1947), pp. 3–20.

> Damn with faint praise

the paradox of praising and condemning at the same time results in a mild shock, so that the reader stops, thinks, reasons his way out of the situation. When two ideas of opposite value are juxtaposed, a similar shock is produced:

> And wretches hang, that jurymen may dine.

The antithesis between the wretch and the person who sits in judgment on him, and the contrast between the man who dies that another man may lunch produces a tension so that each is sharpened by contrast. The discrepancy between the two results in one kind of irony.

When the result is not one we anticipate, when the outcome is not the one that seems appropriate, we say that a discrepancy exists, and that the end is ironic. Richard Cory's fate was ironic: the phrase

> So on we worked, and waited for the light

becomes ironic when the light we finally perceive is death, and an inappropriate one at that.

When a character says one thing and obviously means another, he is being ironic, and the difference between the two may be slight, or may be 180 degrees. When irony has a victim, a target, we call it satire, directed against a social institution, an established convention, a set of standards.

You will remember, of course, that the verb *flay* means to "strip off the skin." Recall for a moment Swift's sentence in *A Tale of a Tub:*

> Last week I saw a woman flayed, and you will hardly believe how much it altered her person for the worse.

The horror with which we react is at least partly due to the realization of the deliberate inappropriateness of the expression for the situation: the understatement.

Language which is more than the situation warrants tends to sharpen our perceptions through exaggeration; such overstatement, or *hyperbole*, is common in our own speech and in poetry. Witness Lady Macbeth's tortured cry:

> Here's the smell of blood still: all the perfumes of Arabia will not sweeten this little hand.

We ask, what is the poet's motive: what is his purpose in writing the poem? In poems whose ironic content is great, the question of motive, and hence of attitude, is paramount. Once we have established the identity of the speaker, and his attitude toward his subject, we can make a guess as to the sound of his voice: is he polite? mocking? sad? sarcastic? regretful?

One of the values of examining poems for their content of antithesis, paradox, irony, hyperbole, and understatement is that a study of these characteristics of language all call for a look at the whole poem, the complete experience. Irony always involves a looking-both-ways; and such examination helps partially to restore a poem to its original unity, and to give it added texture and richness.

How do we teach these things?

First we must examine the presence of these characteristics in our own speech. Our own language is full of shades of irony; we seldom mean just what we say. Unlike the readers of poetry, our listeners are usually aware of the fact. "Nice going!" we say to the child who has just spilled a bottle of ink over our desk. We listen calmly to "I thought I'd die when he asked me to the Prom." If we can get as accustomed to sorting out the real meanings of poetic language as we are of everyday speech, we have a beginning. "GIANTS FLAY PIRATES," says a headline; though the score is not given, the implication, in the light of Swift's use of the word, is that the Pirates were badly beaten.

To study very briefly a familiar example of highly figurative language, consider the first line of Keats' *On First Looking into Chapman's Homer:*

> Much have I travell'd in the realms of gold.

Here the language is metaphoric; the whole poem is based on a travel metaphor. The figure is allusive, since the realms of gold refer to Eldorado, giving us an excuse for the use of Cortez later in the poem instead of Balboa; the figure is extravagant, using overstatement, and we are led to sense finally the extraordinary excitement of Keats, a person to whom the enjoyment of literature was worth all the fabled wealth of the mysterious New World, as he discovered Chapman's translation.

In order to cultivate an awareness of these forces at work in language, we have already suggested two basic principles: a teacher who is familiar with the poem, and a series of questions, leading the student into the heart of the poem, asking for reasoned answers instead of *yes's* or *no's*. We have suggested that the study of figurative language should start early, by studying our own speech; we have suggested having the poem read aloud, by competent persons, if not by professionals on records, or the poet himself.

In order to make qualities of particular poems stand out, and to make differences more obvious, we suggest the use of comparison of two poems, treating the same theme with different methods, or rhythms, or different degrees of subjectivity.

Compare, for instance, Arnold's *Dover Beach* with Hardy's *The Oxen*, for explicit and implicit statement of theme; compare the parable of the Prodigal Son with Robinson's poem, *The Prodigal Son*.

And if the young child has had his experiences guided for him as he reads, he will be ready to build the intellectual meanings for himself, to make himself responsive to the great emotional experiences of poetry. The music and imagery and meanings of words will become part of his own experiences; and what a responsive note will he find, as he listens to the bright, extraordinary voice of one of our most modern poets, no longer obscure to him, as Dylan Thomas reads:

> And I saw in the turning so clearly a child's
> Forgotten mornings when he walked with his mother
> Through the parables
> of Sunlight
> And the legends of the green chapels.[14]

And what excitement will his reading yield, when the student can surmount the barrier of language, and respond to the magnificent treatment of the great themes of human passion, dignity, and endurance, in the language by which men become immortal, "the impassioned expression which is the countenance of all science . . . , the breath and finer spirit of all knowledge." [15]

[14] Dylan Thomas, "Poem in October," *Selected Writings* (New York, New Directions, 1946), p. 77.
[15] William Wordsworth, *Preface to the Lyrical Ballads* (London, Longmans, 1798).

Appendix A: Metrics

The different rhythms tend to stimulate different feelings—a device not limited to poetry alone but much more highly organized in poetry. The fast and slow rhythms are obtained by the arrangement of syllables and sounds. One cannot say arbitrarily that the trochaic rhythm is the light skipping beat and that the iambic is the slow solemn one, for the sounds within the line control the method of saying it. The quantity of the syllable, which is very different from its accent and stress, is the time required to pronounce it. *Meant* is long in quantity; *is* is short in quantity. Usually a syllable is prolonged by open vowels (contrast *see* and *set*) and by the multiplication of consonants, especially by the use of *m, n, ng,* and *l.* In the word *imagine* the stress is on the syllable *ag,* but the other syllables are longer in quantity and take longer to say. Therefore, one iambic foot may take longer to say than another iambic foot, and the amount of time spent on each foot will not be equal. In the line

> Thou still unravished bride of quietness

one spends more time on *un* and *ished* than one does on the stressed syllable *rav.*

Pitch as well as stress helps to focus the attention of the listener upon the poetic concept. The variation of pitch in reading a regularly scanned line of poetry can seem to change the stress from long to short.

Although the term *onomatopoeia* is only applied to words which imitate their own literal meaning, as *bang, fizz, buzz,* suggested onomatopoeia, the sounds of vowels and consonants which do not reproduce but merely suggest what is described, is often used to intensify the concept of the poet. *I* and *a* are allied generally to the idea of littleness and delicacy and of joy and mirth:

> How they tinkle, tinkle, tinkle,
> In the icy air of night!

Broad *o,* long *o,* and Italian *a* (*ah*) suggest breadth, magnitude, and serenity as well as other things of like nature:

> Hear the mellow wedding bells,
> Golden bells!

K, g, gr, cl, r, j, ct, are harsh unpleasant sounds and suggest among other things horror, disgust, fear, and swiftness:

> How they clang, and clash, and roar!
> What a horror they outpour.

Long syllables retard the movement; therefore, they are best suited to solemn, stately, or mournful emotions. Short syllables hasten the movement; therefore, they suggest light, gay, and airy movement.

Although rhythm is one of the strongest influences in poetry, alliteration, assonance, consonance, and rhyme all are used to bind poetry together. These are integrated with rhythm; they involve the repetition of identical or of related sound, and it is this regularity of movement and repetition of sound which not only gives pleasure but gives unity to a poem.

The basic purpose of rhyme is to reinforce the pattern of the stanza. The arrangement of rhyme in set patterns can be so strong a unifying force that it can almost of itself bring harmony to an otherwise bumpy and irregular poem. There are two kinds of rhyme: internal rhyme, words using the same sounds contained within a line, and end-rhyme, words using the same sounds occurring at the ends of two, or more, lines. There are certain rules for end-rhyming; the vowel sound in the word and the succeeding consonant sounds must be identical and the rhyming syllables must be accented. In modern poetry there is a decided tendency to substitute approximate rhymes for perfect ones, such as *beckon—second* and *suddenly—summery.*

Alliteration, the repetition of initial sounds, is the most dangerous of the group we have been discussing, because although it can add unity and emphasis to the author's concept by pointing up certain words, it can, if not used sparingly, become both mechanical and monotonous—a lesson Swinburne did not learn although he was able to make fun of himself for using alliteration to excess.

Assonance is the repetition of identical vowel sounds within the words, and consonance is the repetition of consonant sounds at the end or middle of lines. All of these devices help to emphasize and unify the ideas of the poem. The free verse of Walt Whitman is a striking example of the unifying ability of assonance, consonance, and alliteration.

In comparing conventional verse to free verse, we might note that Miss Elizabeth Drew says:

Free verse is emotional pattern without any regularity of sound pattern. It is of course nonsense to dismiss it as mere lawlessness. It can be as rigidly disciplined as the most complicated stanza construction and it can bring the same complete sense of satisfaction as the formal types of verse but the sensitiveness of the reader must be far more specialized. It is idle to pretend that the appeal of free verse is, or ever can be, as powerful as that of poetry where the emotional rhythm is matched by the regular rhythmical element in the sound pattern.[32]

The most arresting statement from the quotation is that free verse demands more sensitiveness from the reader than conventional verse does.

We must be sure to distinguish between blank verse and free verse as the word "blank" in its connotation is misleading. Blank verse should have been called unrhymed verse, which is what it is. Shakespeare wrote in blank verse—unrhymed iambic pentameter. There is a definite rhythm but no rhyme. Free verse has no rhyme and a very irregular rhythm—sometimes none. It depends for its unity on alliteration, assonance, repetition of the same grammatical structure, or on some such structure. It, too, must be planned and concise, but the two types are entirely different.

The metrical analysis of a poem is never valuable as an end in itself, and how valuable it is to the understanding and enjoyment of a poem is very debatable. In scanning, the tendency today is not to force a pupil to mark off the poems into metrical feet. The divisions have little meaning except to name the meter of the poem. Variations from the basic pattern are so many that it is often impossible to fit a poem into consecutive iambic-anapestic feet. The pupil gets as much training by placing the stress or long marks and the unstressed marks on the syllable as he does by distorting the sense of the poem in order to make it fit a regular metrical pattern. Then, too, authorities often differ on the way a poem is scanned. Shelley's *Skylark* is an example of this difference of opinion. The movement seems to be forward, but the poem,

---

[32] *Discovering Poetry* (New York, W. W. Norton & Company, 1933), p. 184.

except for the last line of each stanza, can be fitted quite conveniently into regular trochaic rhythm. It really does not make any difference to the understanding or enjoyment of the poem whether it is scanned in iambic or trochaic rhythms. Shelley himself probably did not know, for few poets plan before writing a poem just what meter they will use. The stanza pattern is generally planned and the subject matter poured into the form. This fact is especially true of the stylized French stanza-patterns.

Appendix B: Lesson Plans

COURSE: HISTORY OF AMERICAN LITERATURE
UNIT: PORTRAIT SKETCHES OF EDWIN ARLINGTON ROBINSON

Poems to Be Studied:
  Miniver Cheevy   *John Gorham*
  Richard Cory   *Mr. Flood's Party*
  Cliff Klingenhagen

Purpose:
1. To become acquainted with Edwin Arlington Robinson and his place in the development of American literature.
2. To quicken sensitivities so that the mind looks beyond the outward appearance to the psychological reality.
3. To heighten the appreciation of a disciplined technique.

Introduction:
1. Robinson's place at the beginning of a new movement in American poetry.
2. Robinson's life: emphasis upon the loneliness, sense of failure of his early years, and his reticence.
3. Maine background as reflected in the poems:
   a. Great era of shipbuilding gone.

   b. Sea captains' houses along the rivers left as a symbol of a rich past.

   c. Sense of disintegration and decay.

   d. Vigor of old way of life replaced by loneliness, frustration, and failure.

4. Robinson's approach to his portrait sketches:
   a. Realism and directness.
   b. Psychological insight.
   c. Sympathy, tenderness, irony.

Miniver Cheevy:

1. Reading of poem.
2. Interpretation of character: misfit who escapes into a world of romantic dreams.
3. Study of the technique by which Robinson achieves his effects:
   a. Overtones of suggestion in the name *Miniver Cheevy.*
   b. The use of ironic contrasts to bring out the disparity between the real Miniver and the dreams of "days of old."
      (1) Details, images, allusions that evoke Miniver's visions of the heroic and the romantic contrasted to the interlacing verbs of frustration and gestures of futility.
      (2) Ironic juxtapositions.
      (3) Anticlimax.
      (4) Firmness and strength of accented words of one syllable, with their open vowels and clean-cut consonants in contrast to the weaker, softer words.
   c. Relationship of the form of the poem to the meaning:
      (1) Conventional quatrain *a,b,a,b,* a closeknit form, yet one that gives a sense of disintegration and weakness because the masculine rhyme is followed always by the feminine rhyme.
      (2) Regularity of the iambic foot broken by the repeated *Miniver* at the beginning of each stanza, by the effect of truncated lines, and the shortened fourth line of each stanza.
      (3) Review of techniques in relationship to the meaning of the poem.
      (4) Rereading of the poem.

Similar procedure is the study of other portrait poems, with special considerations.

Richard Cory:

    a. Economy of language, suggesting the quiet dignity of Richard Cory with his reticence and his New England way of keeping things to himself, while maintaining an outward appearance of living within an accepted code.

    b. Projection of meaning through verbs and epithets.

    c. Calm directness and understatement of last two lines increasing the shock of the violent action that exposes reality.

Cliff Klingenhagen:

    a. Spare quality of verse in keeping with the stoicism of Cliff Klingenhagen.

    b. Use of symbols.

    c. Relation of Italian sonnet form to the development of the thought.

John Gorham:

    a. Antiphonal effect of alternating stanzas of dialogue; the quality of Jane Wayland's stanzas, capricious in tone, in contrast to the quiet effect of John Gorham's.

    b. Shifting moods of Jane Wayland suggested through shifting imagery.

    c. Play of moonlight throughout the poem, with its culminating effect in the impact of the final image.

Mr. Flood's Party:

    a. Study in loneliness treated with tenderness and pathos.

    b. Gentle humor underlining the pathos.

    c. Remarkable evocations through imagery of stanzas three and four.

    d. Final emphasis on loneliness in the pathetic truth of the closing statement.

Conclusion:

1. Summary of Robinson's subjects and his techniques.
2. Suggestions for further reading:

    How Anandale Went Out
    Karma

Luke Havergal
New England

3. Brief talk on the longer psychological poems of Robinson.
4. Estimate of his place in the development of American literature.

Deering High School,
Portland, Maine

TEACHING PLAN FOR GEORGE HERBERT'S *VIRTUE*

Introduction: This poem is an experience in understanding. Young people are nearly always sympathetic to the idea presented here; that is, they believe it—it is what they *want* to believe. But to *know* it is another thing altogether. That can come only from experience, from having lived long enough to make certain observations and comparisons over and over again till they have grown into conviction. So, in this deceptively simple lyric, George Herbert, the poet, is sharing with us a belief which life itself has convinced him is true.

Read the poem aloud.

Attempt to state the thought:

That simple goodness, a strong character, is lasting, even eternal.

But this thought is almost a cliché; every generation of man has said it again. But then, too, in every generation there have been men whose sad and disappointing experiences have convinced them that goodness does *not* win out, and they have cried out their bitterness in poetry and song that tells us that kindness and gentleness are more often punished or deceived than rewarded.

Show the importance and value of *form* in this poem:

Why, then, has Herbert's poem lasted? Why is it considered "great"? What makes it convincing?

A man's sincere belief that something is true is not enough. Half the world will rise to deny it, to take the opposite side.

Thus, it becomes clear that *how* he expresses his belief is of tremendous importance. Especially if the thought itself be long familiar to mankind, the *form* in which it is expressed is what makes it seem fresh and original and overwhelmingly true.

Consequently, we shall not feel the full and convincing power of this poem until we have analyzed, that is, studied in detail, its form, how it is constructed. This analysis, this taking apart, should not spoil a poem for us. Anyone who understands what a thing is made of, and how it is put together, is far more capable of understanding and appreciating the whole, whether it is a bridge or an automobile or a poem.

Give some groundwork—word meanings:

Naturally, since this poem was written in the seventeenth century, some of the words Herbert uses had a different meaning for him than for us. It is only fair, both to him and to us, that we try to understand what they mean.

Discuss and explain: *virtue, brave, rash, sweets, compacted, music, closes, seasoned, gives*.

Bring out how the seventeenth and the twentieth centuries are alike in their interest in science and their excitement over new discoveries; also that *any* subject (even the formation of coal) is poetic material if the poet feels intensely about it.

Show the parallel construction:

Notice that these all describe something that men consider precious and beautiful: a day, a rose, and spring.

Also, all three are limited, brief, cut off by time.

Point out the use of repetition:

The first three stanzas begin with the same word—*sweet*. (Consider the multiplicity of meanings this word has for every man.) Notice how it is delayed in the fourth stanza by the modifier *only*—in order to focus on the importance of the real subject, expressed in the title, *Virtue*.

The short last line of the first three stanzas is a refrain.

Show how the poem is sharpened by effective contrast and variety:

Point out the changes in the refrain of the first three stanzas.

There is a denial, a positive statement—in the last line of the last stanza.

The total effect of the poem is a balance of truth between the denial and the affirmation.

As the poem consists of four stanzas, the last of which contradicts the first three, so each stanza consists of four lines, the last of which makes a positive statement of exactly half the length and twice the force of each preceding line. (As time allows, bring out the fascination which mathematics had for the seventeenth century mind, and how the poetry of each period reflects what was absorbing to the people at that time.)

Comment on the poet's acceptance of the opposites in life: earth, sky; morning, night; beginnings, ends; sweet, bitter; life, the grave.

Emphasize that the whole poem has unity—it mounts to a climax of affirmation: that, whereas everything else dies, character and goodness are enduring.

Save time to read the poem aloud again.

Give a summary of the techniques and subjects common to all the Cavalier poets.

Read other Cavalier poems, such as:

Go, Lovely Rose! by Edmund Waller
Shall I, Wasting in Despair by George Wither
Counsel to Girls by Robert Herrick
The Constant Lover by Sir John Suckling
Why So Pale and Wan, Fond Lover by Sir John Suckling
To Althea, from Prison by Richard Lovelace
To Lucasta, Going to the Wars by Richard Lovelace

Deering High School
Portland, Maine

TEACHING PLAN FOR JOHN KEATS' *ODE ON A GRECIAN URN*

Grade XII
Purpose:

To teach the importance of beauty in the life of each individual.

To teach that beauty is an individual experience.

To teach that we must bring a receptive mind, that we must be willing to enter into the thoughts of the author and not just to expect to find our own thoughts reflected by them. "If the person who wrote the story (poem) is not wiser than you, you need not read it; if he be, he will think differently from you in many respects." (*Of Kings' Treasuries*—Ruskin)

Introduction: What is beauty?

John Galsworthy says in his essay *Castles in Spain:* "Everything which promotes the real dignity of human life." To illustrate the breadth of the word *beauty* he continues:

Good sportsmanship—to be a good sportsman, a man shuns that which lowers his dignity.
Pleasant sounds
Fine form
Lovely color
Health
Strength
Cleanliness
Balance
Joy of Living
Just conduct
Kind conduct, for there is no beauty in the sight of a tortured thing.

1. Read Keats' poem through without comment (if you do not read well, play a good recording).
2. Explanation of words whose meaning or connotation may not be known or clear, such as *Tempe, Arcady, timbrels, Attic, Fair attitude.* Why *cold* pastoral?
3. Draw on the blackboard, or have drawn, a picture of the figures on the Grecian urn.
4. Brief discussion of the metrical form of the poem. Note the use of assonance. Do the metrical questions point up the idea Keats is expressing? What are they?
5. How does Keats unify his ideas? What is the central thought the following lines are emphasizing?

> Heard Melodies are sweet, but those unheard
> Are sweeter;

> She cannot fade, though thou hast not thy bliss,
> Forever wilt thou love, and she be fair!
>
> Ah, happy, happy boughs! That cannot shed
> Your leaves, nor ever bid the Spring adieu:
> And, happy melodist, unwearied,
> Forever piping songs forever new;

What does Keats mean by the following lines:

> Thou, silent form, dost tease us out of thought
> As doth eternity:
>
> Beauty is truth, truth beauty—that is all
> Ye know on earth, and all ye need to know.

What is the function of the last two lines?

Conclusion:

What is the poem written about? Is it really about a Grecian urn? Read the poem again.

> *Deering High School*
> *Portland, Maine*

A STUDY IN COMPARISONS

Materials:

The Parable of the Prodigal Son (Luke 15:11–32)
The Prodigal Son, a poem by E. A. Robinson (28 lines)
The Prodigal Son, a poem by Weldon Johnson (123 lines)
A dictionary on every desk

Time:

Two fifty-minute periods on consecutive days, a four-day interval, a final fifty-minute period.

Procedure:

1. Have class read orally the Bible version of The Prodigal Son. Discuss as a narrative and as a parable.
2. At end of period, tell them that the next day's lesson will be based on the parable and ask them to be familiar with the following words:

viands	venomous	indigent
acclaim	lentils	anguish
execrate	draggled	monologue

3. On the second day, read the Robinson poem aloud, explaining before you begin that this poem is by an American twentieth-century poet who has taken for granted that the reader knows the original. Each student is to take notes after each of two readings by the teacher. After the third one, he is to write a comparison of the two selections, the poem and the parable. No questions or explanations are to be made. Collect papers at end of period. (After the first reading, allow five minutes for note taking. Reread the poem and allow ten minutes for notes. Reread for third time and allow twenty-five minutes for composition.)
4. Near end of second day, give each student copies of the two poems. With the three selections, they are to write a paper based on the comparisons that they find after careful rereadings.

Instructions:

a. Read aloud the selections several times while you are preparing your notes and outline.
b. Review your notes on imagery, figurative language, on versification and stanza patterns.
c. Title: A Study in Comparisons
d. Paper due four days from now.
e. We will have a final day of discussion when you will receive your corrected papers.
5. Final Day: Return papers with comments. Give orally your general comments as to how well the assignment has been done, strengths and weaknesses. Have the class discuss results, compare notes, and have a few of best papers in each exercise read aloud for evaluation by the class.

NOTE: It is presupposed: that the class has *already* had experience in writing comparisons; that when a student discusses a point such as length, he will treat it fully in one paragraph, using all three selections; that the introduction will tell the points he will use and the materials he will examine for the comparison; that each point of comparison will be in a separate paragraph; that the conclusion will be based on all materials and not just one selection.

Bennington High School
Bennington, Vermont

THE TWA CORBIES

Instructions: Read the poem over slowly three or four times. Do not attempt to do much conscious thinking about the meaning of the poem until your final reading, which may be guided by the questions reproduced below.

On your first reading, listen to the sounds of the poem. Is the tempo fast or slow? Are the rhythms and vowel sounds cheerful or mournful? Don't make up your mind on this matter until you have completed *all* your readings. On your second reading, try to visualize clearly the images (pictures, visual impressions) presented in the poem. On your third reading, let sounds and images blend more fully. What kind of mood do they, together, establish? On your fourth reading, start thinking more analytically (less dreamily), and answer the following questions:

1. Is this a cheerful or mournful poem? What sonic elements most strongly contribute to your feeling or mood?
2. Briefly describe the two or three images or pictures you found most vivid. What specific emotion did each evoke?
3. What emotional associations, if any, did the word *raven* ("corbie") have for you before you started to read this poem? (At this point, the teacher explains the traditional associations of the raven for the benefit of those students for whom it had no associations.)
4. What was your initial feeling toward the corbies (that evoked by stanza one before you had read further)? Was it like or unlike the feelings and attitudes traditionally associated with the bird?
5. Was your initial attitude toward the corbies altered by information you gained subsequent to stanza one? If so, what was the altered emotion, and what information contributed most strongly to your change of attitude?

6. After your fourth reading, should you say that other creatures mentioned in the poem are more disgusting than the corbies? Enumerate, in order of repulsiveness, all creatures mentioned in the poem that are distasteful to you.

7. How did the knight meet his death? Explain briefly how you arrived at your conclusion. (At this point, teacher gives the correct answer to those who missed it.)

8. Now that the answer to the preceding question is known, would you change your answers to Questions 5 or 6? If so, how?

9. What feelings do you think the poet intends you to have ultimately toward (a) the knight, (b) "his lady fair," (c) his hawk and hound?

10. What are intended to be the two most powerful feelings left with you when you have finished the full reading of the poem?

11. This poem is *for* what virtues? *Against* what faults or vices?

12. What does the poem imply about the relative moral superiority or inferiority of human beings to animals? Can you put this in the form of a theme statement?

Supplementary Question

What ironies in the poem support the conclusions at which you arrived in your answers to questions 9, 10, 11, and 12?

NOTE: This is not a test given primarily for the purpose of giving the student a grade but for the purpose of instruction in how to read the poem.

> *Phillips Academy,*
> *Andover, Massachusetts*

A UNIT ON BALLADS

Grade X

Recordings by Burl Ives, Columbia Records, offer as good a link between the present and the beginnings of poetry as the general group of pupils can enjoy. Many other recordings are good.

One record by Burl Ives has, on one side, four examples of ballads: *Green Broom*, a tuneful melody; *High Barbaree*, a pirate story; *I've*

Got No Use for Women, a raucous, amusing song; and *Old Point,* which the pupils suddenly recognize as the theme song of a TV serial.

The tone, rhythm, joy of song and story are well reflected on this record. It makes a good introduction, a gentle passage into poetry. Who can resist the tale of battle, of love and elopement, of suffering and suspense, of agony and hope, all told with a rhythm and rhyme that "give the story a human touch," according to the pupil for whom "most poetry is too deep," in his own words. Ballads work.

Swing Low, Sweet Chariot and *He Never Said a Mumbling Word* are powerful teachers. If a record is not available, read or sing in class. This furnishes even more opportunity to see that the allusions and symbols are understood. Few young people wish to be thought ignorant of what is being said. More and more pupils are saying, "I didn't understand that line." Recordings are excellent and abundant. Not infrequently some pupil (who seldom appears in the school concerts) will have a guitar; another pupil will know a ballad, lead it, and the group will join in the refrain.

Why were ballads so elemental, so earnest, so dramatic, so heart-rending, if not to appeal to every human being? Why was the refrain used, if not to lure the audience? The alternate rhyme of the ballad stanza afforded easy grasp of the words; any irregularity of beat or accent, any repetition was all to the good.

From the old folk ballad to the modern literary ballad no artificial bridge is needed. All have echoes of the past, whether truly mytho-logical or of Davy Crockett; all have easy rhythm, emotion, and dramatic narrative.

After the recordings mentioned (sung by Burl Ives) one might well turn to three ballads in the text.

Ballads of Kents and Fallons by Lucy Furman

This ballad carries the traces of the Scotch clans and their feuds to their descendants in the Kentucky mountains. Depths of emotions are sounded; struggles know no end; but the young hero does his vengeful duty, though he linger in prison for it. All this is sung out in such easy rhyme and rhythm that observation of the *Oh's, O's, a-diving's,* onomatopoeia, alliteration, and occasional techniques can be developed without damage to the ballad or to the pupil's enjoyment of it.

Questions ranging from the cast of characters to quality of law and justice can readily check the understanding of the pupils from the lower to the higher levels of ability.

A Ballad of the Oysterman by Oliver Wendell Holmes

The gossip column narrative quality of the ballad can be noted without a miss by the least able pupil. The parody of the old folk ballad will be almost equally obvious, and the burlesque of the classical myth of Hero and Leander will give occasion to those of more ability to show their powers of recognition and interpretation. Meanwhile all will be seeing what fun an early American author had in writing a poem and how much more fun can be gained by reading a poem, or any composition, if the background of some allusions has been acquired.

Questions as to the characters, form, rhyme, rhythm, allusions, generalizations will be all the testing necessary for the moment.

A Ballad of Trees and the Master by Sidney Lanier

This ballad illustrates the use of Biblical allusions and would surely awaken a pupil to the richness that can be gained by use of them. Symbolism, personification, compression, love, both human and divine —all combine to raise this apparently simple ballad to great heights.

Do not lose hope if some pupils do not know the story of Gethsemane, to say nothing of the symbolism. It is better that they learn it at school than not at all. Some will understand the basic allusion, and from them an interpretation of the symbolism will come. The struggle in a person's soul, the victory of nobility of mind and spirit, the true spirit of sacrifice will be realized. Sidney Lanier's gentle music is appropriate for this theme.

Spaulding High School
Barre, Vermont

A CLASS ON THE ANALYSIS OF SHAKESPEAREAN SONNET CXLVII

General Directions:

A. Read aloud the entire selection carefully.

1. My love is as a *fever, longing* still
2. For that which longer *nurseth* the *disease;*
3. *Feeding* on that which doth preserve the *ill,*
4. Th' uncertain *sickly appetite* to please.
5. My reason, the *physician* to my Love,
6. Angry that his *prescriptions* are not kept,
7. Hath left me, and I *desperate* now approve
8. Desire is *death,* which *physic* did except.
9. Past *cure* I am, now Reason is past *care,*
10. And *frantic-mad* with evermore unrest;
11. My thoughts and my discourse as *madmen's* are,
12. At random from the truth *vainly* express'd;
13. For I have sworn thee fair, and thought thee bright,
14. Who art as black as hell, as dark as night.

B. Read it a second time noting carefully the words that have an interrelationship.

Specific Analysis and Study:

A. Tone:

List one or two adjectives that accurately describe the tone of the poem. Tone is essentially a communication of emotion, and most students can sense this emotion from an initial careful reading and before the intellectual analysis begins to intrude. From discussion we accept as valid for description of the tone such adjectives as *disturbed* and *angry.*

B. Prose statement:

This helps to make concrete the message of the poem and provides a firm basis for the analysis to follow. From class discussion and casual reference to the text arrive at some such acceptable statement as "Although I have found you thoroughly unworthy of my love, this love yet remains; and in spite of all, it drives me mad." This should not take the form of a complete paraphrase; it should be written in plain sight of all students.

C. Basic metaphor:

1. Many poems are founded on a basic comparison. For instance Tennyson's *Crossing the Bar* is founded on the com-

parison, or metaphor, of a ship putting out to sea and the soul putting out to the sea of the future life.

2. List the words and expressions that carry out the basic metaphor.

    a. Students should not *here* refer to the text.

    b. Number lines 1 through 14 on the board, and after each number place the words that carry out the metaphor as given below:

1.		fever	longing
2.		nurseth	disease
3.	Feeding		ill,
4.		sickly appetite	
5.		physician	
6.		prescriptions	
7.		desperate	
8.	death	physic	
9.	cure		care
10.	frantic-mad		
11.		madmen's	
12.		vainly	
13.			
14.			

    c. Ask students to read these silently and to determine the context in which these words usually find an interrelationship. When it has been determined that the metaphor is based on a terrible illness, the sonnet should be reread aloud for two reasons: to find the specific or implied statement of the metaphor, in this case in line 1, and to replace all supporting words into the framework of the poem.

D. Rhythm:

Examine the rhythm in general. Is it smooth and regular or unusual and irregular? The rhythm of a poem usually carries out or emphasizes the tone.

1. Mark the rhythm of the first quatrain. The first two lines are fully regular with the five iambics we have been led to expect in a sonnet. This regularity is immediately dissipated

by "Feeding" in line 3. A further sampling reveals that at least lines 6 and 8 have their irregularities. It is not necessary to scrutinize every foot of every line of the sonnet lest this analysis resolve itself into a mere exercise in metrics.

2. Determine why such irregularities in meter are in keeping with the tone of the sonnet and why they are appropriate to the metaphor. Here the irregularities emphasize the anger of the tone and are appropriate to the metaphor because they bring into relief the wild restlessness of the soul torn by the fever of love.

E. Examine the rhythm in particular, noting particularly the juxtaposition or repetition of the same sound in the same quatrain.

1. Note the multiplication of *s* and *l* sounds in the first two lines; realize that these sibilants and liquids intensify the regular quality of the meter in these two lines and prepare us for the strong contrast of the rough and disturbed sounds in the following lines where we find an irregular meter appropriately introduced. As has been pointed out, we find this irregularity introduced by "Feeding" in line 3, and supported by the introduction of such harsh sounds as provided by "sickly appetite," "Reason," "Angry" (in this word a good combination of irregularity in meter coupled to a hard sound), and "prescriptions." Others can be found, but these are sufficient to prove the point. Again the appropriateness of the use of these sounds to bring into relief the tone, and changes of tone, should be stressed. Mention of their existence alone is not sufficient; demonstration of their integral quality in the fabric of the sonnet should be stressed.

F. The rhyme scheme:

1. Mark down the rhyme scheme using on the board only the last words of the fourteen lines. We find it to be the usual English sonnet rhyme: *a,b,a,b, c,d,c,d, e,f,e,f,* and *g,g.*

2. Notice how each quatrain encompasses within itself a complete thought in the development of the sonnet. Notice also how the completeness of each thought, the transition from one facet of thought to another are emphasized by the end

punctuation plus the changes in rhyme scheme. There are full period stops at the end of lines 4 and 8 and a near full stop at the end of line 12.

3. Notice also that the contrast afforded by the consecutive rhyme of lines 13 and 14 is prepared for by the introductory and transitional word "For" in line 13; not to be overlooked is the final element of poetical strain effected by the juxta-position of "fair" and "black as hell" and "bright" and "dark as night." A further note would be to point out how a certain degree of unity is achieved by the reintroduction in the last line of the *l* and *s* sounds first used in line 1.

G. In a logical statement say whether or not you believe the poem to be successful. Give a complete answer based on conclusions drawn from your analysis.

Stevens High School,
Claremont, New Hampshire

AN EXPERIENCE IN LISTENING BASED ON POETRY

Grades X, XI, or XII (at all levels)

Materials:

Poet's Gold (LM 1813, RCA Victor, $3.98). This is an excellent re-cording of fifteen poems, but we use only three of them for this par-ticular unit:

The Ballad of the Harp-Weaver by Millay (read by Helen Hayes)
The Lake Isle of Innisfree by Yeats (read by Helen Hayes)
The Raven by Poe (read by Thomas Mitchell)

Time:

About four class periods of 50 minutes each.

Procedure:

We do not announce poems ahead of time, nor do we put copies of the poems in the hands of the students. This unit is taught well in ad-vance of the study of Dylan Thomas' *Poem in October* which we give only to seniors. We announce: "Tomorrow we will have an experience in listening that we hope you will find interesting, enjoyable, and thought-provoking."

At the first of the period, the group is asked to review the basic element of *Narrative:*

A. Characters
B. Plot (series of incidents)
C. Setting (time, place, and atmosphere)
D. Theme (the main idea)

and *Lyric:*

A. Contains very little narrative
B. Usually written in the first person
C. The speaker explains an emotion
D. Theme (the main idea)

After discussion period, students are instructed:

"Take any notes that you care to while you listen to *The Ballad of the Harp-Weaver,* written by the American poet, Edna St. Vincent Millay, and read by Helen Hayes. Watch for elements of narrative and lyric. After the record you will have ten minutes to organize your impressions and findings."

"Then we will play the record once more and you will have five minutes to write, after which you will give your notes to our chairman who will have the remainder of the period for oral discussion of this poem. Continual reference will be made to your notes by the chairman."

The next day is given to *The Lake Isle of Innisfree,* and the third day to *The Raven.*

For seniors the fourth day is given over to a discussion of Poe's essay "The Philosophy of Composition" in which he explains in detail how he set about composing *The Raven.*

Each member of the class is given a mimeographed copy of the poem after the class discussion, and a few minutes are allowed for silent reading and self-evaluation.

Measuring Progress:

Use the same procedure but collect notes and self-evaluation sentences.

Poems used for this include:

The Coin by Teasdale
Stopping by Woods by Frost
Da Leetla Boy by Daly (Italian-American dialect)
Two Little Boots by Dunbar (Negro dialect)

Bennington High School
Bennington, Vermont

LISTENING TO *POEM IN OCTOBER*

Grade XII

Materials:

Pleasure Dome (LP ML 4259 Columbia). This is a recording of eight poets reading their own poetry which includes:

Poem in October by Dylan Thomas (pronounced as *dillon;* it is the Welsh word for *water*).

A mimeographed copy of the entire poem for each member of the class.

Procedure:

A. Study helps:

1. Read this poem *aloud* four or five times before you come to class. Get off by yourself and *listen* to your own voice in different parts of the poem. This is one of Thomas' best poems and today's critics rate it very high. What is its significance? Notice its *tone quality* and its rhythm.
2. What parts are literal? What parts figurative?
3. How much is this poem a picture of Thomas' surroundings in Wales? What kind of surroundings? Rural or urban? From what lines do you draw this conclusion?
4. Does the *time* element change during the poem? What signs of October? Be specific.
5. Any suggestion here of a relationship with modern painting? music? (Look up *surrealism.*) What about stanza and rhyme patterns here?

6. Any of it meditative or philosophical? Where? See question 17.
7. What part is narrative? For what end?
8. Does the poet's own reading of his poem help in setting the *tonal values?* How?
9. What are its lyric qualities?
   a. Who is speaking?
   b. What is his attitude?
   c. Is an emotion explained or described?
10. Imagery: Find lines that make sensory appeals.
11. Read Coleridge's *Kubla Khan* and comment on *tone quality* and *imagery*.
    Can you draw any comparisons in the two poems? Which did you enjoy most when you read them aloud?
12. Notice unusual use of "woke" and "stood" by Thomas. What part of speech as here used?
13. Notice use of word "marvel." List some of the details that he could marvel.
14. Poe says the ideal extent of a poem is about 100 lines. How does this compare?
15. Vocabulary: *parable, legends, mussel, beckon, blithe.*
16. Explain "heron priested shore," "white horses," "rain wringling wind," "a child's forgotten morning," "twice told fields of infancy."
17. Whose tears burned whose cheeks and why? How is this tied up to the mystery that sang alive?

B. Play recording of poem before and after class discussion.

Measuring Progress:

Use Whitman's *Out of the Cradle Endlessly Rocking* and Lanier's *The Marshes of Glynn* or *The Song of the Chattahoochee*. Use recordings wherever possible.

This measuring *follows* a period in which every member of the class has selected a poem he likes, has read it to the class, and had an analysis period based on narrative and lyric qualities, imagery and figurative language.

Bennington High School
Bennington, Vermont

OZYMANDIAS

Percy Bysshe Shelley

A series of questions aimed at unravelling the poem through a study of syntax.

The poem is first read aloud, preferably by the instructor.

1. Note the word "survive" in line 7. What is its subject?
2. What is the antecedent of the word "which"?
3. What is the object of the verb "survive"?
4. Whose is the "hand," and whose the "heart"?
5. What is the antecedent of the pronoun "them" in line 8?
6. Who is mocking what?
7. Whose are the "passions" in line 6?
8. What specific details illustrate the abstraction "passions"?
9. What are the instructions Ozymandias gives to those who view the pedestal?
10. To whom is he talking?
11. To whom did he expect to be talking?
12. What are the "works" in line 11?
13. What, then, is the irony in the words spoken by Ozymandias?
14. Who are the three speakers in this poem?
15. What is our attitude toward Ozymandias? Why?
16. What is the relationship between Ozymandias and the sculptor? Is there any irony present? What?
17. What, then, has survived what? Who has survived whom?
18. What is the similarity between the first speaker in the poem and the sculptor?
19. What is the effect of contrasting words like "works," and "wreck," "despair," and "decay"?
20. What is the effect of the choice of words in the last two lines?
21. Will you please read the poem again, aloud?

Phillips Academy,
Andover, Massachusetts

READING A POEM

The following questions to help you read poems are divided into two groups: first, about how the elements of a poem communicate the experience; and, second, how the experience may be defined and evaluated. Not all the questions, of course, are equally important for all poems; some poems need little analysis.

1. Read through the whole poem at least once, preferably aloud, for a *general impression* of the experience communicated, whether or not you understand all the details. Read it again when you've finished with the analysis.

2. What is the *plain sense* of the poem? What exactly does the poem say? Read it for what it says, not for what you think it ought to say. Study the meanings (and etymologies) of important individual *words* as they appear in and are controlled by their context. Use your dictionary. Be sure, also, that you understand the word order and the structure of individual sentences.

3. What use does the poem make of *suggestion?* What picture-making words (*images*) are used? What metaphors? What symbols? What allusions? How do they help reinforce or help communicate the experience?

4. How is the *experience dramatized?*
   a. Who is the speaker? What sort of person (physically, emotionally, intellectually, spiritually)?
   b. Who is the person spoken to? What sort of person?
   c. What circumstance or situation gives occasion for the speaking?

5. What are the parts or steps in the development of thought and emotion? On what principle of *structure*, or organization, is the poem built? What emphasis is given in the poem: story, picture, mood, idea, music?

6. How does the poem control the experience? Does the poet use effectively such *rhetorical devices* as contrast, parallel, climax, irony, paradox, or understatement? How does he avoid sentimentality?

7. How does the poem *sound?* What poetic or formal devices are particularly appropriate or inappropriate? Devices to consider are rhythm, stress or accent, caesura, other pauses; rhyme, alliteration, assonance, onomatopoeia; stanza pattern.

8. What is the *mood* or feeling of the poem? By what means is it

conveyed? Try to restate the mood in a single sentence or phrase in your own words.

9. What is the central idea, thought, or *theme?* Is it individualized or generalized? Try to restate it accurately in a single sentence of your own.

10. What is the *tone* of the poem? What is the poet's or speaker's attitude toward his subject? Toward his reader or hearer? How is the tone made evident?

11. What corroboration or intensification of experience (*recognition*) does the poem provide? What extension of experience (*insight*)?

12. The *key question:* How do the various elements in the poem work together to create the experience of the poem? How well? Of what *significance* is the poem as experience?

Phillips Academy,
Andover, Massachusetts

Bibliography

THEORY OF POETRY, CRITICISM OF POETRY, TEACHING METHODS

ALLEN, Gay Wilson, *American Prosody* (New York, American Book Company, 1935).

ALTICK, Richard D., *Preface to Critical Reading* (New York, Henry Holt & Co., Inc., 1955).

"A Birthday for Poetry," *Life* (November 24, 1952).

BOAS, Ralph, and SMITH, Edwin, *Enjoyment of Literature* (New York, Harcourt, Brace & Co., 1925, o.p.).

BROOKS, Cleanth, *The Well Wrought Urn* (New York, Reynal & Company, Inc., 1947).

BROOKS, Cleanth, and WARREN, Robert Penn, *Understanding Poetry* (New York, Henry Holt & Co., Inc., 1943).

BROOKS, Cleanth, PURSER, John T., and WARREN, Robert Penn, *An Approach to Literature* (New York, Appleton-Century-Crofts, Inc., 1941), pp. 419–511.

COHEN, Felix, "The Reconstruction of Hidden Value Judgements," *Essays,* Leonard F. Dean, ed. (New York, Harcourt, Brace & Co., 1955), pp. 22–31.

COOPER, Charles W., *Preface to Poetry* (New York, Harcourt, Brace & Co., 1946).

CONNELL, Rev. F. M., S. J., *A Study of Poetry* (Boston, Allyn and Bacon, Inc., 1913).

DEBOER, John James, and others, *Teaching Secondary English* (New York, McGraw-Hill Book Co., 1951).

DOUBLEDAY, Neal F., *Studies in Poetry* (New York, Harper & Brothers, 1949).

DREW, Elizabeth, *Discovering Poetry* (New York, W. W. Norton & Co., 1933).

GORDON, Edward, "Teaching Students to Read Verse," *They Will Read Literature* (National Council of Teachers of English, Leaflet 12).

HAYAKAWA, S. I., *Language in Thought and Action* (New York, Harcourt, Brace & Co., 1949).

JARRELL, Randall, *Poetry and the Age* (New York, Vintage Books, Inc., 1955).

JESPERSON, Otto, *Growth and Structure of the English Language* (Garden City, N.Y., Doubleday & Company, Inc., 1955).

LABRANT, Lou, *We Teach English* (New York, Harcourt, Brace & Co., 1951).

Living Language, Grade 12, J. C. Blumenthal, ed. (New York, Harcourt, Brace & Co., 1953).

MACLEISH, Archibald, "The Proper Pose of Poetry," *Saturday Review* (March 5, 1955).

MICHENER, James A., "Idealism Today," *Books in Their Courses,* Vol. X, No. 2 (New York, Henry Holt & Co. Inc., 1949).

PERRINE, Laurence, *Sound and Sense* (New York, Harcourt, Brace & Co., 1956).

REYNOLDS, J. J., and BALDWIN, O., *How to Teach the Required Poetry in the New York City Public Schools* (New York, Noble and Noble, Publishers, 1928).

RICHARDS, I. A., *Practical Criticism* (New York, Harcourt, Brace & Co., 1930).

RIGGS, Thomas, Jr., "What Good Are Poems?" *The Wonderful World of Books* (Mentor Books; New York, New American Library of World Literature, Inc., 1953), pp. 42–44.

SMITH, Dora V., ed., *The English Language Arts* (National Council of Teachers of English Curriculum Series; New York, Appleton-Century-Crofts, Inc., 1952).

STAGEBERG, Norman, and ANDERSON, Wallace, *Poetry as Experience* (New York, American Book Company, 1952).

THOMAS, Wright, and BROWN, Stuart, *Reading Poems* (New York, Oxford University Press, 1941).

WELLEK, René, and WARREN, Austin, *Theory of Literature* (New York, Harcourt, Brace & Co., 1956).

REFERENCE BOOKS

BENÉT, William Rose, *The Reader's Encyclopedia* (New York, Thomas Y. Crowell Company, 1948).

BREWER, E. C., *Dictionary of Phrase and Fable*, rev. ed. (New York, Harper & Brothers, 1953).

BULFINCH, Thomas, *Mythology* (The Modern Library; New York, Random House).

*GRAVES, Robert, *The Greek Myths* (Baltimore, Penguin Books Inc., 1955).

*HAMILTON, Edith, *Mythology* (Mentor Books; New York, New American Library of World Literature, 1942).

HERMANS, M. C., *Stories from the Old Testament* (Boston, Allyn and Bacon, Inc., 1928).

HERZBURG, M. J., *Myths and Their Meaning* (Boston, Allyn and Bacon, Inc., 1956).

MOORE, Annie E., *Literature Old and New for Children* (Boston, Houghton Mifflin Co., 1934).

List of Recordings

JEWETT, Arno, ed., *Recordings for Teaching Literature and Languages in the High School*, Federal Security Agency, Office of Education, Bulletin No. 19 (Washington, Government Printing Office, 1952).

WORKS OF INDIVIDUAL AUTHORS

*AUDEN, W. H., *Law like Love, In Memory of W. B. Yeats* (NCTE, 78 RPM).

* Paperbacks.

BENÉT, Stephen Vincent, *Ballad of William Sycamore* (NCTE, 33 RPM).

———, *John Brown's Body*, read by Tyrone Power, Judith Anderson, and Raymond Massey (SL–181, Columbia, Two 12″ records, 33 RPM).

BYRON, George Gordon, *Destruction of Sennacherib, Keen Fitful Gusts, Ode to Autumn, A Petition to Time* (219, Popular Science Publishing Co., 78 RPM).

CHAUCER, Geoffrey, *The Pardoner's Tale*, Selections from the Debate of the Body and Soul in *The Parson's Tale* (SS–5028, 29, Harvard College Library).

*CUMMINGS, e e, Selections from fifty poems (NCTE).

*ELIOT, T. S., *Difficulties of a Statesman, Fragment of an Agon, Love Song of J. Alfred Prufrock, Gerontion, The Hollow Men, Triumphal March, Journey of the Magi, A Song for Simeon* (Harvard College Library).

*FROST, Robert, *Acquainted With the Night, The Runaway, An Old Man's Winter Night, Mowing, Choose Something Like a Star, Come In, The Mountain, A Considerable Speck, Directive, One Step Backward Taken* (P27, P28, P30, Library of Congress).

———, *After Apple Picking, Birches, Death of the Hired Man* (NCTE, 78 & 33 RPM).

*———, Reading his own poems (RCA Victor, 33 RPM).

LINDSAY, Vachel, *The Congo* (NCTE).

MILTON, John, *L'Allegro* (Popular Science Publishing Co.).

*NASH, Ogden, Reading his own poems (TC 1015, Caedmon).

*RANSOM, John Crowe, *Bells for John Whiteside's Daughter, Janet Waking, Here Lies a Lady, Captain Carpenter* (P21, Library of Congress).

*SANDBURG, Carl, *Readings*, including *The People, Yes* (5135 & 7541, Decca).

*THOMAS, Dylan, *Fern Hill, A Child's Christmas in Wales, Do Not Go Gentle into That Good Night, In the White Giant's Thigh, Ballad of the Long-Legged Bait, Ceremony After a Fire Raid* (TC 1002, Caedmon).

*———, *Lament, Poem on His Birthday, There Was a Saviour*, others, (TC 1018, Caedmon).

WORDSWORTH, William, *Bridge of Sighs, I Wandered Lonely as a Cloud, Composed upon Westminster Bridge, The World Is Too Much with Us* (216, Popular Science Publishing Co.).

COLLECTIONS

Anthology of Recorded Verse, read by Edith Evans and John Gielgud (Voice of Poetry, MM 375, MM 419, Columbia).

* read by the poet.

Appreciation of Poetry, read by Norman Corwin (Masterpieces of Literature, Vol. 1E5, Columbia).

Audio Book of Famous Poems, 74 poems by 38 authors, read by Marvin Miller (St. Joseph, Mich., Audio Book Company, 16 RPM).

Our Common Heritage, 15 poems celebrating milestones in the history of America, read by Bing Crosby, Brian Donlevy, Walter Huston, Fredric March, and others (A 536, Decca).

Pleasure Dome, 8 poets reading their own works: T. S. Eliot, Marianne Moore, e e cummings, William Carlos Williams, Ogden Nash, W. H. Auden, Dylan Thomas, and Isabel Bishop; Lloyd Frankenburg, ed. (ML 4259, Columbia, LP).

Poet's Gold, 15 poems, read by Helen Hayes, Raymond Massey, and Mitchell (LM 1818, RCA Victor).

MISCELLANY

Ballad Hunter, Songs by native singers of American folk songs (Washington, Office of Education).

DYER-BENNET, Richard (35, Stinson; 199–34, Remington; 5046, Decca).

IVES, Burl, *The Wayfaring Stranger* (CL 6109, Columbia).

————, *Ballads and Folk Songs* (5013, 5080, 5093, Decca).

NILES, John Jacob, *Folk Love Songs* (22, Boon).

SANDBURG, Carl, *American Songbag* (4, Lyric).

————, *American Folk Music* (A–356, Decca).

WHITE, Josh, *Ballads and Songs* (5083, Decca).

LAUGHTON, Charles, *Readings from the Bible:* The Garden of Eden, The Fiery Furnace, Noah's Ark, David and Goliath (DU 15, 16, 17, 18, Decca).

17

Teaching Drama:
Julius Caesar

Maynard Mack, *Yale University*

I want to preface my remarks on *Julius Caesar* this morning with one expression of wonderment. Wonderment that there is not more use made of plays—plays of all shapes, sizes, and periods, including Shakespeare's—in our schools. I know that usage in this matter varies somewhat from system to system, state to state, public to independent school, but in general I believe it is fair to say that if drama appears at all in our scholastic English programs outside of the college preparatory course, it runs a poor third or fourth to novels, short stories, poems, and discursive prose. This is an odd state of affairs, I think, not only because drama is far the easiest of all the literary forms to make exciting in the classroom, but because, all things considered, it is also the most effective introduction to the pleasures of reading literature and the skills involved in enjoying it.

The reasons for its outstanding usefulness are not far to seek. The appeal of drama is elemental and instinctive: the infant in his playpen is director, dialoguist, and actor by the time he can talk; his dramatic sense is highly selective before he has a narrative sense at all. Moreover, there is a vast latent experience of drama in children of almost any age, waiting only for the teacher to evoke and build on it. The pupil may never have had acquaintance with poetry or novels outside of school requirements, but he is sure to have met with drama in abundance. He sees it constantly on the motion picture screen and the television tube, and, what is much more important, he is reasonably certain to have participated at first hand, through the normal stresses and strains of growing up, in most of the basic dramatic situations. It will be a rare child who reaches adolescence without experiencing, in his own way and degree, what it is to be tempted and fall, like Macbeth; deceived by appearances or false friendship, like Othello; perplexed and disillusioned, like Hamlet. It will be a still rarer one who gets past adolescence without seeing one or more of his friends walk into disaster by the very steps taken to evade it, as with Oedipus; or become trapped in the unforeseen consequences of a "noble" act, as with Brutus.

For the adolescent, to be sure, such experiences will not ordinarily take place under the kind of pressures that passion builds in the adult world; for him, the escape hatches are usually still open, and he is unlikely, on the whole, to assassinate his guests, marry his mother, or run upon his own switch blade. Nevertheless, the latent connections are there, and it has been my observation that when the public experience of a great play is brought into the right kind of relation with the private experience of the individual student, there comes a flash of illumination into the classroom that nearly crumbles the plaster, as the student contemplates his own image in the play and the play's image in himself. At this moment, what we like to call education, the "leading out" of the intelligence and human spirit, takes place. No one will have to tell that student that reading is a key to understanding, that knowledge gives self-knowledge, that literature has much to say to him about life. He knows.

There is a third advantage, too, in extensive use of drama in the classroom, and this is the unparalleled degree of student participation that it enables and invites, even from pupils of the most modest aptitudes. The practice of assigning parts and informally putting on the scenes of a play takes literature off the page for those who are not verbally oriented, lifts it out of the abstractness of the reading process into the kinetic and sensory world of voice, gesture, movement, stance. The exciting problem of how to interpret a scene—all the more exciting with Shakespeare and the older dramatists since their plays come to us blissfully bare of author's comment—promotes speculation, argument, debate, leading to more and more exacting consultations of the text, and to projects suited to all levels of ability. Those with verbal facility can be given historical or dictionary projects. Those with talent for drawing, for seeing things spatially, can be assigned the job of deciding how to project the ideas of a scene in visual terms, as if on an actual stage. Even those with no apparent talent at all can be set to working out the movements and groupings of persons that they feel will best dramatize the content of a passionate speech. One of the most effective demonstrations of this kind was described to me not long ago by a friend who had witnessed it while visiting a high school in his vicinity in 1953. A trio of boys, whose I.Q.'s, according to the teacher, amounted to about 200 among them, were struggling to bring before their classmates the succession of bodily motions and gestures with which they imagined Antony would have accompanied the phases of his oration to the Roman populace. The effort was crude enough by the standards of the Old Vic, but the assignment had clearly brought to life for those boys the meaning of the situation in Shakespeare's play and also its timelessness. For the postures on which they were quite unmistakably, although apparently quite unconsciously, modeling their interpretation were those of a well-known senator from Wisconsin, whom they had seen all that fall talking on television to the populace of the United States.

As this story suggests, I am one of those who believe that Shakespeare can be taught to almost any sort of audience. I am perfectly aware, of course, of the language problem that Shakespeare presents for today's students, particularly for the nonverbalizers to whom I have already referred; and I am perfectly willing to admit that there are classes to whom it would be preposterous to offer his plays. I would only argue that to any group to whom literature in any form may be offered with a prospect of success, Shakespeare may be offered with equal and usually with greater success. After all, it was not mainly the verbalizers and the "brighties" of Elizabethan London who showed up with their penny at the Globe to stand for two and a half hours in the pit. It was the odoriferous and stupid, the groundlings, capable, as Shakespeare himself said, of little but "inexplicable dumb shows and noise." Yet he had something to say to these people: he *held* them. In the hands of a patient teacher, who will make the most of student participation, he still does—as no other reading but the comics will. And when he does not, I suggest it is almost invariably for one of two reasons. On the one hand, the teacher is a bardolater and holds the play aloft for distant veneration as if it were a thing too refined for human nature's daily food. I had a teacher like this myself. Whenever we came to any of the great speeches in the plays, he would lean back in his chair, close his eyes, and murmur, in a voice you could pour on a waffle, "ah, the magic of it, the magic!" That same magic took me a whole year to get over and almost sent me into chemical engineering.

Then there is the other alternative: the teacher is not actually interested in the play except as a scratching post of the student's memory. In *this* teacher's class, the interminable question is "What next? What after that? What then?" as though the play were a timetable to a destination that will never be reached. I get a good many of that teacher's pupils in my classes here. They know exactly what follows what in the first act of Macbeth, say, but nobody has ever asked them any questions beginning with "Why?" Why does the play *open* with the witch scene? Why is the number of the witches *three?* Is there any significance in the fact that there are also three banquets, three murders, three apparitions, and even three murderers at Banquo's death? And what does the second witch mean by saying "When the battle's lost *and* won"? What battle? and how can it be won and lost at the same time?

Questions like these, I feel, suggest the approach that most of us who are neither bardolaters nor mnemonicists will wish to take to Shakespeare, and if we are taking it with *Julius Caesar*, I think the place we may want to begin is with I.ii; for here, as in the first witch scene in *Macbeth*, most of the play to come is already implicit. We have just learned from scene i of Caesar's return in triumph from warring on Pompey's sons, we have seen the warm though fickle adulation of the crowd and the apprehension of the tribunes; now we are to see the great man himself. The procession enters to triumphal music; with hubbub of a great press of people; with young men stripped for the ceremonial races, among them Antony; with statesmen in their togas: Decius, Cicero, Brutus, Cassius, Casca; with the two wives Calpurnia and Portia; and, in the lead, for not even Calpurnia is permitted at his side, the great man. As he starts to speak, an expectant hush settles over the gathering: what does the great man have on his mind?

CAES.	Calpurnia.
CASCA	Peace, ho! Caesar speaks.
CAES.	Calpurnia.
CAL.	Here, my lord.
CAES.	Stand you directly in Antonius' way
	When he does run his course. Antonius.
ANT.	Caesar, my lord?
CAES.	Forget not, in your speed, Antonius,
	To touch Calpurnia; for our elders say,
	The barren, touched in this holy chase,
	Shake off their sterile curse.
ANT.	I shall remember:
	When Caesar says, "Do this," it is perform'd.

What the great man had on his mind, it appears, was to remind his wife, in this public place, that she is sterile; that there is an old tradition about how sterility can be removed; and that while of course he is much too sophisticated to accept such a superstition himself—it is "our elders" who say it—still, Calpurnia had jolly well better get out there and get tagged, or else!

Then the procession takes up again. The hubbub is resumed, but once more the expectant silence settles as a voice is heard.

SOOTH.	Caesar!
CAES.	Ha! Who calls?
CASCA	Bid every noise be still; peace yet again!
CAES.	Who is it in the press that calls on me?
	I hear a tongue shriller than all the music
	Cry "Caesar!" Speak. Caesar is turn'd to hear.
SOOTH.	Beware the ides of March.
CAES.	What man is that?
BRU.	A soothsayer bids you beware the ides of March.
CAES.	Set him before me; let me see his face.
CAS.	Fellow, come from the throng; look upon Caesar.
CAES.	What say'st thou to me now? Speak once again.
SOOTH.	Beware the ides of March.
CAES.	He is a dreamer. Let us leave him. Pass.

It is easy to see from even these small instances, I think, how a first-rate dramatic imagination works. There is no hint of any procession in Plutarch, Shakespeare's source. "Caesar," says Plutarch, "*sat* to behold." There is no mention of Calpurnia in Plutarch's account of the

Lupercalian race, and there is no mention anywhere of her sterility. Shakespeare, in nine lines, has given us an unforgettable picture of a man who would like to be emperor pathetically concerned that he lacks an heir, and determined, even at the cost of making his wife a public spectacle, to establish that this is owing to no lack of virility in him. The first episode thus dramatizes instantaneously the oncoming theme of the play: that a man's will is not enough; that there are other matters to be reckoned with, like the infertility of one's wife, or one's own affliction of the falling sickness which spoils everything one hoped for just at the instant when one had it almost in one's hand. Brutus will be obliged to learn this lesson too.

In the second episode the theme develops. We see again the uneasy rationalism that everybody in this play affects; we hear it reverberate in the faint contempt—almost a challenge—of Brutus' words as he turns to Caesar: "A soothsayer bids you beware the ides of March." Yet underneath, in the soothsayer's presence and his sober warning, Shakespeare allows us to catch a hint of something else, something far more primitive and mysterious, from which rationalism in this play keeps trying vainly to cut itself away: "He is a dreamer. Let us leave him. Pass." Only we in the audience are in a position to see that the dreamer has foretold the path down which all these reasoners will go to that fatal encounter at the Capitol.

Meantime, in these same two episodes, we have learned something about the character of Caesar. In the first, it was the Caesar of human frailties who spoke to us, the husband with his hopeful superstition. In the second, it was the marble superman of state, impassive, impervious, speaking of himself in the third person: "Speak! Caesar is turn'd to hear." He even has the soothsayer brought before his face to repeat the message, as if he thought that somehow, in awe of the marble presence, the message would falter and dissolve: how can a superman need to beware the ides of March?

We hardly have time to do more than glimpse here a man of divided selves, when he is gone. But in his absence, the words of Cassius confirm our glimpse. Cassius' description of him exhibits the same duality that we had noticed earlier. On the one hand, an extremely ordinary man whose stamina in the swimming match was soon exhausted, who, when he had a fever once in Spain, shook and groaned like a sick girl, who even now, as we soon learn, is falling down with epilepsy in the market place. On the other hand, a being who has somehow become a god, who "bears the palm alone," who "bestrides the narrow world like a colossus." When the procession returns, no longer festive now, but angry, tense, there is the same effect once more. Our one Caesar shows a normal man's suspicion of his enemies, voices some shrewd human observations about Cassius, says to Antony, "Come on my right hand, for this ear is deaf." Our other Caesar says, as if he were suddenly reminded of something he had forgotten, "I rather tell thee what is to be fear'd/Than what I fear, for always I am Caesar."

Whenever Caesar appears hereafter, we shall find this singular division in him, and nowhere more so than in the scene in which he receives the conspirators at his house. Some aspects of this scene seem calculated for nothing else than to fix upon our minds the superman conception, the Big Brother of Orwell's *1984*, the great resonant name echoing down the halls of time. Thus at the beginning of the scene:

> the things that threatened me
> Ne'er look'd but on my back; when they shall see
> The face of Caesar, they are vanished.

And again later:

> danger knows full well
> That Caesar is more dangerous than he:
> We are two lions litter'd in one day,
> And I the elder and more terrible.

And again still later: "Shall Caesar send a lie?" And again: "The cause is in my will: I will not come." Other aspects, including his concern about Calpurnia's dream, his vacillation about going to the senate house, his anxiety about the portents of the night, plainly mark out his human weaknesses. Finally, as is the habit in this Rome, he puts the irrational from him that his wife's intuitions and her dream embody; he accepts the rationalization of the irrational that Decius skillfully manufactures, and, as earlier at the Lupercalia, hides from himself his own vivid sense of forces that lie beyond the will's control by attributing it to her:

> How foolish do your fears seem now, Calpurnia!
> I am ashamed I did yield to them.
> Give me my robe, for I will go.

So far in our consideration of the implications of I.ii, we have been looking only at Caesar, the title personage of the play, and its historical center. It is time now to turn to Brutus, the play's tragic center, whom we also find to be a divided man—"poor Brutus," to use his own phrase, "with himself at war." The war, we realize as the scene progresses, is a conflict between a quiet essentially domestic and loving nature, and a powerful integrity expressing itself in a sense of honorable duty to the commonweal. This duality in Brutus seems to be what Cassius is probing at in his long disquisition about the mirror. The Brutus looking into the glass that Cassius figuratively holds up to him, the Brutus of this moment, now, in Rome, is a grave studious private man, of a wonderfully gentle temper, as we shall see again and again later on, very slow to passion, as Cassius' ill-concealed disappointment in having failed to kindle him to immediate response reveals, a man whose sensitive nature recoils at the hint of violence lurking in some of Cassius' speeches, just as he has already recoiled at going on with Caesar to the market place, to witness the mass hysteria of clapping hands, sweaty nightcaps, and stinking breath. This is the present self that looks into Cassius' mirror.

The image that looks back out, that Cassius wants him to see, the potential Brutus, is the man of public spirit, worried already by the question of Caesar's intentions, the lineal descendant of an earlier Brutus who drove a would-be monarch from the city, a man whose body is visibly stiffening in our sight at each huzza from the Forum, and whose anxiety, though he makes no reply to Cassius' inflammatory language, keeps bursting to the surface: "What means this shouting? I do fear the people/Choose Caesar for their king." The problem at the tragic center of the play, we begin to sense, is to be the tug of private versus public, the individual versus a world he never made, any citizen anywhere versus the selective service greetings that history is always mailing out to each of us. And this problem is to be traversed by that other tug this scene presents, of the irrational versus the rational, the destiny we think we can control versus the destiny that sweeps all before it.

Through I.ii, Brutus' public self, the self that responds to these selective service greetings, is no more than a reflection in a mirror, a mere anxiety in his own brain, about which he refuses to confide, even to Cassius. In II.i, we see the public self making further headway. First, there is Brutus' argument with himself about the threat of Caesar, and in his conclusion that Caesar must be killed we note how far his private self—he is, after all, one of Caesar's closest friends—has been invaded by the self of public spirit. From here on, the course of the invasion accelerates. The letter comes, tossed from the public world into the private world, into Brutus' garden, and addressing, as Cassius had, that public image reflected in the mirror: "Brutus, thou sleep'st: awake and see thyself." Then follows the well-known brief soliloquy (which Shakespeare was to expand into the whole play of *Macbeth*), showing us that Brutus' mind has moved on now from the phase of decision to the inquietudes that follow decision:

> Between the acting of a dreadful thing
> And the first motion, all the interim is
> Like a phantasma, or a hideous dream.

What is important to observe is that these lines stress once again the gulf that separates motive from action, that which is interior in man and controllable by his will from that which, once acted, becomes independent of him and moves with a life of its own. This gulf is a no man's land, a phantasma, a hideous dream.

Finally, there arrives in such a form that no audience can miss it the actual visible invasion itself, as this peaceful garden quiet is broken in on by knocking, like the knocking of fate in Beethoven's fifth symphony, and by men with faces hidden in their cloaks. Following this, a lovely interlude with Portia serves to emphasize how much the private self, the private world has been shattered. We have something close to discord here—as much of a discord as these very gentle people are capable of—and though there is a reconciliation at the end and Brutus' promise to confide in her soon, this division in the family is an omen. So is that knock of the latecomer, Caius Ligarius, which reminds us once again of the intrusions of the public life. And when Ligarius throws off his sick man's kerchief on learning that there is an honorable exploit afoot, we may see in it an epitome of the whole scene, a graphic visual renunciation, like Brutus', of the private good to the public; and we may see this also in Brutus' own exit a few lines later, not into the inner house where Portia waits for him, but out into the thunder and lightning of the public life of Rome. It is perhaps significant that at our final view of Portia, two scenes later, she too stands outside the privacy of the house, her mind wholly occupied with thoughts of what is happening at the Capitol, and trying to put on a public self for Brutus' sake: "Run, Lucius, and commend me to my Lord/Say I am merry. . . ."

Meantime, up there by the Capitol, the tragic center and the historical center meet. The suspense is very great as Caesar, seeing the Soothsayer in the throng, reminds him that the ides of March are come, and receives in answer, "Ay, Caesar, but not gone." More suspense as Artemidorus presses forward with the paper that we know contains a full discovery of the plot. Decius, apprehensive, steps quickly into the breach with another paper, a petition from Trebonius. More suspense still as Popilius sidles past Cassius with the whisper, "I wish your enterprise today may thrive," and then moves on to Caesar's side, where he engages him in animated talk. But they detect no telltale change in Caesar's countenance; Trebonius steps into his assignment and takes Antony aside; Metellus Cimber throws himself at Caesar's feet; Brutus gives the signal to "press near and second him," and Caesar's "Are we all ready?" draws every eye to Caesar's chair. One by one they all kneel before this demigod—an effective tableau which gives a coloring of priest-like ritual to what they are about to do. Caesar is to bleed, but, as Brutus has said, they will sublimate the act into a sacrifice:

> Let's kill him boldly but not wrathfully;
> Let's carve him as a dish fit for the gods,
> Not hew him as a carcass fit for hounds.

Everything in the scene must underscore this ceremonial attitude, in order to bring out the almost fatuous cleavage between the spirit of this enterprise and its bloody purpose.

The Caesar that we are permitted to see while all this ceremony is preparing is almost entirely the superman, for obvious reasons. To give a color of justice to Brutus' act and so to preserve our sense of his nobility even if we happen to think the assassination a mistake, as an Elizabethan audience emphatically would, Caesar has to appear in a mood of superhumanity at least as fatuous as the conspirators' mood of sacrifice. Hence Shakespeare makes him first of all insult Metellus Cimber: "If thou dost bend and pray and fawn for him,/I spurn thee like a cur;" then comment with intolerable pomposity, and, in fact, blasphemy, on his own iron resolution, for he affects to be immovable even by prayer and hence superior to the very gods. Finally, Shakespeare puts into his mouth one of those supreme arrogances that will remind us of the destroying *hubris* which makes men mad in order to ruin them. "Hence!" Caesar cries, "Wilt thou lift up Olympus?" It is at just this point, when the colossus Caesar drunk with self-love is before us, that Casca strikes. Then they all strike, with a last blow that brings out for the final time the other, human side of this double Caesar: "Et tu, Brute?"

And now this little group of men has altered history. The representative of the evil direction it was taking toward autocratic power lies dead before them. The direction to which it must be restored becomes emphatic in Cassius' cry of "Liberty, freedom, and enfranchisement." Solemnly, and again like priests who have just sacrificed a victim, they kneel together and bathe their hands and swords in Caesar's blood. Brutus exclaims:

> Then walk we forth, even to the market place;
> And waving our red weapons o'er our heads,
> Let's all cry, "Peace, freedom, and liberty!"

If the conjunction of those red hands and weapons with this slogan is not enough to bring an audience up with a start, the next passage will be, for now the conspirators explicitly invoke the judgment of history on their deed. On the stages of theatres the world over, so they anticipate, this lofty incident will be re-enacted, and

> So oft as that shall be.
> So often shall the knot of us be call'd
> The men that gave their country liberty.

We, the audience, recalling what actually did result in Rome—the civil wars, the long line of despotic emperors—cannot miss the irony of their prediction, an irony that insists on our recognizing that this effort to control history is going to fail. Why does it fail?

One reason why is shown us in the next few moments. The leader of this assault on history is, like many another reformer, a man of high idealism, who devoutly believes that the rest of the world is like himself. It was just to kill Caesar—so he persuades himself—because he was a great threat to freedom. It would not have been just to kill Antony, and he vetoed the idea. Even now, when the consequence of that decision has come back to face him in the shape of Antony's servant, kneeling before him, he sees no reason to reconsider it. There are good grounds for what they have done, he says; Antony will hear them, and be satisfied. With Antony, who shortly arrives in person, he takes this line again:

> Our reasons are so full of good regard
> That were you, Antony, the son of Caesar
> You should be satisfied.

With equal confidence in the rationality of man, he puts by Cassius' fears of what Antony will do if allowed to address the people: "By your pardon; I will myself into the pulpit first/And show the reason of our Caesar's death." Here is a man so much a friend of Caesar's that he is still speaking of him as "our Caesar," so capable of rising to what he takes to be his duty that he has taken on the leadership of those who intend to kill him, so trusting of common decency that he expects the populace will respond to reason, and Antony to the obligation laid on him by their permitting him to speak. At such a man, one hardly knows whether to laugh or cry.

The same mixture of feelings is likely to be stirring in us as Brutus speaks to the people in III.ii. As everybody knows, this is a speech in what used to be called the great liberal tradition, the tradition that assumed, as our American founding fathers did, that men in the mass are reasonable. It has therefore been made a prose oration, spare and terse in diction, tightly patterned in syntax so that it requires close attention, and founded, with respect to its argument, on three elements: the abstract sentiment of duty to the state (because he endangered Rome, Caesar had to be slain); the abstract sentiment of political justice (because he was ambitious, Caesar deserved his fall); and the moral authority of the man Brutus. As long as that moral authority is concretely before them in Brutus' presence, the populace is impressed. But since they are not trained minds, and only trained minds respond accurately to abstractions, they do not understand the content of his argument at all, as one of them indicates by shouting, "Let him be Caesar!" What moves them is the obvious sincerity and the known integrity of the speaker; and when he finishes, they are ready to carry him off on their shoulders on that account alone, leaving Antony a vacant Forum. The fair-mindedness of Brutus is thrilling but painful to behold as he calms this triumphal surge in his favor, urges them to stay and hear Antony, and then, in a moment very impressive dramatically as well as symbolically, walks off the stage, alone. We see then, if we have not seen before, the first answer to the question why the attack on history failed. It was blinded, as it so often has been, by the very idealism that impelled it.

When Antony takes the rostrum, we begin to get a second answer. It has been said by somebody that in a school for demagogues this speech should be the whole curriculum. Antony himself describes its method when he observes in the preceding scene, apropos of the effect of Caesar's dead body on the messenger from Octavius, "Passion, I see, is catching." This is a statement that cannot be made about reason, as many a school teacher learns to his cost. I have not time at my disposal to do anything like justice to Antony's speech, but I should like to make the following summary points.

First, Brutus formulates from the outset positive propositions about Caesar and about his own motives, on no other authority than his own. Because of his known integrity, Brutus can do this. Antony takes the safer alternative of concealing propositions in questions, by which the audience's mind is then guided to conclusions which seem its own:

> He hath brought many captives to Rome,
> Whose ransoms did the general coffers fill:
> Did this in Caesar seem ambitious?

> * * *

> You all did see that on the Lupercal
> I thrice presented him a kingly crown,
> Which he did thrice refuse: was this ambition?

How well Shakespeare knew his crowds can be seen in the replies to Antony. Brutus, appealing to their reason, was greeted with wild outbursts of uncomprehending emotion: "Let him be Caesar!" Antony appeals only to their emotions and their pockets, but now they say, "Methinks there is much reason in his sayings," and chew upon it seriously.

Second, Antony stirs up impulses and then thwarts them. He appeals to their curiosity and their greed in the matter of the will, but then he doesn't come clean on it. In the same manner, he stirs up their rage against the conspirators, yet always pretends to hold them back: "I fear I wrong the honorable men/Whose daggers have stabb'd Caesar;

I do fear it." Third, and this is largely the technical means by which he accomplishes the stirring up, his speech is baited with irony. The passage just quoted is a typical specimen. So is the famous refrain, "For Brutus is an honorable man." Now the rhetorical value of irony is that it stimulates the mind to formulate the contrary, that is, the intended meaning. It stimulates what the psychologists of propaganda nowadays call the assertive factor. "Are you the one man in seven who shaves daily?" "Did your husband forget to kiss you this morning?" The advertiser's technique is not, of course, ironical, but it illustrates the effect.

Finally, Antony rests his case, not, like Brutus, on abstractions centering in the state and political justice, but on emotions centering in the individual listener. The first great crescendo of the speech, which culminates in the passage on Caesar's wounds, appeals first to pity and then to indignation. The second one, culminating in the reading of Caesar's will, appeals first to curiosity and greed and then to gratitude. The management of the will is particularly cunning: it is an item more concrete than any words could be, an actual tantalizing document that can be flashed before the eye, after the manner of the senator mentioned in my preamble. It is described, at first vaguely, as being of such a sort that they would honor Caesar for it. Then, closer home, as something which would show "how Caesar lov'd you." Then, with an undisguised appeal to self-interest, as a testament that will make them his "heirs." The emotions aroused by this news enable Antony to make a final test of his ironical refrain about the "honorable men," and finding the results all that he had hoped, he can come down now among the crowd as one of them, and appeal directly to their feelings by appealing to his own: "If you have tears to shed, prepare to shed them now."

The success of this direct appeal to passion can be seen at its close. Where formerly we had a populace, now we have a mob. Since it is a mob, its mind can be sealed against any later seepage of rationality back into it by the insinuation that reasoning is always false anyway— simply a surface covering up private grudges, like the "reason" they have heard from Brutus; whereas from Antony himself, the plain blunt friend of Caesar, they are getting the plain blunt truth and (a favorite trick of politicians) only what they already know to be the truth.

But also, since it is a mob and therefore will eventually cool off, it must be called back one final time to hear the will. Antony no longer needs this as an incentive to riot; the mingled rage and pity he has aroused will take care of that. But when the hangover comes, and you are remembering how that fellow looked swaying a little on the rope's end, with his eyes bugging out and the veins knotted at his temples, then it is good to have something really reasonable to cling to, like seventy-five drachmas (or even thirty pieces of silver) and some orchards along a river.

At about this point, it becomes impossible not to see that a second reason for the failure of the attack on history is what it left out of account—what all these Romans from the beginning, except Antony, have been trying to leave out of account: the phenomenon of feeling, the nonrational factor in men, in the world, in history itself—of which this blind infuriated mob is one kind of exemplification. Too secure in his own fancied suppression of the subrational, Brutus has failed altogether to reckon with its power. Thus he could seriously say to Antony in the passage I quoted earlier: Antony, even if you were "the son of Caesar/You should be satisfied," as if the feeling of a son for a murdered father could ever be "satisfied" by reasons. And thus, too, he could walk off the stage alone, urging the crowd to hear Antony, the very figure of embodied "reason," unaware that only the irrational is catching.

Meantime, the scene of the mob tearing Cinna the Poet to pieces simply for having the same name as one of the conspirators (III.iii) gives us our first taste of the chaos invoked by Antony when he stood alone over Caesar's corpse. And as we consider that prediction and this mob, we are bound to realize that there is a third reason why the attack on history failed. As we have seen already, history is only partly responsive to noble motives, only partly responsive to rationality. Now we see—what Shakespeare hinted in the beginning with those two episodes of Calpurnia and the soothsayer—that it is only partly responsive to human influence of any sort. With all their reasons, the conspirators and Caesar only carried out what the soothsayer foreknew. There is, in short, a determination in history, whether we call it natural or providential, which at least *helps* to shape our ends, "rough hew them how we will." One of the names of that factor in this play is Caesarism. Brutus put the point, all unconsciously, in that scene when the conspirators were gathered at his house. He said:

> We all stand up against the spirit of Caesar:
> And in the spirit of men there is no blood:
> O that we then could come by Caesar's spirit,
> And not dismember Caesar! But, alas,
> Caesar must bleed for it.

Then Caesar did bleed for it; but his spirit, as Brutus' own remark should have told him, proved to be invulnerable. It was only set free by his assassination, and now, as Antony says, "ranging for revenge, . . . Shall in these confines with a monarch's voice/Cry 'Havoc' and let slip the dogs of war."

The rest of the play, I think, is self-explanatory. It is clear all through Acts IV and V that Brutus and Cassius are defeated before they begin to fight. Antony knows it and says so at V.i. Cassius knows it too. Cassius, an Epicurean in philosophy, and therefore one who has never heretofore believed in omens, now mistrusts his former rationalism: he suspects there may be something after all in those ravens, crows, and kites that wheel overhead. Brutus too mistrusts *his* rationalism. As a Stoic, his philosophy requires him to repudiate suicide, but he admits to Cassius that if the need comes he will repudiate philosophy instead. This, like Cassius' statement, is an unconscious admission of the force of unreason in human affairs, an unreason that makes its presence felt again and again during the great battle. Cassius, for instance, fails to realize that Octavius "Is overthrown by noble Brutus' power," becomes the victim of a mistaken report of Titinius' death, runs on his sword crying, "Caesar, thou art reveng'd," and is greeted, dead, by Brutus, in words that make still clearer their defeat by history: "O Julius Caesar, thou art mighty yet!/Thy spirit walks abroad, and turns our swords/In our own proper entrails." In the same vein, when it is Brutus' turn to die, we learn that the ghost of Caesar has reappeared, and he thrusts the sword home, saying, "Caesar, now be still."

To come then to a brief summary. Though I shouldn't care to be dogmatic about it, it seems clear to me that Shakespeare's primary theme in *Julius Caesar* has to do with the always ambiguous impact between man and history. During the first half of the play, what we are chiefly conscious of is the human will as a force in history—men making choices, controlling events. Our typical scenes are I.ii, where a man is trying to make up his mind; or II.i, where a man first reaches a decision and then, with his fellows, lays plans to implement it; or II.ii, where we have Decius Brutus persuading Caesar to decide to go to the senate house; or III.i and ii, where up through the assassination, and even up through Antony's speech, men are still, so to speak, impinging on history, moulding it to their conscious will.

But then comes a change. Though we still have men in action trying to mould their world (or else we would have no play at all), one senses a real shift in the direction of the impact. We begin to feel the insufficiency of noble aims, for history is also consequences; the insufficiency of reason and rational expectation, for the ultimate consequences of an act in history are unpredictable, and usually, by all human standards, illogical as well; and finally, the insufficiency of the human will itself, for there is always something to be reckoned with that is nonhuman and inscrutable—Nemesis, Moira, Fortuna, the Parcae, Providence, Determinism: men have had many names for it, but it is always there. Accordingly, in the second half of the play, our typical scenes are those like III.iii, where Antony has raised something that is no longer under his control; or like IV.i, where we see men acting as if, under the control of expediency or necessity or call it what you will, they no longer had wills of their own but prick down the names of nephews and brothers indiscriminately for slaughter; or like IV.iii and all the scenes thereafter, where we are constantly made to feel that Cassius and Brutus are in the hands of something bigger than they know.

In this light, we can see readily enough why it is that Shakespeare gave Julius Caesar that double character. The human Caesar who has human ailments and is a human friend is the Caesar that can be killed. The marmoreal Caesar, the everlasting Big Brother—the Napoleon, Mussolini, Hitler, Franco, Peron, Stalin, Kruschev, to mention only a handful of his more recent incarnations—that Caesar is the one who must repeatedly be killed but never dies, because he is in you, and you, and you, and me. Every classroom is a Rome, and there is no reason for any pupil, when he studies *Julius Caesar*, to imagine that this is ancient history.

18

Individual Reading: Report of the Committee on Extensive Reading

CHARLES M. RICE, *Choate School, Connecticut, Chairman*
CHARLES ABRAHAM, *Roger Ludlowe High School, Fairfield, Connecticut*
FREDERICK ALLEN, *Holliston High School, Massachusetts*
WILBURY CROCKETT, *Wellesley High School, Massachusetts*
DAVID MALLERY, *Germantown Friends School, Pennsylvania*
DOROTHY POTTER, *Bulkley High School, Hartford, Connecticut*

In a day when it takes no prophet to tell us that the young are no longer dependent on books for entertainment, we whose business it is to stimulate an interest in the written word face an increasingly difficult task. That area of our work known as Intensive Reading presents obstacles enough: daily class assignments must compete, on the one hand, with innumerable outside interests which need not be named here and, on the other, with the economic opportunities and necessities of a period of prosperity. Yet we teachers, idealists that we are, go on believing that children must develop enthusiasm for a reading program of their own outside the requirements of the classroom and that we can somehow show them the way and make it so irresistible that they will crowd the gangplanks of those frigates that take them lands away.

We believe we can do this, for we have seen ourselves successful with untold numbers of individuals, and we know that the adult who has no capacity for an interest in the information, the adventure, the human understanding, and the linguistic pleasure of books is doomed to a vapid, restless and profoundly unrewarding life, in spite of unlimited alternatives for public and private entertainment. We believe that reading beyond classroom requirements is so important to our students that they can't do without it. The problem, however, is to get them to believe it while they are still young enough to form the habit.

Though this whole problem has been examined many many times, we consider it the function of this conference to examine it again on behalf of the teachers and students of a new era. Though the phrase "atomic age" is already hackneyed, the effect of this age in domestic life is still a matter of prophecy and speculation. But it seems incontrovertible that the students we are now working with will be deep into it before they are ten years older. We are likely to see an industrial upheaval sudden and extreme. We are told that within five years machines will be in use that will permit four men to do in two days the work that two hundred now do in two weeks. It seems inevitable that leisure time will be multiplied many fold, that the four-hour working day will quickly become a commonplace, and that only training for productive use of leisure time can save our society from a restlessness which would need Dante to imagine and Jung to understand. The mere technical skill in reading, the extended imagination, and the intimate and solitary satisfaction—that disciplined self-knowledge which permits a man to use solitude for philosophic growth and moral refreshment—these things, we believe, come from the habit of reading.

Yet clearly we shall not inculcate this habit by merely saying so. And, more important and more difficult, we are unlikely to inculcate it by merely requiring it. In the highly controlled situations which exist in many private schools, where the classes are small and the teacher-load light, compulsory outside reading assignments can perhaps still establish the old disciplines, though even those schools are dealing with the youth of a new day. But we are concerned here with all the youth in America between the ages of 14 and 18, all 7,700,000 of them this year, all 10,300,000 of them in 1960, 13,000,000 in 1965, 15,000,000 in 1970. The future intellectual life of these students is very much our responsibility. How shall we get them to say, "Reading is so important that we can't do without it"? It would be idle to assume that there is a very new or very easy answer. What we say here is the result of twelve hours of talking together by the group you see here before you, of thinking, which we ask you to supplement at the end of this report.

A TYPICAL TEACHING SITUATION

As we approached this problem, we thought it well to begin with the specific reality. One of us teaches in a school where it is the lot of the English teacher to have 140 students, divided into five classes of 28 each. They meet five days per week. In addition to these five classes every day, the teacher is responsible for one period of supervision of study hall and is adviser to one outside activity or club, such as debating and dramatics. Preparation for the next day's classes, correction of class tests, reading and evaluation of student essays and research papers, individual conferences with students must all come after school hours.

The student finds his time almost equally hedged in. In this particular school eighty per cent of the students have afternoon jobs; though they are legally required to stay until two forty-five, there is constant pressure from both employer and employee for release from school at two. These students cover the fundamentals of grammar and usage, write one paragraph each week and one long composition every six weeks, study in detail examples of essay, novel, poetry, drama, including one play of Shakespeare in each of the high school years, participate in compulsory essay contests (the entries prepared, of course, outside of class), write, in their Junior and Senior years, one research paper each semester. As if this were not enough to cover, class time is taken for public speaking tryouts, and occasional periods are shortened or omitted for assembly programs. The rest of the student's academic time is available for supplementary reading to be done on the outside, the reading which is the subject of this committee's investigation. We know, of course, how little time this is in the life of the average student, with all the social and domestic claims he has upon him.

In the melee of vibrant restlessness, the English teacher finds himself responsible not only for intellectual life but for manners and morals. The homes of many of our students are no longer places of orderly family groups, of quiet security. In the face of what passes for security in our day—which means primarily a yielding to the pressures of advertising—families are together less and less; such books as do get read are unlikely to be the subject of discussion in the home. And it is from these very facts that we must take our clue. We believe that it is no longer feasible to set up a list of established novels as an outside reading program—*Ivanhoe, David Copperfield, Vanity Fair, Silas Marner*. If our students are ever to read these novels, they must come to them on the path of some need, the need for entertainment, for human understanding, or for historical investigation; and while we hope that the Victorian novelists may continue to be read, we believe them to be of consequence to students in our secondary schools only as they compete with contemporary books to give them insights into their immediate world. It is our responsibility, then, to understand the student, to estimate his needs and interests and the sources of his personal satisfactions, and to discover where reading can meet them on the paths of his daily life.

TOWARD INDIVIDUALIZED READING

The real issue here, of course, is how shall our teacher establish an extensive reading program that will really fit his 140 students individually. The old *Ivanhoe, David Copperfield, Silas Marner* solution was far easier. Every student read the same book, every student made the same sort of report, and the teacher was able to evaluate a student in relation to all the others. But the values were questionable, as we all know: students plodded through the books, too youthfully ignorant of history to enjoy the vitality of Gurth and Wamba, too unsophisticated to relish the stylistic humor of Aunt Betsey Trotwood and Mr. Micawber or to grasp the social significance of Eppie's heritage. They quickly developed a conviction that all Victorian novels are dull, particularly those chosen by their teachers, that "classics" persist in our society because teachers have forced them upon their students, and that great books are great only because some one removed from the main stream of life says so. There seemed a strong likelihood that compulsion might kill the desire to read. Many of us have, of course, long ago broken with this tradition, and this report is designed to include some of the methods that we who have done so have found practical and to suggest ways in which these new methods can be made even more effective.

We are all aware of the dangers that lie in abandoning the old tightly controlled program. As with all other concessions to the concept of so-called freedom for the young, we recognize that the direction of a highly individualized program is a task requiring far more subtlety, more imagination, and more dedication. The teacher has always needed to be a psychologist. Today he needs to keep abreast of psychology in all its modern manifestations. One undeniable truth about the modern student is that he lives under a constant barrage of whirling, chaotic, vivid information about the world. Our final service to our students will be that we have brought some order out of that chaos for them. We shall do that through the books to which we bring them and the powers of evaluation which we inculcate in them. A successful program of outside reading, directed, yet generated in and nourished by the student's own vitality, is one way to the achievement of this service, a way as productive, we think, as any we can devise for them.

INDIVIDUAL READING FROM CLASSROOM ASSIGNMENTS

One practical method of initiating such a program of individual reading is to conjure it out of the bubbling brew of our daily classroom. If the teacher must be psychologist, he is also magician, casting his spells and evoking unexpected wonders from vessels that to the layman look empty and unpromising. Our colleagues in this conference have devoted their thinking to the reading for detailed analysis in the classroom, the reading which will be the stuff of daily assignments. They have spoken of the importance of relating the chosen examples of the four literary forms to life as students know it or have it within their power to conceive it. Every essay or poem or novel or play poses a problem in human relationships. If it has been taught so that the culmination of the student's understanding about it is its relation to the enduring concerns of humanity—birth and death, love and hatred, fear, anger, greed, and pain—presented so that they impinge on the student's perception of life, then the ramifications of that essay, that play, are unlimited, both in variety and range. Each student can be shown an area of investigation and reading which appeals to him alone. If the play is *Macbeth*, the student can run the whole gamut of murder, from such literary approaches as Marlowe's *Edward II* to the article on toxicology and the detection of crime through chemical analysis in a recent issue of *Harper's*. And there's always Serge Rubinstein and Murder, Inc. If he sees in Macduff the archetype of the modern political refugee working through the underground to effect revolution in a dictator-ridden country, he can turn to John Buchan, Helen McInnes and all the thrillers, *Watch on the Rhine*, the story of Anne Frank. Lady Macbeth leads to Medea and Lavinia Mannon in the O'Neill trilogy and to any number of wives who have wielded power behind their husbands' thrones and mistresses who haven't. The weird sisters lead from studies in Renaissance necromancy to Marjorie Stark's *Witchcraft in New England*, Arthur Miller's *Crucible*, John Van Druten's *Bell, Book, and Candle*, and the methods of Joseph McCarthy.

If the play is the *Taming of the Shrew*, there is *Kiss Me, Kate* and the use that was made of original lines for the creation of ingenious contemporary lyrics. In one class this led more than one student to Phyllis McGinley and Ogden Nash and then into an incipient but eager grasp of the formal techniques of all verse. In this way a great circle was made back to Pope and Byron and Wordsworth and Shelley.

If the novel is *Arrowsmith*, the embryonic doctors and nurses in the class can be led on to *The Citadel, The Mayo Brothers, Microbe Hunters*, biographies of Florence Nightingale, and dozens of books about doctors and nurses, including *Devils, Drugs and Doctors*, which begins to cross lines with those who went from *Macbeth* to the study of medieval and Renaissance medicine.

The inevitable crossing of many lines of interest leads to a consideration of how the burden can effectively become the student's, once the interest is generated by the imaginative teacher. Class time is precious for the fulfillment of all those other responsibilities which the teacher of English assumes: meeting the requirements of a syllabus, often preparing for departmental examinations under which students will be tested against all others in his school without consideration of the emphasis which the initial teacher may have found productive. Even so, though, as much as one class period per week can be profitably spent on the extensive reading program. Properly used, that time can become, we believe, a stimulus to interest in the intensive program; the resentment which comes of simple compulsion can be turned to pride in the achievement which each student will present to his peers.

The success of any such program will, of course, depend upon the genuine satisfaction of the student. He must make some sort of record of his reading, on filing cards, in a notebook, in whatever way gives him a ready reference when his opportunity comes to present his achievement to his classmates. We must emphasize over and over to the student that none of this reading is of consequence unless it has led to enjoyment, that there is no use in his sharing his experience with his class unless he can be enthusiastic about it. "What do you like?" and "Why do you like it?" are questions that he must be constantly ready to answer, and he must know that the purpose of this program is to share discovery, not to demonstrate mastery. For that reason many of the familiar disciplines can be relaxed: we need not fear uneven, unchecked individual reading; we need not prescribe the number of books to be read; we must not insist that they be drawn from a list. This does not mean that disciplines are to be abandoned, but the student must more and more meet requirements which he himself imposes. Our goal is that this individual exploration be self-motivated. Somehow this kind of reading must do more than merely meet deadlines which the teacher has imposed, though we all know that the teacher must impose them. But much of the value of this reading will lie in the student's feeling that he is discovering new areas of interest to his whole audience, even to the teacher. (At this point some of us may have to curb the pride that makes us want to show that we know "all about that.") The student's outside reading should be as flexible, as exploratory, as much a sequence of unexpected connections as the teacher's own summer reading.

In one school where the specific reading requirements were removed, a kind of competition developed to read and share. Students showed themselves much more interested in each other's recommendations than in the teacher's.

This student-sharing can take place in many ways. Some classes are divided into groups of four, the desks being pushed around to make informal groupings. All four members may have read the same book or have read different books around a common theme. The members question each other, explain their points of view, often develop a conviction about a book merely by virtue of having to explain it to the others. This arrangement makes for much talking in the classroom, but we who go to conferences know what intensity of conversation can be built up within little groups against the hubbub of unrelated talk. It can even be argued that a kind of hypnotic concentration is achieved.

Prepared panel discussions are often effective. A panel of four or five can present their views of a book or of a series of unrelated books and then be subjected to the questioning of their classmates. Some English departments make use of the school paper to present a column entitled *Reading I Have Liked*, in which perhaps ten students make a two- or three-sentence comment. School magazines can do the same thing, printing perhaps more extensive comments.

Any of these devices can be used in focusing on a chosen approach to reading: "What new ideas did you get from reading this book? What new experiences did you meet in it? How does what happens in the book relate to what happens here in my city? What problems do we meet in this book which are common to the human race? What different kinds of experience are possible with this book, recognizing that the central experience of the book will be different for different people?"

In all of this there are a number of attitudes to consider. The teacher must guard against the naïve student notion that the only reading worth doing is that which teaches some kind of lesson. The best thing we can do for our students, perhaps, is to open the doors of simple enjoyment. There will be those who will turn to Benchley and Perelman and Ogden Nash and E. B. White; and we can help them cherish those experiences.

We shall do well to avoid listing books with the credits their reading will net—six points for *War and Peace*, one for *Ethan Frome*. It is inevitable that we give credit for reading, but it must be as recognition for achievement. The teacher will rightly insist that this individual reading be done, but he and the student share the responsibility for finding the appropriate material and getting into it.

The teacher will need the help of collections of bibliographical books and pamphlets and of many lists, such as are appended to this report. He can effectively put a list into the hands of a student with titles checked *for him*. Many teachers, even with maximum classes, manage once a year to put a book into the hands of each student, saying, "I think you might be interested in this because . . ."

Sources for the development of interest are the current Teenage Book Clubs; classroom circulating libraries, to which each student brings a copy of his favorite book and lends it for the year; the newspaper, from which the human interest stories can be used to lead to fiction dealing with the same problems; television and movies. To fail to teach *Romeo and Juliet* in a year when the film is widely shown is to miss one of the most productive sources of interest. Television, bringing everything from *Peter Pan* to *Macbeth* into every other living room in the land, becomes a wonderful instrument for the teaching of discrimination.

A detailed account of a project in one of our large city high schools, where the students were permitted to choose fifty dollars' worth of books for the school library is appended to this report. This project led students to read reviews, to frequent bookshops, to understand more of the cost of books and the responsibility involved in their selection.

Finally, one productive source of interest in new books is book reviews in daily papers and in magazines. The few students who may get the habit of watching reviews will not only illuminate their own interests but will pass on information to others whose interests they find represented and may ultimately generate within a class the idea that it is good to be aware of the new books which the public will be reading.

This sort of stimulus to be "in the know," to participate in the knowledge shared by the discriminating members of a society, is part of the purpose of what we have chosen to call Extensive Reading. We had better, though, think of it as individual reading, for only as it nourishes the individual human spirit, satisfies a man in his solitude, and helps him to establish his separate identity in an all too standardized world, will it become in the hands of us teachers the effective instrument we intend it to be in our great service to the future of the world.

Appendix

THEMES FOR READING

Some examples of human attitudes, problems, and situations which people share in different plays and novels and in our own life experience.

IDEALISTIC PERSON WHO LIVES IN THE MIDST OF THE WORLD'S ACTIVITY

Anouilh's *Antigone*, Rostand's *Cyrano de Bergerac*, Shaw's *Saint Joan*, Ibsen's *Enemy of the People*, Howard's *Yellow Jack*.

HOPES AND ILLUSIONS THAT DRIVE PEOPLE

O'Neill's *Beyond the Horizon* and *Desire Under the Elms*, Steinbeck's *Of Mice and Men*, Miller's *Death of a Salesman*, Synge's *Playboy of the Western World*.

MEETING AND ACCEPTING A NEW IDEA

Shaw's *Caesar and Cleopatra*, Landon's *Anna and the King of Siam*.

THE NEED TO BELONG TO SOMETHING OUTSIDE OF ONE'S SELF

McCuller's *The Member of the Wedding*, O'Neill's *The Hairy Ape*, Brown's *A Sound of Hunting*, Steinbeck's *Of Mice and Men*.

COURAGE IN STANDING UP FOR ONE'S BELIEFS

Melville's *Billy Budd* (or the play by Coxe and Chapman), Sherwood's *Abe Lincoln in Illinois*, Koestler's *Darkness at Noon*, Hersey's *A Bell for Adano*, Moon's *Without Magnolias*.

OUR REACTION TO UNFAIR AUTHORITY

Nordoff and Hall's *Mutiny on the Bounty*, Monserrat's *The Cruel Sea*, Wouk's *The Caine Mutiny*, Walpole's *Fortitude*, Dickens' *David Copperfield*.

WORKING FOR A GOAL: WHAT ACHIEVING IT OR FAILING MAY DO TO
A PERSON

Ullman's *The White Tower*, Lewis' *Arrowsmith* and *Main Street*, Curie's
Madame Curie.

THE PERSON WHO REMOVES HIMSELF FROM SOCIETY: WHY DOES HE
DO IT?

Ibsen's *Enemy of the People*, Stone's *Lust for Life*, Maugham's *The
Moon and Sixpence*.

THE SEARCH FOR A FAITH

Bowen's *The Weight of the Cross*, Eliot's *The Cocktail Party*, Mann's
The Holy Sinner, Shaw's *Saint Joan*.

MAN'S ENDURANCE AND FORTITUDE WHEN HE HAS A PURPOSE

Wright's *Black Boy*, Hemingway's *The Old Man and the Sea*, Dickens'
A Tale of Two Cities.

PEOPLE'S REACTION TO WAR OVER THE WORLD AND THROUGH THE YEARS

The Trojan Women, Crane's *The Red Badge of Courage*, Remarque's
All Quiet on the Western Front, Dos Passos' *Three Soldiers*, the writings
of Tom Paine, Wouk's *The Caine Mutiny*, Simonov's *Days and Nights*,
Boyer's *The Secret Game*, Coward's *In Which We Serve*.

HOW WE DEVELOP AN OBJECTIVE IN LIFE

Fitzgerald's *This Side of Paradise*, Maugham's *Of Human Bondage*, Al-
drich's *A Lantern in Her Hand*.

PEOPLE AT ODDS WITH THEIR ENVIRONMENT

Wharton's *The Age of Innocence*, Michener's *Tales of the South Pacific*,
Lewis' *Main Street*, Phillips' *Search for a Hero*.

THE ROLE OF THE SCIENTIST IN THE MODERN WORLD

Amrine's *Secret*, Lewis' *Arrowsmith*, Hobert's *The Serpent Wreathed
Staff*, Cronin's *Adventures in Two Worlds* and *The Citadel*.

OVERCOMING IGNORANCE AND PREJUDICE

Shute's *The Chequerboard*, Wright's *Black Boy*, Graham's *Earth and High
Heaven*, Hobson's *Gentleman's Agreement*.

THE LUST FOR POWER

Warren's *All the King's Men*, *A Lion in the Streets*, Shakespeare's *Corio-
lanus*.

How People React to Danger

Brickhill's *The Great Escape, The Wooden Horse*, Browne's *The Weight of the Cross*, White's *They Were Expendable*, Vorhee's *Korean Tales.*

Germantown Friends School
Germantown, Pennsylvania

COLLATERAL READING LIST FOR *ARROWSMITH*

I. Drama about small-town life in:
  A. New England
    1. O'Neill, Eugene, *Ah, Wilderness!* (can be found in *Sixteen Famous American Plays*, Cerf and Cartmell, eds.)
    2. Wilder, Thornton, *Our Town* (can be found in either *Sixteen Famous American Plays* or *Modern American Dramas*, Harlan Hathner, ed.)
  B. Midwest
    1. Howard, Sidney, dramatization of Sinclair Lewis's *Dodsworth* (can be found in *Modern American Dramas*)
  C. An unlocalized one act play: Gale, Zona, "The Neighbors" (can be found in *One Act Plays*, Marie Webb, ed.)

II. On science:
  A. Research on Drugs:
    1. Silverman, Milton, *Magic in a Bottle*
    2. Sokoloff, Boris, *The Miracle Drugs*
  B. Haldane, J. B. S., *Adventures of a Biologist*
  C. Public Health
    1. de Kruif, Paul, *Health is Wealth*
    2. Peters, Clarence A., *Free Medical Care*

III. Novels
  A. Fisher, Dorothy Canfield, *The Brimming Cup* (a picture of the convention-bound life of a small Vermont community)
  B. Lewis, Sinclair, *Babbit* (a satire on middle-class life in the United States)
  C. Lewis, Sinclair, *Main Street* (a satire on American small-town life)
  D. Tarkington, Booth, *The Gentleman from Indiana* (of a man's search for truth in politics)
  E. Tarkington, Booth, *The Magnificent Ambersons* (life in a Midwestern town)

F. White, William A., *A Certain Rich Man* (commercialism in the Midwest)

IV. Biographies and Autobiographies
    A. Of people who devoted their lives to scientific research:
       1. Bolton, Sarah K., *Famous Men of Science*
       2. Curie, Eve, *Madame Curie*
       3. de Kruif, Paul, *Hunger Fighters*
       4. ———, *Men Against Death*
       5. ———, *Microbe Hunters*
       6. Ditmars, Raymond L., *The Making of a Scientist*
       7. Dubos, Rene J., *Louis Pasteur, Free Lance of Science*
       8. Fox, Ruth, *Great Men of Medicine*
       9. Holt, Racham, *George Washington Carver*
     10. Wood, L. N., *Raymond L. Ditmers: His Exciting Career with Reptiles, Animals, and Insects*
    B. Of people who devoted their lives to helping others directly through the practice of medicine:
       1. Braddy, Nella, *Anne Sullivan Macy: The Story Behind Helen Keller*
       2. Clapesattle, Helen, *The Doctors Mayo*
       3. Eaton, Jeanette, *David Livingstone*
       4. Grenfell, Wilfred T., *A Labrador Doctor*
       5. Heiser, Victor, *An American Doctor's Odyssey*
       6. Kenny, Sister Elizabeth, *And They Shall Walk*
       7. Nolan, Jeanette, *The Story of Clara Barton of the Red Cross*
       8. Regli, Adolph, *The Mayos: Pioneers in Medicine*
       9. Seagrave, Gordon S., *Burma Surgeon*
     10. ———, *Burma Surgeon Returns*
     11. Woodham-Smith, Cecil, *Florence Nightingale*
    C. Of people who sought truth or to help mankind in different fields:
       1. Gollomb, Joseph, *Albert Schweitzer: Genius in the Jungle*
       2. Parkman, Mary R., *Fighters for Peace*
       3. Sickels, Eleanor, *Twelve Daughters of Democracy*
       4. Thomas, Henry, and Dana Lee, *Fifty Great Americans*

V. Essays and miscellaneous nonfiction materials which provide interesting background information:
    A. On the character and customs of various sections of the country:
       1. *The Midwest, Look at America* series
       2. New England
          a. Botkin, B. A., *A Treasury of New England Folklore*

    b. Mitchell, Edwin Valentine, *It's an Old New England Custom*
    c. *New England, Look at America* series

Wellesley High School
Wellesley, Massachusetts

Bibliography

READING LISTS

Books for You, Grades 9–12 (Champaign, Ill., National Council of Teachers of English).

Good Reading (Mentor Books; New York, New American Library of World Literature).

Lenrow, Elbert, *Reader's Guide to Prose Fiction* (New York, Appleton-Century-Crofts, Inc., 1940).

Reading Ladders for Human Relations (Washington, American Council on Education).

Social Understanding Through Literature (Washington, National Council for the Social Studies).

Teaching of American Ideals (Urbana, Ill., Illinois English Bulletin).

Your Reading (Champaign, Ill., National Council of Teachers of English).

BOOKS ON INDIVIDUAL READING PROGRAMS

LaBrant, Lou, *We Teach English* (New York, Harcourt, Brace & Co., 1951).

Raushenbush, Esther, *Literature for Individual Education* (New York, Columbia University Press, 1942).

Rosenblatt, Louise, *Literature as Exploration* (New York, Appleton-Century-Crofts, Inc., 1938).

Index